D0931674

Comprehensive High School Reading Methods

Third Edition

Comprehensive High School Reading Methods

Third Edition

David L. Shepherd
Hofstra University

Charles E. Merrill Publishing Company
A Bell & Howell Company
Columbus Toronto London Sydney

Published by
Charles E. Merrill Publishing Co.
A Bell & Howell Company
Columbus, Ohio 43216

This book was set in Century Schoolbook and Helvetica.
Production Editor: Judith Rose Sacks

Cover Photo: Lyle Holbrook

Library of Congress Catalog Card Number: 81–86087
International Standard Book Number: 0–675–09881–5
Printed in the United States of America
3 4 5 6 7 8 9 10—86 85 84 83 82

Photo Credits

pp. 1, 18, 53, 98, 130, 191, 228, 254, 329, 375—**Strix Pix**

p. 145—**Michael Hayman/Corn's Photo Service**

p. 169—**Rick Smolan**

p. 208—**Photo by Richard Khanlian**

p. 242—**Dan Unkefer**

p. 357—**Paul Conklin**

Contents

Preface xi

CHAPTER 1 Fusing Process and Content 1

The Reading Process 2
Language and the Content Fields 10
Applying Principles of Learning to Reading 13
Teaching Reading in the Content Areas 14

CHAPTER 2 Vocabulary Development and Word Analysis 18

Reasons for Poor Vocabulary 19
The Bases of Vocabulary Development 20
Principles of Vocabulary Development 22
Vocabulary in the Content Fields 24
Word Analysis at the High School Level 31

CHAPTER 3 Comprehension 53

The Nature of Comprehension 54
Implementing Our Knowledge of Comprehension 64

CHAPTER 4 Reading Study Skills 98

The SQ3R Procedure 99
Organizing Information 100
Using Graphic Aids 107
Following Directions 122
Research Reading 124
Rate of Comprehension 127

CHAPTER 5 Developing Interest 130

Why Do Adolescents Read? 131
What Do High School Students Like to Read? 133
Guidelines for Developing Interest 134
Techniques for Developing Wide Reading 136
The School Library 139

CHAPTER 6 Diagnosis for Effective Teaching 145

Principles of Diagnosis 147
Precautions in Diagnosis 148
Methods of Appraisal 149

CHAPTER 7 Basic Procedures 169

Principles of Learning Applied to Procedure 170
Planning the Lesson 173
General Guidelines to Procedures 188

CHAPTER 8 Individualizing Instruction 191

The Teacher's Dilemma 192
Considerations for Individualizing Instruction 192
Forms of Individualization 193
Materials That Help You Individualize 204

CHAPTER 9 Exceptional Students 208

Superior Readers 209
Slow-Learning Students 218
Disabled Readers 219

CHAPTER 10 Remediation 228

Identification of Remedial Readers 229
Remedial Reading Programs 229

Remediation in the Content Area Classroom 232
Basic Competency 238

CHAPTER 11 Adjusting Materials to the Student 242

Factors Affecting Difficulty of Materials 243
Readability 245
Textbook Evaluation 248
Rewriting 251
Supplementary Materials 252

CHAPTER 12 Applying Reading Skills in English, Social Studies, Science, and Mathematics 254

Applying Reading Skills to the English Class 256
Applying Reading Skills to Social Studies 268
Applying Reading Skills to Science 282
Applying Reading Skills to Mathematics 305

CHAPTER 13 Applying Reading Skills to Business Education, Industrial Arts, and Home Economics 329

Applying Reading Skills to Business Education 330
Applying Reading Skills to Industrial Arts 340
Applying Reading Skills to Home Economics 348

CHAPTER 14 Applying Reading Skills to Foreign Languages, Art, Music, and Physical Education 357

Applying Reading Skills to Foreign Languages 358
Applying Reading Skills to Art 360
Applying Reading Skills to Music 363
Applying Reading Skills to Physical Education 367

CHAPTER 15 The Complete High School Program 375

Parts of a Complete Program 376
Implementing a Complete Reading Program 376

Organizing the Reading Program 380
Success of the Program 385

Appendix Steps in a Unit Procedure 389

Index 395

Preface

This book emphasizes specific and practical methods a teacher can employ to fuse reading and content. The methods, strategies, and procedures suggested focus on developing know-how for reading material in each subject area, a positive and inquiring attitude of mind, and methodical work habits in each subject. Throughout, the content area teacher is seen as the key to effective instruction in reading.

The ability to use language has been characterized as uniquely human. This symbolic medium is a means of thinking as well as the major vehicle with which to transmit and to receive ideas. Through language, especially in its written form, we have been able to store and share knowledge through the ages of recorded history. Language facilitates interaction between people—between teacher and learner as well as between the reader and the writer of the printed page. Each content area teacher is involved with all aspects of language use. Indeed, every teacher, irrespective of content specialty, is a teacher of language as it is used in the subject area.

This text deals with one aspect of language usage—reading—as it applies to different types of printed materials in middle and secondary school classrooms. The effective implementation of this idea rests upon four premises. First, the ability to read and understand the language of the subject influences the learner's mastery of that subject. We, therefore, are concerned with both the developmental linguistic process and linguistic proficiency as applied to the printed form of language. Second, both societal changes and personal functioning in a democracy require independence in learning and communicating through the written word. Third, the teaching of any content area and the ability to read its materials are interwoven. Fourth, the learner must be cognizant of the learning processes in order to become independent and self-directing.

Reading ideas and techniques are presented in this text to show how instruction can take place in any subject area. The first chapter develops a rationale that provides teachers with the *reasons why* certain skills and procedures are suggested.

Next is a discussion of the skills needed to read effectively, with many suggestions that will help students develop these skills. Chapters dealing with vocabulary, comprehension, and study skills encompass these skill clusters. Chapter 5 investigates the area of developing interest in reading, with emphasis on the affective domain. The interrelationship of the cognitive and affective domains is explored. The chapters that follow suggest instructional procedures, beginning with assessing and diagnosing reading proficiency. This is followed by chapters on basic procedures and classroom management that lead toward meeting each student's need. This concept is expanded by a chapter about exceptional students, the gifted, the slow learner, the physically handicapped, and the linguistically different. Since a number of high school students need remedial help, a chapter is devoted to this topic, with special emphasis on help in the subject area classroom.

The next three chapters (Chapters 12, 13, and 14) detail reading in specific subject areas. It is emphasized that while each subject represents a particular style of writing, the styles are not discrete, and many of the same skills are needed in each subject. Therefore, readers of this book should read the material appropriate to all subject areas irrespective of their individual subject specialty. Because of this crossover of skills from one area to another, broad understanding of all areas is useful in accommodating the differences of students and reading material in most classrooms. The final chapter pulls all threads together in describing a complete high school reading program with guidelines for organizing such a program.

The people who contributed to this book are many. They are the high school students in various parts of the United States who have felt the need for instruction in reading in different disciplines. The concerns and ideas of many teachers have also been contributed. These professionals are continually expressing their desire to know how to incorporate more effectively instruction in reading with the teaching of content.

CHAPTER 1 Fusing Process and Content

OVERVIEW

This chapter provides a rationale for including reading instruction in content classes. The process of reading and the developmental stages of learning to read are reviewed. Aspects of the stages of reading development that relate to the secondary school are noted to show that learning to read is a process. Also discussed are the importance of language, the relationship of reading to language, and the various uses of language: listening, speaking, and writing. Finally, general teaching procedures are recommended.

Questions

Consider these questions before you read further:

1. What do you think are the basic aims of education today?
2. What reasons can you offer for teaching reading at the secondary school level?
3. How should reading instruction be included in the secondary school curriculum?

THE READING PROCESS

What is reading? When individuals read, are they merely pronouncing the words fluently, or are they also understanding the ideas presented? At the primary grade level, children learn to call out words by various methods of instruction—is this reading? At the high school level, some students can "read" fluently yet understand very little; because of their years of experience with language, however, these same students often can answer factual questions on the materials. For example, in the reading of mathematics students may be able to pronounce all of the words and memorize a process but have no understanding of what is being done. Is *this* reading?

Authorities on reading agree that reading involves extracting *meaning*—understanding an author's ideas. Hittleman clearly emphasizes meaning: "Reading is the process of reconstructing an author's ideas."[1] Harris and Sipay define reading as deriving meaning from a printed page through the ability to recognize printed words, knowledge of language, and previous reading and life experiences.[2] Thus, reading requires recognition of printed symbols, knowledge of the language and its structure, and a background of information.

At the secondary level, students must become familiar with the unique aspects of writing in specific content areas. Learning of all subject matter depends largely on competence in the language of the subject. Students must understand the vocabulary and syntax, use language skills in learning the information, and be able to communicate it to others. Students must be competent, therefore, in the language arts—reading, writing, speaking, and listening. Further, students must be provided with the background needed for understanding each content assignment.

We also need to realize that reading is a developmental *process*. It is not a subject in and of itself, such as American history, Algebra I, business law, or biology. It is possible in theory, though not in reality, to teach all that is known in most content fields. Not so with reading; as a process, it is infinite. A reader can always make further improvement.

The developmental nature of reading is of relevance to the secondary school curriculum. First, we can discard the traditional notion that reading is taught *completely* in the primary grades and can be ignored thereafter. Most individuals can and do continuously sharpen and expand their reading skills; it is most appropriate, therefore, to teach reading at the secondary level. Second, since learning to read is not finite, we can note broad guidelines for procedure. Teaching any process involves two basic provisions: instruction in how to apply the process, followed by practice—much of it.

Many students resist reading instruction because they consider it to be a primary subject. To overcome this attitude, draw a comparison between learning to read effectively and playing a sport proficiently. Using the Socratic method of questioning to help students arrive at the ideas, point out that even star athletes continue to practice. Further, point out that those who

---

1. Daniel R. Hittleman, *Developmental Reading: A Psycholinguistic Perspective* (Chicago: Rand McNally, 1978), p. 5.

2. Albert J. Harris and Edward R. Sipay, *How to Teach Reading* (New York: Longman, 1979), p. 27.

coach such athletes provide instruction in the skills and specific plays of the sport, and they set strict requirements about the duration and frequency of practice. Other analogies to use include playing a musical instrument, dancing, painting, driving, or any other skill.

Reading is one component of the language arts. Speaking and writing are an individual's means of using language to communicate. Through listening and reading an individual understands the language of others. These four components are interrelated, and competence in one likely enhances competence in the others. For example, if the teacher helps students learn to find the main idea of a paragraph as they read, they can apply the same ideas of structure in trying to write well.

Developmental Stages

There are developmental stages in learning to read. Many authorities have discussed each of these stages in great detail. Here we will briefly review the stages prior to secondary school and how they affect the secondary experience.

Preschool

The first five to six years of a child's life are crucial in their effect on secondary school success. It is during this period that the child learns the oral use of language. Hittleman points out:

> By the time children are four years old, there has been mastery of basic grammatical structures. During the fifth and sixth years, children begin to control the inconsistencies of language, and by the end of the seventh year—roughly corresponding to the end of the first grade—the children have developed a grammar that is almost equivalent to that of adults. What is lacking is the extensive vocabulary and the ability to manipulate the extensive number of grammatical transformations of adult speech.[3]

Although the teacher might assume that secondary students have language competence, they might not be overtly aware of language structure or be able to analyze it to the point of making it work effectively. You will surely need to continue and expand upon students' earlier instruction.

Children's use of language is largely influenced by the language experience they have with adults as well as with their own peers. As infants learn language, they rely at first on imitation. Secondary students with linguistic difficulties may not have had sufficient opportunity to use language, particularly the form used in school. Bilingual students, for example, may have had sufficient practice with the native language but not enough with English.

Preschoolers explore their world with apparently unbounded curiosity. Parents and others who work with preschool children try to provide experience with words and general language competence in discussing these experiences. Another way of building background and fostering a positive

---

3. Hittleman, *Developmental Reading,* p. 57.

attitude toward reading is to read stories to preschool children regularly. In this way, they gain experience and knowledge. In addition, many children's books are informational, serving to increase general knowledge. Some secondary students never had the classics of children's literature read to them, including *Mother Goose Nursery Rhymes,* fairy stories, and *Winnie the Pooh.* Not only have those students missed a great deal of pleasure, but also they will not understand any allusions made to these classics.

Children experience pleasure, excitement, and warmth when adults read to them. This enjoyment fosters a positive attitude toward reading. Teachers of secondary students can continue to encourage a positive reading attitude by reading aloud some article, story, poem, or anecdote that they particularly like.

Primary and Elementary School

This stage of reading development includes grades one through four or five. In this stage, children learn the basic skills for effective reading. At first, the teacher guides children toward the point of *reading readiness*—that is, ready to begin to read. *Beginning reading* is the time during which children learn to recognize graphic symbols to obtain ideas. These two stages usually occur in kindergarten and the early primary grades. In the later primary grades (grades two and three), children become more independent and learn more about obtaining and organizing the ideas they get from reading. In the fourth and fifth grades, they begin to apply their basic knowledge to acquiring information in various subjects—the beginning of content reading. All of these stages require systematic instruction.

Let's look at these stages a bit more closely and note their carry-over to what you do at the secondary level.

Reading readiness. In preparing children for reading, teachers are concerned with all aspects of growth that may affect success in school. For instance, the primary teacher is interested in the following factors which influence learning: general intelligence, specific aptitudes, learning modality (the way the child learns best), understanding of language and its structure, and conceptual knowledge (background). The teacher also is interested in children's ability to comprehend and perceive through the senses—visual, auditory, tactile, spatial, and so on. Of course, the primary teacher must consider physiological development as well as social and cultural factors. In other words, are the children mature enough to learn successfully in school?

If the teacher notes deficits in certain areas, she helps the child improve. She searches the child's background to find areas of strength on which to build. The teacher focuses on improving the child's ability to think by providing direct and indirect experiences and by emphasizing language development. Clearly, the well-managed primary classroom offers almost limitless opportunities for the child to use language and to hear it used. A basic rule is to begin with what the child already knows—the known—and then develop what is new—the unknown.

How does readiness affect what you do at the secondary school level? One aspect of readiness applies very well in helping students read a new selection: assuring them that they do have relevant background before they read. By relating the known to the unknown, the teacher prepares students for understanding new material. Of course, the teacher should provide students with study techniques for doing this on their own. Readiness is indeed one of the basic aspects of effective procedure in the secondary classroom. (For a more thorough discussion of how to develop background before students read, see Chapter 7.)

Beginning reading. When children reach this stage, they should be ready to learn to recognize the graphic symbols associated with word sounds. Emphasizing meaning, the primary teacher tries to develop a sight vocabulary so that children can begin to read for understanding as soon as possible. The sight method (often called "look and say") does not teach students how to recognize the graphic symbols; this method is not sufficient to help children recognize words. Once a word *is* learned, by whatever means, it becomes a sight word. No reader uses techniques of word recognition every time she meets a word. Therefore, secondary students usually know a large number of words at sight.

During this stage of development, children learn techniques of word recognition, including: noting the meaning by context, phonic analysis, structural analysis, and dictionary use. *Context* involves recognizing the word by the way it is used in a sentence. For instance, is the word *pre sent'* or *pre' sent*—a verb or a noun? Context also involves redundancy in the language—various cues to the same meaning in a sentence. In the sentence, *A boy skinned his knee yesterday when he fell from his bicycle,* we note the singular of *boy* through *a, his, he,* and *his*. We note time: *skinned, yesterday, fell.* Sometimes a word is contextually defined directly, as part of the sentence. Secondary textbooks almost always use this technique when new vocabulary words are introduced.

Phonic analysis deals with the sound units of a word, known as *phonemes*. Phonemes may be single letters or a combination that gives a single sound. Most primary reading programs provide intensive instruction in the sound units. Learning of phonemes depends on the ability to distinguish sounds. *Structural analysis* helps the child analyze a word by its meaning components—its *morphemes*. Structural analysis includes the study of roots of words, prefixes, suffixes, inflectional endings, and compound words. Syllables are determined in part through both phonic analysis and structural analysis. Toward the end of third grade or early part of fourth grade, instruction in dictionary use provides further independence in decoding (recognizing) graphic symbols.

Many of the skills and techniques taught at the early stages of reading must be taught at the secondary level as well. For example, structural analysis is closely tied to grammar: prefixes and suffixes that note the word's function in a sentence, and the inflectional endings of tense, plural, and degree. Syllabication is a skill many secondary students need. They regularly encounter multisyllabic words, such as *hydrometer;* they may know the meaning, but they may not know how to break it into pronounceable units. Also, secondary students must refine their dictionary skills. However, primary-level instruction and materials do not prepare students to use those skills with secondary materials. The teacher must guide students in applying their basic knowledge to increasingly difficult materials.

Much instruction in the primary and elementary levels focuses on competence in decoding. The emphasis remains, however, on increasing language competence, concept development, and comprehension. These should be emphasized at the secondary level also.

Many volumes have been written on the various approaches to teaching beginning reading. One very widely accepted approach is *eclectic*—using whatever it takes to ensure optimum progress. You will also do this at your level, since you will encounter as many personalities, learning modalities, backgrounds, values, and experiences as there are students.

The *basal reader approach* is probably the most widely used. It uses a graded set of readers for each grade and, depending on the series, includes other materials such as work-practice books, special instructional materials, tapes, and tests for diagnosis and evaluation. Most of these readers are composed of story-type material—fictional prose. This approach is not usually followed at the secondary level, except for remedial secondary reading classrooms.

The *language experience approach* is also widely used, often along with other methods. Basically, this approach uses children's own language—their own stories—as the reading material. In beginning reading, this approach has many advantages. Children see their language in printed form, and the content is known, Most primary classroom teachers use "experience charts" to record an individual's or the class' experience. At the secondary level, you can use such an approach by translating a textbook into the student's own language. (See Chapter 11 for a detailed discussion of this.)

The *individualized approach* is based upon the philosophy that reading is an individual matter and that children pace themselves as they become more competent. It also emphasizes that children have different instructional needs, develop at an individual rate, and have different backgrounds or intellectual needs. Secondary students also differ in personalities and needs, and you will need to adjust assignments and procedures accordingly. (See Chapter 8.)

The Middle School

The middle school, usually encompassing grades five through eight, is designed to replace the junior high school (grades seven through nine). Whereas the junior high school is departmental, the middle school was designed to provide alternatives. However, many middle schools are organized departmentally with teachers specializing in content areas.

Middle school students are entering puberty—a stage affecting social, emotional, and intellectual behavior. H. Thompson Fillmer describes the middle school student in the following way:

> The middle school pupil is a volatile creature. He is encountering radical physiological changes, his intellectual growth is erratic and may at any given time be quite different from the intellectual behavior of a given peer, and he is striving to develop basic attitudes about himself as a person.[4]

---

4. H. Thompson Fillmer, "The Middle School Student and the Reading Program" in *Reading in the Middle School, Perspectives in Reading No. 18.* ed. Gerald G. Duffy (Newark, Del.: IRA, 1974), p. 17.

The character and organization of the middle school reading program is evolving. Should reading be taught as a subject in a class called *reading*, or should it be taught in each of the content areas, or both? Should the program be for all students or just for those who exhibit difficulty? These are fundamental concerns. However, if we keep in mind what we know of the reading process and the goal of developing thinking and the use of language, we can see clearly the type of program required:

1. A class in reading should build upon primary and elementary reading instruction. Reading skills acquired earlier need to be maintained, and most middle school students are not mature enough to maintain these skills for themselves. Systematic reading instruction involves the use of content readers as well as intensive work on study skills.
2. Reading should be emphasized in each of the content areas. This will help students apply their reading skills and techniques to the writing encountered in content subjects.
3. Wide reading should be encouraged both in the reading class and in the various content classes.

During the middle school years, students begin to apply to specific materials what they have learned about reading. At this stage, instruction should be directed to each student's need. Middle school students have achieved a basic competence in *how* to read; the teacher must focus on encouraging students to read about subjects that interest them and increasing their competence.

The Secondary School

Now we are at your level. Let's look at some significant characteristics of adolescents, the demands the world of technology is placing upon them, and how we can improve their proficiency in reading.

Emphasis must be placed on the following:

1. Skills and techniques taught in earlier grades must be maintained and applied to increasing levels of difficulty.
2. Instruction in reading must be applied in each content field. If this is done, reading instruction occurs throughout the day. Also, students will note the similarities and differences of each area's writing style.
3. Study skills must be emphasized and developed in each discipline, leading toward as much independence as possible.
4. Continue to foster wide reading, for three basic reasons: to increase background, to provide practice in the necessary skills and techniques, and to promote reading as a pleasurable recreational pastime.

Your view of adolescents determines in great measure your success with them. First, it is important to note that adolescents have *ability*. Do not underestimate it. They may seem at times not to want to do school assignments, and they may even lead you to believe that they are unable to do them. However, when students do not perform adequately on an assignment, it is often because they were not taught the necessary skills and techniques.

Second, adolescents are *young adults*. They vacillate between what we consider immature and mature behavior out of uncertainty. Instruction and guidance in reading and study skills will show students how to proceed and will lead to more mature behavior. Treat adolescents as adults by respecting individual views and desires. You need not accept these views, but adolescents need sympathetic, objective reception and discussion.

Third, adolescents do have *interests,* including: how they fit into the school group as well as society at large, what they will become and how they will earn a living, values, the pros and cons of different lifestyles, and their progress through life. These interests can be overwhelming. For instance, many gifted adolescents become distressed because their advanced intellectual abilities are not matched by experience and knowledge.

Adolescents are concerned about the world and society. Through the media they are aware of current issues and problems such as ecology, environmental pollution, energy, the job market, interpersonal as well as international relations, and so on. They see the complexity of the world and wonder what it means to them and how they can cope. A sampling of views about why they are in school often reflects only the immediate concerns, such as "I want to get a good job," or "I'm trying to get into college." If we believe that young people do have ability, are young adults, and have interests, how can we get them involved?

Fundamentally, we must know what we need to accomplish as teachers of young people. We may give as our goal that which Jefferson cited: "Only an educated people could understand their rights, maintain them, and provide for the successful functioning of a democratic-republic."[5] But we may also express more immediate concerns. For example, over the years, in conversation with teachers, the following comments have been noted: "I merely want my students to learn the subject matter. If they become independent in the acquisition of knowledge in the process, good! But I am concerned with the *content.*" "I want them to pass the final exam [or the competency test]. My principal will rate me low if they don't."

To get young people involved, however, we need to consider some characteristics of our modern world. A. W. Combs points out two characteristics which support the importance of reading effectively:

> Two things are happening in the world we live in that guarantee we can never again base our thinking on the concept of a stable society or the certainty of a body of knowledge. There are: (1) the information explosion, and (2) the ever accelerating pace of change.[6]

Thus we see the current emphases on the ability of students to acquire, understand, and use increasing amounts of information, and to adapt to continuously changing conditions. Ziegler suggests broad directions of procedure for leading the student to use, rather than merely acquire, knowledge. According to Ziegler there are three stances we may take to help

5. Bernard Mayo, ed., *Jefferson Himself* (Boston: Houghton Mifflin, 1942), p. 76.
6. Arthur W. Combs, *Myths in Education* (Boston: Allyn & Bacon, Inc., 1979), p. 77.

students adjust to future conditions. One is *preventive*—this is the one usually taken by education, he says, and it is designed to make a forecast about the future obsolete. According to this writer, the preventive stance may be necessary and wise in certain situations. Another stance is *adaptive*, designed to help individuals adjust to changing conditions over which they may have little or no control. The third stance, which Ziegler seems to prefer, is *inventive;* here, there are "acts of creative intervention in the present to bring that desirable future about."[7] Shane and Shane suggest two specific skills which young people should acquire: coping with the future and learning how to plan for the future.[8]

What specific procedures and directions must we use in our classrooms? This book suggests approaches, procedures, and techniques for helping secondary school students become involved in the modern world. The basic emphasis is that the individual must acquire the *skills* and *knowledge* which are foundations to wise choices. As a preview, consider these questions concerning how your daily classroom practice relates to young people's concern about the modern world:

1. How do you expand students' knowledge so that they have information on which to base wise choices?
   a. Do you teach levels of comprehension that require more than recall?
   b. Do you teach how words can be used not only to convey meaning but also to create a point of view or an impression?
   c. Do you relate a topic to its current implications? For example, in biology, what can be the impact of genetic coding on humans?
   d. Do you guide your students to materials other than the textbook?
   e. Do you relate the study of a problem to Ziegler's three stances and discuss the implications of each stance as a means of solving the problem? Do you discuss the pros and cons of each stance?
   f. Do you take a topic and relate it to Shane's skill of future planning, or at least for coping?
   g. Do you discuss how new knowledge about a topic changes our understanding of it?
   h. Do you teach the concept that knowledge is not stable or fixed in completeness? What does this mean vocationally (that specific jobs will become obsolete)? How will the students cope with this?
   i. Do you teach the concept of diversity of options? For example, what are the options for resolving the energy crisis?
2. How do you help your students become independent in communication skills such as reading?
   a. Do you give them techniques of study?
   b. Do you involve them in current projects and assignments that will compel them to use and apply effective techniques?

---

7. Warren L. Ziegler, *The Potential of Educational Futures,* ed. Michael Marien and Warren L. Ziegler (Worthington, Oh.: Charles A. Jones Publishing Company, 1972), pp. 5-6.

8. Harold Shane and June Grant Shane, "Educating the Youngest for Tomorrow," in *Learning for Tomorrow,* ed. Alvin Toffler (New York: Random House, 1974), pp. 191–192.

Any topic in the curriculum can be developed using such questions. These questions require students to sharpen their skills in acquiring knowledge; also, students must go beyond mere fact acquisition to applying ideas to current problems and issues. As a result, your classes engage both teacher and students.

By expanding the students' scope of ideas and their application to modern issues and problems and providing instruction in appropriate techniques of reading, the teacher leads students toward an acceptable level of literacy. In determining the literacy level for our modern society, Chall says:

> We take the position that the "reading problem" in the United States should not be stated as one of teaching people to read at the level of minimal literacy, but rather as one of ensuring that every person arriving at adulthood will be able to read and understand the whole spectrum of printed materials that one is likely to encounter in daily life. In terms of grade levels of difficulty, a meaningful goal would be the attainment of twelfth-grade literacy by all adults—roughly, the ability to read with understanding nearly all the material printed in a magazine like *Newsweek*. As one member of our committee has pointed out, our national educational policy is that every child is expected to complete at least the twelfth grade; we ought then to expect every child to attain twelfth-grade literacy.[9]

Finally, as you work with your students, inform them about the "science" of what you do in the classroom. Show them the steps of your teaching procedure, what your objectives are, what you want to know through classroom diagnosis, and how it will relate to what you will do as a class. Explain why you may use different ways of organizing group participation and individual work. If need be, discuss some theories of learning; encourage students to suggest how these theories can be applied to and by themselves. In short, work *with* the students rather than have them work for you. One outstanding social studies teacher established an atmosphere so engrossing that her eighth grade students, working in groups and independently, often would not hear the class dismissal bell. During the year, this class had been given "mini-courses" in reading skills and techniques, group dynamics, and educational methods, along with the content material. By the end of the year these students had become independent in their study at the eighth grade level.

LANGUAGE AND THE CONTENT FIELDS

Content teachers are dismayed when students are unable to get meaning from printed materials used in their subjects. Postman and Weingartner define meaning as "what *results* from the transaction between language and the language used."[10] They continue by saying that it is a very individual process. In other words, meaning results from the matching of the author's language to the language of the reader.

9. John B. Carroll and Jeanne S. Chall, eds., *Toward a Literate Society: The Report of the Committee on Reading of the National Academy of Education* (New York: McGraw-Hill, 1975), p.8.

10. Neil Postman and Charles Weingartner, *Linguistics: A Revolution in Thinking* (New York: A Delta Book, 1966), pp. 183, 184.

The skills of thinking—judging, imagining, reasoning, synthesizing, and applying—depend upon the ability to use language as a medium of thought. For instance, just to understand a simple sentence, students need to recognize the words, understand the concepts underlying the words as well as the interrelationship of clusters or groups of words, and understand the grammatical structure—the syntax—of the sentence. Knowledge of language enables students to form sentences in speaking and writing. In order to express themselves precisely, they need to know which words to use, their proper order, and their interrelationship. In listening and reading, students need the same basic skills except that they are not the originators but the receivers; they must know the meanings of the words and their interrelationship in order to understand the thought. And since the meaning individuals acquire is personal to them, knowledge and experience contribute markedly to the ability to think.

Each discipline has its own way of using language. Word usage and structure are adapted to the pertinent ideas of each area. A quick look shows that fiction and factual prose differ. For instance, the language in mathematics is terse, with all important details connected by a specific relationship. A story, however, may be filled with descriptions designed to give the reader a general mood or tone, and individual details may not be important. Social studies material is often chronological and can be highly abstract, whereas science material is dense with factual detail in which the student must perceive the organization. Of course, the language patterns used in each discipline or subject are not exclusive. For example, a description of a scientific process would likely be written in a pattern characterized as scientific writing; the biography of the scientist involved would be in a more narrative style, similar to what students would read in English class; and the sociological or political impact of the process might be described in a way similar to social studies writing. If an equation or formula is involved, the material could resemble mathematical writing.

We know also that the same word used in different subjects may have different meanings. This may occur even within one subject. A *guard* on a piece of machinery in industrial arts is different from a *guard* who protects the president, as may be described in social studies, even though the basic idea of both is similar. In mathematics, as in many other subjects, the meaning of a word depends upon the context—for example, a *gross* of eggs and *gross* profit.

Michaels notes that students report having difficulty in mastering subject matter mainly because of language problems.[11] Students did not say that the *facts* were incomprehensible; rather, their responses reveal difficulty with both vocabulary and comprehension. Students may not be aware of the function of language when studying content. For purposeful study in the content areas, they need to understand the central role of language and apply techniques to use it effectively.

---

11. Melvin Michaels, "Subject Reading Improvement: A Neglected Teaching Responsibility," *Journal of Reading* 9, No. 2 (October 1965): 16–20.

The Interrelationship of the Language Arts Skills

Content teaching is based on ideas, which in turn are based upon knowledge. Knowledge is derived from both direct and indirect experiences that an individual has throughout life. It stems from discussion and interaction with others, actual experience, reading about things and people, and from the communications media—television, films, radio, and pictures. Ideas grow from thinking about the information one has acquired.

In order to use knowledge, students must be competent in specific skills of communication and thinking. They must apply skills of language in speaking, listening, reading, and writing to see how they are related. Table 1.1 shows the similarities among the language arts skills.

TABLE 1.1 Language Arts Skills

Speaking (doer)	*Listening* (receiver)
1. Knowledge of word sounds.	1. Recognize word sounds.
2. Knowledge of the meaning of words to express a specific thought.	2. Knowledge of the meaning of words used.
3. Understand how to formulate various sentence patterns and how to express meaning through them.	3. Understand how to get thought from various sentence patterns used.
4. Know how to speak coherently to express a desired meaning. Be able to speak to a main idea. Organize ideas according to purpose.	4. Understand conversation and denote the desired meaning. Note the main point (idea). Note the speaker's plan of organization.
5. Include details to fit purpose and content of the communication.	5. Listen for details—note type and function.
6. Be able to support a main idea with appropriate details; have coherence among details.	6. Listen for interrelationship of main ideas and details.
7. Use clue words to indicate a pattern of thought.	7. Note clue words that indicate a thought pattern.
8. Present information to indicate inference.	8. Listen for information organized to indicate inference.
9. Foreshadow.	9. Anticipate outcomes.
10. Choose words, idiomatic and/or figurative language to express thought.	10. Interpret figurative speech, idiomatic language.
11. Know purpose.	11. Recognize purpose, bias.
Reading (receiver)	*Writing* (doer)
1. Knowledge of word structure. meaning clues sound clues	1. Know how to spell words, prefixes, roots, suffixes, inflectional endings, syllables.
2. Knowledge of the meaning of words.	2. Knowledge of words to express a specific thought.
3. Understand how to get thought from various sentence patterns.	3. Understand how to formulate various sentence patterns; to express meaning through them.

TABLE 1.1 *cont.*

Reading (receiver)	*Writing* (doer)
4. Understand functions of sentences in paragraph; recognize logic of sentence arrangement.	4. Know how to arrange sentences in paragraphs to express a desired meaning.
Recognize the main idea.	Be able to formulate a topic and/or main idea sentence.
Recognize paragraph types.	Understand paragraph types; be able to construct them.
5. Read for details—note type and function.	5. Include details to fit purpose and content of paragraph.
6. See interrelationship of main ideas and details and of details to each other.	6. Be able to support main idea with appropriate details; to relate similar details.
7. Note clue words indicating pattern of thought.	7. Use clue words to indicate pattern of thought.
8. Note inferences.	8. Present information to indicate inference.
9. Anticipate outcomes.	9. Foreshadow.
10. Note and understand styles of writing (figurative speech, metaphors, mood, etc.).	10. Choose words, idiomatic and/or figurative language to express thought.
11. Recognize author's purpose, bias, type of structure.	11. Establish purpose, bias, type of structure.

APPLYING PRINCIPLES OF LEARNING TO READING

Principles of learning are guidelines for effective classroom teaching, and teachers must guide students daily in techniques and habits of efficient learning. Since students must acquire reading skills just as they must learn subject matter, teachers should apply the principles of learning in teaching reading skills. Learning principles that apply to reading include the following:

1. *Learners must have purpose and motivation.* Students who do not read because they lack motivation do not get practice in reading skills. Further, if students lack purpose and motivation, their comprehension suffers.
2. *Learners must extract meaning.* Reading should enable readers to understand information and to determine its significance. If students regularly fail to extract meaning, both comprehension and motivation will decline.
3. *Learners must have a background of experience and knowledge.* New ideas must be connected to existing ideas and information. To build concepts, students must have a background for understanding the vocabulary and applying new ideas.
4. *Learners must be active.* It is nearly impossible for students to master

reading skills if they put forth little effort and do not practice and apply these skills.

5. *Learners must form habits.* When students acquire reading skills and learn how to attack a reading assignment, they acquire techniques—habits—that will insure success and efficiency.
6. *Learners learn by association.* Students comprehend more if they can see the relationship among ideas and can relate new information to their own experience.
7. *Learners must practice.* This is particularly true of learning to read. Students do not master a reading technique merely by being shown; they must use it.
8. *Learners need favorable attitudes.* Students who have developed negative attitudes toward reading will not likely regard it as an effective learning tool.
9. *Learners learn at their own rate and in their own mode.* Teachers must take student differences into account. To be effective, classroom procedure must provide for each individual student.
10. *Learners must know the reason for learning.* Students need to understand how each reading skill can increase their reading competence. Understanding this will not only encourage reading improvement but will also provide motivation.

The goal of reading instruction in school should be to help students develop independence in understanding all kinds of printed materials. Independence consists of the ability to understand the subject matter and to engage in interpretive, critical, and creative thought. Students must acquire the skills of gathering and using information. Content teaching should balance factual understanding with thinking about and beyond the facts.

TEACHING READING IN THE CONTENT AREAS

Four basic premises provide the underpinning for teaching reading in the content fields. If you accept them, you will have a philosophy to use in combining the teaching of reading with the teaching of content.

Reading in the Content Fields Is Part of the Total School Reading Program

A good school reading program is based on two considerations. First, you must instruct in the skills of reading using printed material of all types of content and styles of writing. Second, the students need to practice the skills through a wide reading program.

Reading in the content fields is but one part of a total program. Other parts of a school reading program include:

1. Classes in which reading is taught as a subject, possibly as an elective for students at any level of reading who wish to sharpen their skills.

2. Using reading in the content areas to expand the range of material so that skills can be further developed and applied.
3. Providing a library program and supplementary classroom collections to foster research skills and opportunities for wide reading.
4. Providing instruction for students who need remedial help.

All Teachers Are Responsible for Helping Students Read Their Specific Subject

The teacher with expertise in a specific subject is the one best qualified to adapt reading skills to it. For example, the mathematics teacher is best qualified to extract the mathematics content from the language used and to show students how to do so. Further, students gain competence in a reading skill if they are instructed in its use while they are reading. Therefore, when students are reading a mathematics problem, they need help at that time.

Each content teacher must know how to teach reading in that area. Not all teachers are so trained, however. Call and Wiggin note that an English teacher with no background in mathematics and limited knowledge in how to teach reading was able to teach students to extract meaning from the words and to translate the words into mathematical symbols. Two major conclusions were:

> (1) . . . part of the difficulty which teachers encounter in teaching mathematics is that they are not equipped to teach reading and (2) if by teaching reading instead of mathematics, we can get better results, it seems reasonable to infer that the competent mathematics teacher might get considerably better results if he were trained to teach reading of the kind encountered in mathematical problems.[12]

Change the Focus from Teaching Content to Teaching How to Read and Understand Content

Teaching reading is not an activity separate from teaching content but is a part of it. You are concerned with process. Instead of teaching just the "what" of content, also teach the "how"; of course, in teaching students how to obtain content, they learn the content itself. In this way the teaching of reading and of content is fused.

Some Skills Are Common to All Content Subjects

Obviously, the basic techniques of learning vocabulary and mastering information are essentially the same for all content fields. However, the vocabulary and the style of writing is different in each content area. For instance, the type of writing in fiction is different from that in the highly detailed, factual prose of science. If students learn how to find the main idea of

---

12. Russell J. Call and Neal A. Wiggin, "Reading and Mathematics," *Mathematics Teacher* LIX, no. 2 (February 1966): 157.

a story, they may not be able to apply the same skill in studying science materials.

Reading skills can be grouped in the following basic clusters common to all subject areas:

1. *Word recognition.* This cluster includes all of the techniques students may use to decode the graphic symbols (printed word) to the aural representation in our language, including recognizing words through context, phonic parts, structural parts, and using the dictionary.
2. *Vocabulary meaning.* Current linguistic opinion is that a word's meaning is determined by the way it is used. But the view of this author is that each word represents an idea that is present in all of its contextual meanings.
3. *Comprehension.* Numerous skills are included here, among which is noting the factual content and organization of the information—main idea, supporting detail, sequence, steps of process, and so on. Then there are the areas in which readers apply their own background and reasoning: interpreting the author's thoughts (inference); analogies, such as cause and effect, comparing and contrasting; drawing conclusions; noting connotative use of words. Further, readers may evaluate the author's ideas, judging pertinency, accuracy, bias, and so forth. Finally, readers apply their understanding of the information to practical situations and to themselves.
4. *Study skills.* These reading-study tools are the techniques the reader uses to understand and complete an assignment. They involve reading for a specific purpose; knowing how to use the parts of the book (and reference sources); reading graphic aids such as diagrams, maps, pictures; and adjusting speed and intensity to either purpose or type of material, or both.
5. *Oral reading.* There are specific techniques for effective oral reading, though our emphasis at the secondary level is on silent reading.

When you teach reading in your content area, you must undertake certain preparation. First, note the reading skills pertinent to your subject and how they apply. Second, plan ways to diagnose each student's proficiency in applying the skills to your subject; then you will know what skills to emphasize with each class. Finally, create procedures for fusing the instruction in reading with the teaching of content.

SUMMARY

Reading isn't just a subject—it's a developmental process. Teachers must get across to students not only the content of a subject but also the reading skills necessary for interpreting and using what they have read. In this way, education creates a responsible citizenry capable of self-government—individuals who think independently, understand how to apply knowledge, and communicate effectively.

QUESTIONS AND PROBLEMS FOR YOUR OWN CLASSROOM

For readers who are training to be teachers:

1. List the competencies you wish students to acquire for each topical unit in your subject.
2. What skills of speaking, listening, reading, and writing must the student be able to use in your subject?
3. Consider the implications of the statement, "All subject teachers are teachers of the language of their subject." How does this statement affect your classroom teaching procedure?
4. Consider ways to motivate students to learn.
5. What degree of student independence in learning and direction do you wish to achieve? What approaches will you use?

For readers who are teaching:

1. What are your purposes? List specifically what you wish to accomplish, including basic understandings and attitudes to be developed.
2. How will you implement your purposes in your classroom procedure?
3. What skills do you plan to teach in reading, writing, speaking, and listening?
4. What background and skills do your students need for success in their study? Translate these into cognitive objectives. Are there any affective objectives you would wish to develop?
5. How will you present your subject to the students so that they will see its relevance?
6. What degree of student involvement do you plan? How will you develop and direct it?
7. How will you adjust your teaching procedures to the differing needs of the students, such as learning rates and modalities?

SELECTED REFERENCES

Carroll, John B., and Chall, Jeanne S., eds. *Toward a Literate Society: The Report of the Committee on Reading of the National Academy of Education.* New York: McGraw-Hill Book Company, 1975.

A discussion of the level of literacy required by our society and broad guidelines for achieving it.

Marien, Michael, and Ziegler, Warren L., eds. *The Potential of Educational Futures.* Worthington, Ohio: Charles A. Jones Publishing Company, 1972.

A broad somewhat philosophical discussion of how education should be implemented in the future.

Toffler, Alvin, ed. *Learning for Tomorrow.* New York: Random House, 1974.

Shows the need for educational change and presents ideas for education in a rapidly changing society.

CHAPTER 2

Vocabulary Development and Word Analysis

OVERVIEW

Vocabulary of adequate scope, depth, and precision is basic to effective language use. Indeed, understanding terminology is vital to competence in any subject. In particular, students must have conceptual understanding for comprehension, since vocabulary development relates closely to the ideas of which words are labels. This chapter details vocabulary acquisition in each of the content areas as well as the educational principles underlying acquisition. Also discussed are the dual, interrelated features of vocabulary growth: recognition of the written or graphic symbol and development of conceptual meaning. A number of activities which can be adapted to any subject are suggested as practical ways to work toward increased comprehension.

Questions

Consider these questions before you read further:

1. What is the relation of vocabulary development to concept development?
2. What are the essential conditions for acquiring an adequate vocabulary?
3. How much and what areas of symbol recognition should be taught to high school students?

All content teachers will readily attest that vocabulary competence is paramount in the student's mastery of content. Vocabulary is the language of the subject, and it governs the student's ability not only to communicate pertinent ideas but also to think abstractly about them. A full understanding of the words leads to basic competence in the subject matter. Manzo and Sherk state that vocabulary is "central to concept formation, acculturation, articulation, and apparently, *all* learning."[1]

REASONS FOR POOR VOCABULARY

Many students may be generally competent in reading but, relative to other skills, vocabulary often seems to be their weakest area. The weakness ranges from complete ignorance of words to a superficial or narrow knowledge of them. There are several reasons for the weakness, including a student's social background. Havighurst notes that disadvantaged school children:

> Lack a family conversational experience that answers their questions and encourages them to ask questions; extends their vocabulary with new words, in particular adjectives and adverbs; and gives them a right and a need to stand up for and to explain their point of view on the world.[2]

This statement also can apply to individuals other than those labelled disadvantaged. In view of all the current literature in the field of psycholinguistics (a combination of the psychological fields of child development and acquisition of language), Kenneth Goodman points out the importance of language *clarity*—the receiver must be able to recognize and relate the message to his experience and knowledge, thus acquiring complete and accurate meaning. Simply put, using language in a variety of situations, with many other users, fosters effective usage.

If this is so, then the teacher should use words that both communicate and stretch the student's vocabulary. One teacher made it a practice to use synonymous key words in her speech. For instance, she would say, "What factors or conditions impeded, hindered, interrupted, or caused a snag to __________?" Rephrasing questions and statements helps to attune the class to the sound of less familiar words.

Another cause of insufficient vocabulary is narrow interests, often as the result of limited experience. Vocabulary will develop as the teacher succeeds in enriching the students' backgrounds and stimulating their interest and as students are exposed to and use new words to think about and to communicate experiences.

Still another reason for a poor vocabulary may be the lack of voluntary reading. This tends to keep the background narrow, depriving the student of experiencing words of differing shades of meaning. Faulty habits may stunt vocabulary growth—for example, skipping over difficult words, failing to use context, depending solely on others or on class discussion for word meanings, and avoiding the use of the dictionary.

1. A. V. Manzo and J. K. Sherk, "Some Generalizations and Strategies for Guiding Vocabulary Learning," *Journal of Reading Behavior* 4, No. 1 (Winter 1971-72): 78.
2. Robert J. Havighurst, "Social Backgrounds: Their Impact on School Children," in *Reading for the Disadvantaged,* ed. Thomas W. Horn (New York: Harcourt Brace Jovanovich, 1970), p. 15.

Finally, of course, low intelligence may be the cause. All words are abstractions; words that represent ideas, which are intangible, often are very difficult for the slow learner. Concrete representations of word concepts are necessary in this case and must be related to the student's experience. Actual or vicarious experiences may need to be provided.

Teachers who are alert to their students' backgrounds, capabilities, and habits can note any of these causes of vocabulary weakness. But what can be done about the weaknesses? How can vocabularies be enlarged in scope and in precision? We need first to consider the bases and principles of vocabulary development, some of which have already been implied. Then we need to consider specific classroom techniques.

THE BASES OF VOCABULARY DEVELOPMENT

In the narrow view we are concerned about the student's reading vocabulary. In the broad view, we are concerned about language facility, for reading is just one of the interrelated communication skills of reading, writing, speaking, and listening. Mastery of language enables the user not only to listen and read with discrimination and insight but also to speak and write with clarity and precision. A broad vocabulary increases the student's articulateness and contributes greatly to reading comprehension.

Smith, Goodman, and Meredith note that the reader uses all available *cue systems* in order to comprehend.[3] They list four such cue systems in their psycholinguistic view of the reading process: first, those within words; second, those in the flow of language; third, those within the reader; and fourth, those outside both the language and the reader. The first cue system uses the reader's knowledge of (*a*) phonic generalizations about letter–sound relationships, (*b*) little words within new words, (*c*) affixes, and (*d*) words in the reader's sight vocabulary.

The second cue category relates to the reader's basic knowledge of word patterns, which at the secondary level we recognize as knowledge of sentence structures. Included also are inflectional words—the function words that give little content meaning but alert the reader to the author's direction of thought, emphasis, and organization of ideas. Intonation, which includes pitch, stress, and juncture, is a feature in oral language more than written language. However, a reader does note, through context and structure, whether the word is *pre sent'* or *pre' sent,* for example. Juncture is noted through the marks of punctuation. The contextual meaning of a word (which is important to understand) indicates how the basic concept can be adapted or even altered by other words in the sentence or paragraph. The redundancy found in many oral or written forms is also a cue. For instance, in *The band students play their instruments,* the reader knows that the word *instruments* has to be a noun (N V N). It cannot be an adverb because of the possessive pronoun *their*. Redundancy provides four cues to the fact that the subject is plural: *students, play, their, instruments*. Certainly, syntax instruction in

---

3. E. Brooks Smith, Kenneth S. Goodman, and Robert Meredith, *Language and Thinking in School* (New York: Holt, Rinehart & Winston, 1976), pp. 269–83.

English classes is aimed toward developing the student's competence in structure and usage and relates closely to this second cue category.

The third cue category emphasizes the experiential background of the reader—language facility, dialect differences, and physiology. We will note later the importance of background to adequate comprehension. The fourth cue category includes the reader's use of graphic aids (pictures, diagrams, maps, and models) or concrete objects as a means of developing vocabulary and comprehension.

Vocabulary development is directly related to the ability to conceptualize. Therefore, if students are to think rather than to memorize by rote, they must understand the ideas represented by the word labels. However, conceptualization is accomplished only gradually, since it is dependent upon the student's growth and development in language use.

Forming Concepts

A concept is the basis for vocabulary development and, as such, is basic to comprehension. It is the individual mental construct a student develops. Although it is labelled by a word, the *word* is not the concept; it is merely the representation of the concept. When meaning (as concept) is understood, in whatever context, then only the label needs to be provided; vocabulary development is the result.

A concept is not easy to define. The dictionary suggests that it is a thought, an idea, a mental image of an action or a thing. Marksheffel defines *concept* as the "systematic organization of the total meaning that one has for any idea, process, person, thing, place or word."[4] Russell adds that a concept involves discrimination, generalization and symbolization.[5]

Each person discriminates, generalizes, and uses the appropriate symbolization in order to develop a concept. A simple illustration of this is the concept of *Prime Meridian.* Since the meridian is an imaginary line going north and south from pole to pole, the learner distinguishes the meridian from latitude and sees any meridian as a possible line of longitude. On the other hand, the meridian is the highest point of the sun during the day. This is the noon hour, when the day is at its halfway mark between sunrise and sunset. The learner would need to discriminate between meridian and latitude and also between meridian and longitude, since *meridian* has a more precise meaning than the general term *longitude.* The use of the Prime Meridian (at Greenwich, England) as the starting point for measuring degrees of longitude east and west on the earth would be noted. The next step is to generalize the interrelationship among meridian, Prime Meridian, and longitude: all are different in a precise way, but they all have a common element—placing an imaginary line north and south through the poles to note either time of the day or distance east and west. In this example, symbolization is the word to label the appropriate and precise idea: *longitude, meridian,* or *Prime Meridian.*

---

4. Ned D. Marksheffel, *Better Reading in the Secondary School* (New York: Ronald Press, 1966), p. 242.

5. David H. Russell, *Children Learn to Read,* 2nd ed. (Boston: Ginn & Co., 1961), p. 273.

We know that concepts are not static. They grow and develop as we add information and experience to our background. Suppose the student learns the differences and common elements of the terms *meridian, longitude,* and *Prime Meridian.* He may discover in a study of astronomy another application of the basic meaning—a great circle of the celestial sphere that passes through the poles and the highest point of a given place in the sphere. The concept is continually enriched as the student adds meanings in different contexts from many varied sources. The teacher does not develop a concept totally and completely in one lesson but merely establishes the basic meanings that enable the student to further discriminate, generalize, and apply the concept.

The student develops concepts both from direct experiences and from information acquired through viewing, hearing, and reading. Marksheffel outlines the sources of conceptual development:

> The child first develops his concepts from direct experiences and then as he learns the language, he has an additional aid for acquiring concepts. How do concepts and language development affect his reading? It is most important to understand that a child's success in learning to read and his growth in reading are determined to a large extent by his total background of experience, his meanings, concepts, and language. We must never forget that basic direct experiences are vital to the initial development of concepts; but once established, they need to be supplemented by a myriad of indirect experiences.
>
> Reading will provide the child with innumerable experiences that can be gained in no other way. Without vicarious, or indirect, experiences man's concepts, language, and thinking would be irrevocably restricted to his immediate environment.[6]

Thus we see that developing student competence in reading different types of informational material is vital for building concepts.

PRINCIPLES OF VOCABULARY DEVELOPMENT

Vocabulary study can be dull or exciting. Much depends upon *your* attitude. If students are asked to look up a list of ten to twenty words before each major reading assignment and then to write these words in sentences, most of them will probably look upon vocabulary study as drudgery. But if you introduce a few words at a time, discuss their uses and how they affect meaning, and weave them into your discussion, interest will likely increase. The students' attitude toward vocabulary development, reflecting your attitude and the nature of the assignment, can mean success or failure in reading.

Any successful vocabulary program follows general procedural principles. Under these principles the specific activities can be used with a firm hope of success.

1. *Make vocabulary development an activity that permeates the entire program of study in all content areas.* In class discussions, for instance, always search for the precise term, such as the distinction between

---

6. Marksheffel, *Better Reading,* pp. 243–44.

round and *spherical* when describing a shape. Discuss interesting etymologies when appropriate, such as the origin of the word *chauvinism*. Give students an appreciation of the functions of words by requiring precision in thinking and communicating. For instance, if answers or observations are too general, discuss how they could have been more precise.

2. *Create enthusiasm for vocabulary growth.* Your enthusiasm is contagious. Play with words by adding prefixes, suffixes, and inflectional endings; forming acronyms; investigating interesting derivations; and so on. Show how specific words have emotional impact and affect meaning. Say the same idea in different ways. For instance, what different impressions are created by the following statements?

   The man is fat.
   The man is obese.
   The man is roly-poly.
   The man is robust.

   Many activities can be used; the most important element is to enjoy and have fun with words.

3. *Attack verbosity.* Because of their age and familiarity with language patterns, many high school pupils verbalize very well. They may even fool us on some occasions by creating the impression that they know what they are talking about. And though the students themselves may not be overtly aware of this phenomenon, they do have a "sense of language" that often enables them to supply the correct word(s) or idea in proper form. But, in fact, they may often have only a hazy, indistinct idea. Pin the verbalizers down. Have them explain their statements. Ask them to be more specific or to explain their idea by using other words. Discuss why their statements are too broad or too narrow to be precise.

4. *Use new words repeatedly in conversation.* As a concept is developed in class, provide the word which labels or describes it. Introducing a few words at a time enables you and the students to keep them in mind as class discussion proceeds. Then weave them into the discussion when appropriate. Students begin to feel familiar with words when they use them in their own language constructs.

5. *Anticipate concepts and the appropriate words when introducing a reading assignment.* For instance, if the students are to read a selection about ecology, *ecology* is the word that must be introduced and developed; it is at this point that the new concept is tied to some past experience. Enrichment of the concept will develop as students read and the information is discussed in class.

6. *When introducing a new concept and its label, proceed from the known to the unknown* by using familiar words; recalling relevant past experiences; reinforcing through demonstrations, illustrations, or actual objects; and by using audiovisual aids such as films, recordings, and strip films.

   One social studies teacher illustrated this procedure superbly with a reading assignment about the American Revolution. The teacher developed the basic concept of the word *revolution* prior to the students' reading. She asked the students if they had any idea what the word meant. She elaborated that the American colonies' war of independence from England was called a revolution. "Why is this so?" she asked. "What does it mean?" The class, composed of students who were below average in achievement, thought for some time. Fortunately, she let them think and did not hastily assume that no one knew. Finally, a boy said, "Is it like *rpm*?" She answered, "Yes, what does *r p m* mean?" The student responded, "Well, that's what's on my record player." The teacher pushed further, "What does *rpm* stand for?" The student replied, "Revolutions per minute. It means that the turntable turns around so many times per minute." The teacher noted that the other students in the class understood the term *rpm*. With further short discussion the concept of *turning* was applied to the social studies context. Note that *before* the students read the selection they learned the basic concept of the word *revolution,* developed from their prior experience.

7. *Introduce the dictionary as a source book of interesting information.* Provide practice in dictionary use. Interest in words usually develops interest in source materials such as the dictionary and the thesaurus.
8. *Develop the idea that success in vocabulary growth depends on assuming responsibility for it.* Requiring precision in communication and thought plus a fascination with words will do much to develop students' interest in their own vocabulary development. However, this interest does not develop quickly; rather, it builds slowly throughout the school years.

VOCABULARY IN THE CONTENT FIELDS

The vocabulary of the various content fields can be separated into three groupings. One is the general vocabulary—words that may apply in general communication to more than one field. We associate these words with general and nontechnical writing, but they may appear in technical writing as well. For instance, in "The ambitious Governor Cortez built up his colony of New Spain," *ambitious* is an example of a general word used with social studies material.

The second group includes a nonspecific and general type of word that may have a precise meaning in a given field of study. Such a word would be *court*—to court disaster (general), to be presented to the court (social studies), to play tennis on a court (physical education), or a court of law (social studies or business law). Another such world would be *cell:* cell in living tissue (biology), jail cell (social studies), or battery cell (physics or general science).

The technical terms of a content field comprise the third group. These are the words usually considered when vocabulary in the content fields is studied. An example would be *photosynthesis* (biology), *integer* (mathematics), *federalism* (social studies), *accounts payable* (business), *literary genre* (English), or *cam* (industrial arts). Each field of study has its own vocabulary.

Added to the use of general words that may give students difficulty is the connotative meaning we give to many words. The connotative use of a word is different from its recognized dictionary (denotative) meaning: it is the use of a word for its emotional impact. Words may be used that have a symbolic association for us, such as *gold* or *sunrise,* when we mean something other than the actual (denotative) meaning. The connotative use of words is one way language can be employed to influence people.

Suggested Activities for the Classroom

You can incorporate these specific suggestions for vocabulary development into your lesson procedure. Vocabulary study should be included in every lesson as the words are needed for understanding and thinking about the content. Certainly, the fundamental vocabulary should be introduced before the student reads the text material.

1. Use as many firsthand experiences as possible, particularly in teaching concrete items or situations. For example, when a new word representing a tool or a piece of equipment is introduced, show the tool or equipment. In social studies, for instance, the concept of law may be illustrated by classroom and school rules. In developing such a concept the reasons for the rules, who made the rules, and so on would likely stimulate much discussion that could also enrich other concepts, such as forms of governance and the responsibilities and privileges of citizens. In mathematics, actual models of shapes (such as a cylinder or a polygon), can be shown. All subject areas provide many opportunities for establishing the meanings of vocabulary concretely.
2. Use pictures, objects, dramatizations and audiovisual aids to give concrete illustrations of a word. Many textbooks contain illustrations and diagrams which explain concepts.
3. Discuss the concepts which the words label. Explain them; help the students relate them to past experiences. For example, ask what a word means to them. Note their definitions or illustrations of the word; check the meaning from the textbook or dictionary. Note whether their meaning matches or differs from the textbook meaning.
4. Alert students to *context*—work with them in making an intelligent guess about a word's meaning by the way it is used in a sentence. For instance: *Doris had an insatiable hunger for candy after four weeks of dieting*. Even if the student does not know the meaning of the word *insatiable,* he can still note that Doris had a hunger for candy. He does not know what type or degree of hunger, but he knows that *insatiable* is an adjective that must describe her hunger. Also, from the context he notes that Doris has been dieting for four weeks, and he could infer that she had not had candy. Therefore, the meaning of *insatiable* would likely be *intense*. This is close to the actual meaning of *insatiable*—not capable of being satisfied. Examples from three textbooks follow. (See Examples 2.1, 2.2, and 2.3.)

EXAMPLE 2.1

Geysers (GI zurz) are hot springs that have a small surface opening. Water is forced upward by steam pressure at fairly regular intervals. Heat for the building of steam comes from hot, intrusive igneous rocks. Hot springs occur in the same area as geysers, but openings are not constricted. Calcium sulfate, calcium carbonate, and various sulfur compounds are dissolved in the hot water giving such springs unusual color, taste, and odor.

Reprinted by permission from Margaret S. Bishop, Berry Sutherland, and William H. Rasch, *Focus on Earth Science* (Columbus: Charles E. Merrill, 1981), p. 256.

EXAMPLE 2.2

A rectangle *ABCD* with its diagonal $\overline{AC}$ and midpoint *O* is shown. Under a half-turn about *O*, $\triangle ABC$ goes to $\triangle CDA$, written $\triangle ABC \rightarrow \triangle CDA$. So triangles *ABC* and *CDA* have *exactly the same size and shape*. They are ***congruent.***

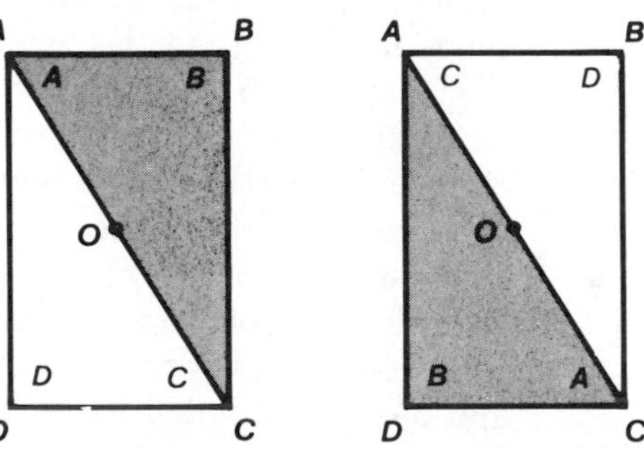

Reprinted by permission from Jay Graening, *Geometry: A Blended Approach* (Columbus: Charles E. Merrill, 1980), p. 118.

EXAMPLE 2.3

His first idea was to divide the work of making guns into different parts. Each person in his factory specialized in making one part of the gun. **Specialization** and **division of labor** mean that each person does one special part of the total job. A worker who specializes can learn to do the job quickly and well, and does not have to learn the whole job.

Whitney's second idea was to make the parts of all the guns exactly alike. The person who made triggers made them all the same size and shape. The person who made barrels made them all the same. This meant that all the parts of one kind were **interchangeable.** One trigger on one barrel could be changed for another and the gun would work just as well. All that remained was for someone to put all the parts together. And that was a simple matter.

Reprinted by permission from Irving Cutler et al., *Urban Communities* (Columbus: Charles E. Merrill, 1978), p. 136.

5. Provide a study of antonyms and synonyms. Develop precision by noting the slight differences of meaning possible in applying synonymous terms. For instance, a *dwelling* is where a person or a family lives. A *home* is also such a place, but it has an additional meaning concerning the interrelationship of family members. Other examples of differences in connotation abound in the various subject areas: *tyranny/dictatorship, section/class, cell/compartment, immunity/exemption.* Antonyms tend to be less subtle—for example, *conservation/waste* and *collection/appropriation.*
6. Study prefixes and how they alter the meaning of the root word. A random sampling from different subject areas reveals many prefixes: *in*vertebrate, *re*production, *anti*trust, *sub*urban, *bi*sector, *con*current, *de*ductive, *exo*thermic, *non*volatile. Also, show the relation of suffixes to the function of a word in a sentence. The words *information* and *inform* have the same root and basic meaning, but their functions in a sentence differ. *Information* is the knowledge or the subject matter of communication. *Inform* is the act of communicating knowledge. One is a noun, the other a verb. Another variation is to build words by adding suffixes: nature, natural, naturally. Encourage students to be precise by observing the function of the word in a sentence. In the example just presented, *nature* is the phenomenon, the noun; *natural* pertains to the phenomenon of nature and is an adjective; and *naturally* is the "how"—the adverbial form.
7. Encourage wide reading as a means of providing exposure to words and variations of word usage. Though this activity is unstructured in helping students to learn words, the reader will discover words with many meanings. For example, the student may encounter the word *food* used as a means of nourishment, as provender, as diet, as a type (bread or meat), as board, as a ration—depending upon the subject and context. Other examples found in the subject areas are *breed* (noun), a group related by a common ancestor, or (verb), to propagate; *area,* as we are using it here, a field of study such as biology, or a surface included within a set of lines, as in mathematics.
8. Stimulate interest in words by discussing idiomatic phrases, figurative language, and interesting word origins. For example, what type of action is described in "He came forward like a two-ton truck"? What is the history of such words as *chauvinism* and *pasteurization?*
9. Keep notebook records of the following:
   a. new words the students meet and learn.
   b. words relating to special subjects.
   c. words relating to hobbies.
   d. new uses and additional meanings of familiar words.
   e. substitutes for overworked words.
   f. words that describe or characterize particular persons, objects, or situations.
   g. words appealing to the senses—those contributing to sensory imagery while reading.
   h. idiomatic phrases.

A classroom dictionary can be a growing reference book, as elaborate or simple as you wish to make it. It is usually a looseleaf notebook with a page for each new word. The word is entered with all appropriate definitions listed. Various forms of the word can be listed, showing prefixes and suffixes and inflectional endings added. Examples can be shown of the word used in different sentences to show changes in contextual meaning. It may be illustrated graphically, when appropriate. A history of the word may also be included.

10. Substitute specific words for general and overworked words used by your students. Note overworked words in student compositions. For instance, students may use the word *said* too frequently in their short stories. To have students become aware of other words that indicate dialogue, they could research several books and list all the ways authors indicate conversation. A class listing could be compiled for the students to refer to when they write stories.
11. Replace slang with standard language. Sometimes students are interested in the reverse of this activity. The class might decide to compile their own slang dictionary.
12. Think of all the words that can be used to describe an object, a time, a person, or a situation. This activity is effective in a class discussion, and it can be embellished in a number of ways. After a complete listing of adjectives has been compiled, students can determine which words are best suited for advertising copy, which words tend to have emotional overtones, which words would give a negative picture. Since all could apply to the object, none would be inaccurate. This exercise may serve as a good introduction to the various techniques of propaganda.
13. Rewrite a paragraph using different words. Note the functions of specific words that give the paragraph the desired meaning or impact. A variation of this is to rewrite the paragraph to keep the same meaning but to present a different point of view through use of connotative words.
14. Point out words that denote categories, such as *tree,* under which many types can be listed. In the subject areas, this activity as a means of outlining new vocabulary to show the organization of information. A variation is to require students to match people, places, and events from terms found at the ends of a chapter or a unit. For example:

    Thomas Paine—*Common Sense*
    Minutemen—Lexington, Concord

    A typical listing of vocabulary at the end of a chapter is: *homosphere, heterosphere, ionosphere, mesosphere, stratosphere, troposphere, thermosphere, atmosphere.* In this listing, *atmosphere* is the classifier or the fundamental term; all of the other terms are names of parts of the atmosphere.
15. Note words that give impressions or appeal to the emotions.
16. Note words that carry a symbolic meaning, such as *sunrise:* hope, beginning, new freshness.

17. Have the students keep a vocabulary file of new words on index cards. Determine the type of information to be recorded on each card—meanings, form of the word, etymology, pronunciation, examples of usage. Use one card for each word. The cards may be organized alphabetically or according to subject unit or categories.
18. Rewrite headlines and articles to take out the words appealing to the emotions. Material for this activity will be found in newspapers, magazines, and trade books. In the social studies, material can be original sources or writings contemporary with periods of history.
19. Write advertising copy for some product, choosing words to give different impressions of the products.
20. Have the students note wordiness and offer a more succinct statement; for instance, changing *met with approval of the principal* to the more succinct *the principal approved.*
21. Note euphemisms such as *funeral director* for *undertaker.*
22. Note acronyms. Many acronymic words are being devised, particularly in science and the social studies; examples include *radar, sonar, laser, NATO,* and *VISTA.*
23. Devise vocabulary "bees," crossword puzzles, dictionary races, and vocabulary games where knowledge of words is the skill of the game.
24. Question students on their understanding of words:
    a. What is the key word in this heading? Why?
    b. What does ______ mean as used in this sentence?
    c. What other meanings do you already know for ______?
    d. What does the glossary in your book say about ______?
    e. How many meanings does your dictionary give for ______?
    f. Which meaning is appropriate in this selection?
    g. What other words may be substituted for this word?
25. Discuss indefinite words such as *few, many, any, large, small, little, much, some, several, most.* Students should realize that these words do not convey precise meanings.
26. Discuss definite words such as *all, always, certain, every, sure, never, right, true, whole.* Alert students to their effect on the meaning of a sentence.
27. Investigate and discuss the history of the English language, its changing form and its various levels of usage—slang, informal English, formal English, technical language. Note how the same idea can be expressed at each level. Investigate obsolete words such as *flivver, galluses, celluloid.*
28. Review the kinds of adjectives that modify nouns. Note these in the vocabulary lists at the end of chapters. A few illustrations:

Noun	*Adjective*
coordinates	polar
resistance	environmental
radiation	adaptive
dome	geodesic
policy	colonial

29. Note words that may be confused. Give the students sentences in which they must supply the correct word according to the context.

For example: *A country usually* (imports, exports) *goods it does not produce for itself.*

30. Some confused words may be called malapropisms or "boo-boos." These are particularly effective in English classes, and students can have much fun with them while learning to use words more precisely. Illustrations of the type of malapropisms that you can evolve are: "What *delusion* to Greek mythology is made in the poem?" or "I was very insulted with the *preposition* the salesman made to me about my car."
31. Discuss words that have multiple meanings, especially in subject areas other than the one you teach. For instance, consider the word *capital:* a type of punishment, the seat of government, the top of a column, a building, wealth, highly important, and excellent.
32. Help students to develop an understanding of word meaning through the use of analogies. Examples: hypotenuse—right triangle; three axes of symmetry—__________ (isosceles triangle, equilateral triangle). Or aorta—large artery; capillary—__________ (vein, artery, connectors of veins and arteries).
33. Use matching exercises. Present two columns, one listing the words and the other listing the definitions. In a variation, the listing of definitions can be greater in number than the number of words.
34. Discussing compound words is one way of noting little words in big words. For example: *longshore, carpetbaggers, commonwealth, income.*
35. Use a variation of the cloze procedure. Have the students complete a passage from which essential words of mood and description or new technical words are deleted. For example:
    In the United States most of the ________ courts are overloaded with ________. A large part of the jam-up in the courts is due to cases of ________ drunkenness, ________ gambling, and prostitution. ________ arrests for property crimes such as robbery and burglary have also greatly ________ in most cities. (increased, cases, felony, illegal, criminal, public)[7]
    The words that need to be put into the blanks are listed out of order. To make the exercise more difficult, list more words than there are blanks.
36. Study commonly used abbreviations, which are closely related to acronyms. Each subject uses its own abbreviations in addition to those in general use—for example; ft., gal., neg., misc., m.p.h., and so on. Incidentally, as all mathematics, shop, and science teachers know, formulae and equations are abbreviated forms of English sentences.

Several methods of study help in vocabulary development: memorization of word lists, wide reading, study of word histories, use of context, use of the dictionary, and prefix-root analysis. But no one of these methods is adequate

7. Irving Cutler et al., *Urban Communities* (Columbus: Charles E. Merrill, 1978), pp. 299–300.

when used alone without consideration of the student's needs and interests. McDonald summarizes the key aspects and benefits of a viable vocabulary program:

> A functional vocabulary program will provide each student with words he needs in such a way that he can master the conceptual categories they represent. The program will be multidimensional, drawing on all of the traditional methods *where appropriate* and in ways consonant with the principles of learning. As an outcome, the student will be able to guess at meanings of unfamiliar words, using one or more methods as appropriate. He will check the guess with the meaning of the whole and (where necessary) with the dictionary. He will look for familiar words used in unfamiliar ways and so gradually extend the range of referent attributes symbolized by each word.[8]

WORD ANALYSIS AT THE HIGH SCHOOL LEVEL

Instruction in the techniques of word analysis traditionally has not been considered important at the high school level. Except for the severely disabled, high school students are able to recognize common letter clusters and to give the appropriate sound for nearly all single-syllable words. However, they have difficulty pronouncing many of the multisyllabic words found in the subject areas. Consequently, techniques of word analysis should be taught.

The goal in word analysis instruction is to boost students' comprehension. Of course, students' background and sense of language play important roles in the ability to analyze an unfamiliar word. High school students can approach unfamiliar words in the following ways:

1. Contextual analysis. This relates directly to meaning, particularly to the word's placement in the sentence and the general sense of the sentence.
2. Structural analysis. This involves knowing the units of meaning—the morphemes—within words, specifically roots, affixes, inflectional endings, and compound words.
3. Phonic analysis. This involves the actual recognition of letter–sound correspondence. Particularly important at the high school level is the ability to divide a multisyllabic word into pronounceable units—syllables—and to note letter clusters.
4. Dictionary usage. The high school student uses the dictionary to discover the meaning of an unfamiliar word when all of the other methods of analysis have proven fruitless.

Although students may not be aware of these options, they do use them. Furthermore, they use a combination of options, going only as far as they need to until they can recognize the word. Competent students check their

---

8. Arthur S. McDonald, "Vocabulary Development: Facts, Fallacies and Programs," in *Teaching Reading in High School: Selected Articles,* ed. Robert Karlin (New York: Bobbs-Merrill, 1969), p. 166.

recognition by comparing the conclusion from one option against the conclusion drawn from another. For example, a student first attempts to recognize a word from its contextual use and then confirms the choice by using phonetic information—does the word start with the same sound? Next she checks meaning units within the word. If these techniques do not help, sounding out the word might; finally, using the dictionary may be necessary. Much of this process is done nearly simultaneously.

In the primary grades other means of word analysis also would be included, such as the sight method and configuration. The sight method, commonly called *look and say,* is a rote memorization of the printed form of the word. The other method, configuration, involves paying attention to the shape of the word. Neither of these methods is taught to any great extent at the high school level. However, we must recognize that high school students do use the sight method. Once a word has been analyzed and its pronunciation and meaning are known, the word becomes a sight word. Effective readers do not analyze every word each time they meet it. Consequently, as knowledge of words and scope of reading increase, fewer and fewer words must be analyzed. To get students to this point of expertise, continual review and reteaching must accompany the presentation of vocabulary in each subject area.

Contextual Analysis

Contextual analysis has often been characterized as "intelligent guessing" by the reader. It is a quick and valid technique but inadequate as the sole method. The ability to use this method depends upon the student's general knowledge of the subject. Also, general knowledge of language usage, such as the function of the word in the sentence, helps to determine the proper pronunciation and function of a word. For instance,

"The dentist will extract two wisdom teeth."
(verb)

"The chef used a vanilla extract in the recipe."
(noun)

One application of contextual analysis is to have students note the meanings of technical words in their textbooks. Most new words are defined in the material when they are first used. Students can expect to read the meaning if the word first appears in italics or boldface print. Sometimes, however, the word is not highlighted typographically. For example: **"Physical properties** are properties or characteristics that can be seen and measured." Then, "Oxides are another important group of minerals. They are combinations of oxygen (O) and some other element or elements."[9] In both examples, the context defines the technical terms as they are introduced.

Besides the direct explanation, the word may be used as a synonym to one the student may already know. For example: "The pirates started firing when their ship was *alongside* or *abeam* of ours." It may also be explained by an example: "*Strip farming* and *terracing* to keep land from washing away are

9. Margaret S. Bishop, Berry Sutherland, and William H. Rasch, *Focus on Earth Science* (Columbus: Charles E. Merrill, 1981), pp. 73, 88.

techniques of *land conservation.*" A word may be used to summarize a description or action; such a sentence might be found in a social studies textbook: "Theodore Roosevelt was successful as a *statesman, soldier, sportsman, explorer* and *author;* he was a *versatile* man."

Help high school students to apply their sense of language structure. Such terms as *for example, for instance, in other words, that is, or to be more specific* signal either illustration or restatement to clarify a thought. Another set of clues to contextual meaning is punctuation—the use of the comma, colon, parenthesis, quotation marks, dashes. An illustration from a high school textbook shows a number of such clues:

> Interest
> Interest—the price of money—is determined by the forces of demand and supply in the market for capital. . . . Buyers (the users of money) are numerous and well informed. Sellers (those who make the savings available) are also numerous and well informed.[10]

Note the use of the dash and parentheses to denote definition.

In another instance, the meaning of the term *incentive* is implied by a question:

> Individual Incentive
> Finally, high taxes are sometimes held responsible for reducing an individual's incentive to work. Why should certain highly paid people work unusually hard if they are permitted to keep only a small portion of the additional dollars they earn?[11]

Is the unfamiliar word a noun that may signify who or what? Is it a verb that may indicate a state of being or what is being done? Is it an adverb that would answer such questions as how, how much, how long, how well? Is it an adjective noting what kind of nature? This type of information narrows the student's choices.

Contextual analysis also makes use of *language redundancy.* In looking for clues that will assist in recognizing a term, students may not realize that the direct explanation or definition given for a word is a redundancy. Restatements, examples, and summary statements all are forms of redundancy.

Suggested Activities

1. Have the student read a sentence from the textbook and note the type of context clue for a specific word:
   a. direct definition—How is the definition included? Is it set off by commas, dashes, parentheses? A subordinate clause? A following sentence? A paragraph?
   b. synonym
   c. summary
   d. restatement

---

10. James E. Brown, Harold A. Wolf, and S. Stowell Symmes, *Economics: Principles—Practices* (Columbus: Charles E. Merrill, 1979), pp. 188–89, 214.
11. Frank Freidel and Henry H. Drewry, *America Is* (Columbus: Charles E. Merrill, 1978), p. 376.

2. Use the cloze procedure in which certain key words are omitted, such as the new and important ones for the subject area. A random listing of the words below the paragraph can help the students. Discuss with the class what clues they got from the context for choosing a particular word for a blank space.
3. Prepare an exercise in which key ideas are presented. Then ask questions that focus attention on certain contextual clues. For example: "Isolationists—people who want to isolate or close off their country from outside problems—had a strong support throughout the United States.[12]
   a. How is the word *isolationists* defined?
   b. How could one country such as the United States be "closed off" from other countries?
   c. Describe an isolationist's view of what our relations with other countries should be.
4. Choose or create sentences in which students are to supply a synonym of the word they must define contextually. For example: "There were four *pertinent* facts in the article on energy." (Synonyms students could supply include *important, essential.*)
5. When students note a word they do not know and they cannot find any contextual clues, help them limit the choices by using their knowledge of syntax to note both the word's function and the type of question it would answer, such as what, how, when, what kind, and so on. A key question is, "What word would make sense?" In other words, ask students to think about the general meaning of the sentence as a clue to the word in question.

Using Morphological Clues—Structural Analysis

Morphological clues to word recognition help in analyzing words with regard to the units of meaning within them. The term is closely related to an older term, *structural analysis*.

In this method, the student uses her knowledge of word-form changes through the analysis of prefixes, suffixes, roots, grammatical inflectional endings, and recognition of compound words. Each of these contributes to the meaning of a whole word. Both teachers and students think of this as a very logical method of word analysis. It relates closely to the meaning of words and the function of a word in a sentence.

Inflectional endings denote tense, number, and degree.

tense:	ask	ask*ed*
	ask	ask*ing*
number:	boy	boy*s*
	speech	speech*es*
degree:	green	green*er*
	green	green*est*

The high school student likely has been taught that inflectional endings change the meaning of the word. The principles of adding inflectional endings

---

12. Freidel and Drewry, *America Is,* p. 432.

to words serve as guides for spelling as well as for correct usage. Though these are included in the curricula of most English classes, they should be carried over when appropriate to all classes. The principles are:

1. When the root word ends in a final *e*, the *e* is usually dropped before an ending that begins with a vowel, as in *produce—produced* (*ed* added), *raise—raised*. However, when the root words end in *ce* or *ge*, the *e* is retained when the ending begins with *a* or *o*, as in the case of *change—changeable, notice—noticeable*.
2. If a syllable or root words ends in a single consonant preceded by a vowel, the consonant is usually doubled when a consonant is added. *Examples: ship—shipped, shipping; map—mapped, mapping*.
3. Words ending in *f* or *fe* usually form their plurals by changing the *f* to *v* and adding the plural ending, as in *half—halves*.
4. When a word ends with *y* preceded by a consonant, the *y* is usually changed to an *i* before an ending is added in such cases as *century—centuries, cavity—cavities*.

Prefixes and *suffixes* are added to the root of a word to condition the meaning of the root. The meaning of the root is not altered but modified. For example, *trace, retrace:* to trace again; *possible, impossible:* not possible. In addition, many suffixes indicate the function the word has in a sentence. For example, *govern* is a verb and denotes an action. *Government* is a noun and is the means or instrument for governing.

Many of the most common prefixes and suffixes are listed below (see Tables 2.1 and 2.2), with meanings and examples given. Wherever possible, in all of the subject areas the appropriate prefixes, roots, and suffixes should be reviewed when used in the words the students are expected to learn.

TABLE 2.1 Common Prefixes

Prefix	*Meanings*	*Example*
Negative		
in-		insensitive
im-		impossible
ir-	not, non-, un-	irresponsible
il-		illegal
un-	not, in-, non-, contrary, removal or privation of	unnecessary
non-	not, un-, in-	nonsense
dis	separation, reversal, depriving, negation	dissuade
mis-	amiss, wrong, ill	misspell
anti-	opposite, against, instead, counter	antitoxin

TABLE 2.1 *Cont'd*

Prefix	*Meanings*	*Example*
Direction, Time, Occurrence		
ex-	out of, off, from beyond, away from, without, thoroughly, formerly—but not now	exit
in-	in, within, into, toward, on	infuse
per-	throughout in space or time, away or over, completely, perfectly, extremely, very; largest or relatively large, highest, or relatively high (chem.)	permit
re-	back, backwards, back from advancing, again	retrace
de-	down; separation, off; away; out of; intensification, completely; reversing, undoing, depriving, freeing from	deface
circum-	round, about, on all sides, revolving about, surrounding	circumspect
sub-	under, below, beneath, lower; next lower than, subordinate to; forming a further division, a repetition, continuation of below the category of but above the category which follows (biol.); situation on ventral side or under (anat.); having less than normal amount (chem.); near base of, bordering upon (geog., geol.); inversely (math.)	subterranean
syn-, sy-, sym-	with, along with, at the same time	synchronize
trans-	over, across, beyond, through, transcending	transport
retro-	backward, back, situated behind	retroactive
Relationship		
auto-	self	automobile
co-	with, together, in conjunction, jointly; corresponding function of the complement of an arc or angle (math.); complement of the delination, latitude (astron.)	cooperate
com-	with, together, in conjunction, very	commit
con-	equal to *com-* before consonants except b, h, l, m, p, r, w	conform
col-	assimilated form of *com-*	collude

TABLE 2.1 *Cont'd*

Prefix	*Meanings*	*Example*
cor-	assimilated form of *com-*	correspond
counter-	opposite or contrary, reciprocal, retaliatory, complementary	counteract
contra-	against, contrary, in opposition	contradict
hyper-	over, above, beyond, beyond the norm; super; extra; denoting position above (anat., zool.); equal to per- (chem.)	hyperactive
super-	above, over; on or at the top of, over and above, more than; that surpasses all or most others of its kind; exceeding, in excess; in addition, extra; secondarily; situated over, on upper part or dorsal side (biol.); having the ingredient in large proportion (chem.)	supercilious
Time and Number		
pro-	priority in place, or time, or order; before	proceed
pre-	before in time, previously, previous, in advance, in front of, ahead of, prior to	precede
post-	after, subsequent, later; behind or posterior (biol.)	postpone
uni-	one, single, have but one	uniform
bi-	two, twice, double; relation to each of two symmetrically paired parts (biol.)	biennial
tri-	having three, into three, thrice, every third, denoting presence of three atoms, groups, or equivalents of that signified by the term to which it is attached (chem.)	triennial
quadr-	four	quadrilateral
tetra-	four	tetrometer
penta-	five	pentagon
quin-	five	quintet
sex-	six	sextet
hexa-	six	hexagonal
sept-	seven	septennial
oct-	eight	octagon
dec-	ten	decade

TABLE 2.1 *Cont'd*

Prefix	*Meanings*	*Example*
centi-	one hundred	centimeter
milli-	one thousand	milligram
kilo-	one thousand	kilogram
hemi-	half	hemisphere
semi-	half; approximately half, partly; precisely half; halved or bisected; coming twice; in one half, in some particular; in low degree, no more than half; little more than, little better than	semicircle
multi-	many, much; having many; many times over; more than two	multiply
Additional (Misc.)		
ante-	before, preceding, in front of, prior, anticipatory, anterior fore	antedate
inter-	among, between, together; mutual, mutually, reciprocal, intervening	intercede
intra-	within, inside, into	intramural
intro-	to, into, within, inward	introduce
fore-	in front, as forerunner, beforehand, preceding, before	forecast

Suffixes indicate the function of a word, and therefore its part of speech. As the student becomes familiar with the various suffixes she should be able to give the correct form of the word as determined by its function in the sentence. Table 2.2 presents common noun, verb, and adjective suffixes.

TABLE 2.2 Suffixes

Suffix	*Meanings*	*Example*
Noun		
-ion	result of	fusion
-sion	the act, quality, condition of, result of	explosion
-ation	the act of	formation
-ity	state or condition	density
-ty		plenty
-ance	quality or state of being	disturbance

TABLE 2.2 *Cont'd*

Suffix	*Meanings*	*Example*
-ence	quality or state of being	presence
-ment	result of or a means, agency, or instrument	government
-ness	condition, state of being	goodness
-hood	condition, state of being	neighborhood
-ship	condition, state of being, ability, or rank	partnership
-dom	rank of, position of, state of being one who has to do with; one of a size, capacity, value, date; resident of; agent	freedom
-or	state, quality, agent, doer	elector
-ant	person or thing acting as agent	attendant
-itis	inflammation	appendicitis
Verb		
-ize	to subject to, to render; to impregnate, treat, or combine with (chem.); practice or carry on	minimize
-fy	to make, to form into	ratify
-ate	combine, impregnate, treat with (chem.)	agitate
Adjective		
-able (-ible)	implication of capacity, fitness, worthiness to be acted upon; tending to, given to, favoring, causing, able to, liable to	serviceable
-ive	having the nature or quality of, given or tending to	deceive
-al or -ial	belonging to, pertaining to, indicating the presence of the aldehyde group (-al, chem.)	natural remedial
-ful	full of, abounding in, characterized by; able to or tending to	masterful
-ish	of the nature of, belonging to	childish
-less	without, distitute of, not having, free from; beyond the range of; unable or without power	selfless
-ary	pertaining to, connected with; a person or thing belonging to or connected with; a place for	residuary
-ous (-ious)	full of, abounding in, having, possessing the qualities of, like; denotes valence lower than that denoted by -ic (chem.); used to form adjectives corresponding to nouns of classification (biol.)	gracious

The words that comprise the English language come from many different languages. Of these, Latin and Greek are considered the primary sources. Many technical words have roots belonging to Latin and Greek. When specific words are being studied, the teacher may call attention to the root, its origin, and its meaning. Students may find that developing their knowledge of roots will gradually improve their skill in recognizing and defining new words. They will also note how many words can develop from a single root. In fact, upon learning a root, they will be able to list a number of related words. For example, if the student is learning the word *photometer* and discovers that the root *photo* is of Greek origin and means light, and *meter* is of Greek origin and means measure, the meaning of the word can be determined: a device to measure the intensity of light. They will also be able to think of other words using the same roots, such as *photoelectric, photogenic, photographic, thermometer, metric,* and *barometer.*

The listing of Latin and Greek roots in Tables 2.3 and 2.4 is highly selective, but it indicates the extensiveness of this aid.

TABLE 2.3 Common Roots—Latin

Root	*Meaning*	*Derivatives*
-aud-, -audit-	hear	auditorium
-avi-,	bird	aviation
-caput-	head	capital
-ced-, -cess-	move, yield	recede
-clar-	clear	clarify
-clin-	lean	incline
-clud-, -claud-, -clus-	shut	seclude
-cord-	heart	cordial
-corp-	body	corporal
-cred-	to believe	credible
-curr-, -curs-	run	current
-dic-, -dict-	say	predict
-domin-	master	dominate
-duc-, -duct-	lead	conduct
-fac-, -fic-, -fact-, -fect-	to make, do	factory
-fer-	bear, carry	transfer
-fin-	end	finish
-fort-	strong	fortitude
-jun-, -junct-	join	junction
-laud-, -laudat-	praise	applause
-let-, -lect-	gather, choose, read	collect
-legis-, -lex-	law	legislature
-lux-, -luc-	light	elucidate
-magn-	great	magnificent
-mal-	bad	malevolent
-man-	hand	manual
-mit-, -miss-	send	missile
-mov-, -mot-	set in motion	motor
-nov-, novus-	new	renovation

TABLE 2.3 *Cont'd*

Root	*Meaning*	*Derivatives*
-pac-	peace	pacific
-pel-, -puls-	urge, drive	propel
-pend-, -pens-	hang, weigh	pensive
-plic-, -plex-	bend, fold	plexiglas
-pon-, -pos-	place, put	postpone
-sci-	know	science
-scrib-, -script-	write	describe
-solv-, -solut-	loosen	solution
-sepec-, -spect-	look	spectator
-sta-	stand firm	stable
-stru-, -struct-	build	construct
-tend-, -tens-	stretch	tendency
-tort-	to twist	distort
-ven-, -vent-	come	convention
-ver-	true	veritable
-vert-, -vers-	turn	reverse
-viv-, -vit-	live, life	vitality
-vid-, -vis-	see	evident
-voc-	call	vocation

TABLE 2.4 Common Roots—Greek

Root	*Meaning*	*Derivatives*
-anthrop-	man	anthropology
-arch-	first, chief	monarch
-aster-	star	astronomy
-bibl-	book	bibliography
-bio-	life	biology
-chrom-	color	chromatic
-chron-	time	chronological
-crypt-	secret	cryptic
-dem-	people	democracy
-derm-	skin	epidermis
-dox-	opinion	paradox
-dynam-	power	dynamic
-gam-	marriage	polygamy
-gen-	birth	eugenics
-geo-	earth	geography
-gyn-	woman	gynecology
-graph-, -gram-	write, written	photograph
-hetero-	different	heterogeneous
-homo-	same	homogeneous
-hydr-	water	hydrometer
-lith-	stone	monolith
-log-, -logy-,	speech, word, study	astrology
-metr-	measure	thermometer

TABLE 2.4 *Cont'd*

Root	*Meaning*	*Derivatives*
-micro-	small	microscope
-path-	feeling, suffering	sympathy
-phil-	love	philosopher
-phon-	sound	dictaphone
-photo-	light	photogenic
-physio-	nature	physics
-pod-	foot	tripod
-polis-	city	metropolis
-psych-	mind	psychology
-scop-	see	microscope
-tele-	far	telescope
-the-	god	atheist
-tom-	cut	anatomy
-zo-	animal	zoology

Many compound words in English are formed by combining two words. These words are pronounced the same as each of the combining forms except for accent, and the student will need to use appropriately all of the various means of word analysis. The meaning of a compound word is the combined meaning of the individual word components. *Examples: rainfall* (rain′fall)—the fall of rain in amount; *earthquake* (earth′quake)—quaking (trembling) of the earth.

Syllabication relates to aspects of both sound units and meaning units within a word. Prefixes, suffixes, and many inflectional endings add one or more syllables to a root. Students should know that each syllable must contain at least one vowel letter and that each syllable has one vowel sound. Then they can easily determine the number of syllables a word contains by saying it carefully and noting the number of different vowel sounds. Further, they can determine the accent by listening for the syllable(s) that receive stress. Many of the new and long words students meet in reading would be recognizable if they could break the words into pronouceable, one-syllable units. At this point, general knowledge of language sounds could be used.

Through continual application in class, students should become familiar with the following principles of syllabication and accent:

1. The number of vowel sounds heard in a word tells how many syllables the word contains. There is one vowel sound for every syllable: *u*m-br*e*l-l*a*, r*e*-c*ei*ve, r*ai*n.
2. If a vowel is followed by two consonants, the first syllable usually ends with the first of the two consonants: le*t*-*t*er, e*x*-cept, ca*n*-*dy*.
3. If a vowel is followed by a single consonant, that consonant usually begins the second syllable. *Examples:* ba-*c*on, pa-*p*er, ti-*g*er
4. If a word ends in *le* and a consonant comes before the *l*, this consonant usually begins the last syllable. *Examples:* tum-*b*le, ma-*p*le, ta-*b*le
5. Generally, consonant digraphs (*ch, th, sh,* and *wh*) and consonant blends are not divided. *Examples:* ma-*ch*ine, wea-*th*er

6. Prefixes and suffixes usually form separate syllables. *Examples: com*-promise, *un*-constitutional, *a*-septic, termin-*al*, hydraul-*ic*
7. When the suffix (inflectional ending) *ed* is added to a word ending in *t* or *d*, a separate syllable is formed. *Examples:* weight-*ed*, expand-*ed*
8. Words of two or three syllables are usually accented on the first syllable. *Examples: ster*-i-lize, *in*-su-late, *sul*-fur
9. Words ending with the suffix -sion or -tion are usually accented on the syllable preceding the suffix. *Examples:* in-*fec*-tion, plan-*ta*-tion, di-*men*-sion
10. Some words are accented differently in accordance with their function in a sentence. *Examples: con*-tract (noun)—con-*tract* (verb); *re*-cord (noun)—re-*cord* (verb)
11. When the last syllable of a word ends in *le*, the syllable is usually unaccented. *Examples: tum*-ble, *ma*-ple, *ta*-ble
12. When one or more prefixes or suffixes are added to a root word, the accent is usually on the root word. The root and the prefix are generally not in the same syllable. *Examples:* dis-*prove*, re-*count*, un-*clean*, a-*bout*, *great*-ly, *deal*-ing, *mile*-age, *rest*-ful

Suggested Activities for Classroom Use

1. *Using endings to determine word function.* Change the following verbs to nouns.

Verb	*Noun*
pay	pay*ment*
transpose	transposi*tion*
diffuse	diffu*sion*
elevate	eleva*tion*
direct	direc*tion*

   The same type of exercise can be constructed to change words to verbs, adjectives, and adverbs.
2. *Building words.* Have the students select a word and make as many new words as possible by adding various prefixes and suffixes. Then determine the basic thread of meaning to all, the way each alters this meaning, and the function of each word as it is used. For example:

	Function	*Meaning*
construct	verb	to build (the basic thread of meaning)
construc*tion*	noun	the state or act of building
construct*ing*	verb-participle	process of building
construct*ed*	verb-past tense	was built
*re*construct	verb	same as above except for the addition of the prefix *re* which adds to the meaning—building again
*re*construc*tion*	noun	
*re*construct*ing*	verb	

3. *Noting words with the same root.* Have the students select a root and determine all of the words which use the root. Have them give the

meaning of the root and the meaning of each word, showing how the change in word function or use of affix alters the basic meaning. For example: *graph, graphy*—write (meaning of root). Samples of the use of the root follows:

photography—	writing with light-producing images on a sensitized surface by the action of light
photographer—	one who writes with light
photograph—	the product of writing with light
autograph—	self *written:* a person's written account of his life experiences
phonograph—	the instrument used to *write* with sound
dictograph—	instrument used to write speech
biography—	a written account of life
bibliography—	the written listing of books
biographer—	one who writes an account of a life
orthography—	correct writing
cartography—	written maps or charts
cartographer—	one who draws (writes) maps or charts
geography—	earth writing—description of the earth or region therein—of its features and life
stenography—	small writing—shorthand
stenographer—	one who writes small

Each of these can be expanded further by grammatical inflections. For example:

photograph	noun
photograph*ing*	verb—participle
photograph*ed*	verb—past tense

A variation of this exercise is to present to the students an outline of word forms which the students are to fill in with words of a single root. One is worked out as an example.

verb: (to) photograph
noun: photograph
adjective: photographic
adverb: photographically
person: photographer
action: photography
thing: photograph

Sometimes the noun and verb forms will be the same. Also, sometimes there may be several forms for a single part of speech.

4. A similar exercise is a listing of words by the student with the use of a single prefix. For example: *in* means not, *in*conclusive means not conclusive. Also, alert the student to assimilated forms of the prefix. For example:

ir	*ir*responsible
il	*il*logical
im	*im*possible
ig	*ig*noble

5. *Dividing words by their structural components.* Have the students divide words from their textbooks into prefixes, roots, and suffixes.

Prefix	*Root*	*Suffix*
multi	—plic	—ation
inter	—nat	—ion al
in	—sol	—uble
ex	—pos	—ition

An extension of this type of exercise is to have each part of the word defined in order to note its basic meaning.

multi-	many	condition of folding many times
-plic-	fold	
-ation-	state, condition	
inter-	between	pertaining to the condition between nations
-nat-	nation	
-ion, al	condition, pertaining	
in-	not	not capable of being
-sol-	dissolve	
-uble-	capable of	
ex-	out of	the act of placing out ("putting out") (writing designed to convey information)
-pos-	place, put	
-ition-	action	

6. *Acronyms.* Some modern words in the English language are formed by using the first letter of each word in a name. For example, NATO comes from *N*orth *A*tlantic *T*reaty *O*rganization. Have the students form lists and define acronyms such as:

CORE	Congress of Racial Equality
SNAFU	Situation normal, all fouled up
LORAN	Long-range navigation
LASER	Light amplification by stimulated emission of radiation
AWOL	Absent without leave
NOW	National Organization of Women

7. Similar to acronyms are abbreviations of terms which do not form acronyms, but are used in place of the full title. Have the student evolve a listing of such abbreviations as:

PTA	Parent-Teachers Association
NBC	National Broadcasting Company
TV	Television
AD	Anno Domini
CPA	Certified Public Accountant

Grapho-Phonemic Skills

Though the English language has been characterized as an irregular one, it has been estimated that 85% of English words are phonetic and therefore can be analyzed in accordance with specific principles.

Although they may not know specific rules or generalizations, high school students have used language over the years and are familiar with various usages. They are familiar with the basic sounds and letter combinations of the language. For example, they probably know the basic vowel sounds as well as the consonants, consonant blends, digraphs and diphthongs and letter clusters. However, they may not realize they have this general knowledge and may need the teacher's help to recognize and use it.

Students should know the following basic information about letters:

1. We have twenty-six letters in our alphabet which are used to spell all of the words in English.
2. There are forty-three different sounds in English called *phonemes,* which are represented by numerous and various combinations of letters.
3. The letters of the alphabet are basically classified as vowels and consonants. The vowel letters are *a, e, i, o, u,* sometimes *y,* and occasionally *w.* The remaining letters are consonants.
4. In many English words a single vowel may represent different sounds. This is true also for some consonants such as *c, f,* and *s.*
5. In many English words some vowels and consonants may be silent and not produce any sound for the word.
6. Certain combinations of vowels and of consonants produce unique sounds.

The most important phonic generalizations that help high school students are as follows:

1. The vowel in a syllable which ends with one or more consonants (a closed syllable) has a short sound. *Examples:* ash, cell, fifth, ton, bud
2. A vowel which is the final letter of a syllable (an open syllable) is usually long. *Examples:* vill*i*, zer*o*, rati*o*
3. A syllable having two vowels, one of which is a final *e,* usually has the long sound of the first vowel with the final *e* silent. *Examples:* nitr*a*t*e*, sec*e*d*e*, l*i*m*e*, n*o*d*e*, c*u*b*e*, d*ye*
4. The sound of a vowel followed by the letter *r* is controlled by the sound of the *r.* Specifically, *a* or *o* followed by *r* is neither long nor short. The vowels *i, e,* and *u* followed by *r* sound the same. *Examples:* *ar*bitrate, v*er*min, int*er*nal, f*or*ce, n*ur*ture
5. In words that contain two vowels together (digraph) such as *ai, ay, oa, ee, ea,* usually the first is long and the second is silent. *Examples:* imp*ea*ch, br*ai*n, st*ea*m, r*ay*, st*ee*l
6. In words that contain two vowels together such as *au, aw, eu, ew, oo,* the vowel letters (digraphs) have a special sound unlike either of the vowels. *Examples:* c*au*stic, past*eu*rize, f*oo*d, s*ew*erage
7. In words that contain two consonants together such as *sh, wh,* th, ch,* the consonant letters (digraphs) produce a single and new sound. *Examples:* *sh*ip, *wh*eat, *th*is, *th*ird, *ch*ange, *ch*orus, *ch*ef
   *The *w* is silent when followed by *o.* *Example:* *who*
8. Some words have a blend of two or more consonants each of which retains its own sound. *Examples:* *bl*ood, *st*omach, *gl*and, *pr*onounce, *tr*ade, *dr*aft, *str*aw
9. Some words have a blend of two vowels (diphthongs) which produces a blended sound. *Examples:* c*oi*l, b*oy*cott, m*ou*th, fl*ow*ery

e, *i*, or *y*, each is usually soft. *Examples:*
ric, gyroscope
a word may cause the vowel to have the
ınd, designated by the inverted *e* (ə), does
tinctive sound. *Examples:* respiration,
l

ınce in analyzing words, the appropriate
ıcher may ask what sound the vowel
ne function is of the silent *e* at the end of a
students' memory and illustrates an
nts do not know or cannot remember, the
nd then ask for other examples.
ymbol relationships, students usually
uild on this interest and cite exceptions.
e exceptions. For instance, help students
guage developed: it evolved through use
the language is not uniform. Also, review
languages on English. For example, we
have "Americanized" the pronunciation.
t is a French ending but is pronounced
en intrigued by such discussions of their
delve more deeply into the evolution of

dely in many subject areas, they need to
ılary. Fortunately, each word they learn
re able to focus attention upon meaning.
omprehension and reading speed, since
inishes the number of words that must be

annot be analyzed by phonic generaliza-
art of students' sight vocabulary. Such
hips that differ from what is normally
silent, and other combinations have
tributable to the letters.
nations include:

th *gn*, the *g* is silent before *n*. Examples:

h *gh*, the *h* is silent following *g*. *Example:*
en preceded by an *i* it is usually silent.

with *kh*, the *h* is silent following *k*.

h *rh*, the *h* is silent following *r*. *Example:*

th *kn*, the *k* is silent before *n*. *Example:*

efore *m*. *Example:* palm
m is silent at end of syllable. *Example:* comb

8. *pn, ps* In words beginning with *pn* or *ps*, the *p* is silent before *n* or *s*. *Examples:* pneumonia; psalm.
9. *tch* t is usually silent before *ch*. *Example:* watch
10. *wr* In words beginning with *wr*, the *w* is silent. *Example: wr*ought
11. *Double consonants* Only one is sounded. *Example:* com*m*on
12. *t* When *t* follows *s* or *f*, the *t* is sometimes silent. *Example:* of*t*en
13. *ck* The *c* is silent when followed by a *k* at the end of a word. *Example:* hac*k*neyed
14. *qu* Since *q* has no sound of its own, it usually takes the sound of *kw*. In English *q* is always followed by *u*. *Example:* e*qu*ivalent
15. *ph* Neither consonant is sounded. Instead, the sound of *f* is used. *Examples: ph*otosynthesis; gra*ph*
16. *que* At the end of a word, the *que* has the sound of *k*. *Example:* opa*que*.
17. There is also variability with the sounds of some consonants. Note:

S	us	s
	fuse	z
G	get	g
	giant	j
C	cat	k
	receive	s

Words that have been borrowed from other languages and incorporated into English are among the 15% of words in English that are exceptions to phonetic principles. Have the class keep a file of such words. For example: *bureau* (French), *mesa* (Spanish).

Using the Dictionary

Though dictionary skills have been taught prior to high school, they may need further refinement and application.

Three basic clusters of skills are needed to use the dictionary efficiently. The *locational skills* involve knowledge of alphabetical sequence, the use of guide words, knowledge that words appear according to the sequence of their letters, and a knowledge of structural analysis (since the word in the context may not be in the same form as the dictionary entry). For example, *excite* will be a dictionary entry, but *exciting* probably will not; *necessary* will be, but *unnecessary* may not.

The *pronunciation skills* involve an understanding of phonetic spellings, the use of diacritical marks, and the use of the pronunciation key. Also, knowledge of the accent mark is important. Usually, students are not required to memorize a diacritical marking system since slight differences occur in dictionaries. Students can better understand and use the phonetic spelling if they apply their phonetic knowledge.

The *discrimination skills* help students discriminate between meanings and select the one appropriate to the context—the one the author means. Also, they need to adapt the meaning to the grammatical, inflectional form of the word in the context. For example, the past tense of a verb in context would require adapting the present tense of the meaning found in the dictionary. This leads to an important responsibility of dictionary users: they must "tune in" to the defined meaning proper for the context. This may be simple or complex. "Tuning in" may require only the substitution of a definition for the unknown word, or it may become increasingly complex as the student needs to transpose the order of words in the context or to completely paraphrase the context.

Suggested Activities

1. *Alphabetizing*. In each column below, number the words in the order in which you would find them in the dictionary.

Sample

4 gouge	____placate	____mansion	____realist
1 fabulous	____piston	____needle	____scribe
3 gossip	____pitiful	____pedestal	____tension
7 haggard	____place	____lava	____tentacle
6 habitat	____pitch	____organic	____union
2 faculty	____plane	____quill	____wave
5 governor	____pivot	____jaguar	____vacuum

2. *Using guide words*. The top of each dictionary page contains two "guide words" (the first and last entries on that page). Guide words help you rapidly determine if the word you are looking up is found on a particular page. You must decide if your word falls alphabetically between the two guide words. Underline the word(s) in Column B which would be on the page indicated by the guide words in Column A.

	Column A	*Column B*
1.	come—command	comedy companion comfort
2.	frank—free	fret freckle fraud
3.	spread—sputnik	sprout squat sport
4.	hinder—historic	Hindu hoist hitch
5.	plan—plaster	plasma plantation plane
6.	minute—mischief	miserable miracle miner
7.	ranger—raspberry	rascal rather rally
8.	trace—transit	transport trademark traitor
9.	weave—weight	weekly welcome weapon
10.	average—awkward	autumn avoid aware

3. Determine the derivation of each of the following words by reading the information between the brackets in the dictionary entry for that word.

radius	indent	erg
perimeter	parenthesis	laser
quadratic	prefix	colloid
factor	conversation	equilibrium
trapezoid	antecedent	galvanometer

4. Use the dictionary to note the syllable(s) accented in the following words. Note that some may have two accented syllables—a heavier or primary accent and the lighter or secondary accent.

investment	interrogatory	streptococcus	reclamation
binomial	correspondence	insoluble	unconstitutional
factorable	homily	protoplasm	indemnity
vertices	personification	vertebrate	execution
equilateral	antithesis	atmosphere	strategic

5. Extensions of the above exercise may include:
   a. Using the dictionary to divide the words into syllables.
   b. Noting vowel sound of each accented syllable as shown by dictionary.
   c. Noting which, if any, of the syllables contain the schwa sound.

6. For each of the following words, write the form that would be found in the dictionary.

rectangles	arguing	fumigating	savageness
retailed	modifier	sterilizing	wharves
companies	synopses	exhalation	oases
radii	delineated	chlorinated	annulled
algebraic	sagas	liquefier	strategically

7. Determine the appropriate dictionary meaning that fits the context in which the word is used in a textbook. Direct students to use the textbook to see how the word is used, or give them sentences with the word included.
8. Have the students use the dictionary to see if the word has a meaning other than in the subject you are teaching. Alert them to such labels as *slang, colloq.* (colloquial), *obs.* (obsolete), *law, math.,* and so on.
9. Discuss with the students the meanings of the abbreviations *n., v., adj., adv., pron., prep., conj., interj.* Note the context in order to select the appropriate meaning. Also have your students note the form and meaning of words in your subject when more than one of the abbreviations are used.

High school teachers should be familiar with various methods of word analysis in order to apply the methods in their subject areas as the need arises. Though students were taught the methods of word analysis in the elementary grades and should be using them, they must be given guidance as necessary with the more complex words usually found in the high school subjects.

The teacher's goal is to develop independence in reading so that the student does not have to puzzle over word analysis but rather can concentrate on the information and ideas. For word analysis to become natural and automatic, students need extensive practice and application.

SUMMARY

At the secondary school level we wish to have students increase their vocabularies, become motivated to learn vocabulary, and ultimately acquire an adequate vocabulary for today's society. We wish also to have them understand the *concept* a word labels, not just the dictionary meaning. Students realize quickly that a word's meaning changes in accordance with the context in which it is used. However, the basic concept of the meaning remains rather constant. When teaching vocabulary we need to be systematic and consistent in our procedure, yet we need to be almost casual to the point of having fun with words.

QUESTIONS AND PROBLEMS FOR YOUR OWN CLASSROOM

For readers who are training to be teachers:

1. Select a passage from a textbook and note the number of concepts the student must know. Note how many should be known from previous instruction. Note the new concepts.
2. Select a concept and plan how you will develop its meaning with the students.
3. Make a listing of general words used with specialized meanings in your subject.
4. Review some textbooks in your area and determine the roots of the technical words the student will need to know.

For readers who are teaching:

1. For your class, plan specific ongoing vocabulary procedures. Invite your students to suggest ideas.
2. Have your students note the new words in an assignment and note the contextual meaning given for the word. Have them explain in their own words what the words mean to them. For example, what number has the same *value* as 1¾? (What does *value* mean?)
3. Have your students divide the new words of an assignment into syllables. Also have them note the use of prefixes and suffixes. Discuss with them the influence of the prefixes and suffixes upon the root.
4. Organize a committee of students who will investigate the etymology of new vocabulary words.

SELECTED REFERENCES

Deighton, Lee C. *Vocabulary Development in the Classroom*. New York: Bureau of Publications, Teachers College, Columbia University, 1959.

A well-known publication on vocabulary development that discusses problems of word analysis as well as word meaning.

Smith, E. Brooks; Goodman, Kenneth S.; and Meredity, Robert. *Language and Thinking in the Elementary School.* New York: Holt, Rinehart & Winston, Inc., 1970.

Although this publication is mostly about the development of language and thought, it has an excellent section on phonemics.

CHAPTER 3

Comprehension

OVERVIEW

Comprehension—understanding—is the essence of reading. But what precisely goes on in the brain that enables us to comprehend? A number of models and taxonomies attempt to explain the logical sequence or structure of comprehension. Each model and taxonomy provides a degree of insight into the comprehension process. Much of the effort toward understanding how we comprehend has been in the cognitive domain. Recent research into the *split-brain concept* is giving us insight into the affective domain of interest, emotion, and attitude and its effect upon comprehension. The types of thought questions students must consider in order to comprehend adequately are discussed. Then, the classroom procedures the subject teacher must use are presented. Finally, specific comprehension problems are dealt with. Guiding and teaching students to comprehend effectively require the application of our theoretical knowledge to specific classroom practices.

Questions

Consider these questions before you read further:

1. What do you think a student has to do and to know in order to comprehend?
2. What kinds of problems do students have in comprehending? How do these relate to the cognitive domain, the affective domain, and to classroom procedure?
3. What kinds of procedures can a classroom teacher use to teach comprehension?

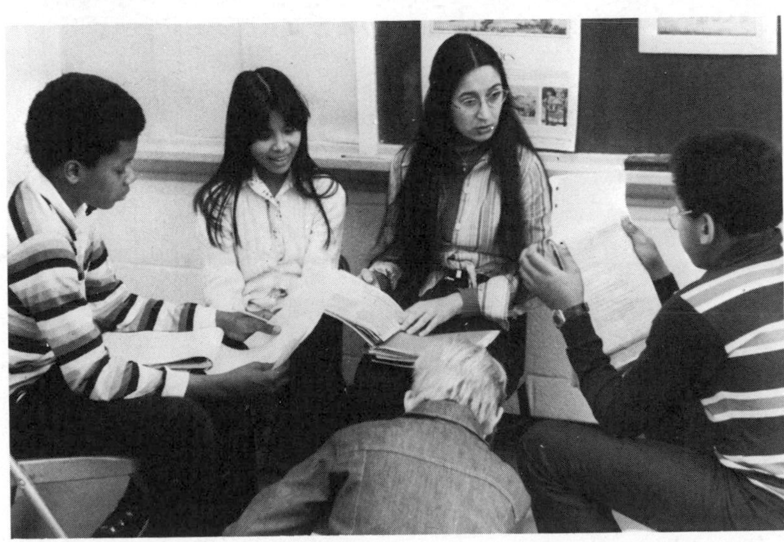

To read in the full sense is to comprehend. It goes beyond decoding or recognizing the graphic symbol, which is a mere step toward using the written form of language. A synonym for *comprehension* is *understanding*. However, we need to consider the complete meaning of understanding, which includes many mental processes: grasping the thought, penetrating the ideas, interpreting the information, construing the significance or its application, inferring what is meant, connoting a point of view or mood, seeing the intentions of the author. In short, to understand is to realize, apply, contemplate, and deliberate—all of which are aspects of thinking. Thinking involves the use of language. Indeed, the goal of each content teacher is to help students to think, to understand, and therefore to comprehend.

THE NATURE OF COMPREHENSION

The Cognitive Dimension

Investigators of intelligence and of the processes of thinking in comprehension have given us valuable insights into what is involved, and there are parallels in the results of the investigations. Most of the work is in the cognitive mode of knowing. However, we need to consider the affective mode as well, since interest in the subject, motivation, and values affect comprehension. As we study and analyze intelligence, we note that there are parallels to comprehension—intellectual factors which are parts of the comprehension process. J. P. Guilford, whose model of intelligence is shown, states: "Reading, when fully developed, is one of our most complex intellectual activities, involving many of the intellectual abilities, which we may also regard as intellectual functions."[1]

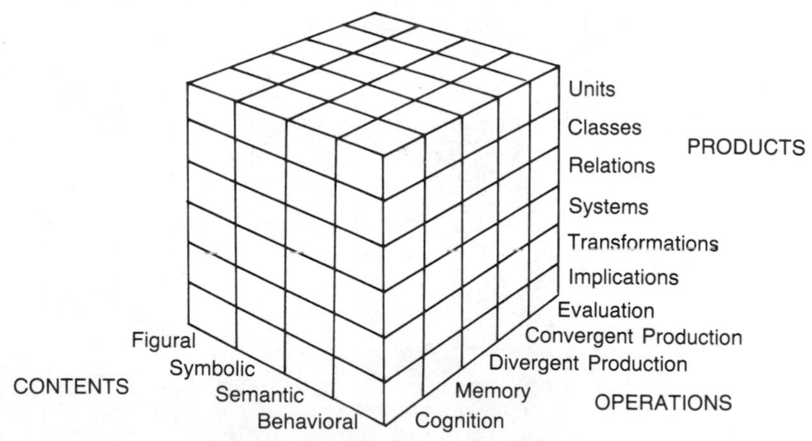

Reprinted by permission from J. P. Guilford and Ralph Hoeffner, *The Analysis of Intelligence* (New York: McGraw-Hill, 1971), p. 19.

1. J. P. Guilford, "Frontiers in Thinking that Teachers Should Know About," *The Reading Teacher* 13, No. 3 (February 1961): 176.

Guilford's model shows the interaction of three categories: *operations* (ways of processing information or of thinking about it), *contents* (kinds or sources of information), and *products* (basic forms of the information or ways it is organized). Each category is made up of classes of abilities that cut across and interact with the others. There are 120 "cubes" in the model that designate specific mental activities. All 120 are not yet identified, and even more than 120 may be ascertained as research goes on. Further, none of these categories and the classes of abilities operate separately; rather, in solving a problem, two or more are involved. For instance, as Guilford states:

> Becoming aware that a problem exists is a matter of cognition, often emphasizing the product of implication. Before progress can be made toward a solution, the problem must be understood; it must be structured, which usually means cognition of a system. Having structured the problem, the individual generates alternative solutions, which is divergent production. If sufficient basis for a unique solution is cognized, there is convergent production. All the way along the problem-solving event there is evaluation, in the form of accepting or rejecting cognitions of the problem and the generated solutions. At any step what happens may become fixated and retained for possible later use, so that memory is involved. When evaluation leads to rejections, there may be new starts, with revised cognitions and productions.[2]

Now let us define the classes of ability in each category forming the structure of intellect and note some implications for comprehension.

Category 1: Operations

Cognition: Discovery or recognition of information in its various forms. The student recognizes the information and grasps the literal or specific information the author has presented.

Memory: the fixation of information. The student retains what he has read and can recall it.

Divergent production: the generation of logical alternatives from given information. The student uses deductive thinking, proceeding from a generalization or principle to particulars. New ideas of a creative nature may evolve. Here, the student goes beyond merely what the author has written to interpreting and possibly applying it.

Convergent production: the generation of logical conclusions from given information. The student draws conclusions from what he has read. This, too, is interpretive—he uses the information an author has presented and evolves an overall conclusion, inference, generalization, principle, or logical outcome. For instance, the proof of a theorem in geometry involves using specific facts to lead to a conclusion (proof).

Evaluation: making judgments as to correctness and consistency. The student reads (thinks) critically. He judges the information an author has presented in accordance with certain criteria involving his own views, background, and systems of thought.

---

2. J. P. Guilford and Ralph Hoeffner, *The Analysis of Intelligence* (New York: McGraw-Hill, 1971), p. 31.

Category 2: Content

Figural: pertains to information in concrete form as perceived through the sensory modalities. The student uses sensory imagery—visual, auditory, and kinesthetic—to construct mental pictures of what an author is describing or relating. This helps the reader understand precisely what the author is stating.

Symbolic: pertains to information in the form of denotative signs that have no significance in themselves. The student must recognize letters, letter combinations, syllables within words, prefixes, roots, suffixes. Also included are isolated numbers and signs in mathematics as well as isolated musical notation.

Semantic: pertains to information in the form of concepts or mental constructs to which words are often applied. Meaningful pictures and diagrams may also convey semantic information. The development of vocabulary meaning in each content area relates closely to the development of concepts and also involves the ability to apply contextual or language clues. Note also that graphic aids such as pictures and diagrams are means of forming or enriching concepts.

Behavioral: pertains to information gained through human interactions involving our own and others' attitudes, needs, desires, moods, intentions, perceptions, and thoughts. Paramount to the reader's evaluation and application of information is his interaction with the thoughts of the author regarding their relevance, accuracy, and effect on the reader's set of values, background, and needs.

Category 3: Product

Units: items of information. In reading, this would be factual content such as important details.

Classes: sets of information having common properties. In reading, a group of related details is a *set* of information; so are words that are classifiers (that categorize information).

Relations: connections between items of information. Making connections involves reading to *(a)* note the relationships among the syntactical parts of a sentence, such as the relationship between the noun and verb; *(b)* relate to a main idea; and *(c)* relate sentences to each other in a well-constructed paragraph.

Systems: organized information that has interrelated parts. The student notes the structure of information when he sees the organization of an author's ideas—part to whole, or cause and effect. The system of a textbook helps the student in noting the organization of thought: paragraph to topic, topic to chapter section, chapter section to chapter, chapter to unit, unit to total book (method of organization for many content books).

Transformations: changes of various kinds of existing information such as redefinitions, transitions, or modifications. The reader makes transformations when he "puts into his own words" the ideas an author has presented, when he rearranges or synthesizes ideas as he does a research report, or as he draws a diagram or chart from material he has read.

Implications: circumstantial connections between items of information which show that the items belong together. This involves the reader's creative use of information. He may note an author's implications, expand upon or amplify them, evolve his own implications, and possibly note the social impact of such implications.

Guilford's model of intelligence relates closely to other analyses of comprehension. One of the first was the categorization by Nila Banton Smith and Constance McCullough. They divided comprehension into four levels: literal, interpretative, critical, and creative.[3]

The *literal level* is the simplest level, since all the students need to do is to reproduce the facts as the author relates them. The skills needed for this level of understanding include noting factual data, sequence, chronology, and enumeration. It is assumed that the student understands the facts, but this is not always the case. Some students are quite glib and can state in a parrot-like manner what the author has written, with little or no understanding.

The *interpretative level*, requiring the student to go beyond the information given by the author, depends upon competence at the literal level. Students are now required to see the significance of the data: to note various relationships such as cause and effect and relation of the part to the whole, to make comparisons, to draw conclusions and inferences, and to make generalizations. Class discussion in which students share ideas is vital for the development of competence at this level.

The *critical level* depends upon the first two. At this level students learn to evaluate and judge the information and the author's presentation of it. Skills at this level are aimed toward *(a)* evaluating the author's use of language for guiding the reader's interpretation, *(b)* noting evidence of the author's fairness or bias, qualifications, point of view, intent, and truthfulness; and *(c)* determining how adequately the information is covered. Recognizing the techniques of propagandists also is included among the skills of critical reading. Class discussion is again valuable, since students will need help in making evaluations and judgments and in realizing that judgments must be made against a standard. This standard may come from factual evidence, or from society's and the students' own scale of values. For example, whether or not an author is truthful could be determined against factual evidence, but whether or not an author is biased must be determined against not only factual evidence but also the students' or society's sense of fairness.

The *creative level* requires the students' involvement with the information presented as they use it to formulate or to rethink ideas. Obviously, readers are best able to think creatively about what they have read when they know what the author has written, have made interpretations basic to their purpose, and have evaluated the relevance of the information. This level is viewed as the culminating one. Questioning at this level might consist of open-ended queries which require students to include their own knowledge, views, and values.

---

3. Nila Banton Smith, "Levels of Discussion in Reading," in *Readings on Reading Instruction*, ed. Albert J. Harris (New York: David McKay, 1963), pp. 285–89; Constance McCullough, "Creative Reading," in *Readings on Reading Instruction*, ed. Albert J. Harris (New York: David McKay, 1963), pp. 289–94.

Detailed classifications, called *taxonomies,* have been created. Two well-known taxonomies that view comprehension in levels of complexity are those of Bloom and Barrett. Bloom's taxonomy of educational objectives in the cognitive domain contains the following levels:

1. *Knowledge.* This level involves the attaining and retaining of factual data and the processes needed for the student to be aware of such data. Specifically, the basic comprehension skills include *(a)* recall of specific information; *(b)* knowing the meaning of specific terminology, such as the words found in each content subject, as well as general vocabulary; *(c)* knowing how knowledge is organized; *(d)* recognizing the main idea and supporting details; *(e)* classifying and categorizing data, sequence, and chronology; and *(f)* techniques of organizing information.
2. *Comprehension.* Two very important aspects of comprehension are translation and interpretation. In translation, the reader restates the ideas of the author in his own words or through some graphic representation (such as a diagram). In interpretation, the reader goes beyond the data presented by the author. The reader may restructure the information; give a new view or unstated relationship; draw conclusions; make inferences; see relationships such as part to whole, cause and effect, comparison and contrast; and relate to the information through the various senses and experiences.
3. *Application.* The reader uses the information he has gained to note how a principle, theory, or idea can be applied.
4. *Analysis.* At this point the reader is able to note the parts of a whole and see how the parts contribute to the whole. This ability includes distinguishing fact from opinion; how and why propaganda and advertisement may be persuasive; how a literary form may set a mood, tone, or point of view; and the accuracy of a line of reasoning.
5. *Synthesis.* This is the ability to organize ideas into a logical structure or pattern. The reader notes specific facts and formulates a generalization. He then sees how the paragraph information centers around one main idea.
6. *Evaluation.* Evaluation, of course, is judging according to some criteria or standards. Often the reader's evaluation is colored by his own set of values but, still, he needs to recognize the standards he is using to make his judgment.[4]

Barrett, who used Bloom's taxonomy of educational objectives, developed a taxonomy of the cognitive and affective dimensions of reading comprehension. Two items are notable: his taxonomy is on comprehension of *printed* material, and he brings in the affective domain as well as the cognitive.

The outline of Barrett's taxonomy follows:

I. Literal Comprehension
   A. Recognition
      1. Details
      2. Main ideas

4. Benjamin Bloom, ed., *Taxonomy of Educational Objectives: Cognitive Domain* (New York: David McKay, 1956), pp. 201–7.

3. Sequence
4. Comparison
5. Cause and effect relationships
6. Character traits

} When explicitly stated

B. Recall
(of all six items listed under *A. Recognition*)

II. Inferential Comprehension
A. Supporting details
B. Main ideas
C. Sequence
D. Comparison
E. Cause and effect relationships
F. Character traits
G. Outcomes
H. Figurative language

III. Evaluation—Judgments
A. Reality or fantasy
B. Fact or opinion
C. Adequacy and validity
D. Appropriateness
E. Worth, desirability, acceptability

IV. Appreciation
A. Emotional response to the content
B. Identification with characters or incidents
C. Reactions to the author's use of language
D. Imagery[5]

Tatham notes that taxonomies are useful in designing questions that promote thinking, thereby enhancing the teaching of comprehension.[6] Also, they are useful guides for teachers who wish to analyze the questions included in most textbooks.

Taxonomy levels may appear to be discrete, but in fact they meld into one another. Also, the student's background can affect his level of functioning within the taxonomy. For instance, for a student who has been involved in prior discussion or reading about a certain topic assigned in class, the higher level of comprehension—such as analysis or inference—might be at his *literal* level. This would not be the case with a student who had no prior knowledge of the topic. Taxonomies do not take into account the background a reader brings to comprehension.

The Affective Dimension

Some writers believe that the total view of comprehension must take into account the reader's feelings about the author's ideas. Category IV of Barrett's taxonomy includes the affective dimension. In Category IV,

---

5. Richard J. Smith and Thomas C. Barrett, *Teaching Reading in the Middle Grades*, 2nd ed. (Reading, Mass.: Addison-Wesley, 1979), pp. 63–66.

6. Susan Musland Tatham, "Comprehension Taxonomies: Their Uses and Abuses," *The Reading Teacher* 32, No. 2 (November 1978): 193.

Appreciation, Barrett notes the emotional impact a reading selection might have upon the reader (subcategory A). Certainly, the emotional reactions the reader has to the ideas in the selection—fear, love, hate, amusement, excitement—will color thinking and comprehension. Barrett suggests that identification with characters or incidents fosters sensitivity to or empathy for the character or incident (subcategory B). Questions to stimulate students' thinking include: "How would you feel if ________?" "What would you do if ________?" "Why do you suppose the character did what he did?" Next, Barrett notes reactions to the author's use of language (subcategory C). In other words, how does the author attempt to color the reader's thinking by his choice of words? What an excellent opportunity to study the connotative use of words! Finally, Barrett notes imagery, which requires the reader's use of the senses: sight, smell, taste, feel, and hearing (subcategory D). The reader uses imagery when he feels he is an "unseen" character in a story; when he finishes a story, he feels he has made new friends and has had a unique type of vacation or experience.

In addition to these four subcategories, the affective dimension also includes the reader's interests, motivations, emotions, and attitudes. These influences are entirely personal and individual ways of reacting, and so they are hard to identify and nearly impossible to measure. They depend upon a reader's concept of himself and of others, his reaction to the physical and social environment, and his view of what the future holds for him. All of these perceptions affect how an individual comprehends and reacts to information.

Many teachers feel unsure about venturing into the affective dimension. Current research into the way the human brain operates can give us some insights. Further, some theories of comprehension regard it as a holistic operation rather than a hierarchical stratification of operations and skills. We may need to draw implications from both approaches in classroom practice.

Split Brain Research

Only recently has the research on reading shifted from considering it as a function of the *whole* brain to examining the interaction of the two hemispheres of the brain (the left and the right). Patricia Fox discusses the significance of current neurological studies and findings:

> Successful reading requires integration of the two modes of symbol processing available to the human mind. Since ancient times, these modes have been dichotomized as logic [cognitive process] and intuition [affective], analysis and synthesis [Bloom uses both of these terms in his taxonomy], pedantry [knowledge and learning] and creativity [innovation], yet only recently have scientists proven that each cerebral hemisphere functions in distinctly different modes. This enormous advance in knowledge about brain functioning has affected theories of thinking and learning.[7]

Gary Steinley maintains the same view as Fox. He states:

> Today split brain research is making concrete what philosophers and poets

7. Patricia L. Fox, "Reading as a Whole Brain Function," *The Reading Teacher* 33, No. 1 (October 1979): 7.

> have said for centuries. That is, humans are capable of two very different modes to thinking. One is rational, the other intuitive. One linear, the other spatial. One stratified, the other holistic . . . .[8]

One might make a simplistic analogy of split brain research as follows: cognitive functioning (detail) is to the left hemisphere of the brain as affective functioning (global impression) is to the right hemisphere of the brain. Fox notes the functions of the respective hemispheres. The left hemisphere, she says, is specialized for the syntactic, logical, ordered aspects of language. Writing, speaking, and reading exercises which emphasize denotative language and literal comprehension also use the left hemisphere. The right hemisphere views information as a *whole* and processes imagery, connotation, and nonverbal responses. She summarizes by stating the different functions: "The left hemisphere is concerned with detail but lacks coherent organization, while the right hemisphere apprehends global characteristics but ignores detail."[9]

Noting the dichotomy between the analytic, cognitive structure (left) and the global, impressionistic structure (right), Steinley uses the terms *hierarchical structure* and *web structure,* respectively. The web structure is not a stratification of levels but is rather an enmeshing of circles of influences—such as interest, motivation, emotions and attitudes—that increase global understanding. However, Steinley points out that these two approaches (extremes) are not opposed to each other but rather are on a continuum.[10] Our classroom procedures should use both. Indeed, as the cognitive dimension and the affective dimension both influence how a reader comprehends, we need to use the detailed, skill-oriented approach along with the global feeling and reacting approach. Now, let's consider some implications of interest, motivation, emotions and attitudes upon comprehension.

Interest

When a student is interested in a topic, he directs his attention to finding out more about the topic, and he usually has specific questions to which he wants answers. When he reads under these conditions, he will use all of the levels of comprehension—though he may not be aware of doing so. For instance, to use Bloom's taxonomy, we find that when a student is reading to satisfy an interest, he will:

1. Read to gain knowledge.
2. Translate it into his own words.
3. Make interpretations and see the significance as a whole.
4. Apply the information to practical uses pertinent to his purposes or desires.
5. Analyze the application.

8. Gary Steinley, "Structures and Strategies in Reading Comprehension," in *Research on Reading in Secondary Schools,* Monograph #4, ed. Joseph L. Vaughan (Tucson: University of Arizona, 1979), p. 30.

9. Patricia Fox, "Reading as a Whole Brain Function," pp. 8–9.

10. Gary Steinley, "Structures and Strategies in Reading Comprehension," p. 31.

6. Synthesize or review the steps of his logic.
7. Evaluate, or say to himself, "Does it make sense?"

Mike, a sixth grader, was tested to have a reading level of second grade. Though his intelligence seemed to be average, he was unable to do the class work. Mike had a hobby which also furnished him with spending money. He hatched and raised game birds and then sold them to parks and hunting preserves. The unique phenomenon here is that Mike could read and comprehend any material presented to him on the subject of game bird culture. For example, he had sent for and could understand pamphlets on the subject published by the U.S. Government Printing Office. Mike's face would light up when he talked about game bird culture.

Why was it that Mike, who was at a second grade level in reading, could comprehend the material of his interest as high as the ninth grade level? He could not recognize a number of words in the game bird material, but he used his sense of language to build more and more background. As it grew, Mike acquired further knowledge to translate the material into his own words, interpret it, and continue through the other levels of comprehension. Once, he read the pronoun referent *it* when he could not read the subject of the sentence, which was *partridge*. He said, "*It*—they mean one bird or type of bird. The word starts with *p*—that must be *partridge*." Here Mike used redundancy (pronoun referent), beginning phonetic skill (the letter *p*), and his background to recognize the word. Clearly, Mike's interest motivated him—he wanted to know all he could about game birds.

Interest affects comprehension by increasing a reader's background, which means that an individual can refer to an increased body of knowledge. Bloom points out that

> All of the affective classifications make use of or are based upon knowledge. Thus, it is generally held that interests are developed as the result of an increase in information; likewise, attitudes and appreciations are regarded as having some bases in knowledge or information. . . . Problem solving or thinking cannot be carried on in a vacuum, but must be based upon knowledge of some of the "realities."[11]

We may infer from Bloom that an individual's interests grow as his scope of knowledge expands.

Motivation

Similar to interest, motivation is the stimulating and sustaining force that leads individuals to undertake and carry through a project. When a student is motivated, his comprehension is enhanced.

One often hears in the teacher's lounge: "I just can't seem to get my classes motivated to do anything," or "I wish I knew how to get them turned on," or "How do you get students motivated today?" Motivation is a real concern among teachers. We all know that the motivated individual learns more effectively and works harder than an unmotivated person.

A student's motivation is tied closely to his reasons for learning.

---

11. Bloom, *Taxonomy of Educational Objectives,* p. 33.

Different students will have different reasons. One student may be motivated because he wants to get good grades, or he may wish to establish and maintain a good relationship with his parents, other family members, his teachers, his peers. Another may have a vocational goal that sustains him, or curiosity, or a wish to solve some problem or to know more about himself. Basic to all of the reasons is that the learning is *relevant* to the individual and will help his understanding in some way.

Helping the student to see the relevance of everything we need to teach him is most challenging. An effective way to involve students in discussion is to pose open-ended questions. Such discussion involves cognition, memory, divergent and convergent thinking, as well as evaluation—all parts of Guilford's operations in his intelligence analysis. Questions that lead the student to apply the information to himself make use of all of Barrett's and Bloom's levels of comprehension. Some examples follow.

In literature:
What do you think will be the results of what [character] did?
What would you have done?
Can you think of a situation you have seen or experienced which is similar to this?

In social studies:
How has your life been affected by our Federal Constitution?
How will it be affected in the future?
Are there any changes you would like to see in the Constitution?
What do you see as a result of these changes if they were made?
How would you have handled [situation or event] if you had been the President?
You saw the activities of the underground group in France during WW II. What would you have done if you had been French?

In science:
In what ways does the cycle of life affect us?
Can you see any practical uses of chemical bonding?
In light of our electronic machinery [computers], in what ways do we still use the simple machines (lever, pulley, etc)?
As you view the future, how will they be used?

In business:
Everyone uses this specific form in accounting to note deposits. Can you give any reasons why we have standardized the form?
Is there other information that should be there?
If you were to start your own business, what records do you think you would need?

In mathematics:
What uses can you see for the Pythagorean theorem?
Have you ever had to use it?
Can you think of any situations where you might?

In homemaking:
Why do we need to follow [recipe/sewing instruction sheet] carefully?
What would happen if you doubled one quantity and not the rest?

In industrial arts:
Why do you think we have steps in doing this process?
What would happen if one [specify] were left out?
If you do not follow a safety rule [specify], what might happen?
Do you know of a situation where safety rules were not followed?

Emotions and Attitudes

Emotions and attitudes have long been known to affect an individual's perception and comprehension of information. Emmett Betts summarized the effect of attitudes upon thinking:

1. How a reader interprets a selection depends upon what he takes to it of information, of techniques of inquiry, and of attitudes.
   a. Unfavorable attitudes tend to contribute to inaccurate interpretation, to interfere with comprehension.
   b. Ideas in harmony with the learner's attitude are more easily learned.
   c. Ideas contrary to attitudes contribute to confusion and irritation.
   d. The stronger the attitude, the more it influences interpretation.
2. Attitudes influence recall of ideas.
   a. Ideas in harmony with the learner's attitudes are more likely to be recalled than those in conflict.
   b. Vividness of recall depends upon the strength of the attitude.
3. The tendency to rationalize is increased to the degree that an idea conflicts with attitudes.
4. A disinclination to read on a topic is increased to the degree that attitudes toward the ideas are unfavorable.
5. The older the child the more his interpretation is influenced by attitudes.[12]

The influence of emotions and attitudes upon comprehension compels us to lead the reader into objective, logical thinking. Asking open-ended questions, such as those just presented, will help students to think and then to counter the views of others. Other procedures can be used, such as problem solving, using language connotatively, distinguishing fact from bias or opinion, and noting the author's intent and organization of the information.

In summary, comprehension is complex, involving the interplay of the cognitive and affective modes. Of great importance are a background of knowledge (cognition), the organization of information (which relates both to cognition and understanding language structure), and the relevance of information to the student's interests.

IMPLEMENTING OUR KNOWLEDGE OF COMPREHENSION

Understanding the comprehension process should make us aware of the direction we must take and the kinds of things we must do in the classroom. Sanders points out:

12. Emmett A. Betts, "Reading as a Thinking Process," *The National Elementary Principal* 35, No. 1 (September 1955): 90–91.

> A teacher who has mastered the taxonomy of questions [based, for example, on Bloom's taxonomy] can use it in a number of ways to improve the intellectual climate of his classroom. It offers a means for him to answer this question: "Am I offering all appropriate intellectual experiences in my classroom or am I overemphasizing some and neglecting others?" The answer can easily be found by classifying the questions asked on examinations, homework, and orally.[13]

Asking appropriate questions, then, is vital for teaching comprehension.

Questioning

The kinds of questions we ask reflect in part our view of the goal of education. We need to ask ourselves, "Is the purpose of our subject merely to fill the students with knowledge, or is it to teach *thinking* and *reasoning,* during which process the content is taught?"

There are appropriate questions for each level of comprehension. Typical questions of the four levels as listed by Smith and others are:

Literal:
List the steps of the photosynthesis process.
What was the reaction of the colonists to the Stamp Act?
What materials and equipment do you need for the experiment?
Where did the robber hide the stolen money?

Interpretative:
Explain why the photosynthesis process is essential to life on earth.
Why was the Stamp Act an unwise law?
Why do you need to have exactly two grams of sodium sulfate for the experiment?
Explain how the hiding place for the stolen money showed the robber's ingenuity.

Critical:
Explain scientist X's point of view about the photosynthesis process when she stated that forest cutting must be highly controlled and kept to a minimum.
How might an author favorable to the British cause have viewed the colonists' reaction to the Stamp Act?
What would be the result of your experiment if you used three grams of sodium sulfate?
Judge the validity of the young man's arguments for leaving his job.

Creative:
Give your views about the importance of the photosynthesis process. Support your answer with factual evidence.
How would you have reacted if you were a colonist at the time of the Stamp Act?
What is the most crucial part of the experiment? Why?

---

13. Norris M. Sanders, *Classroom Questions: What Kinds?* (New York: Harper and Row, 1966), p. 5.

What would you do if you found yourself face to face with the robber in the story?

These questions, while not difficult to formulate, do require some preparations.

1. Read the material prior to class.
2. Ascertain the level of comprehension the students should employ with the material, which is determined by the importance you place on the information.
3. Formulate the key questions *before* class for the levels of comprehension required.

Questions signal to the student what his purpose should be as he reads—what he is to look for. He can then adjust his reading to the level of comprehension required. For example, "Read to find out what the old man did when he lost his fortune" does not require the same careful reading that the question, "How did the old man feel when he lost his fortune?" requires. In the first, the action of the story will reveal the answer. In the latter question, the reader will be searching for clues, such as specific words and descriptive action, to formulate the answer.

Now, let's note questions which would generate specific types of thinking and begin to implement the taxonomies we have reviewed. Examples 3.1 and 3.2 are short selections from high school textbooks with accompanying questions a teacher might use (Tables 3.1 and 3.2).

Even if the teacher formulates clear questions and knows the level required by the questions, he may find that the student does not know how to *record* the answer although he basically understands the question. You may need to review with your students the questions from the textbook as well as your own to note those words that indicate the form of the answers. You will also need to review with them the key words of each question as they skim to find the answer. For instance, one teacher discussed with his class questions such as those shown in Table 3.3.

Directions:

1. a. Note the key words which indicate the form of the answer.
2. b. What form can or should the answer be?
3. If the student were asked to skim, what key words would be used from each question?

Table 3.3's questions are typical of those found in high school textbooks. Sanders maintains that "many textbooks offer only recall questions at the end of each chapter."[14] This, indeed, seems to be the case. As you look at the analyses beside each question, note that of the twenty-one questions listed, ten are at the cognitive and memory levels of thinking—literal comprehension. Five others are at the reorganization or the translation level. This leaves only six which aspire to higher levels of comprehension. However, Sanders makes a very interesting point with regard to the classification of questions:

14. Sanders, *Classroom Questions,* p. 6.

EXAMPLE 3.1

Preparing for War

The United States had begun to prepare for possible war before 1917. Ideas that had brought about new inventions and improved others were used to make new military machines. The automobile had been developed by many people in the late nineteenth century. By 1917, it was greatly improved. Knowledge gained from making cars was put to use in making trucks, tanks, and ships called submarine chasers. Orville and Wilbur Wright had made the first successful airplane flight in 1903. Since then, knowledge for making and flying airplanes had grown. World War I was the first time that military plans included the use of airplanes.

Changes in the ways of manufacturing goods also helped industries meet new military needs. Before the growth of the automobile industry, people worked separately on different parts of the product. These parts then were carried to another place to be assembled, or added to the final product. By 1917, many factories used moving assembly lines where belts carried the parts from one worker to another until the product was finished. This method saved a great deal of time which could be used to make more products.

To make sure that the country would be able to supply the armed services as well as the people at home, the government set up agencies with power to regulate the economy. The Railroad Administration, for example, took over control of all the nation's railroads. It ran them without competition as one system. The Food Administration planned ways to increase the amount of food grown. Herbert Hoover, its director, announced that the government would buy the entire crop of wheat grown in 1917 at $2.20 a bushel. Farmers felt that the price was a good one for them, and more wheat was grown that year.

Before the United States declared war on Germany, the army had only eighty thousand soldiers. Congress passed the Selective Service Act, or draft law, in 1917. Under it, all male citizens between the ages of twenty-one and thirty had to register with their local draft boards. They were then selected by chance from the register lists to serve in the army. With this system, plus those who volunteered, the number of soldiers grew to two million.

Reprinted by permission from Frank Freidel and Henry N. Drewry, *America Is* (Columbus: Charles E. Merrill, 1978), pp. 377–78.

Teachers working with the taxonomy of questions often disagree on the classification of a question as you might have in the prior illustrations and that all parties to the dispute can make good cases for their positions. Fortunately, this is not a severe handicap in the uses anticipated for the classroom teacher.[15]

Effective Classroom Procedures

Appropriate questioning is indeed one very important procedure for teaching comprehension. It is not sufficient alone, however. Herber and Nelson recognize the value of appropriate questioning but note a caution:

> When one directs students' reading with questions, there is an implicit assumption that students already have the reading skills necessary for a successful response to those questions. If the students do indeed possess those skills, then such questioning is perfectly valid.[16]

15. Sanders, *Classroom Questions,* pp. 7–8.

16. Harold L. Herber and Joan B. Nelson, "Questioning Is Not the Answer," in *Classroom Strategies for Secondary Reading,* ed. W. John Harker, (Newark, Del.: IRA, 1977), pp. 48–49.

TABLE 3.1 Questions for Example 3.1

Barrett's Taxonomy	Bloom's Taxonomy	Type of Thinking
Literal When were airplanes first used in a war?	*Literal* ⟶	Cognition Memory
Reorganization Two agencies are mentioned that were set up to make sure that both the people at home and the armed services would be supplied. What are the two agencies mentioned? State in your own words what the main function of each was.	*Translation* ⟶	Cognition Memory
Inferential comprehension Why was the Selective Service Act of 1917 passed as part of the preparation for World War I?	*Interpretation* ⟶	Convergent production
synthesis	*Application* In light of what you have read about the preparation for WWI, what would the United States have to do today to prepare for a major war?	Divergent production
	Analysis Explain how the U.S. used ideas that had brought about new inventions and had improved others in preparing for war.	Convergent production
application	*Synthesis* When an invention evolves from an idea, what has to be done before it can be used practically & economically? What often happens when an established	Divergent production

	product such as an automobile has (a) redesigned feature(s)?	
Evaluation In your judgment, was the Selective Service Act of 1917 a fair law?	*Evaluation* →	Evaluation
Appreciation (Affective Mode) What would determine how you would feel if the United States were to prepare for war today?		
How would you react to the increased government regulation on the activities of people and business when the country is involved with a national emergency such as a war?		Divergent production Evaluation

EXAMPLE 3.2

13:5 Camouflage and Other "Tricks"

Adaptations involving deception and camouflage (KAM uh flahj) are widespread in nature. **Camouflage** is a kind of "disguise" to blend with the environment. The color of peppered
3. moths is a type of camouflage in which the moths blend with
their environment. Thus, it is hard for predators to see them. This type of protection is called **cryptic** (KRIP tik) **coloration.**

An organism with cryptic coloration blends with its environment.

Camouflage not only serves the hunted but can also help the hunter. A tiger's stripes break up the general body outline of the animal so that another animal may not see a tiger approaching.

Many animals can change colors in different environments (Figure 13-9). They can change colors because they have special cells called **chromatophores** (kroh MAT uh forz) which are cells filled with one or more pigments. When the pigment spreads throughout the entire cell, one color pattern is seen. When the pigment shrinks to one part of the cell, another color is seen. These changes are probably triggered by the action of nerves and hormones. The animal's vision and other senses may be involved.

Some organisms can change color by means of special cells, chromatophores.

Point out that not all animals having protective coloration and/or shape are actually protected. The population, however, profits.

A chameleon (kuh MEEL yuhn) is a reptile with a complex coloration pattern. This pattern is determined by the interaction of three pigments—black, yellow, and red. As a result, a chameleon can display several colors.

and disuse

In addition to camouflage by color, some animals "hide" by means of their shape and behavior. The dead-leaf butterfly and many other insects have wings shaped like leaves (Figure 13-10a). The veins within the wings have a central vein from which many smaller veins branch like the veins of leaves. Also, the insect may remain very still. Pipefish (Figure 13-10b) can resemble the algae among which they live by swimming in an upright position. Many insects look like the twigs of plants upon which they rest. In all these cases, the combination of color, shape, and behavior provides protection. How would Lamarck have explained the origin of these adaptations? How can they be explained using Darwin's theory of evolution?

Shape, as well as color, is an important aspect of deception.

Variations which promoted the deception were selected for. Organisms lacking these variations were more vulnerable and were selected against.

Warning coloration involves a display of bright colors and 4.
patterns which announce rather than hide animals. The yellow and black stripes of a bumblebee warn predators that the bee is distasteful and can sting. A predator which once ate a bumblebee or got stung would learn to avoid bumblebees later. Often, behavioral adaptations are important in warning coloration. Some animals show their presence by sudden movements or changes in position.

Some distasteful or harmful organisms advertise their presence by warning coloration.

Mimicry (MIM ih kree) is a type of deceptive adaptation. In 4.
mimicry, organisms with a pleasant taste have evolved a color pattern like that of distasteful organisms. The robber fly (Figure 13-12) is a *mimic* (MIM ik) of the bumblebee which is called a *model.* The two insects are not closely related, but their likeness in color deceives predators. As a result, predators ignore the mimic just as they do the model.

In mimicry, a tasty organism or one that cannot effectively harm a predator has a color pattern similar to that of a distasteful or harmful organism.

The origin of a mimic's color and pattern is genetic. By chance, variations occur which cause one group of organisms to look like another group. Organisms which have the variation are less likely to be eaten, so they will survive to produce offspring with the same pattern. Gradually, through continued change and natural selection, the mimic population closely resembles the model population. Mimicry does not have to be complete. Any slight change which improves the chances of survival and reproduction can be selected.

This type of mimicry is called Batesian mimicry.

Reprinted by permission from Raymond F. Oram, *Biology: Living Systems* (Columbus: Charles E. Merrill, 1979), pp. 275–76.

TABLE 3.2 Questions for Example 3.2

Barrett's Taxonomy	Bloom's Taxonomy	Type of Thinking
Literal What is the definition of camouflage?	*Literal* →	Cognition Memory
Reorganization Describe how warning coloration works for the benefit of animals which use it.	*Translation* →	Cognition Memory
Inferential Comprehension Explain why mimicry adaptation has evolved as a means of camouflage.	*Interpretation* →	Convergent production
Explain the statement, "Camouflage not only serves the hunted but can also help the hunter."	→	
	Application What might you wear to increase your success as a duck hunter? How does a duck hunter hide his presence? (One student said, "Costume like a mother duck." How would you grade this answer?)	Divergent production Convergent thinking involving background of knowledge
	Analysis List the three types of camouflage and show the differences among them.	Cognition Convergent production
	Synthesis What other ways besides hunting do we use camouflage? If you were scouting in enemy territory at night, how would you camouflage yourself? Why do you not camouflage yourself when riding a bicycle at night?	Divergent production
Evaluation If camouflage relates to the survival of a species, are there times with both animals and humans when it might not be desirable?	*Evaluation* →	Evaluation
Appreciation (Affective Mode) What would be some instances when you would consider camouflage to be devious and stealthy? Is there anything you can do to discern camouflage?		Divergent production

TABLE 3.3

Questions	Form of Answer	Level of Comprehension
1. Give the reasons why Texas was refused admission to the Union in 1837 but admitted in 1845.	list	literal
2. Trace the steps by which the United States acquired Florida.	flowchart	
3. Why was California's status as a territory so brief?	sentence paragraph	literal interpretation
4. In your opinion could the Spanish-American War have been averted? Support your position.	column opinion/reason	
5. In what ways did the Spanish-American War change the status of the United States as a world power?	list	synthesis literal
6. What were the main raw materials and natural resources of each of the American possessions?	chart	literal
7. Describe the two Cabinet departments which were set up in 1965 and 1966.	paragraph	translation
8. Summarize the military activities in the campaign for the control of New York City.	paragraph list	translation
9. Give examples of "red tape" in government and discuss what in your judgment can be done to eliminate—or at least decrease—such red tape.	list ⟶ paragraph	literal/application
10. Analyze the problems which are likely to develop because of the huge number of agencies and departments in government.	list ⟶ paragraph	analysis
11. List the major reasons why the number of civil service employees has greatly increased in recent years.	list	literal
12. This story is not about one gift of love, but many. What gift of love did each of the four main characters make? How would you define "gift of love"?	sentence	interpretation literal
13. What did the boy come to recognize about Shane?	sentence paragraph	analysis
14. Look up the word philosophy in a complete dictionary and discuss the meanings you find there. Is earth science a philosophy? Explain your answer.		
15. Why does the United States have more hours of daylight in June than in January?	sentence	interpretation
16. Name some fields of study that are related to the study of the earth.	list	literal/application
17. Explain the difference between mass and weight. How have measurements of the earth's mass been obtained?	paragraph	translation/literal
18. Construct a table contrasting typical metallic properties with the coresponding properties of nonmetals.	columns	translation

TABLE 3.3 *Cont'd*

Questions	*Form of Answer*	*Level of Comprehension*
19. Convert 384 mg to grams.		
20. Make a list of the uses of Roman numerals in modern times.	process list	translation
21. Round to the nearest hundredth: 409.736, 627.55, 859.	process	literal synthesis

Key: ═ form of answer; —— skimming.

Suppose the student cannot answer the question—then what? The teacher must have strategies in mind to lead the student toward appropriate answers. But *are* students being taught to comprehend? Durkin's study, entitled "What Classroom Observations Reveal about Reading Comprehension Instruction," presents a rather dire situation:

> Before the present study was undertaken, it had been assumed that at least some of the time they are teaching reading, teachers adhere to a sequence like the following: instruction, application, practice. The data that were collected, however, do anything but support that assumption. Instead, they portray teachers as being "mentioners," assignment givers and checkers, and interrogators. They further show that mentioning and assignment giving and checking are characteristic whether the concern is for comprehension or something else. Just as comprehension instruction was slighted, therefore, so too were all other kinds.[17]

Hodges, however, suggests that teachers are doing more than Durkin indicates. She considers all aspects of teaching procedure that contribute toward instruction in comprehension, even though it may not be the obvious goal the teacher has in mind. She notes interesting and valid aspects of procedure that may be conducted in the classroom. In her view, comprehension is taught whenever a teacher helps students with a reading assignment through questions and suggestions of pertinent techniques, gives direct verbal instructions and guidance, prepares students for reading a selection and, through questioning, provides feedback about how well the students understand.[18] Even these procedures, however, will not be enough in many instances. Chapters 7 and 8 present a full discussion of procedures to teach comprehension.

Comprehension Problems

Different content subjects require different types of thinking. While we know that the general reading skills apply to all subject areas, each area has its own organization. The organization may range from narrative, descriptive, or fictional material to the detailed explanation of a process. Science and math

17. Dolores Durkin, "What Classroom Observations Reveal About Reading Comprehension Instruction," *Reading Research Quarterly* 14, No. 4 (1978–79): 523.

18. Carol A. Hodges, "Commentary: Toward a Broader Definition of Comprehension Instruction," *Reading Research Quarterly* 15, No. 2 (1980): 299–306.

usually require intensive reading for details and their interrelationship. Social studies and English materials require large quantities of reading and may comprise much anecdotal material. The connotative uses of words, the author's intent, and relationships such as cause and effect are important in these areas.

Students may not know how to adjust to the demands of each subject. Consequently, the teacher must teach appropriate techniques of reading and study for each subject area. The business major encounters all types of prose; business law is like social studies; office machines like science; business arithmetic and bookkeeping like mathematics; shorthand like mechanics of English, and so on. In music, reading about musical theory would involve both scientific and mathematical type prose. But in a book on musical appreciation which describes musical movements historically, the material is like social studies. Or it can be like English if biographical accounts of composers are presented. Similarly, materials in art may be precise prose when a process is described, or more loosely written when the material is about appreciation. In industrial arts, the prose is usually very exact, giving specific steps of a process and factual information. The same is true of home economics, with the addition of social studies type materials when the student is reading about current problems of family living. Industrial arts and home economics both include some mathematical reading about measurements. Physical education may have materials that state rules of a game, how to accomplish a specific technique, or scientific type material if health is included.

The Student Equates "Word Calling" with Reading

This student emphasizes recognizing words and reading fluently. She recognizes only the surface structure of the language and uses mostly the written symbol and sound cues. She is glib—she can say the correct words but is unclear about the author's ideas. She pays little attention to the syntactical cues and none to the semantic ones. This student must be taught to look for specific information while reading, thus shifting attention from word calling to the information contained in the words. Try to help her develop the habit of anticipating what the author will state. Most textbooks have headings within chapters that give clues about the information that follows. For example, if the heading is "The Three Main Advantages of the St. Lawrence Seaway," the student can anticipate the information that will follow. (To the mature reader it is obvious that the text will discuss the three advantages. However, many students fail to use the topical headings in this fashion.) Nor is the student always able to formulate a question from the topic heading, as simple as such a technique may seem.

The author had a college student recently who complained that she could not understand her economics textbook. When the student was asked how she read the textbook assignments, she answered, "I just turn to the page and read." Then with a shrug she added, "But I don't get anywhere with it." When the suggestion was made to restate the topic headings in the form of questions, she seemed to understand and agreed to try. However, when she tried to restate one heading, she could not do it. Essentially, this student had been only calling words. We need to focus upon reading as a problem-solving process—one in which the reader is searching for information.

The Student Does Not Read for a Well-Defined Purpose

Many students read an assignment because they were told to. When questioned, they may have only a fuzzy idea of what they are to learn except "the information in Chapter 2 or on these pages," or "my teacher said we are going to have a test tomorrow," or "we have to answer the questions at the end of the chapter." Many students are merely doing the assignment with the belief that in doing it they will absorb the information. As part of your teaching procedure, you must make the purpose—what to find while reading—very clear. Leading students to evolve their own guide questions for reading is also valuable, as Andre and Anderson note: "student generation of questions during study produces greater learning than the rereading method of study. Findings indicate that training students to generate main idea questions may enhance their comprehension of written materials."[19] Start by pacing the students through an assignment and guiding them to formulate questions from the topic headings. This study technique must become a habit if students are to learn to apply the SQ3R (SURVEY, QUESTION, READ, RECITE, REVIEW) study formula independently. (See Chapter 4).

The Student Does Not Distinguish the Central Idea from Details

Some students read all of the factual data and may even understand it, but only as isolated and unique bits of information. They note very little of the interrelationship of ideas. Such students need help in noting the chapter organization and paragraph structures. Again, the topical headings in a textbook are of value; they serve as the author's outline of the information. Teach the student that just as the Table of Contents can show the organization of a book, so the topical heads in a chapter can show the organization of the chapter.

Anticipating what an author may write about a subject is a means of suggesting the main topics. For example, if the students are to read about photosynthesis, prior to reading have them list what type of information the author is likely to present. (They should include a definition of photosynthesis, a description of the process, the importance of the process, and the way the process affects humans and other living organisms.)

You may also find that these students have difficulty sorting the information given in a paragraph. They may not know how to spot sequence, chronology, steps of a process, or sort important from unimportant details, and anecdotal material from factual information. James McCallister points out the importance of having the student learn to recognize different paragraph patterns and lists several roles paragraphs can play:[20]

1. *The central thought supported by details.* Though this may be the commonest form of paragraph structure, it is by no means the only one. In this structure, the central idea statement often is expressed in the first sentence, or the last. The other sentences of the paragraph include the details which may give additional information about the central thought, conditioning information which qualifies in some

19. Marlie D. A. Andre and Thomas H. Anderson, "The Development and Evaluation of a Self-Questioning Study Technique," *Reading Research Quarterly* 14, No. 4 (1978–79): 621.

20. "Using Paragraph Clues as Aids to Understandings," *Journal of Reading* 8, No. 1 (1964):11–16.

way the central thought, or examples of application of the central thought. (See Examples 3.3, 3.4, and 3.5.)

EXAMPLE 3.3

Main idea →

Details categorized by:
performer
listener

Concluding statement

Most schools have an active program made up of a number of musical performing groups, vocal and instrumental. Many of you have or will have the opportunity to either perform with these groups or listen to them. As a performer you have the splendid opportunity to make music along with other students for your individual or combined pleasure. This is a wonderful thrill in itself, and you need not have outstanding talent to be able to perform in many of the school organizations. As a listener and a member of an audience where music is performed, you have the pleasure of enjoying music through quiet listening. Again, it is important that you try to get as much as you possibly can from the music. Whether you are busily involved in performing music or listening to it, a better understanding of the music would increase your enjoyment of it.

Reprinted by permission from Samuel L. Forcucci, *Let There Be Music* (Boston: Allyn & Bacon, 1969), p. 5.

EXAMPLE 3.4

Main idea →

Paragraph has three sentences:
develops from main idea (general) to specific
1. main idea
2. detail-what the bacteria do.
3. illustration (example) of work of bacteria.

Nitrogen compounds are added to soil through the action of **nitrogen-fixing bacteria.** These bacteria have the unique ability to take nitrogen gas from air and change it into nitrogen compounds called nitrates and nitrites. For example, sodium nitrate ($NaNO_3$) and sodium nitrite ($NaNO_2$) are two of the compounds formed.

Reprinted by permission from Charles H. Heimler and Charles D. Neal, *Principles of Science* (Columbus: Charles E. Merrill, 1979), p. 216.

EXAMPLE 3.5

Main idea not stated in one sentence at the beginning. Student has to construct the main idea as shown by the underlining.

Heading

Most American players, unless they have played soccer, are unfamiliar with this particular skill. It consists in propelling a ball that is in the air by means of bouncing it off your head in a desired direction. In heading a ball, jump into the air with your neck rigid and your head slanted in the direction you wish the ball to go and play the ball off the thickest part of your skull, directly over the eyes.

Reprinted by permission of the American Alliance for Health, Physical Education, Recreation, and Dance, 1900 Association Drive, Reston, VA 22091.

2. *Introductory statements.* This type of paragraph is often found at the beginning of selections or units and chapters in textbooks. These are a great help to the student because they can give her a mental set that aids greatly in comprehension. In the introductory paragraph, the purpose of the author usually is stated, a preview of a selection is given, a plan of organization is indicated and questions sometimes are cited to guide the reader. See Examples 3.6, 3.7, and 3.8.

EXAMPLE 3.6

Practical illustration

Main idea →

General definition of forces

Two subtopics as part of introduction—overview.

Huge cranes, such as the one shown here, can lift, hold, and move amazingly large amounts of materials. A crane is an example of a machine. Machines are used to do work. They help us lift and move things we couldn't easily lift or move by ourselves.

Work and machines are part of the study of mechanics, the topic of this unit. By reading this unit you will learn more about machines and work. You will also learn about forces and how forces affect objects. Forces are needed to do work, to hold objects in place, and to cause motion.

Reprinted by permission from Charles H. Heimler and Charles D. Neal, *Principles of Science* (Columbus: Charles E. Merrill, 1979), p. 85.

EXAMPLE 3.7

Specific objective stated for student.

Transition—recall of prior study

Topic of chapter

Three points to be considered in measurement. Will be developed in chapter.

Thus far, we have discussed two properties of matter: inertia and energy. We often refer to properties as we consider materials. Thus, it is helpful to learn how to measure properties of matter.

In order to make a measurement, we must meet three basic requirements.

(1) We must know exactly what we are trying to measure.

(2) We must have some standard with which to compare whatever we are measuring.

(3) We must have some method of making this comparison.

Reprinted by permission from Robert C. Smoot, Jack Price, and Richard G. Smith, *Chemistry: A Modern Course* (Columbus: Charles E. Merrill, 1979), p. 19.

EXAMPLE 3.8

This paragraph notes three considerations that will be investigated.

CHAPTER 6 **Buying a Car**

Someday you will want to buy a car. In this chapter, we will discuss purchasing a car and the kinds of cars you might want to purchase. Then we will take a look at what it will cost you to operate a car. You will need to know all of these costs before you can decide how much you can afford to spend on a car.

Reprinted by permission from Jack Price; Olene Brown; Charles Michael; and Miriam Lien Clifford, *Mathematics for Everyday Life* (Columbus: Charles E. Merrill, 1978), p. 99.

3. *Paragraphs of definition.* These paragraphs develop concepts or define technical terms pertinent to the information. Usually the new term or word is printed in italics the first time it appears. Competent readers give special attention to paragraphs of definition because such paragraphs furnish background for further information and understanding. See Examples 3.9, 3.10, and 3.11.

EXAMPLE 3.9

Explanation of definition of heat.

Definitions

Effect of heat flow

Relationship of the two terms is implied.

2:4 Temperature

"What a hot day it is!" What does this expression mean? It means that the heat content per unit volume of air that day is greater than usual. What is heat? **Heat** is a form of energy. Heat always flows from a region of higher intensity to one of lower intensity. **Temperature** is a measure of heat intensity. Heat flows until the heat intensity (temperature) is the same everywhere. If one end of a metal rod is heated, the other end eventually becomes warm.

Reprinted by permission from Robert C. Smoot, Jack Price, and Richard G. Smith, *Chemistry: A Modern Course* (Columbus: Charles E. Merrill, 1979), p. 13.

EXAMPLE 3.10

Definition

Both paragraphs give practical illustrations of force which would be within the students' experience.

5:1 Force

Every time you walk, jump, or pedal a bicycle, you use a force. Walking and jumping make your body move. When you push on the pedals of a bicycle, your force sets you and the bicycle in motion. The harder you push, the greater the force, and the faster you go.

A force is any push or pull on a body. The pull of a car on a trailer being towed is a force. So is the push of your hand against a ball when you throw it. When two people arm wrestle they clasp each other's hand and push hard. The person who pushes with the most force usually wins.

Reprinted by permission from Charles H. Heimler and Charles D. Neal, *Principles of Science* (Columbus: Charles E. Merrill, 1979), p. 87.

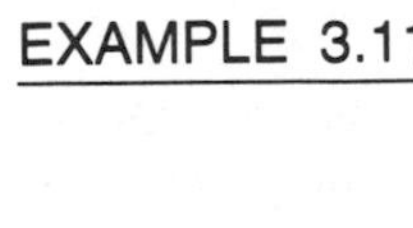

MELODIC CONTOUR

Definition

Our foregoing discussion of the tonality frames of melodies leads logically to another basic aspect of melodic structure. While the pitches of the tonality frame represent the "floor and ceiling" of the pitch line, the general motion up and down within these limits forms what we may call the *melodic contour.* This basic shape of up and down is merely another way through which we can describe the combined space-time structure of any melody.

A tune like *Joy to the World* traces a very simple down-up contour, forming an arc that fills in the limits of the tonality frame.

Example 1-17

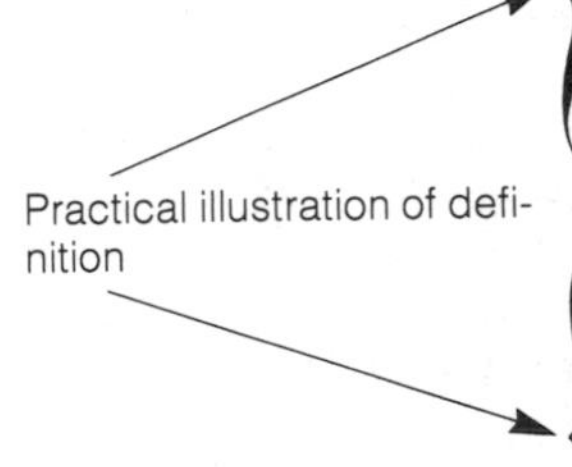

Reprinted by permission from William Thomson, *Introduction to Music as Structure* (Reading, Mass.: Addison-Wesley, 1971), p. 15.

4. *Principle explained by illustration.* Sometimes the author attempts to make an abstract principle or process easier to understand by giving illustrations or examples that may be similar to situations the reader has experienced. Some readers, however, may confuse the illustration with the principle that the author is explaining. This confusion stems from the fact that often the language of the illustration is more readable, and as a result the illustration attracts more attention or is more interesting to the reader. Competent readers differentiate carefully between the author's thought and the illustrations. See Examples 3.12 and 3.13.

EXAMPLE 3.12

Main idea

Illustration
One that students can relate to.

Prejudice can obviously lead to all kinds of unfairness when it is directed against people. Suppose, for example, that you are an expert mechanic looking for work. A gas station manager refuses even to interview you because you are a woman. He has the prejudiced view that women can't fix engines. Because his view isn't based on fact, it's unfair to you.

From *Creative Living: Maclean Hunter Learning Resources,* 708 Third Avenue, New York, New York 10017.

EXAMPLE 3.13

Main idea—information

Illustration

These two paragraphs could have been joined together.

9:11 Polyatomic Ions

There are a large number of ionic compounds that are made up of more than two elements. In these compounds, one of the ions consists of two or more atoms covalently bonded. However, the particle as a whole possesses an overall charge.

For example, consider the hydroxide ion (OH^-). The oxygen atom is bonded covalently to the hydrogen atom. The hydrogen atom is stable with two electrons in its outer level. The hydrogen atom contributes only one electron to the octet of oxygen. The other electron required for oxygen to have a stable octet is the one which gives the 1− charge to the ion. Although the two atoms are bonded together covalently, the combination still possesses an ionic charge. Such a group is called a polyatomic ion. Polyatomic ions form ionic bonds just as other ions do. Table 4-4 gives some of the more common polyatomic ions with their charges.

Reprinted by permission from Robert C. Smoot, Jack Price, and Richard G. Smith, *Chemistry: A Modern Course* (Columbus: Charles E. Merrill, 1979), p. 223.

5. *Comparison and contrast.* An author may use this pattern to clarify specific points he wishes to make. The reader should keep two questions in mind: "What main point does the author intend to convey?" "What likeness or differences does he use to reinforce the point?" See Examples 3.14 and 3.15.
6. *Cause and effect.* Interpretation in reading often depends upon seeing relationships among the facts. An author may cite causes and effects but does not often label them as such. See Examples 3.16 and 3.17.
7. *Problem solution.* Some paragraphs are designed to present problems and then offer solutions. The reader focuses first upon the problem, then the evidence, and finally the proposed solution. Sometimes the reader may draw her own conclusions or solve the problem from the evidence presented. Such paragraph patterns are often found in scientific and social studies materials. See Examples 3.18 and 3.19.
8. *Enumeration or summary.* These paragraphs are often found at the end of chapters or sections within a chapter. They are usually a compilation of the main ideas presented throughout the selection or chapter. Because they are highly concentrated, the reader may need to read these paragraphs slowly and intensively. At other times, an enumeration paragraph is used for a listing of details. If the reader needs to remember the details, slow and intensive reading again is required. See Examples 3.20, 3.21, and 3.22.
9. *Transitional paragraphs.* Their function is to shift the reader's attention from one aspect of a topic to another, or to vary an argument or shift time. Many times, simple transition is done by just a sentence at the beginning or the end of a paragraph. See Examples 3.23 and 3.24.
10. *Descriptive paragraphs.* These occur in literature and sometimes in social studies materials. Their purpose is to help the reader create a

mental picture and to note the mood or tone the author wishes to convey. Often they do not have a central idea sentence but merely one that labels the object, person, place, or event being described. See Examples 3.25 and 3.26.

EXAMPLE 3.14

Paragraph shows the similarities and the differences of the reasons for the settlement of each colony.

Among the colonies of the North, Middle, and South there were many <u>similarities</u> as well as <u>differences.</u>① The colonists' right to worship as they pleased was an important reason for the settlement of the Plymouth Colony as well as for the settlement of Rhode Island and Connecticut. The first Southern colonies were inspired more by a search for② new opportunity than by a search for religious freedom, although later Southern Colonies, especially Maryland, were settled by colonists seeking religious freedom. In the Middle Colonies, Pennsylvania was settled by Quakers, although New Netherland (later New York and New Jersey) was③ settled for commercial gain.

Three reasons given for settlement:

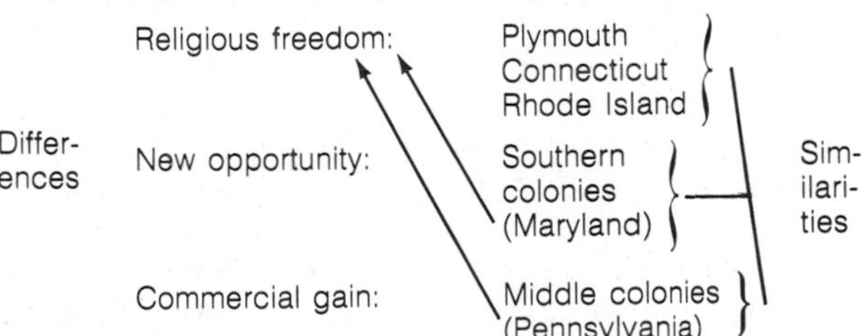

Reprinted by permission from Landis R. Heller and Norris W. Potter, *One Nation Indivisible* (Columbus: Charles E. Merrill, 1971), p. 43.

EXAMPLE 3.15

Shows basic contrast

We have selected this piece as our second example of sonata-allegro form not just because it represents simplicity in relatively modern dress, but also because it affords one view of the malleability of the basic design. While Mozart's sonata movement (and a majority of sonata-allegro movements) contains a middle section clearly occupied with developing *thematic patterns first heard in the exposition section,* the Hindemith movement represents a new twist: here it is the transitional or *bridge* patterns which form the basis of the development section. You will notice that this entire section is occupied with an ostinato bass, a short pattern derived from the three-tone motif first heard during the exposition section.

Reprinted by permission from William Thomson, *Introduction to Music as Structure* (Reading, Mass.: Addison-Wesley, 1971), p. 243.

EXAMPLE 3.16

Cause

Effect

More Temptations

It's no accident that the first things you often see as you enter a clothing store are especially attractive, expensive-looking items. These are usually displayed in eye-catching ways. Scarves may be arranged in a rainbow pattern, or sweaters may be decorated with autumn leaves. The items in such a display usually earn the store a good profit. The display encourages people to buy them.

Reprinted by permission from Josephine A. Foster; M. Janice Hogan; Bettie M. Herring; and Audrey G. Gieseking-Williams, *Creative Living* (New York: Butterick, 1979), p. 161.

EXAMPLE 3.17

Definition

Cause

Effect

This paragraph is a combination of definition and cause and effect.

During the 1940s American pilots discovered strong belts of wind near the tropopause layer. These narrow belts of wind called, **jet streams,** flow from west to east. The jet streams form where the warm air from the tropics meets the cold air from the poles. The jet streams resemble a very fast-moving, meandering river. Wind speeds in the jet streams may reach 180 kilometers/hour in the summer and 220 to 370 kilometers/hour in the winter. The jet streams change their positions in latitude and altitude from day to day and season to season. Unusually severe storms occur when the jet streams interfere with the surface wind systems described above.

Reprinted by permission from Margaret S. Bishop; Berry Sutherland; Phyllis G. Lewis; and William H. Resch, *Focus on Earth Science* (Columbus: Charles E. Merrill, 1981), p. 159.

11. *Narrative paragraphs.* These story-type materials relate an anecdote or sequence within a story. There may not be a central idea statement. A sequence of events is often included in this type of paragraph. Example 3.27, though from a chemistry textbook, is narrative.

EXAMPLE 3.18

This paragraph is introductory but also poses a practical problem. The solution is not given, nor the steps toward the solution. But instruction in how to solve these problems will be the content of the chapter.

Conjecture with the students how the problem can be solved.

CHAPTER 9 **Student Supply Store**

The members of a special musical group at Vista High School wish to perform in a music festival next summer. They have received permission to start a student supply store to raise money for their trip. There are 26 students in the group. Four adults will go along as chaperones. Five people can travel in one car. The trip is 310 miles one way. The cost of driving one car is 14¢ per mile. What is the cost to travel to the festival and back by car?

Reprinted by permission from Jack Price; Olene Brown; Charles Michael; and Miriam Lien Clifford, *Mathematics for Everyday Life* (Columbus: Charles E. Merrill, 1978). p. 159.

EXAMPLE 3.19

Paragraph begins with a question—problem.

Evidence presented by illustration.

Two conclusions.

Application to field of study last sentence (underlined).

What are some of the reasons for classifying living things? One is the desire for order and organization. Coins are more useful for study orderly arranged rather than jumbled together in a box. Once a system has been set up, it is much easier to locate and study a certain coin and new coins can be compared with other coins. Likewise, a new organism can be studied and easily added to the proper group.

Reprinted by permission from Raymond F. Oram, Paul J. Hummer, Jr., and Robert C. Smoot, *Biology: Living Systems* (Columbus: Charles E. Merrill, 1979), p. 289.

EXAMPLE 3.20

An enumerated summary of main ideas

Summary

1. Ionization energy is the energy necessary to remove an electron from an atom, leaving a positive ion.
2. Four factors determine ionization energy.
3. First ionization energy is the energy required to remove the first electron from an atom.
4. Ionization energies also provide support for our theories of atomic structure.
5. Ionization energies are measured in kilojoules/mole.

⋮

17. Polyatomic ions possess an overall charge just as other ions. However, they are composed of groups of atoms bonded together by covalent bonds.
18. Polyatomic ions form ionic bonds just as other ions do.
19. Electron clouds act as hard spheres when two nonbonded atoms approach each other. The radius of this imaginary sphere is called the van der Waals radius of the atom.

Reprinted by permission from Robert C. Smoot, Jack Price, and Richard G. Smith, *Chemistry: A Modern Course* (Columbus: Charles E. Merrill, 1979), p. 229.

The Student Does Not Sense the Author's Purpose

Some students miss the significance of the material. They may understand the facts presented, but they do not understand why they are important or what the relationship to other ideas may be. They are unaware of the author's intent other than to present information and are unable to draw conclusions or to infer adequately. As we have noted before, paying attention to introductory paragraphs will help in detecting the author's

EXAMPLE 3.21

An enumerated summary of main ideas

THE CHAPTER IN PERSPECTIVE

1. Economic instability is the result of drastic changes in aggregate demand, or the total volume of spending.
2. An increase in total spending at a time of unemployment will bring about an increase in production rather than an increase in price levels. If the economy is operating at full employment and total spending increases, the result is inflation. A decrease in total spending with unemployment brings about more unemployment, while decreased spending during full employment will help to check inflation.
3. Two types of government policy which influence aggregate demand and economic stability are monetary policy and fiscal policy.
4. Monetary policy, which consists of manipulating the money supply and the interest rate to attempt to influence the national economy, is implemented by the Federal Reserve System.
5. An easy money policy, which makes more money available, helps to expand the economy. In order to implement this type of policy, the Federal Reserve Board lowers the interest rates and increases the reserves available to member banks.
6. When there is danger of inflation due to an excess of total spending, the Federal Reserve Board could reduce bank reserves and raise interest rates—a tight money policy.
7. The five tools which the Federal Reserve can use to bring about looser or tighter money are open market operations, a change in the discount rate, a change in the reserve requirement, specifying margin requirements, and moral suasion.
8. The greatest weakness of monetary policy is its inability to directly affect national income.
9. Fiscal policy is the federal government's manipulation of its revenues and expenditures to produce desired effects on the economy.

Reprinted by permission from James E. Brown, Harold A. Wolf, and S. Stowell Symmes, *Economics: Principles and Practices* (Columbus: Charles E. Merrill, 1979), p. 323.

purpose. Also, the preface of a book or the "Foreword to the Student" found in many textbooks will alert students to the author's purpose. In editorials, newspaper columns and essays, background about the author may indicate an author's point of view.

The Student Does Not Follow the Author's Organization

Unless students can see the author's organization of ideas, many bits of information and ideas seem unrelated and isolated from each other. Such students rely on rote memorization of a myriad of facts in order to master the content.

Students can employ a number of techniques to follow the author's organization:

1. The Table of Contents of a textbook will help students to see the scope of the material included as well as the order of the specific topics.

EXAMPLE 3.22

From a science textbook

Chronology leading to the establishment of the U.S. Coast Guard

Function of Coast Guard also noted

Colonists traveling to the new world in the 16th and 17th century depended on small wooden ships for their safe arrival on the shores of North America. Many times these early travelers did not reach their destination. Violent storms or sudden attacks by pirates resulted in the loss of much life and property. There was little or no hope for rescue when disaster struck the seagoing passengers and crews.

However, by 1830, volunteer groups along the eastern shores of the newly developed United States saw the need to provide rescue services for ships in distress. By 1850, the United States government began to construct life boat stations along the coast. The U. S. Lifesaving Service was later established by Congress in 1871. The Service used beach patrols which dispatched small boats from shore. In 1915, an agency called the United States Coast Guard was formed. This new agency was responsible for both enforcement of marine laws and search and rescue missions. The Coast Guard extended its service to inland lakes and rivers as well as oceans and bays.

function →

Reprinted by permission from Margaret S. Bishop; Berry Sutherland; Phyllis G. Lewis; and William H. Resch, *Focus on Earth Science* (Columbus: Charles E. Merrill, 1981), p. 216.

EXAMPLE 3.23

Underlining shows transition

Also alerts student to previously studied data

5:6 Molecular Formulas

We have, thus far, calculated empirical formulas from experimental data. In order to calculate a molecular formula, we must know one more experimental fact, the molecular mass. In one of the examples in the previous section, the empirical formula calculated was CH_2O. If we know that the molecular mass of the compound is 180, how can we find the molecular formula? The molecular formula shows the number of atoms of each element in a molecule. Knowing that the elements will always be present in the ratio 1:2:1, we can calculate the mass of the empirical formula. Then we can find the number of these empirical units present in one molecular formula. In the substance CH_2O, the empirical unit has a mass of 12 + 2(1) + 16, or 30. It will, therefore, take six of these units to make 180 or one molecular formula. Thus, the molecular formula is $C_6H_{12}O_6$.

Reprinted by permission from Robert C. Smoot, Jack Price, and Richard G. Smith, *Chemistry: A Modern Course* (Columbus: Charles E. Merrill, 1979), p. 96-97.

Depending upon the detail of the Table of Contents, major subtopics related to each of the major chapter or unit headings may be listed.

2. The topical headings within a chapter clearly show the author's

EXAMPLE 3.24

Underlining shows transition

Conclusion

New condition that will be explained. The structure word *But* signals change in thought.

(These two paragraphs could have been joined together to form a paragraph of transition.)

You have learned how prices are determined in the two extremes of economic markets—pure competition and pure monopoly. You have also seen that these markets rarely exist in pure form in our economy. Thus, price determination takes place under conditions of almost-pure competition and near monopoly.

But between these extremes in the spectrum of economic markets are the vast majority of market situations in the United States. Some display very little of the monopoly element, but still do not possess all of the characteristics of almost-pure competition. These markets are referred to as monopolistic competition.

Reprinted by permission from James E. Brown, Harold A. Wolf, and S. Stowell Symmes, *Economics: Principles and Practices* (Columbus: Charles E. Merrill, 1979), p. 151.

EXAMPLE 3.25

Descriptive comparison

Urge students to see the pictures drawn by the descriptions in their mind.

The United States government moved to the new federal city of Washington in 1800. In that year, the young city was a clear example of the difference that can exist between dreams and reality. In the dreams of government leaders, Washington was a magnificent capital with lovely parks, beautiful public buildings, and grand avenues. In reality, it was a small village of rough fields, half-finished buildings, and muddy paths.

Reprinted by permission from Frank Freidel and Henry N. Drewry, *America Is* (Columbus: Charles E. Merrill, 1978), p. 142.

outline of the information. Students should first read the topical headings in a chapter, then read the chapter in detail.

3. Students could read a chapter title or a section heading and think before reading about the type of information that will be included. They could jot down their listings and see if the author includes the same type of information.
4. Knowledge of composition can be applied to a reading selection. Have students note the basic structure in a unit or chapter—introduction, body, and summarizing statement.
5. If students do not seem to have the concept of organization, some practice in categorization would be a starting point. For example, vocabulary about the classification of matter may be listed as:

EXAMPLE 3.26

Excerpt from a letter by Abigail Adams.

As I expected to find it a new country, with Houses scatterd over a space of ten miles, and trees [and] *stumps in plenty with, a castle of a house—so I found it—The Presidents House is in a beautifull situation in front of which is the Potomac. . . . The country around is romantic but a wild, a wilderness at present.*

I have been to George Town. . . . It is only one mile from me but a quagmire [deep mud] *after every rain. Here we are obliged to send daily for marketting; The capital is near two miles from us. . . . but I am determined to be satisfied and content, to say nothing of inconvenience. . . .*

Reprinted by permission from Frank Freidel and Henry N. Drewry, *America Is* (Columbus: Charles E. Merrill, 1978), p. 143.

EXAMPLE 3.27

Biographical narration from a science textbook

Presents a viewpoint by a scientist about algae

In 1970, Dr. Earle led a team of women divers and scientists in special underwater research. For fourteen days the women lived and worked in an undersea laboratory called Tektite II, which was located near the Virgin Islands 50 feet below the surface. During this time the scientists gained valuable experience in saturation diving. Dr. Earle explains that as a resident of the underwater environment it is possible to get a much better understanding of marine life. During their investigations aboard Tektite the scientists also identified over 150 types of plant life growing in the warm waters. Dr. Earle's work is devoted to the study of marine plants called algae. She has had the opportunity to discover and name dozens of these plants. Dr. Earle believes the role of algae in marine ecology is very important. She considers algae to be the living organisms on which all life on the earth depends.

Viewpoint

Reprinted by permission from Margaret S. Bishop; Berry Sutherland; Phyllis G. Lewis; and William H. Resch, *Focus on Earth Science* (Columbus: Charles E. Merrill, 1981), p. 196.

Matter
- elements
  - solid
  - liquid
  - gas

compounds
  solid
  liquid
  gas
mixtures
  solid
  liquid
  gas

or vocabulary about crime and justice:

Crime	Jury	Trial
sentences	petit jury	arraignment
capital punishment	grand jury	change of venue
rehabilitation	hung jury	prosecuting attorney
probation		double jeopardy
parole		testimony
indeterminate sentences		verdict
		convicted
		appeal

6. Students should note *structure words* (also called *signal words, clue words, connectives,* or *empty words*) in the material to discover how the author thinks, the direction of his thought, as well as the interrelationships and the degree of importance he wishes to give to ideas. Commonly used structure words are listed below.

I. Structure words indicating additional ideas

A. Words pointing to coordinate ideas, adding to the total thought and signalling similarity of ideas:

AND	FURTHERMORE	BESIDES	LIKEWISE
ALSO	PLUS	TOO	SIMILARLY
ANOTHER	OTHERWISE	AFTER THAT	AGAIN
IN ADDITION	MOREOVER	AS WELL AS	SINCE
SINCE THEN	NOT ONLY BUT ALSO		

B. Words pointing to final or concluding ideas:

CONSEQUENTLY	IN CONCLUSION	THEN
THUS	IN SUMMATION	TO SUM UP
HENCE	AT LAST	IN BRIEF
THEREFORE	FINALLY	IN THE END
AS A RESULT	IN RETROSPECT	ACCORDINGLY

II. Structure words indicating a change in ideas by reversing, qualifying, or modifying ideas already presented:

IN CONTRAST	ON THE OTHER HAND	FOR ALL THAT
TO THE CONTRARY	BUT	NEVERTHELESS
OPPOSED TO	IN SPITE OF	YET
CONVERSELY	ALTHOUGH	STILL
HOWEVER	EITHER-OR	EVEN IF
EVEN THOUGH		

III. Structure words indicating concrete application of a thought:

BECAUSE	SPECIFICALLY	PROVIDED
FOR EXAMPLE	FOR INSTANCE	LIKE, AS

IV. Structure words pointing to relationships among and between ideas:

A. Time relationships

IN THE FIRST PLACE	LAST	PREVIOUSLY
AT THE SAME TIME	NOW	HEREAFTER
THEREAFTER	LATER	AT LAST
IN RETROSPECT	AFTER	AT LENGTH
MEANWHILE	BEFORE	FOLLOWING
FINALLY	IMMEDIATELY	

B. Space relationships

HERE	CLOSE	BY	FURTHER ON	TO THE EAST
THERE	FAR	AWAY	ABOVE	WESTWARD
YONDER	NEAR	UNDER	ACROSS	BENEATH
EVERYWHERE				

C. Related in degree

MANY	LITTLE	SOME	BEST	FEWER	GREATER
MORE	LESS	ALL	WORST	FEWEST	GREATEST
MOST	LEAST				ABOVE ALL

D. Pointing to show emphasis

THIS	THAT	ONE	SOME	FEW
THESE	THOSE	SEVERAL		

E. Cause and effect

BECAUSE	SINCE	SO THAT	AS A RESULT

The Student Encounters So Many Strange Words That the Passage Means Little to Him

In this situation, the obvious and best solution is to replace the material with easier material. New concepts and the words which label them are expected in instructional material. The usual ratio is a maximum of one strange word out of every twenty. When this ratio increases, the material becomes frustrating, even with teacher instruction and guidance.

However, when there is no other material available, you can still help the student by following these techniques:

1. Spend as much time as needed developing the vocabulary prior to reading.
2. Use audiovisual aids to develop a background of information.
3. Explain the information included in the reading selection thoroughly before the student reads. As each point is explained, direct the student to the section or paragraph in the material which makes the same point.
4. Call the student's attention to the graphic aids (pictures, maps, graphs, tables) which help to illustrate and give concreteness to the information.
5. Be sure the student has well-defined and specific purposes before she reads.

Ideas Entirely Outside the Student's Experience Are Introduced

In this instance you have a clear-cut responsibility: increase the background of the student so that the information and ideas will have some meaning. To comprehend adequately, the student must have a background of information or experiences to which she can relate the ideas presented in the material; that is, new ideas must be related to old or known ideas. You may use any of the many appropriate aids—films, filmstrips, recordings, pictures, models, field trips, anecdotes, explanations, experiments. These means of increasing background are presented prior to reading and again during the ensuing discussion.

The Student Fails to Relate What She Reads to Previous Experiences

Often students do have related background information that they do not recall or do not relate to the material. In the introductory discussion previewing the material, you can help students recall this information by probing through questioning ("What do you know about ______?") and by relating similar experiences you know the students have had. In probing, students must have time to think. Do not always expect immediate recall.

Richards and Hatcher point out that interspersing meaningful questions throughout a text passage is quite effective in enhancing comprehension and recall. Such questions help the student note the relationship of main ideas and details and see the author's organization.[21] Questions such as "do you

---

21. John P. Richards and Catherine W. Hatcher, "Interspersed Meaningful Learning Questions as Semantic Cues for Poor Comprehenders," *Reading Research Quarterly* 13, No. 4 (1977–78): 538–52.

know?" or "have you had an experience like this?" will spark discussion and will also jog students' memory of personal experiences or information that relates to the topic.

The Student Has Difficulty with Sentence Complexity

In order to formulate ideas, students must have an understanding of how language is structured. They must know the meanings of words and how these meanings interact in various sentence patterns. By the time students are in high school they have heard and used various sentence patterns. However, they may not be able to identify the parts of sentences or know principles governing the function of the parts. Allen points out that a grammar is needed that will help students recognize the sentence units in the more complicated sentences they will meet in their reading. He goes on to say, "Above all, such a grammar must *not* be a grammar that emphasizes words. It must be a grammar that teaches students to regard a sentence as a hierarchy of constructions within constructions, on different levels, rather than as a string of words in linear sequence."[22] Ives follows the same theme: "pointing out syntactic distinctions in . . . class can, it seems likely, help comprehension and serve as preparation for more systematic teaching of the grammatical system.[23]

Students can have fun building sentences as a brainstorming session. Start with a kernel sentence (noun–verb) and then have students add to it the first thing that comes to mind. The sentences will be hilarious and nonsensical, which intrigues them and at the same time shows clearly the relationship of additions to a kernel sentence.

A related activity is one suggested by Combs: have students practice combining sentences. Two or more simple sentences are presented and the students "play with" these sentences to combine them in various ways. The simple sentences also could be incomplete (a variant form of the cloze procedure). For instance:

1. A trait is an (adaptation).
2. A trait improves (survival).
3. A trait must also improve the chance of (reproduction).
4. A trait is not (selected) if it interferes with reproduction.
5. A trait not selected will not be (spread) throughout the species.

These sentences could be combined to read as follows:

A trait is an adaptation *that* improves survival *that* must also improve the chance of reproduction *or else* it will not be selected *and* spread throughout the species. Note the connectives (in italics) which the students would have to use. In combining the five simple sentences, the student would have to see how they relate.[24]

22. Robert L. Allen, "Better Reading Through the Recognition of Grammar Relationships," *The Reading Teacher* 18, no. 3 (December 1964): 194–96.

23. Sumner Ives, "Some Notes on Syntax and Meaning," *The Reading Teacher* 18, no. 3 (December 1964): 178–83, 222.

24. Warren E. Combs, "Sentence Combining Practice Aids Reading Comprehension," *Journal of Reading* 21, No. 1 (October 1977): 18–24.

A technique that is often used to check comprehension is to require the student to restate a sentence in his own words. To restate a sentence in one's own words is an activity similar to transformational-generative linguistics, in which the same idea is expressed in various syntactical patterns. For instance, see the following sentence from a textbook:

"Most electric meters consist of several dials—one for each place value position."[25]

	N	*V*
Kernel sentence:	meters	consist

The sentence could also be expressed as follows:

1. Each dial on most electric meters has a place value position.
2. The dials on most electric meters represent specific place value positions.
3. Each place value position is shown by a dial on most electric meters.
4. Most electric meters show place value positions by dials.

Also, subject area teachers may, on occasion, need to help their students in analyzing sentences to improve comprehension. For example:

Inventors in the United States worked to make production easier or faster.[26]
Subject — Predicate—showing results of work.

A stairs, a mountain road, and a ramp are examples of inclined planes.[27]
Multiple subject — Predicate—stating what multiple subject is. (Plural verb indicates multiple subject)

Special triangles can be used to construct a building called a geodesic dome.[28]
Subject — Predicate—how special triangles can be used and what that use is called.

Deighton maintains that there are two types of sentences: one denotes action and the other is attributive. For example, "Inventions in the United States worked to make production easier or faster" denotes action, whereas "A stairs, a mountain road, and a ramp are examples of inclined planes" identifies *examples* and is attributive. Deighton notes that the words following the verb refer to the words preceding the verb. This occurs with all linking verbs such as *look, remain, stay, sound.* The meaning in such sentences is that of identification, characterization, or description. The verb *have* is also used in descriptive sentences.[29] For example:

---

25. Price, Brown, Charles, and Clifford, *Mathematics for Everyday Life* (Columbus: Charles E. Merrill, 1978), p. 72.

26. Frank Freidel and Henry N. Drewry, *America Is* (Columbus: Charles E. Merrill, 1978), p. 293.

27. Charles H. Heimler and Charles D. Neal, *Principles of Science* (Columbus: Charles E. Merrill, 1979), p. 134.

28. Price et al., *Mathematics,* p. 206.

29. Lee C. Deighton, "The Flow of Thought Through an English Sentence," in *Vistas in Reading,* ed. J. Allen Figurel (Newark, Del.: International Reading Association, 1967), p. 323.

Americans *have seen* great change and growth in the first fifty years of their nation. They *have* confidence in the future of their country.

When the student reads complicated sentences—such as those of two independent clauses joined by a conjunction (compound), those with independent and subordinate clauses (complex), and the long sentences which are both compound and complex—he has a more involved job of understanding. Not only must he understand the interrelationship of the parts of each clause as in a simple sentence, but he must also see the interrelationship of the *clauses* themselves. The student can note the interrelationship of large units of complicated sentences by the use of specific structure words (connectives), such as *although, and, because, but, for, however, if, so, that, thus, when, where, which, who,* and *yet.* In a study of the effect on comprehension of understanding connectives, Robertson states that:

> Although children acquire language structures using connectives early in life, they gain mature understanding of them gradually throughout their school years. Children use clauses in speech before they go to school but they do not develop a sufficient understanding of the meanings of connectives in print for a number of years after that. Therefore, children should be given systematic training through the reading program so they may develop more facility at an earlier age in understanding increasingly complex communications from the printed page.[30]

The subject teacher can help students by alerting them to the use of structure words as they read complicated sentences. A passage taken from a social studies text shows the use of structure words (see Example 3.28).

EXAMPLE 3.28

indication of application of thought

time relation

condition qualification

The Threshing Machine. As a result of better plowing and harvesting methods, the grain grower's crops were greatly increased. He could now grow and harvest large amounts of wheat, oats, or barley with relatively little help. However, he still needed a more efficient way to separate the grain from the stalk. The threshing machine was the best answer to this problem.

Reprinted by permission from Landis R. Heller and Norris W. Potter, *One Nation Indivisible* (Columbus: Charles E. Merrill, 1971), p. 335.

A sentence from an algebra text shows also a qualification of thought:

If the graph of a parabola is folded along its axis of symmetry,

Indicates condition for the result

the two halves of the parabola coincide.[31]

Result if condition is met

30. Jean E. Robertson, "Pupil Understanding of Connectives in Reading," *Reading Research Quarterly* 3, No. 3 (Spring 1968): 416.

31. Alan G. Foster, James N. Rath, and Leslie J. Winters, *Algebra One* (Columbus: Charles E. Merrill, 1979), p. 391.

Teaching sentence comprehension, traditionally considered the domain of the English teacher, is actually the responsibility of each content teacher. Indeed, this knowledge is as much a part of professional preparation as the acquisition of the subject matter of the discipline to be taught.

The Student Does Not Visualize Words

The ability to construct mental pictures from reading material is both evidence of comprehension and a basis for developing interest. Students' reactions to and sensory images of words enable them to sense the mood and tone of a selection. Visualization is necessary for a full appreciation of selections in literature, particularly poetry. Many poems are best comprehended through the images as well as feelings they evoke. Visual imagery is also employed in the content subjects when there are descriptions—for example, sequential development of processes in science; political and social events in history, particularly in sensing the feelings of a people; as one of the first steps in solving a mathematics problem; and in visualizing the end product in home economics or industrial arts.

To help students use sensory imagery, you can:

1. Discuss the meanings of words. Ask students to state quickly the mental picture or the sensory feeling a word indicates to them.
2. Investigate the connotative uses of specific words and alert students to the emotional impact of the words.
3. Guide the reading by posing questions or problems that require sensory imagery. For example, "How would you feel if ______?" "What is the situation taking place in this math problem?" "Describe your feelings if you lived in the cramped quarters of a whaling ship for two years before reaching home port." "Show by simple sketches the various techniques of land conservation."
4. Dramatize situations from literature and social studies.
5. Ask students to draw pictures to show how they visualize a descriptive passage.

The Student Does Not Understand Figurative Expressions and Subtle Meanings

Deficiencies in this area largely are due to a lack of background and unfamiliarity with idiomatic expressions. Many of our idiomatic expressions originated when people lived in a less technological and urban society. Hence, many are outside the students' experience. They must learn that idiomatic expressions and figures of speech are not translated literally but rather are symbolic—terms derived from the literal meanings. Figures of speech should be taught as such, particularly those that appear in the reading material of a subject.

Sherer states that instruction in figures of speech should follow four steps:

1. Students must recognize nonliteral language as such. Ask students to pick out nonliteral words and expressions from passages.

2. Students should realize that much of figurative language, such as similes and metaphors, is based on comparison. Of course, as Sherer points out, similes are easier for noting comparison because they contain the word *like* or *as*.
3. All confusing words on both sides of the comparison must be defined denotatively. Obviously, if students are unfamiliar with the words, the symbolic meaning to figurative language would be unknown.
4. Students must understand the author's purpose for making the comparison and then decide what comparisons the author wants to draw. Sherer states that this is often the most difficult step. But, it is a most important one if the student is to realize the full impact of the figurative language used.[32]

Students will also enjoy attempting to create their own figures of speech. Figures of speech add to the flavor of a selection, making it more interesting.

The Student Cannot Weigh Evidence and Draw Valid Inferences and Conclusions

Weighing evidence and drawing conclusions are abilities based on two factors. One is the student's background of information. Valid inferences and logical conclusions cannot be made in a vacuum. The reader needs some information against which to gauge his inference or conclusion. Second, he needs depth and precision of vocabulary to catch subtle meanings and connotative usage. Once these prerequisites are met, you can guide the student in obtaining comprehension so that he knows what the author has written. Then, help him to apply various skills of critical reading to note the author's point of view, bias, and intent. Questions that might be helpful in this area are:

"What is the author attempting to do in this selection, and how does he try to accomplish it?" "What evidence does the author give? Show whether or not the author's arguments are logical." "What is the significance of the information the author has presented?" "What conclusions can you draw?"

Work through questions such as these with the students before requiring them to answer independently. Questions involving both convergent and divergent thinking as well as Bloom's steps of interpretation, application, analysis, synthesis, and evaluation would be useful here. Finder points out that comprehension may be identified by showing that the reader is able to identify the effects intended by a reading selection and explain the elements within the selection which produced the effects.[33]

The Student Cannot Interpret Special Materials Such as Graphs, Tables, Maps, and Diagrams

Most high school teachers expect students to know how to use the graphic aids in a reading selection. Probably they have been taught, but many high

---

32. Peter A. Sherer, "Those Mystifying Metaphors: Students Can Read Them," *Journal of Reading* 20, No. 7 (April 1977): 559–62.

33. Morris Finder, "Comprehension: An Analysis of a Task," *Journal of Reading* 13, No. 3 (December 1969): 199–202, 237–40.

school students either cannot or do not use them. It is possible that these aids are not emphasized; to teach them or to use them extensively would be considered tantamount to returning to primary reading levels. However, they are valuable aids for any student at any level, particularly for the poor reader. Many poor readers find the standard text easier to grasp after working with graphic aids. The use of these aids is considered to be a reading study skill.

SUMMARY

In teaching comprehension, the emphasis must be on the recognition and development of *ideas*. All techniques must be kept subordinate to the ideas presented by an author. In this way we can incorporate both the cognitive and affective domains—that is, the factual information and the effect of the facts upon the reader. Through the investigation of ideas, we also bring in and develop other important aspects of comprehension: background, the author's organization of information, and the language structure used.

QUESTIONS AND PROBLEMS FOR YOUR OWN CLASSROOM

For readers who are training to be teachers:

1. Select a passage and identify the paragraph patterns.
2. Select a passage and note the structure words. How do they affect the meaning, import, and relationship of the ideas?
3. How would you relate a topic to the students' experiential background? What would you do to increase their background?
4. Select a passage which you consider as a typical assignment and plan how you would teach a comprehension skill, such as noting the main idea and the content at the same time.

For readers who are teaching:

1. Before your next reading selection in class, formulate comprehension questions for each of the literal, interpretative, critical, and creative levels. Then, formulate questions to implement Bloom's taxonomy or Barrett's taxonomy.
2. Analyze questions at the end of a chapter or your own questions and determine the words indicating the form of the answer.
3. In your lesson procedures, identify questions of purpose to guide the students' reading. Evolve some questions from them. Determine with them the rate and intensity of reading required.
4. Examine a reading assignment for your students and do the following:
   a. Make a listing of the general words used with a specialized meaning.
   b. Identify the paragraph patterns.
   c. Note the structure words and determine how they affect the meaning, import, and relationship of the ideas.

5. Select a comprehension skill—such as noting the main idea, drawing conclusions, evaluating the significance, and so on—and plan instruction in it to accompany your coverage of subject matter.
6. Select a reading assignment and determine how you can use and develop aspects of the affective mode. How would you motivate students and develop interest? How would you handle student emotion and attitude toward the selection?

SELECTED REFERENCES

Bloom, Benjamin S., ed. *Taxonomy of Educational Objectives; The Classification of Educational Goals, Handbook I, Cognitive Domain.* New York: David McKay, 1956.

The taxonomy is thoroughly explained and its relation to comprehension is discussed extensively.

Clymer, Theodore. "What Is Reading?" *In Some Current Concepts: Innovation and Change in Reading Instruction,* edited by Helen M. Robinson. Chicago: National Society for the Study of Education, The University of Chicago Press, 1968.

Clymer presents Barrett's taxonomy, which does include a category in the affective mode. Clymer also briefly discusses other analyses of comprehension not presented in the present text.

Guilford, J. P., and Hoeffner, Ralph. *The Analysis of Intelligence.* New York: McGraw-Hill, 1971.

Chapter I gives an overview of the analysis of intelligence.

Sanders, Morris M. *Classroom Questions: What Kinds?* New York: Harper & Row, 1966.

Sanders follows Bloom's taxonomy and gives excellent suggestions for forming appropriate questions.

Spache, George D. *Toward Better Reading.* Champaign, Ill.: Garrard Publishing Company, 1963.

The application of Guilford's analysis of intelligence to reading is the most thorough found in the literature.

CHAPTER 4

Reading Study Skills

OVERVIEW

The reading study skills should be considered the techniques that students use to aid understanding. They are aimed at developing independence in gaining information from printed materials. Students use these skills when working by themselves. Of course, students must have instruction and guidance in ways to become independent. They need guided practice in completing a textbook assignment, in research reading, in seeing the author's method of organization, and in organizing information.

Questions

Consider these questions before you read further:

1. How do you help your students study the material in class?
2. In what ways do you use graphic aids to help students comprehend?
3. How much research reading do you require your students to do? What help do you give them in doing research reading?

McKay states that the study skills include any technique students use in learning school assignments.[1] The study skills—sometimes called *reading study skills*—are those used by students when they need to understand and remember information from a reference book, such as a textbook. Harris calls this *assimilative* reading.[2]

Obviously, the student needs many specific skills to master the information contained in reading study assignments. In fact, nearly all the skills of reading, ranging from word recognition (decoding) skills to the various comprehension (encoding) skills, at some point will be used. As might be expected, different scholars in the literature of reading have different lists of the reading-study skills. Yet, each uses as a core the techniques of studying assignments independently. In fact, the goal of the study skills is total independence in gaining information.

For students who are able to decode words, know the vocabulary, and understand basic syntax, there are reading-study skills which will help them to be more productive in their efforts. Those to be discussed in this chapter are:

1. The SQ3R study procedure
2. Organizing information
3. Using graphic aids
4. Following directions
5. Research reading
6. Adjusting rate of reading

Teaching study skills along with content does not detract from or hinder the coverage of the content. Rather, content acquisition increases. McKay supports this position when he says,

> Study skill instruction in the various content fields is preferred because the skills are taught and practiced where they are needed and in proper combination for the particular subject area, rather than in isolation. In addition, the actual materials of the course are used for the teaching and practice so that students can see the usefulness of the skills.[3]

THE SQ3R PROCEDURE (SURVEY-QUESTION-READ-RECITE-REVIEW)

Francis Robinson's procedure for individual and independent study is probably the best known for use at the secondary and college levels.[4] Though there are variations of the formula, all follow the same basic steps as the original:

---

1. William McKay, "The Nature and Extent of Work-Study Skills," in *Teaching Reading Skills in Secondary Schools: Readings,* ed. Arthur V. Olson and Wilbur S. Ames (Scranton: International Textbook Company, 1970), p. 160.

2. Albert J. Harris, "Research on Some Aspects of Comprehension: Rate, Flexibility, and Study Skills," *Journal of Reading* 12, No. 3 (December 1968): 205-10, 258-60.

3. McKay, "Work-Study Skills," p. 161.

4. Francis P. Robinson, *Effective Study* (New York: Harper & Row, 1961), pp. 13–48.

1. An introduction to the selection by a preview and the delineation of a purpose question
2. Reading the selection for the determined purpose
3. A summing up that involves the students in thinking about what they have read, making an annotation or taking notes (thereby translating the information into their own words), a review of the material similar to the preview, and finally a possible self-testing.

When you study Table 4.1 you will note that different terms are used to explain the same step, certain steps are added for particular emphasis, and some study procedures are designed for certain types of written material or subject.

Students have been instructed and advised to use this procedure, but many still seem unaware of it or its effectiveness. In one instance I taught the method only to have a student say, "Look, you're lucky if I even read the material once, much less survey, question, recite and review! I'd never get my homework done!" This student, of course, failed to appreciate the efficiency of the method; he saw it only as taking more time for no greater return. Teachers have found that students should not only be instructed in the method but also shown its value.

An effective method for orienting students positively toward the study procedure is to have them read two comparable selections, one by their usual method and the other by monitoring them through the SQ3R method. When they are quizzed for recall on both selections, they usually have greater recall and understanding with the SQ3R.

The steps of the procedure are:

Survey—Surveying the introductory statement, the headings, and summaries quickly to get the general idea and scope of the assignment. Readers may also give general attention to the graphic aids and the questions at the end of the chapter.

Question—The students formulate their own purpose questions. They may use the headings or a question which the survey of the material may have prompted. Teacher-directed questions (the assignment questions) may serve as purpose questions, though it is wise for the students to become independent in formulating their own. Even at the college level, students are unable at first to formulate questions from topical headings. You may need to review some headings from the textbook and see if the students can rephrase them in the form of questions. If they cannot, a vital step of the individual study procedure will not be accomplished.

Read—Students read the material to answer the purpose question(s).

Recite—The students pause to relate to themselves the answer to the questions. They may also recall the main ideas of the author and the author's organization of information.

Review—The students look through the selection to perceive again the organization and basic ideas and to make notes.

ORGANIZING INFORMATION

For effective study, students must be able to organize data into a structure that shows logical interrelationships. There are two aspects of organizing

TABLE 4.1 Comparison of Reading Study Procedures

Basic Three Steps	SQ3R	SQRQCQ (Math)[5]	PQRST (Science)[6]	PARS[7]	PANORAMA[8]	OARWET[9]
Introduction	Survey Question	Survey (Reading of problem —General nature) Question (What is the problem)	Preview Question	Purpose (Why read) Ask (Purpose question)	Purpose (Why read) Adaptation (Determine rate to use) Need to Pose Question (Purpose question) Overview	Overview Ask
Read	Read	Reread (Note details, Interrelationships) Question (Process?) Compute	Read	Read	Read and Relate	Read
Sum up	Recite Review	Question (Correct? Does it make sense?)	Summarize Test (Check summary against selection)	Summarize (Put principle ideas into own words)	Annotate (Taking notes) Memorize (Using notes) Assess (Judges if essential information according to purpose is attained)	Write Evaluate Test

5. Leo Fay, "Reading Study Skills: Math and Science," in *Reading and Inquiry,* ed. J. Allen Figurel (Newark, Del.: IRA, 1965), p. 93.

6. Fay, "Reading Study Skills," p. 94.

7. Carl B. Smith, Sharon L. Smith, and Larry Mikulecky, *Teaching Reading in Secondary School Content Subjects: A Bookthinking Process* (New York: Holt, Rinehart & Winston, 1978), pp. 252-58.

8. Peter Edwards, "Panorama: A Study Technique," *Journal of Reading* 17, No. 2 (November 1973): 132–35.

9. Maxwell H. Norman, *Successful Reading: Key to Our Dynamic Society* (New York: Holt, Rinehart & Winston, 1968), pp. 12–13.

TABLE 4.1 *cont.*

Basic Three Steps	PSC[10]	REAP[11]	EVOKER (Poetry Drama)[12]	PQ4R[13]	PQ4R (Math)[14]
Introduction	Preview		Explore (General reading of selection) Vocabulary (Note new key words)	Preview Question	Preview (General reading of problem) Question (What is question of problem)
Read	Study (Reading, Writing a summary, Reviewing—comparing summary with selection)	Read	Oral read	Read	Read (List all facts in logical order)
Sum up	Check (Review of all summary notes)	Encode (Student translates into own words) Annotate (Student writes message according to purpose) Ponder (Thinks about author's ideas)	Key ideas (Theme of selection Evaluation (Relation of key words & sentences to main ideas) Recapitulation (Reread)	Reflect Recite Review	Reflect (What is the unknown quantity) Rewrite (Translate the problem into mathematical terms. Compute) Review (Substitute answer for unknown quantity. Does it make sense?)

10. Vincent P. Orlando, "Training Students to Use a Modified Version of SQ3R: An Instructional Strategy," *Reading World* 20, No. 1 (October 1980): 65-70.

11. Marilyn G. Eanet and Antony V. Manzo, "REAP—A Strategy for Improving Reading/Writing/Study Skills," *Journal of Reading 19,* No. 8 (May 1976): 647-52.

12. Betty D. Roe, Barbara D. Stoodt, and Paul C. Burns, *Reading Instruction in the Secondary School* (Chicago: Rand McNally, 1978), p. 177.

13. Ellen Lamar Thomas and H. Alan Robinson, *Improving Reading in Every Class* (Boston: Allyn & Bacon, 1972), pp. 115–28.

14. Anthony C. Maffei, "Reading Analysis in Mathematics," *Journal of Reading* 16, No. 7 (April 1973): 546-49.

information effectively: noting, as one reads, the organization used by the author, and the reader's own ability to organize information through note taking and outlining. Consider the following points when assisting students in organizing information:

1. The students need to be able to note patterns of thought in paragraphs and larger segments of written material.
2. The students need to acquire and apply skills of outlining, summarizing, and note taking.
3. The students need continuous motivation to apply the skills of noting and producing organized information.

Organizing content information requires intense concentration and sustained study; it is not a casual exercise. Therefore, high school students must appreciate how the skills of organization can benefit them.

A number of successful teachers have commented that students want to be able to comprehend well and efficiently, but many do not know how to proceed. You are the key person to develop the organizational skills as they apply in your content area. McKay underscores this position and suggests ways the teacher can help the student:

1. By being aware of [the material's] values and patterns.
2. By asking the kinds of questions which encourage students to observe the structure of what they have read.
3. By surveying the next lesson with his class, calling attention to the organization they are about to study.
4. By alerting them to headings which almost outline the material.
5. By reading materials to his class and asking anticipatory questions with a focus on structure.
6. By using visual aids such as colored overlays on an overhead projector.
7. By showing students *how* to take notes and *how* to outline.[15]

What McKay is saying points to elements of classroom procedure. By asking questions that emphasize the structure or organization of the information we are engaged in Bloom's steps of analysis and synthesis.

In your classroom, guide the students' thinking by posing such questions as:

What two points did the author make about ________? Where did you find these points? What were the principal ideas presented by the author? How did he relate the ideas? (Or, In what order did he present them?) Then, if the students cannot answer such questions, you need to help them to see the structure, which may involve the plan shown by the topical headings or other typographical features, or the pattern of the paragraphs. Evolve with them a sketch showing the organization.

McKay also cites the necessity of surveying the assigned material before it is read (see Chapter 7 for a detailed discussion of previewing). He suggests alerting students to headings, which comprise the outline. Then, he mentions anticipatory questions. A common question of this kind in literature is: What

---

15. McKay, "Work-Study Skills," p. 160.

do you think will happen next? A particularly effective procedure is to ask students before they read the selection to imagine how a topic might be developed by an author, and then compare their ideas with what the author actually did. For instance, did the author use chronology, comparison, cause and effect, the steps of a process or phenomenon, or a combination? Finally, McKay advises teachers to show students how to take notes and how to outline.

Note Taking

One teacher told her students that they should never do any study-type reading unless they had a pencil in hand to take notes. This teacher offered two reasons for taking notes: first, note taking makes study active, compelling the students to think about what they are reading when they restate it in their own language; second, reviewing becomes easier, particularly if the students have developed the ability to make their notes brief. Notes then become memory joggers rather than a restatement of the textbook. Note-taking ability depends upon identifying the author's structure through the use of introductions and summaries, boldface headings, paragraph analysis, and alertness to structure words that signal direction in thought. Students will need systematic instruction in the skills of note taking.

Notes may take several forms. The student may outline the information, write a precis, or devise a chart of the material. Whatever form is used, specific principles must be observed. First, the notes should be in the student's own words. Phrases and sentence fragments often are sufficient unless the notes are in the form of a precis. Quotes should be kept to a minimum. Most often the quote used would include the author's specific definition of a word, or formulas. Second, the notes should be brief. One way for a student to do this is to select only the outstanding points—the major ideas. Brevity in note taking also helps the student to see in almost a graphic form the total structure of the information. Third, the student should note hints to structure—words such *as first, more important, finally,* and so on. In summaries, the student should be alert to the main ideas by such clues as *remember, the essential difference in,* etc. Fourth, the student should be urged to devise a code of abbreviations and symbols to save time and reduce the length of the notes. These are uniquely his own, particularly since the notes are for his use solely. Fifth, the notes should be orderly and consistent in form. If an outline is used, its form should be consistent throughout. Caution students on this point since one of the goals on note taking is to have the notes make sense after a lapse of time. Finally, the notes should be filed in consecutive order and dated.

Additional considerations and practices are involved when the student takes notes from various references in preparing a research report. Usually such notes are from books and materials that will be read only once. The student should keep in mind the following:

1. Keep the notes as brief as possible, but realize that their length and detail will depend on the amount of material and the purpose.

2. Use cards so that the notes from several references can be reorganized into proper sequence for the report.
3. Record on each card the complete bibliographical reference and the main ideas and details relevant to the purpose.

When should students take notes—while reading, or after they have read the selection? In the SQ3R procedure, the fourth step—*recite*—is the one in which the students think about what they have read and try to recall the information presented. At this time it would be well for them to write down the key points. (Variations of the SQ3R procedure use the term *summarize* or *annotate.*) Students may find, certainly at first, that to read an entire selection and "recite" is too formidable a process. If such is the case, instruct them to take notes after reading the material under each topical heading. The *review* (or *test,* as some study procedures suggest) is a check of the notes against the information in the selection. The review, then, not only acts to check on the students' notes but also helps them to fix the information in memory, thereby aiding recall.

Even in the lecture format, students should take notes, either during breaks in the lecture or after it. Kelly and Holmes state that "students refrain from taking notes during lecture, but instead engage in an intensive listening and thinking process."[16] Their students are given a purpose for listening: they copy the objectives of the lecture as well as any new terminology. Though this author does not view the lecture procedure as the most effective (discussion, with the interaction it involves, seems much more productive), such a note-taking procedure is certainly appropriate when students give reports in class. The rationale for student reports is to present information which the entire class does not have time to study in depth. All students, then, should take notes from the reports, and they need to be instructed in how to do so.

Another form of note taking is the *summary.* To summarize, students must be able to discern the main ideas and the subordinate details, to see the development of the ideas and their relation to one another. Students need to realize that a summary is a listing of main ideas or a compilation of main ideas in paragraph form.

As you teach, you can incorporate instruction in note taking into your regular class procedures. First, read the chapter or section with the students and suggest the ideas which should be recorded in the notes. Second, discuss specific material with the students and evolve with them the most efficient form for their notes. Notes can take the form of an outline, a list, a chart, a time line, parallel columns comparing two or more entities, a flowchart to show steps of a process, or any other form which the students find helpful. Third, guide the students to take notes in class by writing the main points on the blackboard as the lesson progresses. Help students to note the items to be included under each heading. Fourth, use a newspaper article to teach students to take notes that answer the questions of *who? when? what? where? why?* and *how?* Fifth, outlining is the form of note taking most effective in helping students to sort out information in order to see the interrelationships

16. Brenda Wright Kelly and Janis Holmes, "The Guided Lecture Procedure," *Journal of Reading* 22, No. 7 (April 1979): 602.

of main ideas and related details. Students will need guidance in correct outline form, but this is not difficult if they can note the main idea and the factual details relating to it. Therefore, your teaching involves a dual process. The first and most basic is to improve the students' ability to see the structure of information, which may involve paragraph analysis and chapter or unit organization in the textbook. The other is the more mechanical skill of outline form. Students may learn the basic form through direct instruction followed by guidance in applying it to selected passages. Once they have mastered this, more latitude can be granted to develop their own personal form. Clarity and the proper relationships of ideas must still be apparent, or else the outline will be of little value.

Most textbooks in the subject areas try to organize the subject matter clearly. The relationship of the main ideas and subordinate ideas can be noted as follows:

Title of the Book
Unit title
Chapter title
Chapter section
Topical headings
Paragraphs

The title of the textbook presents the overall area of study. The unit and chapter titles, and often the chapter sections, can be examined in the Table of Contents. For example, one typical science textbook is organized in this manner:

Principles of Science
Unit I Science, Matter, and Energy
Chapter 1—Science and Measurement
Science—Product & Process
Scientific Methods
Experiments
Theory and Law
Using Science
Measurement
Metric System
Length and Area
Mass and Weight
Volume[17]

The students may be stimulated to think about the subject matter organization by conjecturing the kinds of data that would be included. Also, as they investigate the Table of Contents, students can begin to acquire some familiarity with the concepts covered.

The organization of the textbook into unit, chapter, and chapter section is helpful to students if they are aware of such textbook aids. If students have been assigned to read about the classification and characteristics of matter, for example, they should be guided to see the overview of the topics. In Unit I, entitled "Science, Matter, and Energy," the chapter they should refer to is Chapter 2, "Matter," which is broken up into the following sections:

---

17. Heimler and Neal, *Principles of Science,* Bk I, p. v.

Gases, Liquids, and Solids
Properties of Matter
Density
Buoyance
Elements, Compounds, and Mixtures
Symbols and Formulas
Atomic Theory of Matter
Molecules

As the students read the assigned chapter, their purpose-for-reading question would probably be, "How is matter classified?" By noting section headings and supporting details as they read, they will then obtain a clear outline of the answer to their purpose question.

USING GRAPHIC AIDS

The graphic aids of a textbook include maps, diagrams, charts, tables, graphs, pictures, cartoons, and time lines. They are intended to aid students in understanding the expository information, but often they are not used to full advantage. There may be several reasons for this. There may be little emphasis on the use of such aids in the classroom. Some teachers believe that only beginning readers need them and feel that high school students are beyond needing graphic materials. It is incorrect to assume that the use of graphic aids is unnecessary because anyone should be able to obtain pictorial information. High school students often do not know how to use these materials effectively—they do not know what purposes to keep in mind when using them, or they do not wish to take the time. Yet, the text is often interspersed with references to the graphic materials as a means of making the exposition more concrete. This is their major purpose.

Students cannot always experience at first hand all of the data to be learned in the various subjects. In many subjects, they are confronted with abstract concepts. Graphic aids can aid comprehension by giving some concreteness to these abstractions, as Summers notes:

> Audio-visual aids play an important role in developing understandings of abstract concepts at all levels of learning. Often a simple picture, model, or film adds measurably to the interpretation of the verbal message of printed material. In particular, the visual aids in the reading materials of a subject such as maps, charts, tables, graphs, diagrams, pictures and cartoons add to interpretation and understanding. If students can profit from such aids, their acheivement in a subject is enhanced. However, visual aids are a means to an end and not an end in themselves. The only rationale for the inclusion of visual aids in reading is the contribution they make to creating interest and adding to the understanding of content.[18]

---

18. Edward G. Summers, "Utilizing Visual Aids in Reading Materials for Effective Learning," in *Developing Study Skills in Secondary Schools*, ed. Harold E. Herber (Newark, Del.: International Reading Association, 1965), pp. 98-99.

Maps

Much of the world's information has been recorded on maps of various types. Usually the subject in which map reading skills are used most often is social studies. However, map study pervades the entire school curriculum. Maps are an essential tool of modern life.

The type of information gained from maps depends upon the type of map used. They may be listed as follows:

1. *Street maps* show the streets of a city and may show information leading to a study of local problems, such as the placement of redevelopment or urban renewal plans, location of cables, telephone lines, power lines, or railways.
2. *Road maps* show distances between cites, types of roads, natural park areas.
3. *Relief maps* show the physical features of the terrain, usually represented by a scale of color and lines to note elevation above sea level. These maps can also indicate information about the location of cities, roads, industries and crops.
4. *Physical maps* are closely related to relief maps, and indicate land use and type, potential boundaries and population centers.
5. *Vegetation maps* show the types of vegetation of a region and often are superimposed upon a physical map.
6. *Political maps* show political divisions of cities, counties, states and countries, and may show shifts of political control over areas.
7. *Product maps* show the principal products, crops, resources, and goods of a region.
8. *Pictorial maps* use pictures or cartoon figures to show historical and natural features, natural wild life, dress of the people.
9. *Population maps* show the centers of population in a region.
10. *Historical maps* show explorers' interpretations of the world's land forms in centuries past, the boundaries of ancient countries, lines of explorations, battle arrangements.
11. *War maps* show where battles took place and the strategy used.
12. *Weather maps* use a specific set of symbols to give information about current and future weather conditions—high and low pressure centers, type of precipitation, air movement.
13. *Blank outline maps* are mostly used in schools for helping students become competent in map usage.

Just as with types of paragraphs, a map may be a combination of two or more types. For example, a historical map may use pictorial symbols and may also give political information. Basically the types of information that can be obtained from maps are land and water forms; relief features; direction and distance; social, political, and scientific data; and evidence of human habitation.

The skills of map usage are similar to the comprehension skills. Both use symbols and abstract representations. The basic level is the ability to use the features of the map to gain specific information. This level corresponds to the literal comprehension level in reading. Students may then need to make interpretations or inferences and draw conclusions from the data. They may need to compare one area with another; to note facts as well as distortions; to think critically of the relationships between facts on maps, and between maps and current events. Map reading is essentially the same as reading language.

As with reading skills, map reading skills should be taught in a consistent and systematic manner. Review basic map reading skills (telling direction, understanding longitude and latitude, using map scales, locating places and making inferences about the correlative patterns as well as the association of people and things in particular areas) and teach the more advanced secondary skills. Thralls presents the major map skills which junior and senior high school students should possess:[19]

Junior High School

1. Read information from weather maps and understand the value of these maps to the individual and to industry.
2. Interpret world pattern maps that show different types of distribution (for example, of products or resources).
3. Understand that parallels and meridians on some maps may be curved lines.
4. Understand that the map scale depends on what is to be shown.
5. Know map vocabulary such as *world pattern, isoline, isotherm, isobar, cold front, warm front, wind direction, wind velocity, ocean current, warm ocean current* and *cold ocean current.*

Senior High School

1. Read all commonly used map symbols.
2. Read descriptive facts from regional and world distribution maps.
3. Draw inferences or raise questions from information shown on two or more maps.
4. Use longitude and latitutde for location.
5. Make inferences about the climatic conditions of a country or region.
6. Use large-scale maps of cities and special areas and be able to relate these to small-scale maps showing a large area.
7. Understand that a map may be distorted deliberately.
8. Understand a polar map and how it is used.
9. Know the advantages and disadvantages of different types of projections.
10. Know how maps may aid in understanding some current event.

Examples 4.1, 4.2, and 4.3 show maps taken from a social studies textbook. Each identifies the type of knowledge needed to read the map. Questions pertinent to each map are also included. Some questions may require further research and inferential thought.

---

19. Zoe A. Thralls, *The Teaching of Geography* (New York: Appleton-Century-Crofts, Inc., 1958), pp. 59, 62–63.

EXAMPLE 4.1

Historical Map

In order to read the map students must know where to locate:

North-South directions
East-West directions
Atlantic Ocean
Pacific Ocean
Gulf of Mexico
Mississippi River
Appalachian Mountains
Rocky Mountains
Great Lakes

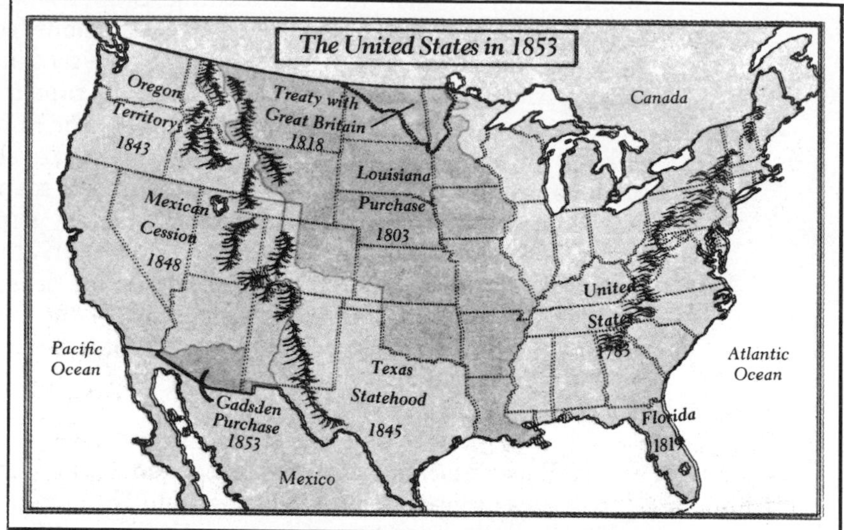

Questions:
1. What part of the country was included in the Louisiana Purchase?
2. How do the boundaries of the United States in 1853 compare with the continental boundaries today?
3. From what territory did we establish the state of California?

Reprinted by permission from Frank Freidel and Henry H. Drewry. *America Is* (Columbus: Charles E. Merrill, 1978), p. 202.

EXAMPLE 4.2

Historical-Political Map

Students must be able to read the key. In order to read the map students must know where to locate:
- Union states and territory
- Confederate states
- North-South, East-West
- The Mississippi River
- Washington, D.C.

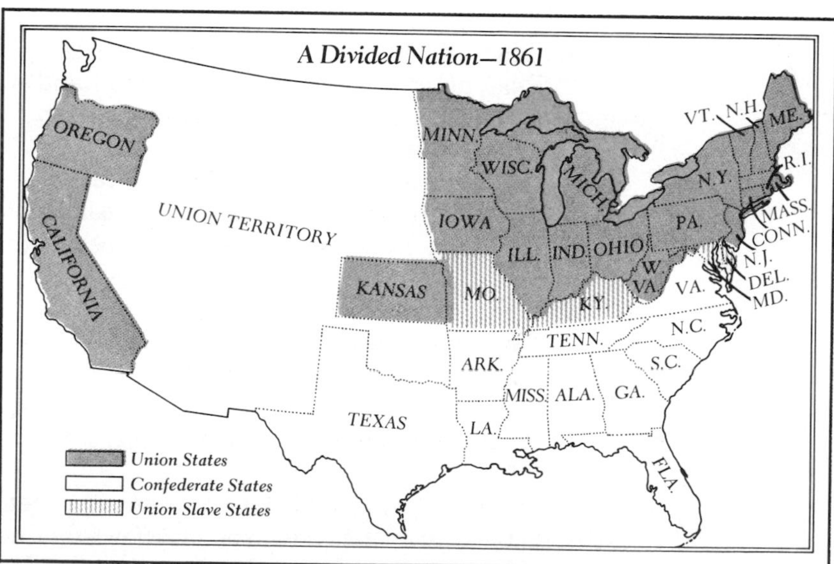

Questions:
1. How would you compare the Union land area to the Confederate land area?
2. Why is the area Union Territory not divided into states?
3. Why was the location of Washington, D.C., vulnerable?

Reprinted by permission from Frank Freidel and Henry H. Drewry, *America Is* (Columbus: Charles E. Merrill, 1978), p. 249.

EXAMPLE 4.3

Geological Map

In order to read the map students must be able to locate:

- North-South, East-West
- Continents
- Oceans

FIGURE 16-8. According to plate tectonics theory, the earth's lithosphere is divided into several rigid blocks or plates.

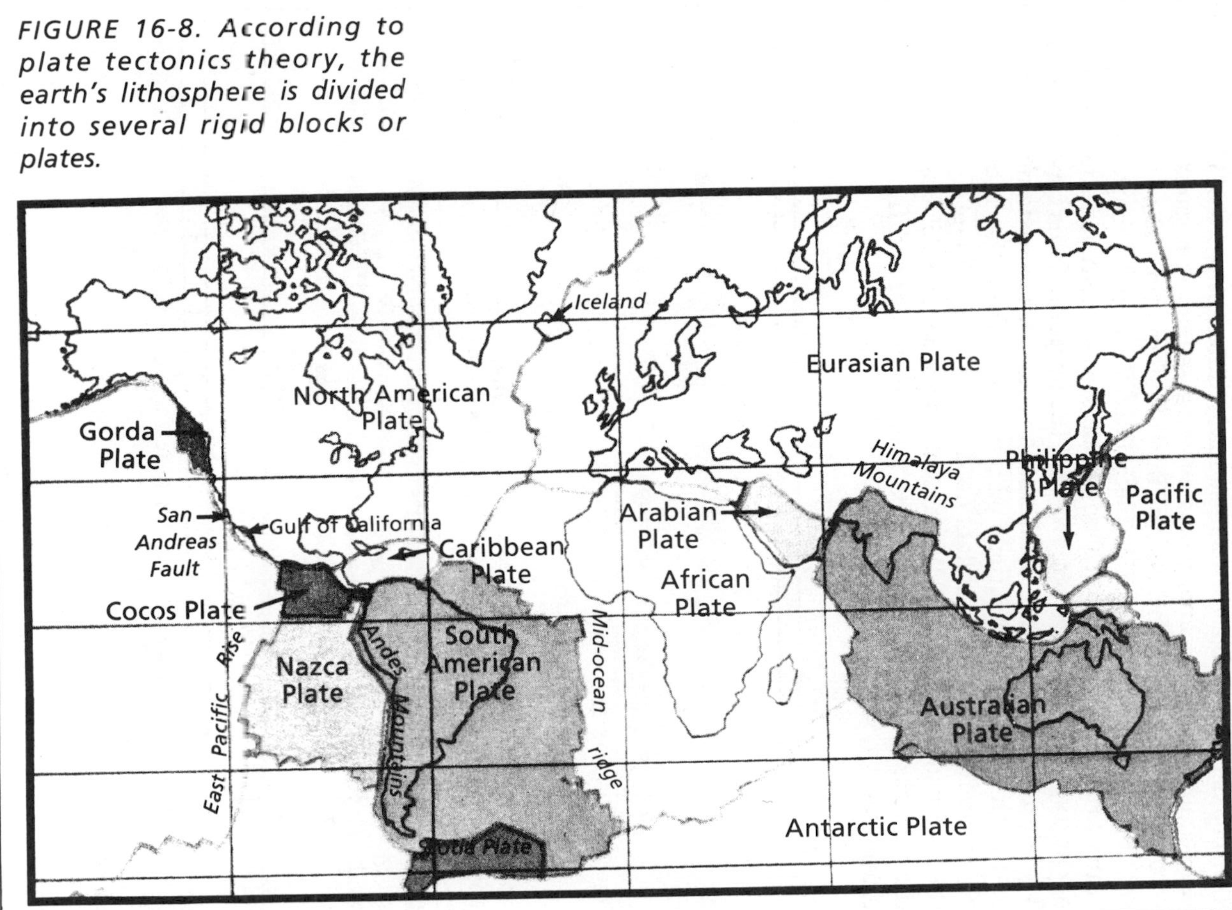

Question:
1. How do the plates relate to the continents and the oceans?

Reprinted by permission from Margaret S. Bishop, Berry Sutherland, and William H. Rasch, *Focus on Earth Science* (Columbus: Charles E. Merrill, 1981), p. 312.

Charts

Textbooks in the subject areas use many different types of charts, such as time lines, diagrams, and charts showing sequence, organization, process, comparison, development, and the flow of information. They supplement the text by displaying information pictorially. Sometimes charts and diagrams summarize text information. One reason that some students fail to make use of charts is that they are not aware of the purpose of this type of visual aid. The student must be able to extract the information contained in the chart and then draw generalizations or conclusions from the data. When using charts and diagrams, the student needs to ask: What type of chart is it? How is the information presented? What symbols are being used? For example, note the information and relationships that can be derived from the charts in Examples 4.4, 4.5, and 4.6.

EXAMPLE 4.4

Students must:

1. See interrelationship of cabinet to President.
2. Know areas of responsibility of each cabinet member. Symbols serve to give clue.

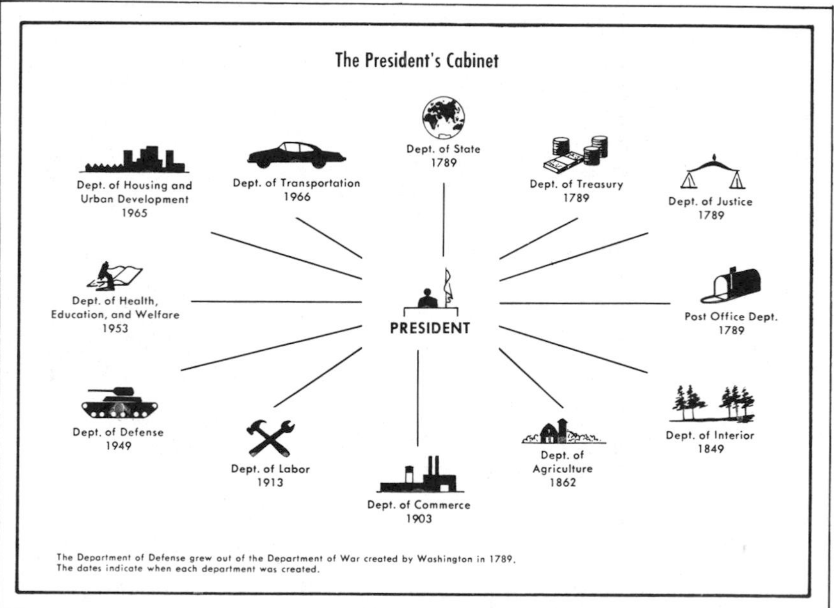

Reprinted by permission from Fred H. Duffy, *The Great Law of Our Land* (Columbus: Charles E. Merrill, 1970), p. 23.

EXAMPLE 4.5

To understand chart, student must:

1. Know the meaning of each term used.
2. Understand the relationships as indicated by arrows.

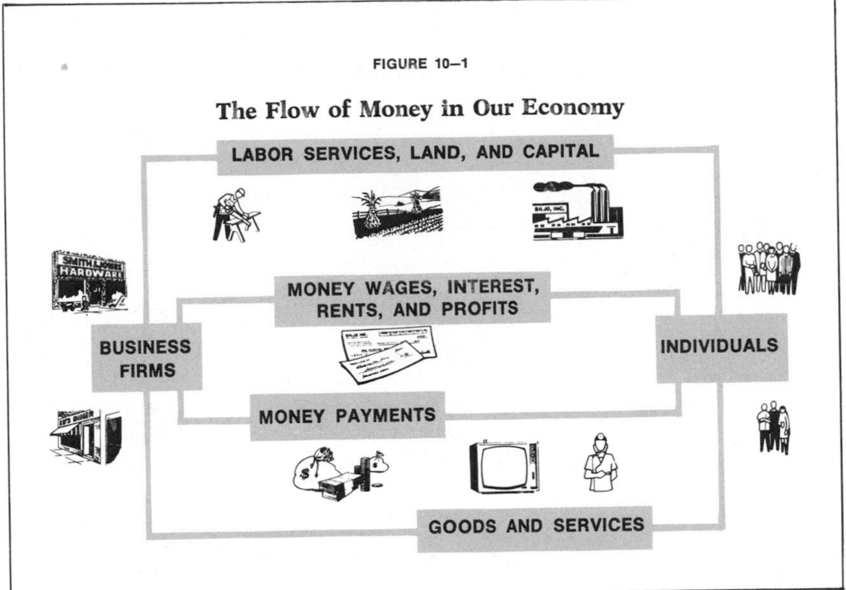

Reprinted by permission from James E. Brown, Harold A. Wolf, and S. Stowell Symmes, *Economics: Principles and Practices* (Columbus: Charles E. Merrill, 1979), p. 166.

EXAMPLE 4.6

Four functions of the Federal Reserve are shown. Each function is described.

Map reading skills are also required.

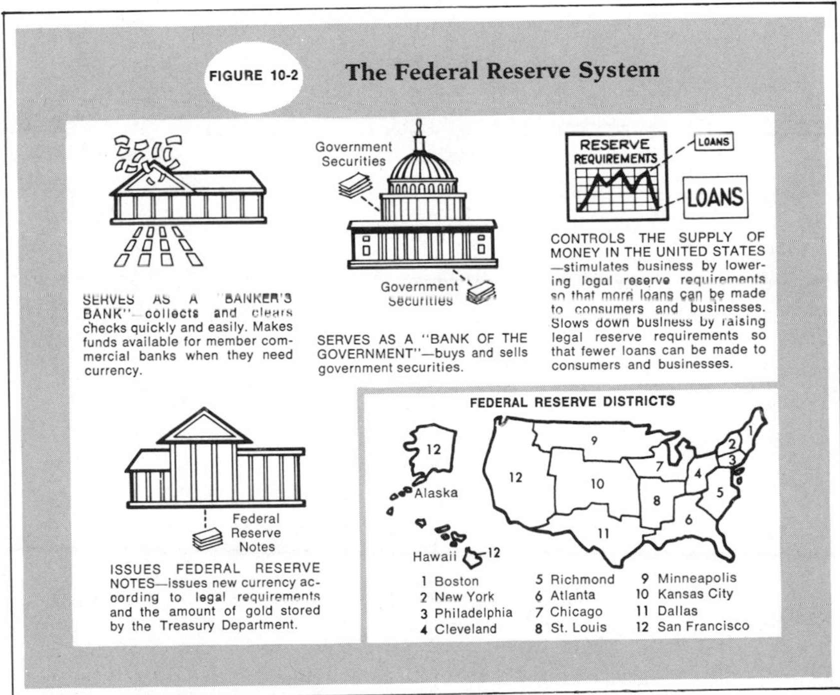

Reprinted by permission from James E. Brown, Harold A. Wolf, and S. Stowell Symmes, *Economics: Principles and Practices* (Columbus: Charles E. Merrill, 1979), p. 172.

Diagrams

Though they are not pictures, diagrams are drawings that explain processes. Students must learn to analyze them in order to understand written materials, and many will need instruction and practice in order to do so. See Examples 4.7, 4.8, and 4.9.

EXAMPLE 4.7

A textbook example showing students how to read diagrams.

Deceptive Packaging

Consumer Skills

Many shapes and sizes of containers are used to package agricultural products. Some containers are designed to appear to hold more than they actually do. The volume of a container can be approximated by using the formula for volume of a cylinder, cone, prism, or pyramid.

Answer each question about the containers at the right.

1. Which *appears* to hold more, A or B? B
2. What is the volume of container A? 343 cm³
3. What is the volume of container B? 297 cm³
4. Which holds more? How much more? B; 46 cm³
5. Which *appears* to hold more, C or D? C
6. What is the volume of container C? 216 cm³
7. What is the volume of container D? 225 cm³
8. Which holds more? How much more? D; 9 cm³
9. Which *appears* to hold more, E or F? F
10. What is the volume of container E? 401.92 cm³
11. What is the volume of container F? 392.5 cm³
12. Which holds more? How much more? E; 9.42 cm³
13. Which one *appears* to hold the most, G, H, or I? answers vary
14. Which one *appears* to hold the least, G, H, or I? answers vary
15. When comparing several containers of different shapes, how can you tell which one has the largest volume? answers vary Check the label if it has one.

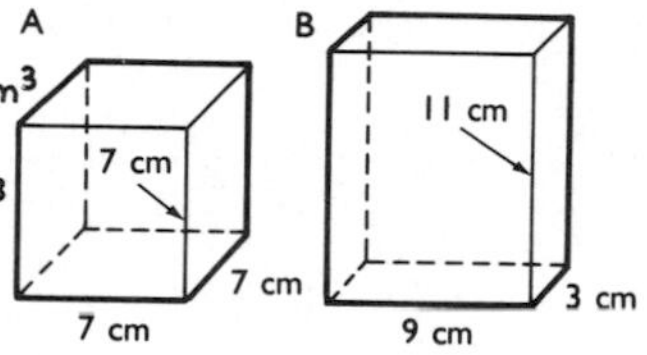

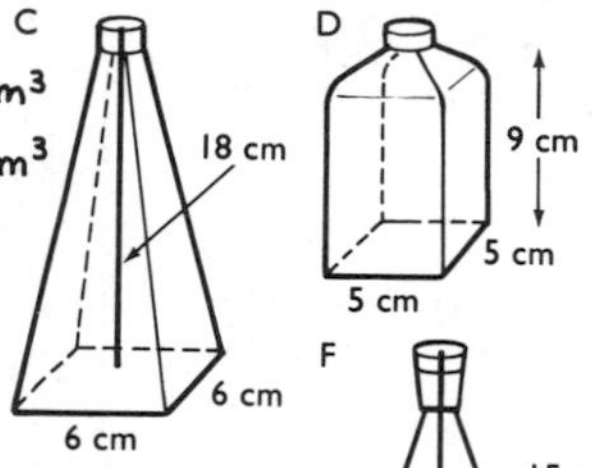

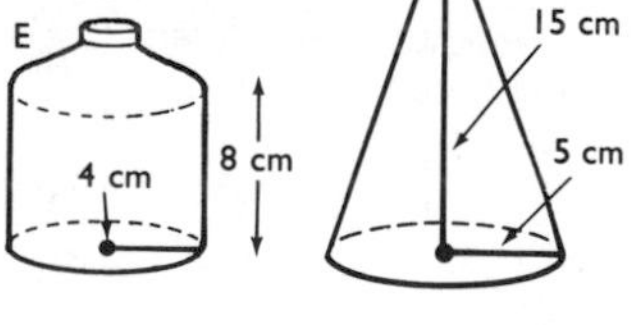

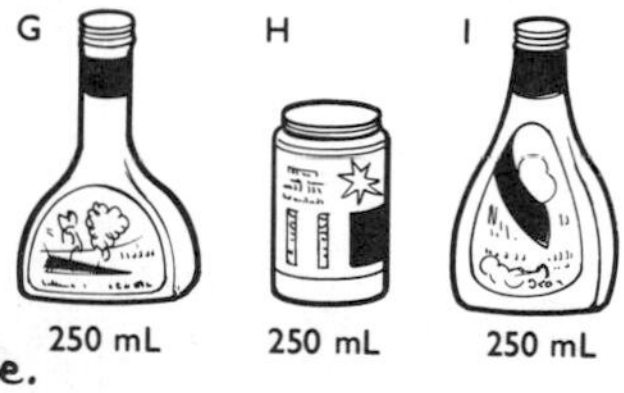

A: 7 cm, 7 cm, 7 cm
B: 11 cm, 9 cm, 3 cm
C: 18 cm, 6 cm, 6 cm
D: 9 cm, 5 cm, 5 cm
E: 4 cm, 8 cm
F: 15 cm, 5 cm
G: 250 mL
H: 250 mL
I: 250 mL

Reprinted by permission from Vannatta and Stoeckinger, *Mathematics: Essentials and Applications* (Columbus: Charles E. Merrill, 1980), p. 325.

EXAMPLE 4.8

Problem using diagrams.

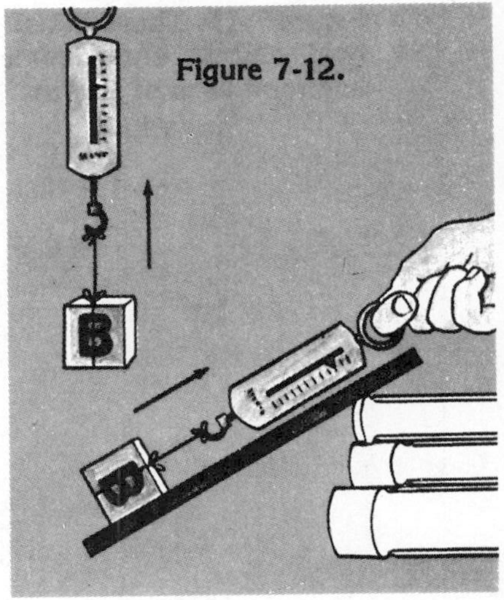

Figure 7-12.

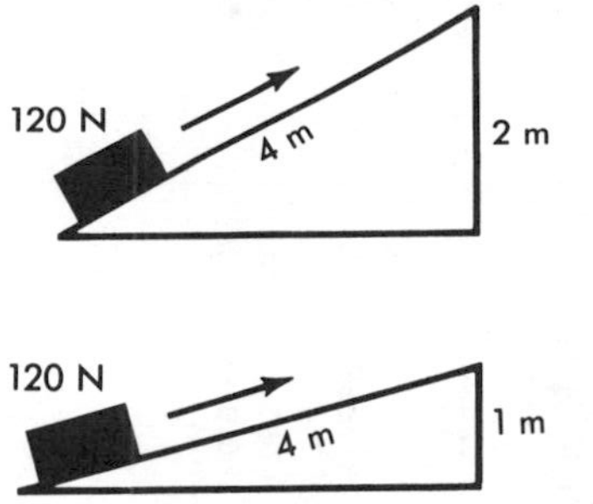

120 N

4 m

2 m

120 N

4 m

1 m

PROBLEM

16. The I.M.A. of an inclined plane is its length divided by its height. Find the I.M.A. for the inclined planes in Figure 7–13. Then find the effort force needed to move the object up each of the inclined planes. Ignore the effect of friction when solving these problems.

Reprinted by permission from Charles H. Heimler and Charles D. Neal, *Principles of Science* (Columbus: Charles E. Merrill, 1979), p. 135.

EXAMPLE 4.9

Diagrams (almost in the form of a flow chart).

Students must see the significance of the arrows to determine what eats what and when there are steps (links) in the process (chain).

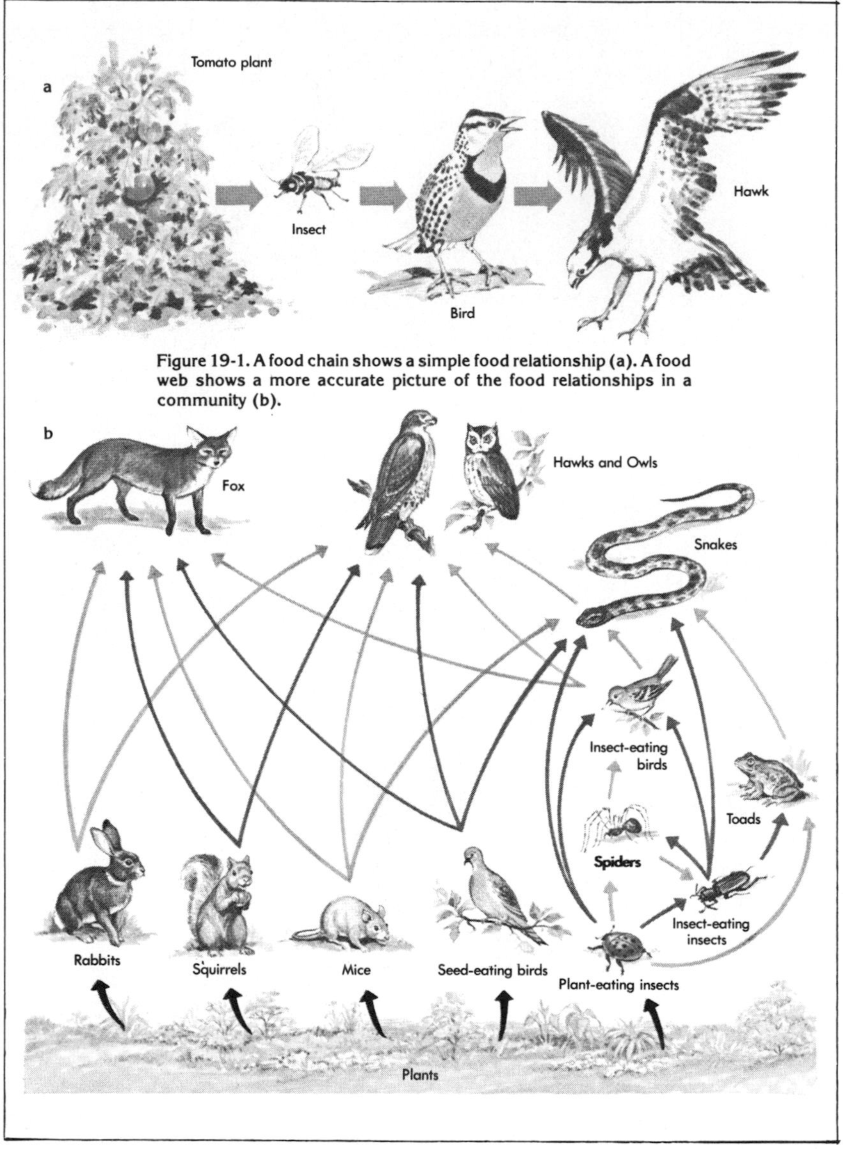

Figure 19-1. A food chain shows a simple food relationship (a). A food web shows a more accurate picture of the food relationships in a community (b).

Reprinted by permission from Charles H. Heimler and Charles D. Neal, *Principles of Science* (Columbus: Charles E. Merrill, 1979), p. 404.

Tables

Tables generally present statistical data which supplement the descriptive passages in the text by adding concrete detail. To read tables adequately, students need to answer these questions:

1. What is the title—what does the table represent?
2. What units of measurement are used?
3. What do the columns and rows represent?
4. What special explanations (footnotes) are used?
5. What is the significance of the data of the table?

See Examples 4.10, 4.11, and 4.12.

EXAMPLE 4.10

Understanding of percentage is required

Table 3-1. Major Uses Of Energy In The United States

	Percent
Heat for Industry	35.0
Transportation	24.0
Heat for Buildings	18.0
Electricity for Industry	12.0
Water Heating	4.0
Air Conditioning	2.3
Refrigeration	2.1
Lighting	1.3
Cooking	1.3

Reprinted by permission from Charles H. Heimler and Charles D. Neal, *Principles of Science* (Columbus: Charles E. Merrill, 1979), p. 47.

EXAMPLE 4.11

Students must know the use of the asterisk

TABLE II

Workers' Average Yearly Wage

Year	Farming	Manufacturing	Government	Average for all Workers*
1919	$725	$1264	$1151	$1220
1920	830	1497	1375	1424
1921	567	1306	1429	1311
1922	551	1255	1473	1294
1923	614	1372	1510	1382
1924	629	1394	1515	1394
1925	642	1417	1545	1421
1926	651	1442	1593	1450
1927	648	1467	1642	1459
1928	646	1500	1673	1478
1929	651	1508	1703	1489

* This also includes wages of workers in mining, trade, construction, finance, transportation, and services.

Reprinted by permission from Frank Freidel and Henry H. Drewry, *America Is* (Columbus: Charles E. Merrill, 1978), p. 405.

EXAMPLE 4.12

To use this table:

1. Students must know what squares and square roots are.
2. Students must know the symbols: n, n^2, $\sqrt{n}$.

Students should be given practice in reading the table as appropriate content is studied.

SQUARES AND APPROXIMATE SQUARE ROOTS

n	n^2	$\sqrt{n}$	n	n^2	$\sqrt{n}$
1	1	1.000	51	2601	7.141
2	4	1.414	52	2704	7.211
3	9	1.732	53	2809	7.280
4	16	2.000	54	2916	7.348
5	25	2.236	55	3025	7.416
6	36	2.449	56	3136	7.483
7	49	2.646	57	3249	7.550
8	64	2.828	58	3364	7.616
9	81	3.000	59	3481	7.681
10	100	3.162	60	3600	7.746
11	121	3.317	61	3721	7.810
12	144	3.464	62	3844	7.874
13	169	3.606	63	3969	7.937
14	196	3.742	64	4096	8.000
15	225	3.873	65	4225	8.062
16	256	4.000	66	4356	8.124
17	289	4.123	67	4489	8.185
18	324	4.243	68	4624	8.246
19	361	4.359	69	4761	8.307
20	400	4.472	70	4900	8.367
21	441	4.583	71	5041	8.426
22	484	4.690	72	5184	8.485
23	529	4.796	73	5329	8.544
24	576	4.899	74	5476	8.602
25	625	5.000	75	5625	8.660
26	676	5.099	76	5776	8.718
27	729	5.196	77	5929	8.775
28	784	5.292	78	6084	8.832
29	841	5.385	79	6241	8.888
30	900	5.477	80	6400	8.944
31	961	5.568	81	6561	9.000
32	1024	5.657	82	6724	9.055
33	1089	5.745	83	6889	9.110
34	1156	5.831	84	7056	9.165
35	1225	5.916	85	7225	9.220
36	1296	6.000	86	7396	9.274
37	1369	6.083	87	7569	9.327
38	1444	6.164	88	7744	9.381
39	1521	6.245	89	7921	9.434
40	1600	6.325	90	8100	9.487
41	1681	6.403	91	8281	9.539
42	1764	6.481	92	8464	9.592
43	1849	6.557	93	8649	9.644
44	1936	6.633	94	8836	9.695
45	2025	6.708	95	9025	9.747
46	2116	6.782	96	9216	9.798
47	2209	6.856	97	9409	9.849
48	2304	6.928	98	9604	9.899
49	2401	7.000	99	9801	9.950
50	2500	7.071	100	10000	10.000

Reprinted by permission from Foster, Rath, and Winters, *Algebra One* (Columbus: Charles E. Merrill, 1979), p. 482.

Graphs

Much information presented in tabular form can also be shown by graphs. However, graphs are more effective for showing quantities, growth or decline, or the size of relative parts. Direct instruction in graph use is usually most extensive in the mathematics classes, but textbooks in all subjects use graphs. Therefore, all teachers should help students gain information from graphs and to apply what they have learned in their mathematics classes. Graphs include several different types: line or profile, bar, circle or pie, and pictographs. See Examples 4.13 through 4.17.

EXAMPLE 4.13

A textbook example showing students how to read graphs.

Reading Graphs

Graphs are often used to help visualize the relationship between two variables. To fully understand the information presented in the graph, ask yourself the following three questions.

1. What does the title indicate will be represented in the graph?
2. What variable is represented along each axis?
3. What units are used along each axis?

Apply each of the three questions to the graph below. The bar graph shows information from a survey.

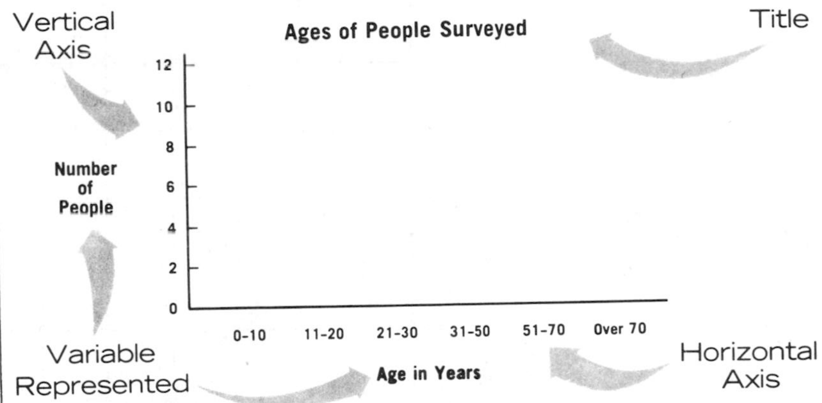

On the graph, the title indicates that the graph shows the number of people of each age who were surveyed. The vertical axis shows the number of people in each age group. The horizontal axis shows age groups in years. Each unit on the vertical axis represents two people. The horizontal axis is labeled to show what age groups were used. Notice that the units used for each axis do not have to be the same.

Exercises Turn to page 326, *Misleading Graphs.* Answer the three questions about the graphs.

1. Brand Preference 2. Percent Choosing Each Brand, and the two brands given as choices 3. Left graph: 0, 25%, 50%, 75%, 100%; right graph: 45%, 50%, 55%; both graphs: Brand A and Brand B.

Reprinted by permission from Foster, Rath, and Winters, *Algebra One* (Columbus: Charles E. Merrill, 1979), p. 307.

EXAMPLE 4.14

Bar Graph

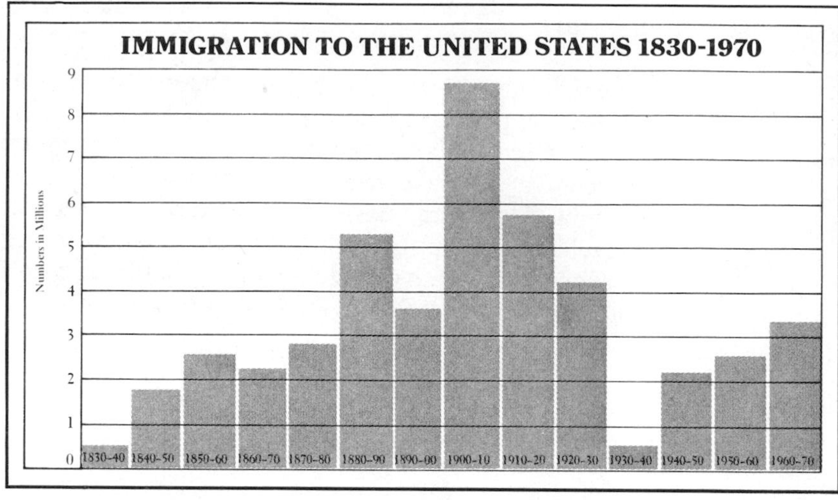

Questions:
1. In what ten-year period was the greatest amount of immigration?
2. How do you account for so little immigration between 1930 and 1940?

Reprinted by permission from Frank Freidel and Henry H. Drewry, *America Is* (Columbus: Charles E. Merrill, 1978), p. 320.

EXAMPLE 4.15

Line Graph

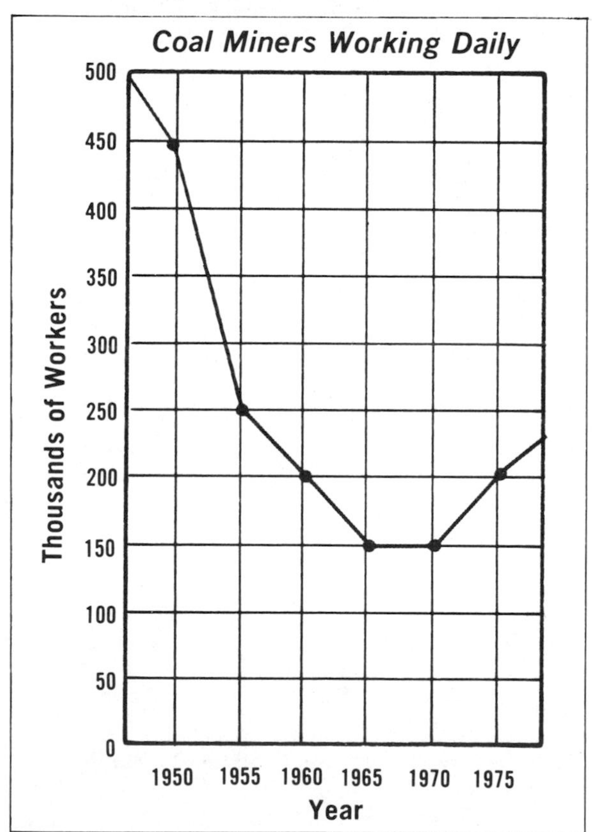

Questions:
1. In what five-year period were the fewest coal miners working?
2. How can you account for the increase in the number of coal miners working since 1970?

Reprinted by permission from Vannatta and Stoeckinger, *Mathematics: Essentials and Applications* (Columbus: Charles E. Merrill, 1980), p. 260.

EXAMPLE 4.16

Circle Graph

Pictoral representation of amounts in percent
Also evidence of where most of the gold is mined.

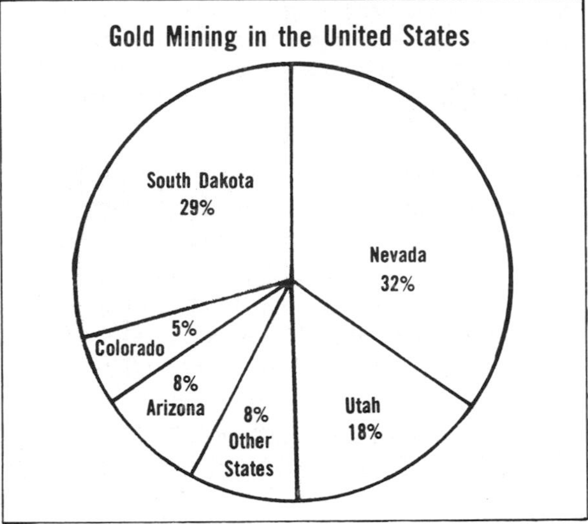

Reprinted by permission from Vannatta and Stoeckinger, *Mathematics: Essentials and Applications* (Columbus: Charles E. Merrill, 1980), p. 262.

EXAMPLE 4.17

Pictograph
Key (check its use with students)

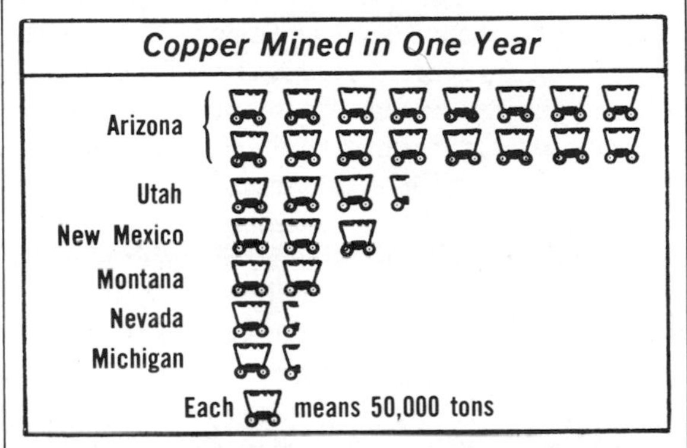

Reprinted by permission from Vannatta and Stoeckinger, *Mathematics: Essentials and Applications* (Columbus: Charles E. Merrill, 1980), p. 257.

Students should keep the following considerations in mind when interpreting graphs:

1. The type of graph.
2. The kind of data presented.
3. The unit measurement.
4. The arrangement of the data.
5. The numerical guides of the horizontal and vertical axes.
6. The significance of the information.

Pictures

These are probably the most widely used graphic aids. They supplement the information while boosting interest and motivation, and they help to make a textbook look manageable rather than formidable. Summers points out that:

> With pictures the learner gets more and clearer ideas than he does with the text material alone. Pictures, through realism, can expand experience and help to avoid misunderstanding. Pictures are particularly effective in showing step by step developments, contrasts and comparisons, and the status of things, processes, scenes, and events.[20]

To obtain information from a picture, students must have a purpose in mind when they look at it. They need to recognize the objects shown, describe details and draw inferences from what they see, and make generalizations about the question or reason for looking at it.

In one class students were asked to look at a picture showing a sod house on the prairie. It was a panoramic picture showing the vastness of the prairie grasslands. No trees were in the picture. The teacher asked why the house was built out of sod. No one in the class had the answer. The teacher then asked leading questions—such as "What kind of vegetation do you see?"—until the students drew the appropriate conclusion. When the teacher pointed out that the legend under the picture contained the answer to her first question, one student commented, "I didn't know that that was part of the picture."

Cartoons are a special type of picture. Used widely in social studies, cartoons present a message or a point of view through symbolism and exaggeration. They can be viewed as a pictorial form of figurative language. Some students, however, are not aware of the symbolism used, or they do not have a broad enough background about the topic to detect the exaggeration. Students must first recognize the technique used in the cartoon—humor, an appeal to emotion, satire, symbolism, caricature. Next, they need to identify and analyze the message the artist is attempting to show. They may need to have the symbols identified and explained. Finally, they need to draw an interpretation or generalization. The students should also learn to evaluate the cartoon for bias, emotional tone, and prejudices. Classroom discussion about the content of the cartoon, the techniques used, and the message intended is useful in helping students learn to understand this form of representation. Students also enjoy drawing their own cartoons.

FOLLOWING DIRECTIONS

Following directions is an essential skill that requires an intensity and precision not demanded by most other reading. You can help students in two ways: make your directions as clear and unambiguous as possible, and alert students to techniques of reading directions correctly. The usual procedure is to have students read the directions in their entirety to get a general picture of what is to be done, read each step, do what is directed, reread the step to check, and go on to the next step, until the activity is completed. Then reread the entire set of directions as a final check. Students must be instructed in reading so carefully. You will need also to check with them for meaning. For example, *compare, superimpose, match, select* and other such words are

---

20. Summers, "Utilizing Visual Aids," p. 146.

general, and students may have a general idea of what they mean. The specific meaning as applied to a particular set of directions, however, may elude them.

A teacher of photography employed a unique procedure in teaching students to understand directions. The school darkroom contained several pieces of complicated photographic equipment for developing and enlarging pictures and for creating special effects. He first had the students write their own directions for using the equipment. Then he had them read one another's directions and note what parts were incorrect, ambiguous or vague, or omitted. This proved to be an excellent way to teach the students (*a*) a useful and readable format for directions, (*b*) the meaning of process words, and (*c*) precision in language.

Study the set of directions shown in Example 4.18. Note what would make the directions clearer, the words the student must know precisely, and the purpose of the diagram.

EXAMPLE 4.18

Words the student must understand:

Direction words:

locate	cross
left side	center
draw	continue
upright	parallel
representing	axis
opposite side	mark
represents	top
dotted line	meets
side view	right
measure	

Content words:
- real image
- focal lengths
- principal focus
- principal axis
- centimeters
- convex lens
- ray

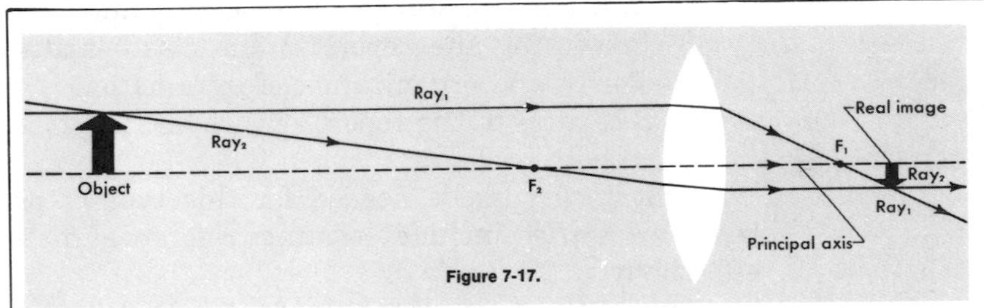

Figure 7-17.

ACTIVITY. You can locate a real image with a diagram. On the left side of a piece of paper, draw an upright 2-cm arrow. The arrow represents the object. Fifteen centimeters to the right of the arrow, draw a side view of a convex lens 5 cm high. With a ruler, draw a dotted line across the paper through the center of the lens to show its axis. Then measure two 5-cm focal lengths: one to the right of the lens and one to the left of the lens. Mark the principal focus to the left as F_2. Mark the principal focus to the right as F_1.

Now draw a line parallel to the axis from the top of the arrow to the lens. This line represents a light ray. Continue the line from the lens to the principal focus F_1. Draw a second line from the top of the arrow through the principal focus F_2. Continue the line until it meets the lens. As the ray leaves the lens on the opposite side, continue the ray parallel to the principal axis. The point at which the two lines cross is the top of the real image (Figure 4–17).

Reprinted by permission from Charles H. Heimler and Jack Price, *Focus on Physical Science* (Columbus: Charles E. Merrill, 1977), p. 368.

This set of directions is stated simply but would be easier to follow if each step were numbered in a list. There are fifteen steps in all. One part of the directions is not clear: there is no indication that the arrow should rest on the dotted axis line. However, the diagram the student is to draw is shown above the set of directions.

RESEARCH READING

Research reading requires students to use a variety of references supplementary to the textbook to find information. It also involves applying the skills of comprehension in locating, selecting, and evaluating information. Reference reading, usually to prepare reports, is the student's opportunity to develop independence in gaining information. All of the reading skills—word recognition, vocabulary, comprehension and study skills—are required. Of course, the techniques must be taught prior to assigning students a research project or report.

If we review the full scope of a research report, we can see an excellent application of the four aspects of the language arts, including:

1. Locating and comprehending information—all of the *reading* techniques
2. Taking notes and synthesizing them into a report—the *writing* skills in which the student becomes the author
3. Presenting the report to the class—skills of *speaking,* including clarity and organization of information
4. *Listening* to the report—in which the class takes notes

The library skills needed for this type of project, sometimes called *reference skills,* include locating reference materials and using them effectively.

One of the first prerequisites is that you understand the nature and content of the reference materials in your discipline and be interested in teaching your students how to use these materials. You must also see that the reference materials are available. One source for both you and the students is the school librarian. He can be invaluable in helping to locate information. However, no librarian has the time to guide students step by step through a project requiring reference reading. Therefore, in addition to the skills of comprehension and note taking, you need to teach the locational skills. They are:

1. Using the alphabet
2. Locating materials using the Dewey decimal classification or the Library of Congress system
3. Using the card catalog
4. Using such indexes as *The Reader's Guide to Periodical Literature*
5. Using specific reference materials
6. Using guide words
7. Determining the best sources of information
8. Differentiating between factual sources and fictional sources
9. Listing a source of information properly in a research paper
10. Acquiring the ability to skim.[21]

---

21. David L. Shepherd, "Using Sources of Information," in *Developing Study Skills in Secondary Schools,* ed. Harold E. Herbert (Newark, Del.: International Reading Association, 1965), p. 46.

Locational skills must be taught as soon as the students need them. This is *very important!* Obviously, students must know how to use a tool before they try to use it. For example, one high school student who was enrolled in an honors social studies class, at the college level, was given a research assignment. He was to use a minimum of five references in his bibliography. The assignment was given on Thursday, and the report was due to be turned in on the following Tuesday. The teacher had given the student one reference book to get him started—a reference of 700 pages. The student was very upset and complained, "Look, I have this report to do in four days. I have to read, digest, and write a report by then; and one reference—this one—is 700 pages! How is this possible when I have four other references to read? I feel like just not doing any of it!" However, when he was advised to check the index of the reference, the student found that only ten pages referred to his topic. The student's face showed amazement and relief!

The teacher was sure that such an excellent student would know to use the index. However, the teacher should have *checked* to see if his students knew this simple procedure. He could have, in thirty seconds, given them the necessary guidance. *Do not assume that the students know.* In fact, research skills often have not been taught—research assignments usually dictate only the topic, how long the report should be, how many references are required, and when the project is due. How inadequate!

Steps of Research Reading

The general steps of a research project requiring reference reading are:

1. Selecting a topic or problem in order to determine what is to be found.
2. Discussing pertinent resource material—type, where to find, how used, etc.
3. Applying all of the reading techniques that have been taught.
4. Teaching and reviewing the techniques of note taking.
5. Guiding the students in techniques of organizing their information into a report.
6. Discussing how the information should be presented to the class with clarity and organization.
7. Discussing with the class how they can take notes from the report.

If committees are working on group reports, standards for committee work and the responsibilities of the committee chairperson must be specified. This would be done before instruction in the types and uses of resources material.

Following is a general plan for getting students started on reference reading.

The teacher plans the research assignments with the students. Usually, problems for research emerge after the students have acquired a basic knowledge of the topic. From the textbook and other required readings, the students develop a background for working with the teacher to identify topics or problems for research. In many classes, the problems are determined through class discussion as both the teacher and class express interest in further information.

When research problems are assigned, the teacher then needs to insure that the students will be able to carry out their projects competently. For example, students may need help in analyzing problems to determine the key words (or *entry words*). Sample problems should be analyzed in class, with the students determining the key words and then checking to see if they lead to the appropriate information. For instance, let us look at two sample topics similar to those found in textbooks to see what the entry words are:

"What is *spelunking?* Is it of any scientific value? What are some of the dangers and how can they be avoided? Report on the work of some discoverers of famous caves." The key word is *spelunking,* which the students will enter in the card catalog and in an index. The topic also gives the students areas to direct their reading toward:

definition of *spelunking*
its scientific value
dangers and how they can be avoided
accounts of some famous discoverers of caves

"After doing research on probation and parole, evaluate these alternatives to imprisonment as a means of handling offenders convicted by the courts." *Probation* and *parole* are the obvious entry words; however, the student may be referred to the word *crime,* which is not mentioned in the topic. The topic also gives the student direction through the word *evaluate.*

Report Writing

Students often find it difficult to write informational material. Many people consider writing more difficult than reading. However, writing can be made a less difficult task. If you have been teaching students how to note an author's organization as they read, they have a frame of reference for their own report writing. In effect, they become the author in report writing and simply move from being the receiver (reader) to the producer (writer). If you have encouraged your students to imagine how an author will organize information and then checked how she actually did it, the students should find such an exercise useful for their own report writing. Analyzing paragraphs to note the type of organization and what an author is trying to do also helps the students, as does reviewing such basic organization as introduction, body, and conclusion or summary. In assigning the research project, discuss topics and problems with your class and brainstorm with them about the scope of each topic and how it can best be organized. Further, of course, you will need to teach the students the techniques of proper bibliographical form, use of quotations, and use of footnotes.

If your students have had little or no instruction in the skills required for research reading, you may find it helpful to organize a class research project, in addition to the individual or group projects. During the class project you can give instruction and monitor each step of the individual or group projects. Students find this procedure very helpful since first there is general instruction, then application to the individual or group project with the teacher. Thus, you are free to give small-group or individual help on trouble points. In other words, your procedure is teach, apply, and reteach (individualize) as necessary. Such a procedure probably will need to be used only once, at the beginning of the school year.

RATE OF COMPREHENSION

As high school students become interested in reading improvement, one of their first concerns often is their reading speed—the number of words they read each minute. They wish to complete their assignments quickly. To a degree their concern with speed is valid. Smith and Dechant point out that "no one actually reads faster than he comprehends, but many read much more slowly than their comprehension would permit. Generally the limiting factor to rate improvement is the mind rather than the vision."[22]

For instance, one student was found to be extremely slow in completing her reading assignments. The teacher discovered that the student was reading each paragraph *three times* before going to the next one. The student remarked, "I am so afraid of not remembering all of the information." The teacher quickly noted that this student required much guidance and instruction, particularly on the skill of taking notes, since she was so concerned about forgetting.

Perhaps a better term than speed is the term *rate of comprehension,* since the reader's quickness of understanding in large measure regulates the speed of coverage. Also, a distinction must be made between reading nontechnical or story-type information and study reading. The latter requires much slower and more analytical reading. In applying the SQ3R formula to assignments for the content areas, students need to skim for the overview, read intensively for the purposes of the assignment, and then read slowly (review) as the demands of the material require. Rate of comprehension depends upon (*a*) the difficulty of the material, (*b*) the student's background with the topic, and (*c*) his purpose for reading.

Mature readers are able to select and adjust their rate of reading to the demands of the material and the assignment. They are flexible in rate not only with different types of material but also within a single selection. They read faster when familiar with the information and when the author gives illustrations of an anecdotal nature. They slow down when the author is presenting and developing concepts and arguments, or when they wish to savor the beauty of a literary passage.

To improve rate, students should learn how to *scan* to find a specific fact or material related to the topic and to *skim* to get a general overview. Both skills are needed in reference reading. To scan, students must do the following:

1. Determine clearly the information desired by identifying the specific key word or figure to look for.
2. Look down the page for the key word or figures (use finger as guide).

---

22. Henry P. Smith and Emerald Dechant, *Psychology in Teaching Reading* (Englewood Cliffs: Prentice-Hall, 1961), p. 222.

3. As soon as the key word is spotted, read carefully to determine whether the desired information is included.

To skim, students must:

1. Use introductory paragraphs, Table of Contents, and the preface.
2. Use topical headings.
3. Read first or last sentences of major paragraphs.
4. Note italicized words.
5. Note graphic aids.
6. Read summaries.

Skimming, which is essentially the same as previewing or doing an overview, is advised before undertaking a slower, more careful reading.

SUMMARY

The study skills are the tools and techniques students use to obtain information. Students progress through the same steps in learning them as they would in learning a craft, working up from novice to master. As in learning a craft, students acquire the study skills by working within a cycle of instruction, demonstration, practice, and evaluation that repeats until they have mastered these techniques.

QUESTIONS AND PROBLEMS FOR YOUR OWN CLASSROOM

For readers who are training to be teachers:

1. Plan to guide your students in the steps of the SQ3R formula.
2. Plan a research project and note the tasks the students will have to do in order to complete the project successfully. Then plan to incorporate appropriate teaching.
3. Plan questions which students are to answer by using only graphic aids such as maps, pictures, charts.
4. Investigate the topics included in your subject area and determine the reference materials you would consider important for students.
5. Investigate the printed material pertinent to your subject area and determine the various ways you might teach the students to organize their notes—for example, outline, comparative columns, diagram, chart.

For readers who are teaching:

1. Use a group of research topics and through class discussion evolve the subtopics, the most appropriate sequence, and interrelationships.
2. Analyze a set of directions with the students to note the equipment needed, the number and order of steps, and important details.

3. After giving an assignment, ask students how they will plan their study.
4. In various assignments, evolve with the students an appropriate organization of notes, i.e., outline, comparative columns, diagram, charts.
5. Discuss with your students appropriate reference materials pertinent to your subject.
6. Analyze the graphic aids in an assignment. What are the skills the student must know in order to use each aid? What purpose must the student realize in order to know the type of information he should obtain?

SELECTED REFERENCES

Herber, Harold L., ed. *Developing Study Skills in Secondary Schools, Perspectives in Reading, No. 4.* Newark, Del: IRA, 1965.

All of the major study skills are treated in depth. Summers has contributed a thorough chapter on using visual aids.

Robinson, Francis P. *Effective Study.* New York: Harper & Row, 1961.

The author explains in detail his basic study formula, SQ3R.

CHAPTER 5

Developing Interest

OVERVIEW

Using adolescents' interests is an excellent way to foster wide reading. But how can our classrooms compete with their interests beyond reading and with other media that seem more immediate and exciting? There *are* ways to compete; we will explore these and investigate the important functions of the school library.

Questions

Consider these questions before you read further:

1. What interests do adolescents have?
2. How important is it in your subject area to have students read widely?
3. In what ways can you use the school library in your subject area?

Why is interest so important? Spache states that "interest itself is a dynamic, motivating force: it leads to action."[1] Adolescents pursue their interests as a way of growing toward adulthood. Adolescents are at the threshold of adulthood, and they are both fearful of it and looking forward to it. They are fearful of adulthood because the world of today seems ever-changing and chaotic, yet they look forward to adulthood because it signals independence.

Adolescents' interests fall into four general categories. One is *vocational*. Most adolescents are very concerned about what they will do, the kind of career they will have. This is a time when they are searching for the type of work which will be satisfying to them. Related to this are their *social* interests, involving getting along with people—such as on the job and in social situations with the opposite sex. Their *special* interests—artistic, literary, sport, or craft—reflect talents and proclivities. Adolescents also pursue *technical* and *scientific* interests in an effort to learn about their environment.

Of course, interests can be developed. A person becomes interested in a subject only after he or she knows something about it. It is generally recognized that schools should attempt to widen and develop new interests. However, students develop interest only when they can see how the new information satisfies a specific need. Therefore, it is important for teachers to *discuss* with the students how what they are learning is applied and how it affects them personally.

No two students have exactly the same interests. For instance, two students with vocational interests may still differ on the *type* of job that attracts them: one student may be interested in veterinary practice, and the other in business management. No one knows how or why a particular interest develops within an individual, but interests are influenced by a number of factors: age, sex, intelligence, family background, aptitudes, and stimuli from the environment (such as the mass media and specific personal experiences).

The four categories of interests can provide us with general areas of reading for high school students. Since it is possible to develop interests, teachers should make an effort to widen background and to have a variety of books available.

WHY DO ADOLESCENTS READ?

Of course we assign material for students to read because there is a body of knowledge they must acquire. We also assign them various selections of literature to enhance their appreciation, with the hope that the students will enjoy reading. The skillful teacher works to make the material relevant and to increase understanding and enjoyment. But assigned reading is not our concern here. Instead, we are concerned about the students' desire to read on their own—to *choose* to read for their own personal satisfaction.

---

1. George D. Spache, *Good Reading for Poor Readers,* 9th ed. (Champaign, Ill.: Garrard Publishing Company, 1974), p. 1.

As with interests, adolescents have several similar yet differing motives for reading. Perhaps the one basic motive is to derive personal satisfaction. This basic motive can be analyzed into several related areas. Students read for information to help them with their *personal needs*—reading about vocations that interest them or about how to do or build something or to act in a certain way. They like to read about people as a means of evaluating their own actions. Reading, therefore, is often for *personal improvement*. Adolescents are at an uncertain time of their lives. They often wonder how to behave in social situations. Consequently, they read as well for *personal security*, in order to be more certain and to gain a perspective about society and their environment.

Sometimes adolescents read for *reinforcement* of their beliefs and attitudes. In their search for values, students are encouraged when they find that others think and feel in ways similar to their own. During a reading assignment in a tenth grade English class, one boy blurted out while reading, "That's exactly what my mother does!" In the story, the protagonist (who was the same age as the student) discovered that his mother opened his mail. The student who spoke out in class was most interested in the hero's reaction to this because it was similar to his own. Then, he read avidly to see how the situation was resolved.

Students also read to *live experiences vicariously*—experiences which they find exciting and ones they may wish to have. Often they identify with a character in a story or biography. Reading for *relaxation* is another motive. Reading can also provide an *escape* into perhaps a more ordered environment or into a fascinating situation which can renew one's energies to cope with the world. Finally, some students read for the beauty of the language. They may enjoy the sensory images that a description conveys or the total *aesthetic* quality.

Though we know that high school students have reasons to read, many do very little or no reading on their own. Why should this be? Let's look into some possible reasons. Obviously, one reason may be that the students do not read well. Reading is difficult and they get no pleasure from it. Their self-esteem in school may be disastrously low because they have never been able to read well. Such students usually seek satisfaction from other activities they can succeed in; this is a natural reaction. Another reason may be that there is no time. After completing the assigned reading, some students do not wish to spend more time in a similar activity. Students who feel this way are not only those who are inadequate readers but also those who are very competent and are enrolled in courses with time-consuming reading demands. A third reason may be competition from other activities. Many high school students have part-time jobs or are involved in sports, music, club, or social activities.

Still another reason may be that reading is not a habit. Perhaps because they were not read to as children, some students do not view reading as an enjoyable leisure time activity. Perhaps the lifestyle of parents and friends is oriented toward "active" recreation such as sports and crafts rather than reading. Gentile and McMillan state another very interesting reason: "A lot of these students who don't read are pressured at home as well as in school to read! read! read! Persistent stress proves counterproductive."[2] They go on to say that parents and teachers are more effective as models, and that pressuring can actually dissuade students from reading. This phenomenon occurs in high school remedial classes in which far more emphasis is placed on techniques than on ideas or content. The class becomes merely *practice, practice, practice*. Students who already know that they need to improve their reading begin to think, "If this is what reading is, I want no part of it. I will read only when I have to."

WHAT DO HIGH SCHOOL STUDENTS LIKE TO READ?

Even if you know the general interests of your students, to find the specific types of books they like you will need to assess their interests. As you get to know your students, you will discover many of their interests. However, you may wish for a more structured method. Two very effective ways are through class discussion and by means of a questionnaire. Take time for a class discussion about their interests and the kinds of reading material they like. From such a discussion you will learn many things in addition to their favorite types of books. You will also discover if they do read, if they have time to read, if they will take the time to read, what they read other than books, and generally how they view reading as a pastime. You may also get some interesting views, pro and con, about reading literature in school.

The questionnaire (often called an *interest inventory*) is an effective tool because you can obtain information about each student, which is difficult in a discussion. The inventory can be as simple or as complex as your needs demand. The types of questions you might ask are:

1. What kinds of books do you like?
2. What kinds of books have you read in the past year?
3. How would you rate each book?
4. Do you read the newspaper?
5. What parts do you read?
6. Do you read magazines?
7. What kinds of magazines do you like best?
8. How much time do you spend reading?
9. When you have leisure time, do you like to spend it reading?
10. How do you view ways a person should spend their leisure time?
11. What hobbies do you have?
12. Do you read material about your hobbies?
13. About what subject do you like to read?

The answers to these and other questions can serve two purposes: they can guide you in your planning and can provide interesting material for the

2. Lance M. Gentile and Merna M. McMillan, "Why Won't Teenagers Read?" *Journal of Reading* 20, No. 7 (May 1977): 652.

students. In planning your discussion with the students, refer to the various surveys and studies that describe the interests of their age group. Your students will be interested in how they compare with others.

Elliott and Steinkellner compared the reading preferences of urban and suburban secondary students.[3] Their major findings were:

1. Stereotypical ideas about student reading interests were invalid. For example, the urban vocational students reported a less negative response to poetry than did the suburban comprehensive high school students enrolled in a typical college preparation curriculum.
2. Student interest was stable over types of media. Those who expressed interest or noninterest in a topic liked or disliked it whether it appeared in a magazine, newspaper, or book.
3. There was a consistent pattern to student interests. If one topic were indicated as a high interest area, there was a high correlation between the topic and others similar to it.
4. Almost all students reported a strong interest in newspaper reading. Even those who reported little or no interest in other topics reported a positive interest in reading newspapers.
5. Interests were not related to grade level. Tenth and twelfth graders could not be distinguished by their reported reading interests.
6. There were clear sex differences in reading interests.

GUIDELINES FOR DEVELOPING INTEREST

Foster Wide Reading

Consider how your classroom procedures foster reading by asking yourself these questions:

1. Do I know my students' interests and how these relate to the classroom work?
2. Do I know my students' reading strengths and weaknesses so that I am able to recommend appropriate reading material and provide guidance if necessary?
3. Do I require my students to read only the textbook?
4. Do assignments lead the students to a wide variety of materials pertinent to my subject?
5. Do I alert students to current newspaper and magazine articles about the ideas they are studying?
6. Do I merely teach facts which the students need to know, or do I teach ideas?
7. Do I use questions that ask for interpretations, evaluations, analyses, and applications of the ideas?
8. Do I discuss with students how the ideas apply currently to the world and society?

---

3. Peggy Gordon Elliott and Lesley Linde Steinkellner, "Reading Preferences of Urban and Suburban Secondary Students: Topics and Media," *Journal of Reading* 23, No. 2 (November 1979): 121–125.

9. Does my classroom stimulate reading through bulletin board displays and displays of relevant books?
10. Do I view reading as a pleasurable and fulfilling activity for my students?

On occasion, teachers have used reading as a punishment for undesirable behavior. Of course, this is an association we must strive to avoid.

Develop a Classroom Library

An obvious way to develop interest and skill in reading is to surround the students with books. Books related to the topic under study should be placed around the classroom. Very few students can resist looking at interesting and related books within easy reach. Classroom libraries are just as important at the high school level as in elementary classrooms.

The classroom library should include three to five books per student. The books should cover various facets of the topic being studied and should range in difficulty. They can include single or multiple copies of reference material, textbooks other than the one used for intensive study, and trade books. The collection would include both fiction and nonfiction. You can keep the cost of the classroom library to a minimum by using paperbacks, collections checked out from the school and public libraries, and books that students bring in. The classroom library should grow over a period of years, with new titles being added constantly.

Show Your Enthusiasm for Reading

Teachers serve as models when the students see them read, note how well-informed they are about current developments in the topic under study, and as teachers share articles, books, magazines, and so on in class. One teacher of seventh grade English taught a unit on Greek mythology. In class, she used newspaper advertisements and articles to note references to names, places, and events stemming from myths. The students were so struck by the relevance of these ancient legends that they decided to examine current materials. By the time the unit was completed, the class had assembled a large bulletin board display of all the allusions they had found.

Provide Time to Read

Though students do find time for their interests, many adolescents have daily schedules that preclude wide reading. The typical student's schedule—school, homework, extracurricular job or responsibility, interests, and social activities—is a full one. Therefore, make a point to set aside some time in class for students to read—even if you feel that your curriculum is already under time pressures to complete the year's study. Once you get students started in reading material of interest to them, many will make time outside of class to continue it.

Use Materials at Different Levels

None of us voluntarily chooses material that is too difficult to read. Students may choose highly technical material if it is about a strong interest of theirs and is pertinent to a problem they are trying to solve. In general, however, students must feel competent with the material if they are to read it voluntarily.

Note the Style of the Material

The *style* of writing students enjoy relates closely to their reading level. For example, long and involved syntax, figurative language, and descriptive passages are not barriers for competent readers, but slow and reluctant readers are very sensitive to the style of the material. Their reading skills are usually inadequate, affecting their attitude toward reading; for such students, reading is not an activity in which they can appear competent. Therefore, these students react best to a style that is simple though not condescending: simple, direct sentences and short paragraphs that include mostly familiar words. These readers like a fast-moving story with little description and mood setting—a story that pulls them along with a lot of dialogue, a simple plot, and familiar situations. In nonfiction, reluctant readers like easy-to-comprehend material with many pictures and other graphic aids. The book should look attractive but not too difficult. Yet slow readers often resent reading a book that looks like it is intended for the primary or elementary grades.

The Material Must Be Pertinent

High school students read for the same reasons that the population as a whole reads: for enjoyment and for information pertinent to their concerns. Sometimes, however, adolescents are not aware that there are books about their interests or about experiences similar to those they have had. Your knowledge of materials related to your subject combined with that of the students' personal interests will enable students to find books they will consider pertinent. The school librarian can be a valuable resource as well.

TECHNIQUES FOR DEVELOPING WIDE READING

Teachers can include techniques for increasing interest and competence in reading in their lesson procedures while still carrying out the purposes of the lesson. Techniques to increase interest are most effective when they emerge naturally from the lesson, rather than being taught in isolation. Suggested techniques include:

1. Establish in each classroom a library corner for browsing. Books related to study units should be available.
2. Discuss books with students. Encourage students to voice their

reactions (judging none as correct or incorrect) and to tell related personal experiences.

3. Let students illustrate stories.
4. Let students write a dramatization of a story.
5. Use "story-teasers." Tell or read a story up to the climax and leave off at that point so that the students must read the story to discover what happens.
6. Assign research reading, in which the students find additional information on a topic the class is studying. Use the problem-solving approach, which includes:
   a. all of the locational skills—reference and library skills as well as parts of a book.
   b. adapting the manner of reading to the type of material and the purpose.
   c. skills needed for exact understanding—main idea, sequence, etc.
   d. interpretive skills—checking the validity of information, seeing relationships, etc.
   e. skills involving drawing conclusions and making inferences.
   f. skills of organizing the information into a complete report—sequence, relevant vs. irrelevant, etc.
7. Have a group of students prepare an annotated bibliography of references for a topic to be studied in class.
8. Have committees of students prepare bulletin board displays of favorite books or stories. Bulletin board displays should be changed often to avoid becoming stale.
9. Display a sampling of books related to a unit of study in the classroom, especially at the beginning of the unit. Talk about the books.
10. Set up a place map, using a map of the world, region, or country, with a pin marking where a story takes place. Attach a ribbon to the pin, labelling the story title.
11. Take a sentence from a story and let the students develop their own story. Let them compare their story with the story from which the sentence was taken.
12. Let students compare points of view from stories. For example, one author may be laudatory of some person or animal and another may be deprecatory.
13. Pose questions to the students concerning their reactions. Such questions require the students to use their own background and bring their beliefs and values to bear upon the point under discussion. Here are examples of such questions:

    How is this story true or not true to life?

    What do you like or dislike about the main character?

    How would you have solved the problem facing ________?

    What do you think was the author's purpose when he wrote the story?

    Why do you think the author is concerned about ________?
14. Have students research the conditions of life during the year they were born. This is an excellent activity in social studies or an

economics course. Students usually are fascinated and they also develop insights as they note clothing styles, price of goods of various sorts, government and world leaders, special historical events and any current effects of these events, the best movies of that time and whether any have been reshown or refilmed since, the popular television shows, special social concerns of that time (for example, the interest in environmental protection then as compared to now). The types of comparisons students could make are innumerable.

15. As students read a biography, have them think of their own lives and how they could be made into interesting biographies. What would they emphasize? What statements or opinions would they voice?
16. Keep a file of reviews of favorite books. As each student reads a book, he is to add a one- or two-sentence review to the file. This can be an exciting catalog of student recommendations. Structure the brief reviews by such questions as: Why I liked or disliked the book; What I found most exciting [or interesting] in the book; Why I would or would not recommend this book.
17. Select a current issue at the local, state, or national level. Have the students read newspapers and other materials and prepare a panel discussion about the issue and its possible resolution.
18. Build a collection of paperback books for your classroom library. Have a committee of students work with you, choosing titles pertinent to their interests. In science you could start a collection of science fiction; in mathematics, books about math puzzles; in English, humorous stories, and so on.
19. After your students have each read a book, use the following variation of the cloze procedure: delete a word from each title of more than one word, and ask students to supply the correct word. Of course, the student who has read the book remains silent. This activity has many variations: After the title has been completed, conjecture what the book might be about. The student who has read the book can verify the guesses. If an incorrect word is supplied to the title, *then* what would the book be about?
20. Have students keep a graph showing the number of books they have read. The graph could be in the form of a thermometer or track which the student would complete after reading a number of books during a specified time. A variation of this is to have places on the graph calling for a book on a different topic or genre than ones previously read.
21. Allow time for browsing, especially after new books have been added to your collection. Teach students how to browse—read quickly through the first chapter to get the flavor of the book and then spot-read a paragraph here and there throughout the book.
22. Read recipes and discuss with the class if the recipe promises to taste good, how would they improve it, what would happen if an ingredient were left out or included in an incorrect quantity. This is easily done in home economics, and students may also try out some of the recipes. A variation of this is possible with science experiments.
23. Use choral reading, especially with poetry and stories in which there

is much conversation. Note how tone, pitch, and stress affect the meaning.

24. Give the students a description and have them draw what is described. Point out that the pictures, though accurate, are different. Conjecture with them why this can be so.
25. Have the students imagine they are publishing the book they have read. How would they advertise it in order to get people to read it?
26. Feature a "Book of the Week," to be chosen by a committee of students. Have a short discussion about why it was chosen.
27. Organize a book club as part of the extracurricular offerings of your school. For each meeting the club members read a book pertinent to a subject—for example, one month, science; another, social studies; another, a famous literary classic; and so on.
28. Have the students imagine that the book they are reading has just been found 3000 years from now. What information would the people learn about the way we live and about our concerns and problems? What misconceptions might these people have about us? This activity is particularly interesting in a world history class.

THE SCHOOL LIBRARY

The school library is central to all school reading programs. It is valuable to both teachers and students as a resource for stimulating wide reading for pleasure as well as for information. Library materials enrich the class by enabling the teacher to expand upon a textbook offering, to get materials on varied levels, and to individualize instruction. Students can find in-depth information about their interests and assigned topics as well as materials which give them pure pleasure. However, the students may not be aware of the "treasure trove" that can be found in the school library. Often, the library seems a cold and forbidding place—certainly not a place a lively teenager would choose to spend time.

Many school librarians are quite successful at attracting high school students to the library. In one case, the librarian organized a committee of students to assist her in selecting new books. She described:

> I have to order references that various departments need, but I have a part of the library appropriation to order general books, fiction and fact, that will be of interest to the students. When I first became a librarian, I placed the new books on the shelves, but I found that only a very small number of students were aware of the new books or seemed to be interested in them. I talked to the English teachers and with their help I was able to organize a committee of 12–15 students from all grades to assist me in choosing the new books. The committee has become sort of a library club. We meet regularly once a week and go over the catalogs from which I order books. The students read the annotations and decide if they and their classmates would be interested. They do a splendid job. I find that we are getting a very balanced collection covering many topics of interest.

Since the committee was chosen from English classes, all students knew of its existence. Comments started to come in from the student committee: "I'll be glad when [such and such] comes in," or "We chose some neat books yesterday. One was __________!" Student interest was indeed mounting, largely because student representatives were active in choosing books. The students felt strongly that the new books were relevant to their interests.

Then this librarian further fostered student interest by placing the new books on a table in front of the check-out desk to encourage browsing. A big sign about the new books was on the browsing table. Attractive notices were placed at key places in the school announcing the new books. This librarian did not spend all of her appropriation at once but instead used it throughout the year so that new books were always coming in. The browsing table always had students around it. They came to the library whenever they had a few free minutes, and circulation went up markedly.

In another instance, the librarian was essentially an "actor" disguised as a librarian—he was a talented oral reader. In December, just before the holidays, he invited all of the English classes, one at a time, to the library. He set the stage with attractive decorations, candle-light, and a beautiful Christmas tree and read appropriate literature of the season aloud to the students. For each English class, that visit proved a sheer delight. It became a tradition in the school, and students looked forward to this celebration of the holiday season. The librarian noted two important results: first, students came into the library for a pleasant, relaxing time instead of for research for an assignment; second, book circulation increased.

In these two instances, students were made aware of the library and its offerings in a very positive way. They became acquainted with the many activities which could be of interest to them. Ellsworth and Wagener list activities other than independent study that students may engage in when using the library:

> Find answers to specific questions that arise either from the teaching process or from ordinary curiosity.
>
> Go alone or as a member of a committee sent to get information.
>
> Carry out study hall assignments; that is, spend a specific amount of time studying in the library.
>
> Find material for projects such as a written report, a book review, a debate brief, or a research paper.
>
> Learn how to use the keys of a library—card catalogs, bibliographies, reference books, periodical indexes, etc.
>
> Look at motion-picture films, filmstrips, or other audio-visual materials. Study with a teaching machine, listen to phonograph records or tapes, listen and record voice for language study.
>
> Locate quotations, excerpts, or data for speeches or projects.
>
> Read just for the fun of reading—one book or a hundred.
>
> Browse through current magazines and newspapers or look at the new book shelf.
>
> Talk with other students.[4]

The library is the school repository of reference materials that students can use in all of their content courses. Some reference materials are common to all subject areas, and there are materials specific to each. Common

4. Ralph E. Ellsworth and Hobart D. Wagener, *The School Library* (New York: Educational Facilities Laboratories, 1963), p. 25.

reference materials found in most school libraries are encyclopedias, *The World Almanac, Who's Who, Who's Who in America, Atlas, Bartlett's Familiar Quotations, Book Review Digest, Vital Statistics of the United States,* dictionaries, and so on. Each subject teacher knows the references for that area. Students need to learn to use the reference materials. Reference materials today take many forms in addition to printed matter: the film, filmstrip, transparency, programmed book, disc and tape recording, microfilm and videotape.[5]

Library skills needed for research are the abilities to (*a*) determine the key or entry words of the topic, (*b*) know the appropriate reference sources for the topic, and (*c*) know how to find as well as to use the reference. Finding the reference involves such basic skills as using the alphabet, knowing the library cataloging system, understanding how to use the card catalog (and knowing that it is organized by both author and subject), and translating the abbreviations and using the entries in *The Reader's Guide to Periodical Literature.* After locating the reference material, students need to be shown how each specific reference is organized and used. With general references, it is necessary to know parts of a book, especially the Table of Contents and index. At this point, the students rely on the other study skills that have been taught: skimming, reading with attention to the purpose of the topic, taking notes and synthesizing them, and organizing and writing the report. Research reading gives the student excellent reinforcement and practice in the study reading skills discussed in Chapter 4.

Let's determine what a student would need to know from some sample topics.

Example of a research problem in social studies:

PROBLEM: *Determine the section of the United States that is showing the greatest growth in industry and population.*

Students might use any or all of such sources as *The World Almanac, The Reader's Guide to Periodical Literature* and *Vital Statistics of the U.S.*

Students will realize that the key or entry words are *industry* and *population.* They should further reason that the information will most likely be found in tables and charts which show the growth of industry and population.

The World Almanac, which would be an important source of information for this topic, gives the highlights of news statistics. Students will find that broad topics such as industry and population are arranged alphabetically in the Table of Contents. Specific detailed items are listed alphabetically in the index. *Vital Statistics of the United States* would give figures about population. *The Reader's Guide to Periodical Literature* would be used to locate general articles on the problem which might present a rationale for the findings.

For the problem as stated, students would need to be able to read and interpret carefully. The problem asks what region *is showing* the greatest growth in industry and population. No dates are given. Therefore, they

5. Jean Key Gates, *Guide to the Use of Books and Libraries* (New York: McGraw-Hill, 1974), p. 25.

should understand that the problem is concerned about the present, indicated by the words *is showing*. The tables they consult should be the most recent in a specific span of years.

Example of a research problem in literature:

PROBLEM: *Read the Greek Myths and determine all of the modern-day references to them that you can.*

The sources would be such library volumes as *Bulfinch's Mythology* and *The Dictionary of Mythology, Folklore, and Symbols.*

At first, students should consult the library card file to locate books about mythology. The key word would be *myth.* After locating the appropriate books, they would note the myths and the names of the gods and goddesses.

In this problem, students must realize that it is necessary to know the Greek myths in order to note modern-day references to the names of the gods and goddesses. An awareness of names used today depends largely upon the student's background knowledge, though specific periodicals might contain articles about modern references to myths. In such a case, the students would need to use the *Reader's Guide.*

Example of a research problem in science:

PROBLEM: *What are the latest findings of research in oceanography?*

The key word is *oceanography*. The major sources of information would be *The Reader's Guide to Periodical Literature* and possibly *The World Almanac*. The students' skill in using these references should be checked so that instruction can be given prior to research if necessary.[6]

Each of the content areas offers problems and topics for research in which the student needs to demonstrate proper use of sources of information.

Some specific types of assignments requiring the use of reference materials are:

1. Use open-ended questions which require numerous references. For instance, instead of a topic assignment such as the Gold Rush of 1849, ask a question such as "What was the effect of the Gold Rush of 1849 upon the westward expansion of the United States?" Use the problem-solving approach.
2. Organize groups and committees of students to work together in developing a report.
3. Use the reference material to develop background for a topic under study in class.
4. Encourage the students to organize panels, demonstrations, debates, as a means of presenting their topic.
5. Use reference material as sources of background information for field trips, for current events.

The librarian is a valuable resource. Whenever time allows, librarians do instruct students in reference reading techniques, especially the locational

6. David L. Shepherd, "Using Sources of Information," in *Developing Study Skills in Secondary Schools: Perspectives in Reading, No. 4* (Newark, Del.: IRA, 1965), pp. 50–53.

skills. However, you cannot rely completely upon the librarian because time is simply not available. Librarians can aid teachers in the following ways:

1. By preparing bibliographies to help in research and reference projects.
2. By providing books and materials to aid professional study and improve inservice training programs.
3. By assembling material which would help improve instructional methods.
4. By participating in curriculum committee work and assisting in the development of new courses of study and units of work.
5. By helping teachers interpret test data and gain an understanding of the reading difficulties of the students.
6. By discovering the reading interests of pupils by means of reading records.
7. By assisting counselors in observing students' personality traits—day-dreaming, dawdling, worrying, and reading difficulties—and leading the students to books and materials that will help the problem.
8. By giving instruction to students on using the library materials effectively.

You or your department chairperson can provide guidance to the librarian by suggesting general references to obtain. One good source is the bibliography or selected references for further reading found at the ends of chapters or units in many textbooks. Many schools obtain such references as soon as a textbook is chosen, thereby insuring that the materials are available for students at the appropriate times.

SUMMARY

The teacher's attitude toward reading is an important influence on high school students' interest in books and reading. Communicate a love of reading. Choose books that are relevant to adolescents' interests. Enriching the subject areas with materials other than textbooks not only makes our classes more interesting but also enlarges a general background of information. The major goals of bringing the library into classroom procedure are to promote independence in study and to encourage using the library for both research and pleasure. Developing interest is a major step toward the goal of developing literate students.

QUESTIONS AND PROBLEMS FOR YOUR OWN CLASSROOM

For readers who are training to be teachers:

1. Delineate your attitude about the purposes of reading.
2. As you study the methods courses in your subject specialty, note where and how you can foster wide reading.
3. Conduct research through your library or with a group of adolescents

and determine what their interests are. Compare those interests listed in the literature with your actual findings.

For readers who are teaching:

1. Discuss with your students the interests they have. Compile a list of interests.
2. Review your subject curriculum and determine the topics that could be used for enrichment and research reading.
3. Review your subject curriculum and note where and how you can foster wide reading.
4. List the specific references pertinent to your subject area.
5. Determine how you and the school librarian can work together.
6. List the books you would like to have in a classroom library.

SELECTED REFERENCES

Herber, Harold L., ed. *Developing Study Skills in Secondary Schools: Perspectives in Reading, No. 4.* Newark, Del.: IRA, 1965.

A discussion of reading research tasks is included.

Russell, Ivan L. *Motivation.* Dubuque: Wm. C. Brown Company, 1971.

Much insight is given about the nature of motivation.

Shapiro, Jon E. *Using Literature and Poetry Affectively.* Newark, Del.: IRA, 1979.

Many suggestions are given for boosting students' desire to read.

CHAPTER 6

Diagnosis for Effective Teaching

OVERVIEW

Effective teaching encompasses more than just the transfer of information from the teacher to the students. It also includes adjusting instruction to their needs, desires, and capabilities. To be effective as a teacher, you must *assess* your students—investigate, determine needs, and plan for their optimum development. A good curriculum considers the individual's strengths and weaknesses as well as the manner in which he or she learns best—information that is obtained through diagnostic assessment. Diagnosis is both objective and subjective, standardized and informal; teachers should feel free to use any assessment devices that provide insights about the students.

Questions

Consider these questions before you read further:

1. What means of diagnosis do you use in your classes?
2. What is the purpose of your diagnosis?
3. How do you relate your diagnosis to class instruction?
4. Other than performing diagnostic tasks, are students involved in diagnosis in any way?

In assessing for more effective teaching, we collect and judge information about the students and their modality for learning. In reading we are concerned about how well they read, what their strengths and weaknesses are, and how they can best learn. Both diagnosis and evaluation are aspects of the total assessment of reading proficiency. In this volume the term *diagnosis* will be used more than *assessment* or *evaluation* in order to emphasize what needs to be done in the classroom. Assessment implies knowing where the student is, and this is important. However, we need to know more. Diagnosis implies that a condition needs correction, and you diagnose to find what that condition is. Even students who read adequately or well can be taught to read more effectively. (Remember, reading is a *process* that allows for continuous improvement.)

Diagnosis occurs in a range of settings and conditions, from daily teaching activities in the classroom to the highly technical investigations into deficiencies of the severely retarded reader. At one end of this continuum is the general appraisal of daily classroom work; at the other, testing (psychological, medical, educational) in a clinical situation. Strang lists seven levels or stages of diagnosis:

1. Information describing the student's reading performance obtained through classroom instruction and from informal and standardized reading tests.
2. Investigation which seeks clues to other aspects of the student's behavior that influence his reading performance. Such clues are noted through observation, interviews and personality tests.
3. An analysis of the student's reading process to note specific strengths and deficiencies so that specific remedial measures and practice can be prescribed.
4. An analysis of mental abilities which underlie success in reading such as visual memory and association.
5. A clinical analysis of personality traits and values which may provide insight into the student's reading performance and may indicate need for psychotherapy preliminary to or concomitant with reading instruction.
6. Neurological examination to determine the possibility of brain damage.
7. Introspective reports by the student stating his view of his reading difficulties and how he attempts to accomplish various reading tasks.[1]

As a classroom teacher you will not perform diagnosis at all seven levels. The first level, that of providing diagnosis through daily classroom teaching, is well within your responsibility. Burnett makes a strong case for the teacher as a diagnostician:

> Effective classroom instruction can take place . . . because there is a teacher, who, within the framework of his classroom organization, is looking for individual problems that come up in the course of instruction. He varies his instructional approach enough from day to day to strengthen weaknesses that become

1. Ruth Strang, *Reading Diagnosis and Remediation* (Newark, Del.: International Reading Association, 1968), pp. 4–6.

> apparent, and to expand and reinforce certain basic learnings that have been covered before but now need expansion and reinforcement. This effective kind of teaching approaches what has been called "diagnostic teaching."[2]

This level of diagnosis incorporates the factor of *prevention*. Teachers should reteach, expand, and reinforce as necessary in order to offset possible problem areas.

Strang's second level is also within the classroom teacher's province—especially skillful observation and the interview. For both techniques you need to know what to look for and how to interpret the evidence gathered.

For the most part, the remaining five levels require the time and training which classroom teachers do not have. However, some teachers may be able to begin an analysis of a student's reading strengths and weaknesses through purposeful classroom activities and evaluations. For instance, during class discussion you might note areas of difficulty by identifying what skill is needed to answer the most important questions asked. This, of course, requires preplanning and an analysis of the reading material.

Level seven provides insight into how the student obtains and uses information. Melnick states:

> Among the insights revealing reading proficiency, the teacher may note evidence of the following:
>
> 1. The student's approach to a reading passage;
> 2. His tendency to relate ideas rather than merely seize on isolated details;
> 3. His ability to uncover the author's pattern of thought;
> 4. His ability to organize and show the relation among details;
> 5. His tendency to let his emotions or prejudices and personal experiences influence his comprehension;
> 6. His tendency to relate what he reads to other knowledge he has gained;
> 7. His ability to communicate in writing what he has gained from reading.
>
> Diagnostic questions, then, reveal rather than conceal individual differences.[3]

In short, diagnostic findings must be incorporated into classroom teaching, and each classroom teacher must know how to find out what the students are able to do. Diagnostic teachers adjust materials and activities to the students' needs. Bond points out, "most of the adjustment is made by the teacher who knows the needs of each child and who makes modifications to correct any confusion before it becomes seriously limiting to a child's future growth in reading. Such a teacher is a *diagnostic teacher*."[4]

PRINCIPLES OF DIAGNOSIS

1. Instruction must be pertinent to each individual child; therefore, diagnosis must also be individual.

---

2. Richard W. Burnett, "The Classroom Teacher as a Diagnostician," in *Reading Diagnosis and Evaluation,* ed. Dorothy L. DeBoer (Newark, Del.: IRA, 1970), p. 4.

3. Amelia Melnik, "Questions: An Instructional-Diagnostic Tool," *Journal of Reading* 2, No. 7 (April 1968): 512.

4. Guy L. Bond, "Diagnostic-Teaching in the Classroom," *Reading Diagnosis and Evaluation,* ed. Dorothy L. DeBoer (Newark, Del.: IRA, 1970), p. 138.

2. Diagnosis must be continuous, paced with the student's development. Since the student is not static but is constantly changing, instruction for each individual must keep pace with the changes.
3. Diagnosis assesses all aspects of students' physical and psychological character as they relate to reading ability. For instance, a severe vision difficulty may contribute strongly to a reading problem. Similarly, failure to progress in reading in accordance with one's potential may belie a negative self-concept.
4. Understand the limitations of measuring instruments, and use discretion when interpreting findings. Measuring instruments are not perfect; there is a margin of error. Even a standardized test gives only an indication of the student's level and strengths and weaknesses. Some students do not perform well on a test because of anxiety.
5. Diagnosis must determine the general nature of the problem, the specific areas of difficulty in reading, and the severity of the difficulties. Conditions that contribute to the reading problems (such as psychological, medical or environmental) also should be determined.
6. The degree and nature of the diagnosed reading difficulty should indicate where the problem can best be treated—in a regular classroom, clinic, or outside agency.
7. The diagnosis should indicate the type of instruction needed and the type and level of materials.

GUIDELINES FOR DIAGNOSIS

Diagnosis of each individual student is a personal interaction between teacher and student. It should be a joint effort toward success. Do not withhold the diagnostic findings from the student, or announce authoritatively the plan of corrective action. Instead, explain the results to the student and involve him in deciding upon the most logical and profitable alternatives for correction. Students make greater progress in correcting their reading deficiencies if they know what they must do and why, especially if they have been given the opportunity to think constructively about the diagnostic findings.

Successful diagnosis results from two major factors: an understanding of the personal relationship between teacher and student, and the teacher's expertise in professional technique. Following are the guidelines for successful diagnostic assessment:

1. *Establish rapport with the student.* The diagnostician should not appear an inquisitor but rather a calm, helpful, and positive person. Enlist the student's cooperation and interest by being objective, realistic, and hopeful. An anxious student usually does not perform well in diagnostic sessions. If the student appears anxious, use informal techniques instead.
2. *Study the learning situation as well as the student.* Note the levels of

material at which the student performs well and at which he has difficulty. Note his reactions to the various activities of the diagnosis—how he attacks words, performs a reading task, and applies reading skills.

3. *Take nothing for granted.* Check on all possible areas that may have a bearing on the student's difficulty. No diagnostician jumps to conclusions. Base all conclusions on definite evidence.
4. *Discover traits and habits through testing and conversation.* The teacher can note an ineffective attack on a reading selection by watching the student read. Talk with the student to discover his attitude toward reading, goals, desires, anxieties, and interests.
5. *Keep written records of the diagnosis.* Of course, the results of individual diagnosis cannot be trusted to memory. Records also provide a basis for measuring the student's development over a period of time.
6. *Help the student to analyze his problem.* This provides the student with insight about his reading problem, and the teacher gains a better understanding of the student's mode of thinking.
7. *Use several different types of tests.* Diagnosis is more accurate if there is more than one source of information about the student's reading status and needs. One source may help explain or reinforce the other. Use both standardized and nonstandardized tests.

METHODS OF APPRAISAL

A complete diagnosis uses many different instruments and techniques, both formal and informal, objective and subjective. Among the many instruments we may use are, standard tests, informal tests, school record of progress, developmental history, observation, interview, daily schedule, autobiography, and the cloze procedure. The choice of instruments or technique depends upon the nature and purpose of the instrument and the type of information we need. For instance, if we wish to find out the student's attitude toward reading, the interview or the reading autobiography would likely reveal it.

A classroom teacher can use the results from standardized tests for a number of purposes, such as comparing the class with norms based on comparable classes and noting a reading level *as a rough guide* (a standardized test usually records the student's frustration level of reading). Davis points out that most students try to score as high as possible on a standardized test, but this effort cannot be sustained for any extended period; therefore, in evaluating reading level, Davis says "we subtract at least a year from the total score."[5] Results from standardized tests are also useful in parent guidance conferences because the results are objective. However, even if the primary purpose of the testing is evaluation, you can find information which points toward the mode of instruction to use in the classroom.

The answer sheet from a standardized test reveals more than just a total

---

5. William Q. Davis, "Functional Use of Standardized Tests," *Reading Diagnosis and Evaluation,* ed. Dorothy L. DeBoer (Newark, Del.: IRA, 1971), p. 81.

score or subscores of the test. Analyzing each of the student's incorrect responses will show the type of question on which the student has difficulty. Many test manuals include an item-by-item analysis of the test questions that indicate the specific skill the student needs for each question. You may discover a class deficiency, or groups of students may show the same needs. This information will help you plan different classroom groupings based on both level and need.

Standardized test scores also give students insight about their strengths and weaknesses. Seeing their answer sheets and plotting their progress provides students with a realistic, objective picture of their reading performance. They can note those skills in which they are competent and those in which they need practice. This type of information can boost self-direction and motivation.

Still another use of standardized tests is to prescribe a specific course of study or corrective program for a student. This use, called the *diagnostic-prescriptive approach,* is what diagnosis is all about. Although such an approach lends itself well to individualization, it can also be used for groups as class patterns emerge.

Standardized tests can provide diagnostic information for instructional guidance, but they are not foolproof. Teachers will need to check each test's *validity* (does it measure what it purports to measure?) and *reliability* (does it measure the same proficiencies all the time?).

A test may provide inaccurate scores in measuring a student's reading ability for a number of reasons:

1. It may overestimate the student's reading ability, which you will discover if you note that the student cannot read successfully at the grade level of his test score.
2. It may lose validity at certain age levels or competence levels. For instance, a test may fail to measure adequately the reading abilities of a highly competent student because its ceiling is too low.
3. Comparable forms of the same test may not be parallel, thereby failing to show accurate gains or losses.
4. Student guessing may unduly raise scores.
5. The student's work speed may affect the score. For example, a slow, thorough, and accurate student who completes only a portion of the test may get a low score.
6. The norms for evaluating the score may be based on a population not comparable with your students.
7. An individual's performance differs from day to day for a number of reasons, thereby affecting the score.
8. Any test measures only a limited number of reading skills, particularly the skills as applied to the content fields.

Most of the tests yield scores for general reading comprehension—fiction, factual material, or both—vocabulary, and speed. Very few investigate all of the pertinent skills of any specific content area, though some do have relevant subtests of that type. Some of the most appropriate diagnostic tests for content areas are:

1. *Diagnostic Reading Tests,* published by the Committee on Diagnostic Testing, Inc. at Mountain Home, North Carolina 28758. The range extends from the kindergarten to fourth grade level, lower level (grades four–eight), and upper level (grades seven–thirteen). The lower level is published in four forms (A,B,C, and D) and the upper level is published in four forms (A,B,C, and D) for the diagnostic battery. The test is also published as a survey test which has eight forms (A,B,C,D,E,F,G, and H). The diagnostic sections are untimed, while the survey sections take from forty to eighty minutes.

   The upper level survey sections yield a measure of the student's comprehension, vocabulary, and rate of reading. The lower level includes the same general reading skills plus word recognition. At both levels the vocabulary section provides scores on words per minute; general vocabulary; vocabulary comprehension; specialized English literature, mathematics, science, and social studies vocabulary. The rates of reading sections give separate measures of timed and untimed rate of general reading, social studies, and science materials.
2. *Reading Versatility Test,* published by Educational Developmental Laboratories, Inc. The range extends from basic (grades five–eight), to high school (grades eight–twelve), to advanced (grades twelve–sixteen and adults). There are four basic forms; testing time is forty to fifty minutes. This test measures the student's reading flexibility by comparing the rate of reading under different sets of instructions.
3. *Iowa Silent Reading Tests,* published by Harcourt Brace Jovanovich, Inc. There are three levels ranging from grade six through grade sixteen. For level one (grades six–nine) there are five scores: vocabulary, reading comprehension, total score, directed reading and reading efficiency. Level two (grades nine–eleven) consists of the same five scores. Level three (grades eleven–sixteen) consists of four scores: vocabulary, reading comprehension, total score, and reading efficiency.
4. *The Iowa Tests of Educational Development,* grades nine–eleven, published by Science Research Associates, Inc. Forms X-4 and Y-4 consist of eleven scores: understanding of basic social concepts, general background in the natural sciences, correctness and appropriateness of expression, ability to do quantitative thinking, abilities to interpret reading material (social studies, natural science, literary, total), general vocabulary, total score, use of sources of information.
5. *Iowa Tests of Basic Skills,* 1972, grades three–nine, (published by Houghton Mifflin Company.) Fifteen scores can be obtained: vocabulary, reading comprehension, language (spelling, capitalization, punctuation, usage, total score), work-study skills (map reading, reading graphs and tables, knowledge and use of reference materials, total score), mathematics skills (mathematics concepts, mathematics problem solving, total score), total score of all subscores.

6. *The Traxler High School Reading Test,* published by Bobbs-Merrill Company, Inc., Test Division. There are two forms and a range from grades ten to twelve. The testing time is fifty to sixty minutes. Four subscores are given: reading rate, story comprehension, main ideas in paragraphs, and total comprehension.
7. *The Traxler Silent Reading Test,* grades seven–ten, published by Bobbs-Merrill Co., Inc. This test has four forms; testing time is forty-six minutes. Five subscores are derived: reading rate, story comprehension, word meaning, paragraph meaning, and total comprehension.
8. *SRA Reading Record,* grades six–twelve, published by Science Research Associates, Inc. It consists of five scores: reading rate, comprehension, everyday reading skills, vocabulary, and total score. Everyday reading skills tested here are similar to the skills found on basic competency tests issued by various state departments of education.
9. *Botel Reading Inventory,* grades one–twelve, published by Follett Publishing Company. It is designed to ascertain the instructional reading level of the student and for the placement of reading materials. Test *A* is phonics mastery: consonants, vowels, syllabication and nonsense words. Test *B* is a word recognition test, and Test *C* is a word opposites test. These last two tests yield four ratings: the free reading levels, the highest instruction level, the highest potential level, and the frustration level. Test *C* can be administered either as a reading or listening test.
10. *High School National Achievement Test,* grades seven–twelve, published by Psychometric Affiliates. The tests yield six scores: vocabulary, word discrimination, sentence meaning, noting details, interpreting paragraphs, and total score.
11. *Diagnostic Reading Test: Pupil Progress Series,* grades 1.9-2.1 (Primary 1), 2.2-3 (Primary 2), 4-6 (Elementary), 7-8 (Advanced), published by Scholastic Testing-Service, Inc. The test is known by various titles; however, the title in the catalog is "Pupil Progress Series Reading." The advanced level consists of thirteen scores: knowledge and use of sources (functions, best sources, use of index and the table of contents, total), rate of reading for meaning, comprehension (word meaning, reading for recall of information, reading for meaning, reading to locate information, reading for directions in procedures, reading for descriptions, and total).
12. *SPIRE Individual Reading Evaluation,* grades one–six, four–ten, published by New Dimensions in Education. The SPIRE (Student Problem Individual Reading Evaluation) test consists of two tests which yield a diagnostic reading evaluation and a quick placement test. There are two levels, SPIRE 1 and SPIRE 2. Eight scores are given which consist of three diagnostic scores: individual word recognition, oral reading and silent reading; two quick placement scores: individual word recognition and reading; and three derived scores: instructional reading level, frustrational reading level, and independent reading level.

13. *California Achievement Tests: Reading,* grades one.five–two, two–four, four–six, and nine–twelve, published by McGraw-Hill Book Company. The two higher levels have two forms, A and B. Three scores are given: vocabulary, comprehension, and total.

None of these tests measures all of the skills pertinent to any one content area, but all of them contain subtests which measure skills pertinent to one or more content areas. Therefore, you can obtain some diagnostic measures of competence in a few of the skills pertinent to some content areas, but no single test will give a thorough diagnosis.

Informal Teacher-Made Tests

Assessing how well students handle assigned classroom materials is fundamental to diagnostic teaching. The easiest way to make such an assessment is to devise a test using these materials. For each content field, the test can assess such skills as using parts of the book, arriving at word meanings through context, and noting main ideas and gaining information from pictorial representations (maps, pictures, graphs, charts).

The teacher-made *group test* (or *inventory*) has many advantages. First, it provides immediate diagnostic information. Second, it can be administered whenever you are ready for it; there is no wait for a school-wide testing program or for answer sheets to return from machine scoring. Third, the teacher-made test is based on material that students will use and thus is pertinent. In contrast, the material of commercial or standardized tests often is not closely related to the material the students actually read in class. Fourth, the group test is geared to *instruction.* Since you formulate the questions, they will be similar to those you will ask in assignments. In this way you can note a clear relationship between the students' responses on the test and those they make in class. Fifth, the test is easy to score. It is wise not to assign any grade to the test; instead, use it only to note strengths and weaknesses. Have the students correct their own tests in class, and discuss the accuracy and appropriateness of specific responses. Sixth, the test becomes a teaching instrument. Discussing responses in class serves as an informal method of teaching. For instance, it may not be necessary to devote an entire lesson to explaining the difference between an index and a table of contents; a simple explanation pertinent to one question on the test often will suffice. Seventh, the test aids students in their self-appraisal. As they correct their own papers they see immediately—at a time when motivation is highest—what their strengths and weaknesses are. Finally, similar tests can be administered throughout the school year to determine progress. Students often are motivated by observing their progress.

Teacher-made tests are quite easy to devise, although the first one may require some time. There are two areas on which you may need some background. First, decide which skills to test. Second, formulate questions pertinent to the skill being investigated. Detailed directions for making and administering the group tests are included here to guide you in devising your own questions.

English—Group Reading Inventory

Directions for the diagnostic survey test are based on an English literature textbook.

I. Use between thirty-four and forty questions.

II. Use questions designed to measure the following reading skills in the proportions shown below.
  A. Using parts of the book (three questions in all)
    1. Table of Contents
    2. Index of titles
    3. Glossary
    4. Biographical data
    5. Introductory paragraph to story
  B. Vocabulary needs
    1. Meaning (seven–eight questions)
      a. General background of word meanings
        1. Select correct meaning from several dictionary meanings
        2. Antonyms, synonyms
      b. Contextual meanings
    2. Word recognition and attack (fourteen–fifteen questions)
      a. Divide words into syllables
      b. Designate the accented syllable
      c. Note and give meaning of prefixes and suffixes
      d. Changing the part of speech of a word (noun to verb, adjective to adverb, etc.)
  C. Comprehension (eleven–twelve questions)
    1. Noting the main idea
    2. Recalling pertinent supporting details
    3. Drawing conclusions, inferences
    4. Noting the sequence of ideas
  D. Reading rate. Have student note the time it takes to read the selection. Then, figure reading speed in words per minute.

  Example: Words in selection: 4000
  Time to read: 10 minutes
  $\frac{4000}{10}$ equals 400 words per minute

  Time may be recorded by student noting clock time for starting and stopping or by teacher recording time on blackboard every 30 seconds (1′, 1′30″, 2′, etc.)
  E. Skimming to locate information (two–five questions)
  Use selection different from the one used for comprehension and speed purposes.

III. Choose a reading selection of not more than four pages.

IV. In administering the inventory:
  A. Explain the purpose of the inventory and the reading skills it is

designed to measure. When the inventory is given, advise the students which skill is being measured.

B. Read each question twice.
C. Questions on using the parts of a book are asked first. Students will use their books.
D. Introduce the reading selection, establishing necessary background on the topic and giving the students a question to guide their reading.
E. Read selection silently. Note and figure speed.
F. Ask questions on vocabulary. Students will use book for questions measuring ability to determine meaning from context. They will not use the book for other vocabulary questions; these should be written on the blackboard.
H. Skimming. Use a new selection. Books will be used.

V. Students are considered deficient in any one specific skill if they answer more than one out of three questions incorrectly, or more than two incorrectly when there are more than three questions measuring a specific skill.

VI. Since this inventory is administered to a group, it does not establish a grade level. Nonetheless, those who score above 90 percent may be considered to be reading material that is too easy for them. Those scoring below 65 percent may be considered to be reading material that is too difficult for them. If the material is suitable, the scores should range between 70 and 90 percent.

VII. Form of tabulation of results—see page 159.

VIII. Sample Form of Inventory

Parts of book

1. "On what page does the unit [section] entitled *Exploring One World* begin?"
2. "What section of your book would you use to find out something about the author of a story in the book?" (Determines knowledge of section on biographical data.)
3. "In what part of the book can you find the meaning of a word that you might not know?" (Determines knowledge of glossary.)

Introduce story

Explore student background of experiences on the subject of the story and set up purpose questions.

Vocabulary

4. "What is meant by the word *crab* as it is used in the story?" (Read the sentence in which the word is used.)

Contextual meaning

5. "What is meant by the word *eliminated?*" (Read the sentence in which the word is used.)

Synonyms and antonyms	6. "What word means the opposite of *temporary?*" 7. "Use another word to describe the coach when he looked amazed."
General knowledge of meaning	8. "Select the proper meaning of the word *entice.*" a. to lure, persuade b. to force c. to ask d. to caution 9. "Select the proper meaning of the word *initial.*" a. the last or end b. the beginning or first c. the middle d. a letter of the alphabet 10. "Select the proper meaning of the word *rectify.*" a. to do wrong b. to make right c. to destroy d. a priest's home
Word recognition: syllabication; accents	"Divide the following words into syllables and show which syllable is accented:" 11–12. eliminated 13–14. amazed 15–16. undemocratic 17–18. fraternities
Prefixes and suffixes	19. "What does the prefix *un* mean as used in *undemocratic?*" 20. "What is meant by *pre* in the word *pre*scription?" 21. "Change the verb *astonish* to a noun." 22. "Change the noun *boy* to an adjective." 23. "Change the adjective *democratic* to a noun." 24. "Change the adjective *slow* to an adverb."
Comprehension: main ideas; details	25. "What is a ________________? What happened when ________________?" 26. (Such questions as applicable here; ask for 27. only the main points of the story.) 28. (Questions to ask for specific bits of information 29. about the principal characters or 30. ideas of the material.)
Drawing conclusions; inferences	31. (Questions, the answers to which are not com- 32. pletely found in the textbook. Questions begin- 33. ning with "why," making comparisons, or predicting what may happen. e.g. "Why did Bottle imagine he could perform such astounding athletic feats as setting the state high school record in jumping?")
Sequence	34. (May be omitted.) Questions asking what hap- 35. pened as a result of ________, what steps did the police use to solve the mystery, etc.

Skimming

36. Use a new reading selection. (Questions designed
37. to have the pupil locate some specific bit of information)

Social Studies—Group Reading Inventory

Directions for the diagnostic survey test are based on a social studies textbook.

I. Use between 26 and 30 questions.

II. Write questions designed to measure the following reading skills in the proportions shown below.
   A. Using parts of the book (five questions)
   B. Using resource (library) materials (four questions)
   C. Using maps, pictures, charts, etc. (four questions)
   D. Vocabulary (three questions)
   E. Noting the main idea (three questions)
   F. Noting pertinent supporting details (three questions)
   G. Drawing conclusions (three questions)
   H. Noting the organization of the material (one question)

III. Choose a reading selection of not more than 3 to 4 pages.

IV. Have questions of skills II D through H based on the reading selection.

V. In administering the inventory:
   A. Explain the purpose of the test and the reading skills the test is designed to measure. As the test is given, let the students know the skill being measured.
   B. Read each question twice.
   C. If students are to refer to the textbook, write the page reference of each question on the blackboard as the question is read.

VI. Students are considered to be deficient in any of the skills if they get more than one question in any of the skills wrong.

VII. Sample Form of Inventory

Parts of book

1. "On what page would you find the map that shows [name of map]?" (Shows use of map table found in front of book.)
2. "On what page does Chapter ____ begin? What is the title of the unit of which it is a part?" (Shows use of Table of Contents.)
3. "How can the introduction on pages ______ help you in your study?" (Shows understanding of unit introduction.)
4. "Of what value are the questions, activities, and vocabulary shown on pages ______ for under-

standing the material in the textbook?" (Shows understanding of specific textbook study aids.)

5. "In what part of the book would you look to find the page references of this topic: __________?" (Shows purpose of index.)

Use of resources

6. "What library aid will tell you the library number of the book, ______________, so that you can find it on the shelves?" (Shows knowledge of card catalog function.)
7. "What is a biography?" (Shows knowledge of one type of reference book.)
8. "Name one set of encyclopedias. How are the topics in them arranged?" (Shows knowledge of a type of reference material.)
9. "Name a library guide that will help you find a specific magazine article. If you were to give a report in class and you knew that most of your information would be in current magazines, what guide would tell you which magazines and which issues to use for information on your topic?" (Shows knowledge of a type of library guide to research.)

Use of maps, charts, etc.

10. "What does the map on page ___ show you?" (Shows an understanding of fundamental idea on map.)
11. "What do the black areas [or some other feature] shown on the map on page ___ represent?" (Shows ability to read information from a map.)
12. "Turn to page ___." Ask for some specific bit of information that is shown by the chart. Example: chart showing organization of federal government—"What are the three branches of our federal government?" (Shows ability to understand charts, diagrams.)
13. "Turn to page ___." Ask for some specific bit of information that is shown by the picture. Ask also for interpretation. Example: picture showing sod house on the prairie—"What is the settler's house made of? Can you tell why that type of building material is used?" (Shows ability to understand and interpret picture.) "Read pages _______."
14. "Define _______."

Understanding vocabulary

15. "What did So and So mean when he said _______?" (word or term to be defined from the comment must be pointed out) (Contextual meanings)
16. "What is a _______?"

Noting main ideas

17. Questions to ask for only the main points of
18. information—main ideas of the longer important
19. paragraphs.

Noting details	20. 21. 22.	Questions to ask for specific bits of information about the principal characters or ideas of the material.
Drawing conclusions	23. 24. 25.	Questions, the answers to which are not completely found in the text. Questions beginning with "why," making comparisons, predicting events, measure drawing conclusions. Example: "Why did the pioneers brave the dangers to move west?"
Seeing organization	26.	"Each author follows an outline in writing the information in your textbook. In looking through Chapter [one from which the reading selection was taken], write down the author's first main topic." or "If you were to outline the material that you have read, what would be the I, II, III main topics of your outline?"

Science—Group Reading Inventory

Directions for the diagnostic survey test are based on any science textbook.

I. Use approximately 30 questions.

II. Write questions designed to measure the following reading skills in proportions as shown:
   A. Using parts of the book (four questions)
   B. Using resource (library) materials (three questions)
   C. Using vocabulary (four questions)
   D. Noting the main idea (four questions)
   E. Noting pertinent supporting details (four questions)
   F. Following directions (three questions)
   G. Drawing conclusions (three questions)
   H. Applying theoretical information (three questions)
   I. Understanding formulas and equations (three questions)

III. Choose a reading selection of not more than three pages.

IV. Have questions on skills II C, D, E, G, and H based on the reading selection. Items F and J may be based on this or another reading selection.

V. In administering the inventory:
   A. Explain the purpose of the inventory and the reading skills the inventory is designed to measure. As the inventory is given, let the students know the skill being measured.
   B. Read each question twice.
   C. Write the page reference of each question on the blackboard as the question is read.

VI. Students are considered to be deficient in any of the skills if they get more than one question in any of the skills wrong.

VII. Sample Form of Inventory

Parts of book

1. "On what page would you find the chapter entitled __________?" (Shows use of Table of Contents.)
2. "Of what value to you are the questions under the chapter section titled __________?" (Shows understanding of specific textbook study aids.)
3. "How are the chapters arranged or grouped?" (Shows understanding of textbook organization.)
4. "What sections of the book would you use to find the page reference for the topic __________?" (Shows knowledge of purpose of the index.)

Library

5. "How are topics arranged in a reference book?" (Shows knowledge of organization of reference book under consideration.)
6. "What is a biography?" (Shows knowledge of a type of reference material.)
7. "Explain the difference between science fiction and science factual materials." (Shows knowledge of important types of science reading materials.)

"Read pages ______."

Vocabulary

8. (For contextual meanings—Example: "How is the
9. word used by the author when he states____?"
10. For recall—Example: "What does this word
11. mean?" or "Use this word in a sentence." or "What
is the word I have just defined?")

Main ideas

12. "What is a __________?" (Questions to ask for
13. only the main points of information—main ideas
14. of a longer paragraph; Chapter headings, sub-
15. headings, marginal headings, introduction and
summary.)

Pertinent details

16. (Questions to ask for specific bits of information
17. about the principle, definition and laws such as
18. descriptive words, aspect of a process, applications
19. of a law, or principle steps in an experiment, life
cycle, life of a scientist. Use words that select the relative importance of details—how author shows the importance of specific details. All similar details are grouped around one main idea—each main idea has its qualifying details.)

Following directions

20. (Questions to show sequence of steps or ideas
21. for solving a problem or performing an experi-
22. ment.)

Drawing conclusions

23. (Questions whose answers are not completely found
24. in the textbook: questions beginning with "why,"
25. asking for the significance of a finding, deciding the

value of the finding of an experiment, or the implication of a description of some species or natural phenomena. Cause and effect. What happens if certain natural conditions are present, comparing two or more chemicals, telling chief likenesses, etc.)

Application 26. 27. 28. (Questions that show how scientific laws and principles can be put to practical use, often the same as drawing conclusion questions.)

Formulas, symbols 29. 30. (Questions showing meanings attached to symbols given or used in textbook.)

Mathematics—Group Reading Inventory

Directions for the diagnostic survey test are based on a mathematics textbook.

I. Each subject in the mathematics area will require its own constellation of skills. Generally, the skills to be included are the following:
   A. Reading verbal problems and stating them in one's own words.
   B. Adjusting one's reading to the requirements of the problem.
   C. Translating words into symbols.
   D. Knowing the meaning of symbols.
   E. Understanding vocabulary.
   F. Noting the relationship in formulas and equations.
   G. Obtaining information from charts, tables, and graphs.

II. Explain the purpose of the inventory and the reading skills it is to measure. As the inventory is given, let the students know the skill being measured.

III. It will not be possible to administer this inventory orally; it will have to be duplicated. If there are questions to measure the ability to understand explanations and to use special features in the textbook, direct students to specific pages as necessary.

IV. Sample Form of Inventory (four to five questions per skill)

Restating verbal problems Use typical verbal problems for the subject. Have students read the problems and write the situations they posed. Questions may ask also for what is given and what is asked for (detailed reading). Questions which ask students to note the basic mathematical processes may also be used (interpretative reading).

Adjusting one's reading Students may be asked to state how they would read specific problems, what steps they would use, whether they would read rapidly or slowly, or how they think the reading of mathematical problems differs from story-type reading.

Translating words to symbols	Ask students to underline the words and phrases in a problem that should be converted into mathematical notations. The appropriate symbol may be required of specific words or phrases.
Knowing symbol meanings	Give specific symbols and have the students write the meanings of each.
Understanding vocabulary	Include questions of both generalized and specialized vocabularies: A. Words representing ideas of quantity (*big, bigger, long, wide,* etc.). B. Words used to represent number figures. C. Words used to represent number processes. D. Words used to represent kinds of measurement. E. General terms (*plus, minus, more than, increased by*). F. Specialized technical words (*radius, isosceles*).
Noting relationship in formulae and equations	Use a problem and have the students express the relationship in the form of a formula or equation. Also, an equation may be used expressing the relationship in words.
Obtaining information from charts, tables, and graphs	Reproduce charts, tables, and graphs and ask questions requiring students to use the graphic representations. Present a problem and have students make a graphic representation of it.

As students score their own papers, they see for themselves their strengths and areas of difficulty in reading the classroom material. Students should tabulate on the front of the paper the number wrong (or right, as preferred) for each specific skill. The total score is not as important as the subscores for each skill. If the students score below 65 percent, however, further diagnosis of their difficulties is needed. Such a score indicates the need for easier material.

You can easily make a class profile, as shown below:

Name of Class ________________ Section ________ Teacher ________________

Name	Use of parts of books	Vocabulary	Meaning	Contextual meanings	Synonyms and antonyms	General knowledge	Word recognition	Syllabication	Accent	Prefixes and suffixes	Part of speech	Main ideas	Supporting details	Drawing conclusions	Sequence of ideas	Skimming	Speed in wpm	Comments
Jones, J.																		
Brown, R.																		

(Check wherever pupil is deficient)

When you read the summary chart horizontally, you can see the skill needs of each individual. Reading vertically shows class patterns. For instance, only certain students may show the need for instruction in getting the main idea, while the entire class may show a weakness in vocabulary. The class profile is very useful for grouping according to need, and it indicates clearly what skills the class needs to develop.

Since the inventory is not standardized, it can be altered to suit your specific purposes. The examples of inventories shown here do survey the essential skills the student needs, but you can add questions to assess additional skills if you think it necesasary. You may also center your diagnosis on just a few select skills.

Other Techniques of Diagnosis

Diagnosis helps teachers to gear instruction to the students. Instruction always must follow diagnosis. In monitoring students' performance each day, you sometimes will need more information than testing alone provides. Then, you will use other techniques.

Observation

One other technique available to you is to observe the students as they read, study, and participate in classroom activities. You can gather general information by watching for specific skills, such as:

1. how the students approach an assignment
2. how they apply reading study techniques, such as survey
3. how well they read to find the main idea or to note how information is organized
4. how well they ascertain the meanings of new or unfamiliar words
5. whether or not they can use context clues
6. whether they use locational skills in a book
7. whether they can use reference skills

The specific purposes of your observation will depend largely upon the nature of the work in class and the students' response to it.

Like many other techniques, observation is more useful if you keep a systematic record of each observation. Some teachers use a weekly graph showing the names of the students with spaces opposite for each day of the week:

Week of__________	*Mon.*	*Tues.*	*Wed.*	*Thurs.*	*Fri.*
Names__________					
__________					
__________					

You may have such graphs dittoed as soon as class enrollment has stabilized at the beginning of the school year. By using a code of your own invention, you can note the results of observation immediately. For instance, if the student is having trouble with questions requiring noting the main idea, you may record on the chart "-MI." If the student is competent in this skill, the notation could be "+MI." In another instance, if the student does not survey before she reads, the notation might be "-survey." Or, if vocabulary is the problem, the notation could be "-voc," or more detailed "-voc—context," or "-WR:syll" (*needs word recognition, syllabication help*).

One of the major advantages of keeping a daily record is that you have information readily available for planning the next day's instruction. Do not expect to record a comment about each student each day; instead, note signals from the students as shown by their activities in class. Some students may respond in such a manner that you record many observations, whereas for others (such as students who perform adequately and do not stand out from the group) this may be unnecessary. By keeping a chart of observations, you can see very quickly which students do not prompt recorded observation. You can plan to observe some performances of these students as well.

Observation and recording also reveals the *pattern* of student development over the period of a school year or semester. You can see student progress in many specific ways. Chronic and new needs also will be noted. Continual observations are necessary in order to note the growth of students as individuals, not just as students. Observations of past performance are of interest only insofar as they aid your understanding of present performance.

Observations are very subjective, and there are several cautions to keep in mind when using the observation technique. Your educational philosophy and first impression of the student may color the type of observations you make. Also, the observations will occur in only one segment of the student's life. More information from other sources is needed to determine strengths, weaknesses, interests, and attitudes.

Talking with Students

During the school day you may find opportunities to talk with students individually or in small groups—while they are working on assignments, before or after class on the school day, or by special appointment. Since there is usually no intensive probing, these conversations cannot be considered interviews. In fact, they are often very casual. But if you are alert for the opportunities, you will find that such conversations can have diagnostic value.

Meeting with students can provide much insight into their behavior, attitudes, and accomplishments. You may note a student's attitude toward school and toward reading in particular. You may uncover concerns and fears about school work or other problems both in and out of school. Recreational interests, study habits, voluntary reading, and vocational desires can be ascertained. Such information can be used in planning the subject curriculum. For instance, in a history class, a student who is interested in costume design may find a project on the manner of dress during certain periods of history interesting and worthwhile; this would, in turn, give the student practice in reading-research skills.

Conversations with students can reveal very little or very much, depending on your alertness. You must be willing to *listen*. The conversation is not a time for you to lecture or moralize. Your comments and questions should help the student to crystallize his ideas; they should be stated simply and should show respect for him. Try to understand his point of view, respect his opinions, and be willing to explore ideas.

Talking is a good time for making other observations. You can observe much about habits, self-concept, and relations with others by noting personal appearance (cleanliness, appropriateness of dress, posture, expressive movements of hands and face, and mannerisms); pitch, rapidity, and articulateness of speech; attitude (cooperative or hostile); and reactions to problems and situations in everyday experience.

Cumulative School Records

The cumulative school record provides information about the student's development, enabling a teacher to see the student as a unique individual. The summary of academic progress, medical history, family background, special problems and attributes of the student over the years, teacher evaluations, and past interviews with parents all are valuable information that is available before you meet the student for the first time.

There are dangers in relying excessively on cumulative information. You must realize that the student is a developing person, and that his past needs and problems may not be his current ones. Nevertheless, these records do provide insight, and you can add information to the records based on your daily contact.

Daily Schedule

If students complain about not having enough time to read or study, suggest that they keep a daily record of activities to see how they spend their time. Students can keep a record for a day, a weekend, or a week, with each day divided into half- or whole-hour segments. Students often are amazed to see how they spend their time, and you can quickly see what kind of reading they do, whether they spend an inordinate amount of time on homework, or whether they are overloaded with outside activities and responsibilities. Once such a record is kept, both you and your students can use this information to plan for more efficient and productive use of time.

Student Analysis of Reading—The Autobiography

Students are aware of their own reading abilities and, if given the opportunity, they can provide you with much information. Through an autobiography, they can give you insight into specific reading problems. This autobiography should be a confidential report. It may address such questions as:

1. What is your problem in reading as you see it?
2. When did you first begin to learn to read?
3. Can you give the history of your learning to read since you entered school?
4. What do you think is necessary to improve your reading, or to overcome your difficulties?
5. How much time outside of school do you spend reading?
6. What kinds of books and materials do you like to read?
7. What do you do when you do not know a word when reading?
8. How do you find the main idea of a paragraph, a chapter?

The Cloze Procedure

The cloze procedure is based on the Gestalt idea of *closure,* which is the desire to supply a missing part to make a structure whole. As a diagnostic instrument, it can be used to determine the readability of a passage or a textbook. According to Thelen, the cloze method can be used accurately and quickly to screen each student's ability to understand the text.[6]

Bormuth states what he terms an "oversimplified description" of the cloze readability procedure:

> (a) passages are selected from the material whose difficulty is being evaluated, (b) every fifth word in the passages is deleted and replaced by underlined blanks of a standard length, (c) the tests are duplicated and given, without time limits, to students who have *not* read the passages from which the tests were made, (d) the students are instructed to write in each blank the word they think was deleted, (e) responses are scored correct when they exactly match (disregarding minor misspelling) the words deleted. When the tests have been made properly, a student's score can be interpretated as a measure of how well he understands the materials from which the tests were made.[7]

Selected passages should have 250–300 words each, each passage should begin at the beginning of a paragraph, the readability tests should have 50 deleted words each, and students whose scores fall between 44–57 percent (these figures differ slightly according to the authority) on the passage are considered to have adequate reading skills (at the instructional level). For students whose score is above 57 percent, the materials are suitable for use at the independent level, at which no instructional assistance is needed. Conversely, those scoring below 44 percent are at a frustration level, where normal classroom assistance is not adequate.

When used as a diagnostic measure of readability, the cloze procedure taps specific factors that determine the ability to reproduce language patterns similar to those used by a writer: (a) grammatical skills and familiarity with language, (b) intelligence, and (c) related past experiences. The more the students are aware of the language patterns of society and the more background knowledge they possess of the subject used in the cloze test, the better they can score.

There are many variations of the cloze procedure which offer "cloze-type" exercises. They can be used either for diagnosis or evaluation. For example, in teaching pronoun referents, you could supply a group of sentences or paragraph(s) in which all of the pronouns are deleted. Your purpose would be to see if the students could supply the appropriate pronoun (correct in gender, number, and so on). The pronouns could be listed randomly or left off the page.

Of course, the exercise is more difficult if the deleted words are not listed—hence you have a means of grading the level of difficulty. The easiest form is the random listing of the deleted words; next in difficulty would be the random listing of the deleted words with several extra related words added; and the hardest would be no listing of the deleted words at all. Giving such an

---

6. Judith Thelen, *Improving Reading in Science: Reading Aid Series* (Newark, Del.: IRA, 1976), p. 6.

7. John R. Bormuth, *Readability in 1968* (Champaign, Ill.: National Council of Teachers of English, 1968), p. 40.

exercise to the students prior to instruction would serve a diagnostic purpose—to help you discover how thoroughly you need to develop your instruction. If the procedure is given after instruction, then it could serve as an evaluation. Other variations include (*a*) paragraphs in which new vocabulary terms are deleted, (*b*) mathematics problems in which words denoting process are deleted, (*c*) paragraphs in which adverbs or adjectives are deleted and you instruct the students to supply terms that would set a particular mood or point of view, and (*d*) sentences or paragraphs with prepositions deleted.

The value of the cloze procedure is enhanced if you discuss with the students the reasons for correct responses. The focus is on *meaning*. This procedure highlights the areas in which students may need help: vocabulary, syntax, punctuation, phrases, clause structure, and so on.

SUMMARY

As a classroom teacher, you will obtain most of your diagnostic information through the classroom. You must teach more than content. Your teaching must investigate how the students get and relate to the content; then you are better able to guide them in techniques of reading and study as well as to instruct toward mastery of the content. Diagnostic teaching shows concern for the students. It requires working with them as partners in the learning process.

QUESTIONS AND PROBLEMS FOR YOUR OWN CLASSROOM

For readers who are training to be teachers:

1. Explain the relationship between continuous diagnosis and diagnostic teaching. Evolve ways to strengthen the relationship.
2. Prepare an informal inventory for your subject area.
3. Choose a topic and formulate questions which require competence in a specific skill.
4. After giving an informal inventory, you note that one group of students seems to have difficulty in noting main ideas, while another is weak in vocabulary. How would you plan classroom procedure to accommodate the weaknesses?
5. In your classroom diagnosis, what conditions would indicate the need for referral to (*a*) the reading teacher, (*b*) the guidance counselor, (*c*) the department head or supervisor, (*d*) the school nurse, (*e*) the parent, (*f*) the principal, or (*g*) a combination of persons?
6. If your students are reading at the secondary school level, what should be your major concern—to increase level or to correct deficits and develop specific skill areas? Explain reasons for your choice.

For readers who are teaching:

1. As you plan each day's lesson, note how you will continue diagnois and

how you will use the information obtained from diagnostic teaching of previous days.
2. Prepare a chart for your class for recording observations. Determine the code you would use.
3. Prepare an informal inventory for your subject area.
4. Formulate questions on the topic you are currently teaching which require competence in a specific skill.
5. Set up your program as a teacher for the complete diagnosis you need for your classroom teaching.
6. Work out an item analysis of the standardized achievement test given in your school. Apply your analysis to a student who shows some deficiencies.
7. Construct a cloze passage from the textbook you are using. Have your students complete it so that you can determine its readability for your students.
8. Construct two cloze passages from material you will assign to the students. Have the students complete one before reading the material. Have them complete the other after the material has been studied and explained in class. Is there any difference in the scores? If so, to what do you attribute this change?

SELECTED REFERENCES

Farr, Roger. *Reading: What Can Be Measured.* Newark, Del.: IRA, 1969.

A thorough discussion of testing in the field of reading.

Strang, Ruth. *Diagnostic-Teaching of Reading.* New York: McGraw-Hill, 1964.

The relation of diagnosis to teaching procedure is thoroughly explained.

CHAPTER 7

Basic Procedures

OVERVIEW

The goal of most classroom teachers is for all students to become independent in the ability to think about and use the understandings of the subject. Some teachers emphasize content, with the hope that as the students absorb information they will become competent in thinking and reasoning. Mastery of information is necessary, but it is not enough for independence. Specific *habits* and *attitudes* also are important, particularly the habit of inquiry. This chapter presents the steps of basic effective procedure for teaching the reading skills and content.

Questions

Consider these questions before you read further:

1. As you analyze your current teaching, what are the steps of your procedures?
2. What is your goal of instruction—to cover subject matter, to teach thinking, to teach a fusion of content and thinking?
3. What aids do you give your students in acquiring the knowledge in your subject area?

Mature students wish to know and strive to find out. *Independence* in the study of a discipline means that students do not need to be told all that they need to know—they inquire and discover. The teacher can encourage the habit of inquiry by providing students with the necessary tools of study.

The *problem-solving procedure* is a means of discovery. Students formulate a question—inquiry—and use the following steps of problem solving to discover the answer:

1. Realize what information is needed.
2. Identify specifically the area or problem.
3. Collect and organize pertinent information.
4. Consider hypotheses and choose the most likely one.
5. Draw conclusions and make generalizations.
6. Implement the conclusion.

Inquiry, discovery, and problem solving have in common the fact that each requires *thinking*—effort, activity, and involvement on the part of the students. Many teachers lament the lack of active involvement which their students display. They seem to read without any activity on their part other than looking over the line of print in a left-to-right pattern. Such students do not have a purpose for reading. Reading of this kind results in little comprehension; there is no inquiry, discovery, or problem solving, and therefore no active thinking. When you note this type of attack on a reading assignment, you will need to implement classroom procedures that require active learning.

Let's go back to Guilford (pages 54–57), who describes five levels of thinking in his category of *operations*. The first is *cognition,* in which the students understand literally what an author is writing. Next is *memory,* which is the ability to retain and recall. Guilford then mentions *divergent thinking,* which involves elaboration upon given information that may go in many directions. Next there is *convergent thinking,* in which the students gather information about a topic from numerous sources in order to arrive at carefully thought out conclusions, the most comprehensive generalizations, and the most appropriate answer in view of the evidence given. Finally there is *evaluation,* which encompasses knowing whether two units are identical or not identical, whether there is a logical consistency in relationships, and whether the information is workable. Evaluative thinking also includes sensitivity to problems and the ability to perceive implications. The type and level of thinking used, Guilford maintains, is determined by two factors. One is the material—whether it stimulates the imagination of the reader, leads toward a specific conclusion, gives alternatives, and calls for checking and listing facts and arguments. The other factor is the creativity of the teacher in using the material in provocative ways, largely through skillful questioning.[1]

PRINCIPLES OF LEARNING APPLIED TO PROCEDURE

Classroom procedure derives from the teacher's educational philosophy as well as the specific goals of instruction and information to be taught. The

1. J. P. Guilford, "Frontiers in Thinking That Teachers Should Know About," *The Reading Teacher* 13, No. 3 (February 1960): 176-82.

teacher whose goals include developing ability to study and learn independently will keep in mind the following principles of learning.

Purpose and Motivation

Students are motivated when they know specifically what they are to find from their reading. This setting of purpose should occur at the introduction of a topic. The purpose should be related to things the students wish to know, to their concerns. Effective procedure involves eliciting these purposes from the students as you preview the material together and review their background, and as the students air their opinions and impressions about the topic.

Background for Understanding New Information

Hanzell sees the task of content teachers as one of "convincing the students that they know more than they think they do about my subject."[2] Help students remember and relate what they know by asking questions and discussing the topic with the students *prior* to reading. If students do not have an adequate background, basic procedure then requires that the teacher provide those concepts and understandings of the topic that help students relate to the material. In this way, they can begin to think about it. Audiovisual materials can be used for this purpose; previewing the material to point out facts, concepts, and organization also can help.

Relevance of Information

The personal satisfaction students get from the material and its relevance to their lives increase interest and motivation. In order to assist students in seeing relevance, the teacher must know their past school records, their reading proficiency, their interests, and their goals. He must know them as individuals. Unless he does, the class is nothing more than a period for the dissemination of information.

Individual Differences of Students

No two people are alike. Many people share similarities of interest, desire, and personality, but each individual is unique. Therefore, for classroom procedure to be effective, it must apply to each individual. This is where classroom procedure often falters. Many teachers give up in frustration and resort to mass instruction, aiming toward the median of the group. Getting to know and planning for each individual in a class is difficult, especially at the secondary school level where you meet a new class group each hour comprising a daily total of approximately 125 students. But there *are* techniques you can use; Chapter 8 discusses individual differences in detail.

---

2. T. Stevenson Hanzell, "Increasing Understanding in Content Reading," *Journal of Reading* 19, No. 4 (January 1976): 309.

Active Learning

Learning in the classroom takes place as a result of the students' own effort. The teacher's procedures and techniques cannot enforce learning; rather, they provide explanations and guidelines. Instruction should enable students to learn by helping them organize information and appreciate its significance in everyday life. The teacher is really a resource person for students.

Practice

Reading is a process and requires practice. As in any other process, such as learning to play a musical instrument, the students' performance depends upon the amount of productive practice they do. For practice, students should be encouraged to do wide supplementary reading, both for research and for recreation. Each classroom should have a library of supplementary books, and assignments should encourage their use. Devote time in class to reading supplementary materials and discussing their contents; the textbook alone often is not enough.

Emotional Attitudes

Emotional attitudes affect understanding in two ways. Consider, for example, the student who has a history of reading deficiency. Such a student is "turned off" by reading; he finds it too much work to engage in voluntarily. His reading does not improve because he does not practice through voluntary reading. In this case a wide range of materials should be available so that the student can read some material with mastery. *Success* is supremely important. Of course, this student also needs instruction in the basic skills pertinent to his need.

The other instance of how emotion affects understanding is the students' feelings toward a topic or an issue. Students may find that the information presented by an author differs widely from their own ideas and beliefs. This can be disturbing, and the students may turn away from the material. The teacher's role in this case is to develop the students' abilities to read for inquiry and to read critically. The problem-solving approach of drawing conclusions from evidence is helpful because students must rely more on rational judgment than on their attitude.

Reading and Language Use

As one of the language arts, reading should be taught not in isolation but as a way language is used. Teaching subject matter effectively depends on the students' facility with language as it is used in all forms of oral communication.

PLANNING THE LESSON

The principles cited above can serve as guidelines for planning instructional procedure. Beyond these guidelines is the specific planning for each lesson, which may encompass one to several class periods. Whatever steps of procedure are followed, the students' strengths and weaknesses in reading will determine the emphases on reading skill instruction and content. These two focuses of teaching are fused largely through adjusting the content instruction to the students' background and proficiencies. For example, if students are weak in noting the main idea, instruction should focus largely on the main ideas of the subject matter and how they are discerned.

As you review, for the purpose of planning instruction, the needs of the students and the requirements of the subject, behavioral objectives will help you define specific goals. *Behavioral objectives* are statements that describe what students should be able to do after completing the instruction pertaining to a body of content. The objective specifies the degree of student achievement expected and in what form and under what conditions students will exhibit this achievement. For example, "Without the use of class notes or other references the students will be able to describe the cycle of the photosynthetic process, showing how each part leads to the next." When considering a specific reading skill, "The student will note the main ideas and details of the material describing the photosynthetic process and record them in the form of an outline." Another example: "Given the formula for the area of a right triangle, $A = \frac{1}{2}ab$, the student will be able to compute the area when a and b are given a quantity." The reading skill objective might read, "Given the formula for the area of a right triangle, $A = \frac{1}{2}ab$, the student will be able to identify each part of the formula, i.e., A is ____, a is ____, and b is ____."

Behavioral objectives for reading instruction in the different content fields are in two domains: the cognitive and the affective. The cognitive domain involves learning and using the knowledge of each subject. Cognitive objectives include the following:

1. Recalling the important ideas, methods, processes, structure, classification and categories.
2. Knowing the vocabulary.
3. Understanding the structure of thought by being able to study, organize, and evaluate it.
4. Communicating by conventional forms of language, both oral and written.
5. Judging facts, opinions, hypotheses, and principles.
6. Using the problem-solving procedure as a pattern of inquiry.
7. Knowing and applying principles and generalizations.

The affective domain involves attitudes, values, and beliefs that determine how students respond to the environment. Interest and attitude toward a topic and the value students may place upon it also are in the affective area.

The Reading Lesson Applied to the Content Fields

Scholars of the reading process agree that reading is a thinking process, and there is a basic plan of classroom procedure for teaching the reading-thinking process. The plan has been developed for teaching the story-type material in basal readers. Though there are minor variations from one basal series to another in the reading-thinking procedure, the fundamental steps remain the same. Students are guided to (*a*) read for specific purposes; (*b*) relate the information to their background of experience and knowledge; and (*c*) make judgments about the significance, accuracy, and pertinence of what they read. Stauffer states that declaring purposes, reasoning, and judging are fundamental to the reading-to-learn process; he also adds a fourth step, which is refining and extending ideas from the reading material.[3]

As the following outline indicates, the reading-thinking process is as applicable to the content areas as it is to the basal readers of the elementary school.

The Basic Plan: Directed Reading-Thinking Applied to Content Fields

I. Preparation for reading
   A. Investigating and expanding the background of student experience.
      1. Finding out what the students know.
      2. Noting misconceptions of the students.
      3. Filling in with information to give the students an adequate background for understanding.
      4. Arousing student interest.
      5. Giving them an awareness of the significance of the information.
   B. Preview the reading material.
      1. Noting the basic structure of the information—the introduction, summary, specific sections.
      2. Discussing the title and subtitles.
      3. Directing attention to the graphic aids: maps, pictures, diagrams, etc.
      4. Noting study aids: summaries, questions, vocabulary lists.
      5. Noting new vocabulary (usually italicized in a textbook).
   C. Introduce the vocabulary pertinent to the fundamental concepts.
      1. Clarifying basically the fundamental conceptual terms, usually one to five in number.
      2. Analyzing the structure of the words, if necessary, to aid word recognition.
      3. Assisting students to bring their experiences to bear on the meanings of words.
      4. Alerting students to the specific meaning as the word is used in the text.
   D. Evolve purposes for reading.
      1. Evolving purposes in terms of the student's own background and

3. Russell G. Stauffer, *Teaching Reading as a Thinking Process* (New York: Harper & Row, 1969), pp. 14–15.

needs, those of the group, and the understandings desired from materials.
2. Helping students to think of purposes as well.

II. Reading the material silently
   A. Noting the students' ability to adjust their reading to the purposes defined and to the material.
   B. Observing students to note specific areas of need.
      1. Vocabulary: recognition of the word, specific meaning as applied to the content.
      2. Comprehension: organization of data, finding answers to purposes, noting relationships within data.

III. Developing comprehension
   A. Discussing answers to purpose questions.
   B. Clarifying and guiding further development of the concepts and vocabulary, introducimg new vocabulary if needed.
   C. Assisting the students in noting organization of information and in recall of pertinent facts.
   D. Noting need for further information from both the text and other source materials.
   E. Redefining purposes; setting new purposes for reading.

IV. Rereading (silent or oral, in part or in entirety)
   A. Clarifying further the essential pertinent information and concepts.
   B. Giving specific skill training in comprehension as indicated by needs of individuals and the group.
      1. Seeing organization of data.
      2. Interpreting data: drawing conclusions, making inferences, making generalizations, seeing interrelationships of data.
      3. Evaluating: making judgments, noting author's intent, seeing the significance of the material, noting the use of language.
      4. Applying information to real-life situations, formulating new ideas, reorganizing old ideas.
      5. Noting use of words: emotive, new meanings, contextual, technical terms, indefinite and general terms.
      6. Setting up areas for further reading and research.

V. Following up the information
   A. Setting up problems requiring further information.
      1. Using problem solving; delineating the problem.
      2. Locating additional information.
      3. Reading to get additional information.
      4. Selecting and organizing pertinent ideas related to problem.
      5. Concluding and generalizing from data.
      6. Preparing the presentation of the report.
   B. Choosing supplementary recreational reading related to topic to develop and extend interests, attitudes, and appreciations.

C. Extending further understandings and clarifying further concepts as necessary.
D. Analyzing the information and helping students to relate it to their own lives.

Students are not merely assigned a specified number of pages to read as the basis of a class recitation. Instead, students are *guided* through the reading material three times for different reasons: to establish background and concepts, to clarify, and to apply the reading skills needed for understanding. The reading-thinking plan goes beyond rote learning and memorization; students seek information, evaluate it, and apply it. Skills should be incorporated into the plan at each stage to give the students the tools they need. A discussion of each step follows to show further how the reading-thinking plan operates.

Preparation for reading, Step I, is probably the most vital step of a reading lesson. Preplanning to relate the information to the students' background and selection of objectives to be accomplished insure reading success. Sometimes this step is considered the same as the assignment, but it is a great deal more than merely telling the students what they are to read for and how.

In the four aspects of this step—establishing background, previewing the material, clarifying basic concepts, and evolving purposes—the teacher must perform a delicate balancing act. He needs to provide knowledge of the topic, but he must also allow students the satisfaction of inquiring and discovering for themselves. The goal should be to provide just enough background and guidance to enable students to continue learning with success and competence.

The students' ability to learn new information is affected by their background of information. Sometimes this has been expressed as "the more students know about a topic, the more they can get from other specific information." Judging the amount of background information that students need is part of *preplanning.*

Experienced teachers know the value of graphic materials, models, diagrams, and various other audiovisual aids. Reading information from sources outside the textbook can be valuable on occasion. Questions to probe the students' knowledge will help them remember relevant information and ideas.

Another means of providing background information is to preview the content material to be studied. Previewing the material is a warm-up for students. They can note the scope and depth of the information and the author's form of organization—(the topics included and their interrelationship). Previewing serves both to build additional prereading background and to alert students to the nature of the information. Through the preview they may note new vocabulary as well as questions posed by the author which can provide purposes for reading. With your help they can learn to restate topical headings in question form as a means of formulating specific questions of purpose.

The teacher can clarify new terms during the preview—although this must be kept to a minimum. The nature of the material will determine the number of new terms or words, but the number clarified at the preview stage should be no more than five. Other words can be clarified in the discussion of the lesson. For example, in reading about ecology, the basic terms might be *ecology, pollution,* and *conservation*. Students should understand these basic words prior to reading. Subsequent terms, such as the various types of land conservation, will be developed later. Two reasons for introducing only a few words at a time are that (*a*) the teacher and students can keep the terms in mind and use them in discussion, perhaps in sentences of original composition, and (*b*) terms that are not basic to understanding the information are left for students to learn by using the context and their knowledge of word and sentence structure.

The fourth aspect of preparation for readiness is evolving purposes for reading. Purposes stimulate both curiosity and thinking; they motivate. Stauffer notes:

> When pupils have become involved in the dynamics of a purpose-setting lesson, the self-commitment on an intellectual as well as an emotional level has tremendous motivating force . . .
>
> The reader, having helped to create the reading climate, will strive to maintain it. Its tempo is geared to the finding of answers and to the proving or disproving of conjectures. He will want to move forward to test his ideas, to seek, to reconstruct, to reflect, and to prove. What is most astonishing about all this is the integrity with which the reader operates. He is out to seek the truth, and this is his dedication.[4]

These four aspects of the readiness step are not handled separately. They are interwoven. As you preview the material with the students, background will be enriched and expanded, new vocabulary will be clarified, and purposes will evolve. How long you spend on this step depends on (*a*) the extent of the students' background (if the background is meager, obviously more time will be needed), (*b*) the length and difficulty of the material, and (*c*) the importance of the information. Some preparation for reading can take only five minutes of class time, whereas other selections may require a class period or more. Your task is to know how much preparation is needed and to provide adequate preparation regardless of the time it takes.

Reading the material silently, Step II of the lesson procedure, provides an opportunity to extend assistance to any student who has a question or who has difficulty in reading the selection. Many secondary teachers claim that they do not have opportunities to give attention to individual students because of the large number of students they meet in class each day. However, when the students read silently in class, you are free to offer help when a student needs it and the material demands it. At this time you can address specific needs which you may have noted from previous class work. Silent reading often is assigned for outside of class, and this is also proper procedure. In such cases the students must be independent in reading—a skill they must acquire. But, of course, no individual help can be given when the assignment is read outside of class. A balance should be struck such that some assignments are read or at least started in class, and others outside.

Developing comprehension, Step III of the lesson, accomplishes the following:

---

4. Stauffer, *Teaching Reading,* p. 25.

1. Purposes are clarified.
2. New vocabulary terms are discussed—especially those the students have not mastered independently and the teacher considers important to understanding the material.
3. Important understandings are developed.
4. The basic structure of the information is noted—the interrelationships of main ideas to details, cause and effect relationships, author's purpose, and so on.
5. Pertinent reading skills are developed and needs of the class and of individuals are noted.

This step corresponds to the traditional *recitation* period in classes of times past, in which the teacher both tested informally and clarified understandings. This step still contains the ingredients of a recitation. However, there is an added dimension: through discussion the students are guided to apply pertinent skills. For each lesson the teacher delineates objectives for specific tasks the students must accomplish.

Rereading, Step IV, is done for clarification. The entire selection or parts only may be reread, and new purposes must be set. Rereading can be done for a written assignment, or it may be done during class discussion to clarify some specific point. It may be silent or oral. The students can use information acquired thus far to extend their understanding of details, relationships, conclusions, nuances, and so on. Rereading also may pinpoint the application of a particular skill taught in Step III. Step IV may be thought of as the "clincher": the student applies both knowledge and skill. Groundwork may also be laid for extended reading and research.

Follow-up, Step V, is designed to increase the students' knowledge and to give them the opportunity to apply their basic knowledge to related problems. In the follow-up the following can be accomplished:

1. Develop and extend interests, attitudes, and appreciations.
2. Develop further the ability to evaluate data in terms of point of view expressed, emotive language, use of facts or opinions, author's qualifications, and the students' own views and prejudices.
3. Conduct research on a problem related to the content.

In this step, students can engage in various projects related to the problem that might involve creative writing (plays, essays, and so on) and various art activities (murals, models, pictures, and so on). In addition to allowing students to apply skills and information, the follow-up is also another prime opportunity for you to offer individual assistance.

No specific time limit can be placed on the directed lesson procedure. As we have noted, the time spent on a specific selection depends upon the students' background, the length and difficulty of the selection, and the selection's importance to the total curriculum. A lesson may take only a class period or it may take more than a week. For material that is not fundamental to the understanding of the subject and is used only for enrichment, Steps IV and V may be deleted. (It is not always necessary to reread or to follow up with various activities.) Rereading at times may be incorporated into Step III, *Developing Comprehension.*

The class procedure is *teacher-directed.* You guide, instruct, and develop the students' ability to think about the material. The procedure is similar to the SQ3R study formula, which students use on their own when studying an assignment. Alert students to this similarity and to the lesson procedure's steps so that they can begin to realize the fundamental steps of study procedure in general. Table 7.1 displays the similarities of the SQ3R and the directed lesson.

TABLE 7.1 Comparison of Directed Lesson and SQ3R Formula

Directed Lesson	*SQ3R Study Formula*
Preparation for reading Preview	Survey
Establish purpose	Question
Read	Read
Develop comprehension	Recite
Reread	Review
Follow-up	

The steps of the basic directed reading lesson can be adapted easily to any content area. Subjects that mostly involve reading assignments follow in the "pure" form. But the procedure can be followed even with subjects in which there is a "hands on" approach, such as industrial arts (shop) courses, home economics, and many of the fine arts courses (printing, pottery, photography, chorus, and so on). Teachers of different subject areas can refer to the study formulas on pages 101–102 as a guide for adapting the basic procedure. Some of these formulas are designed for a specified subject.

Let's look at some short illustrations of lesson procedure in social studies, science, mathematics and home economics.

Social Studies

The lesson is based on the first part of a chapter about the origin of cities. The short reading selection (about 1½ pages) is a conversation with Socrates in Plato's *Republic.*

I. Preparation for reading
   A. Find out what the students know, stimulate their thought and relate to their background by asking such questions as:
      What are cities?
      Why do you suppose cities develop in certain places?
      What do you think caused ______ (a city close to you or in which you live) to develop?
   B. Quickly preview the chapter, noting the question at the beginning of the chapter, "How did cities start and grow?" (You may have partially answered this question already.) Also look at the topical headings, maps, pictures and various questions posed by the author(s).
   C. Clarify concepts (vocabulary) for the short reading selection. You have already established the meaning of the word *cities.* Conjecture

with the students about the meaning of *origin.* Note that the selection they will read features Socrates. Establish who he was (the text notes that he was a fourth century Greek philosopher). Establish the time period (possibly by a time line drawn on the blackboard), where Greece is located, and what a philosopher does. Get as much information from the class as possible.

D. Establish purpose by eliciting it from the students—that is, ask, "What do you think Socrates will talk about?" Note that they should determine the reasons Socrates gives for the establishment and growth of cities.

II. Silent reading of the selection

III. Comprehension

Begin your discussion with the purpose question, which is literal comprehension (cognitive knowledge). List on the blackboard all of the reasons Socrates gives. (The taxonomies and levels of thinking discussed in Chapter 3 may be helpful in planning the types of thinking you wish to develop.) How important this topic is to your subject will determine how deeply you develop it. You may also wish to defer the questions that parallel the taxonomies until you have completed more of the chapter than just this introductory part. If you do wish to develop this section, you might ask and discuss such questions as:

Translation (memory)—In one sentence list all the reasons Socrates cites.

Interpretation (convergent thinking)—Of all the reasons Socrates cites, which is the most fundamental one?

Application (divergent thinking)—How does this basic need of people apply to ________ (city where student lives)?

Analysis (divergent thinking)—How do all of the other reasons Socrates cites apply to ________?

Synthesis (convergent thinking)—If you were to establish a city, what would you have to consider to insure its success?

Evaluation—In what ways do you think cities are needed? Should there be limitation to city growth today?

If students are unable to answer any of the questions, you will need to teach techniques of reading that would help them. This represents a fusion of content with reading; you will teach technique while at the same time insuring that your students master the content. For example, if the students are unable to list the reasons for cities as noted by Socrates, go back to the selection and pace the students through it, noting each major reason and how one depends upon and leads to the others. Perhaps a flow chart could be diagrammed on the blackboard. It is best not to do this by lecturing but rather by posing specific questions, such as: "What is the first reason Socrates mentions in the first paragraph?" "How does this major reason lead to the next given in the second paragraph?"

IV. Rereading

For this short selection, rereading would probably be in the form of reading orally to prove or interpret points that answer the purpose question for reading. Rereading would be done in Step III, *Comprehension.*

V. Follow-up

This step probably should be deferred until the entire chapter has been read and discussed. (The chapter covers the reasons for the development of cities in early times and the history of urbanization, especially during the Industrial Revolution.)

Science

The reading selection is about animal behavior, covering three major headings: kinds of behavior, inborn behavior and acquired behavior, and a section of seven pages in which there are many illustrations. The directed reading lesson would parallel that of social studies with one major exception—activities (experiments) are suggested.

Of course there are three major terms to develop before the students read: *behavior, inborn,* and *acquired.* The activities are placed in the plan where they best suit your purposes. They could fit into three possible places in the procedure. One is the *preparation* step; you would demonstrate the activity in order to motivate the students or establish basic background for reading. The second place is the *rereading* step; the students would have to reread sections in order to draw conclusions about and implications from the activity. The third is the *follow-up;* at this stage, the activity is an application and enrichment of the topic.

If you follow the PQRST formula (page 101), the *summarize* step is equivalent to the *Comprehension* step of a directed lesson, and the *test* step is equivalent to *rereading*. Questions may parallel the taxonomies and levels of thinking.

Mathematics

Two adaptations usually are required in this field—one in reading the steps of a process, and the other in reading and computing verbal problems.

You may wish to lead the students through the study formula, PQ4R (page 102). An example of its application:

1. Skip Johnson delivers evening papers to 50 customers, 6 times a week.
   a. He pays 6½ cents per paper. Find his weekly cost of the papers.
   b. He collects 60 cents per week from each customer. Find the amount he collects weekly and then find his weekly profit.

First part

Preview

a. First reading of problem–visualize–restate (discuss) situation:
   Skip Johnson has a paper route with 50 customers to whom he delivers papers 6 days each week. He pays 6½ cents per paper.
b. List—clarify unknown words and phrases:
   1. 6 *times* a week
   2. *per* paper
   3. *weekly* cost of the papers

Question

a. Second reading
b. Direct question of problem:
"What is his weekly cost of the papers?"

Read

a. Third reading
b. List all word facts of problems in logical order:
    1. 50 customers
    2. 6 times a week
    3. pays 6½ cents per paper

Reflect

a. Fourth reading
b. What is the unknown quantity: the total weekly cost of the papers.
    1. Need to know total number of papers delivered per week and then the total cost
    2. Change 6½ cents to a decimal: .065

Rewrite (Before student works problem, have him estimate cost)

a. Rewrite numerically
50 × 6 × \$.065 =
50 × 6 = 300
300 × \$.065 = \$19.50

Review

a. Does answer come close to estimate?
b. Substitute answer in equation:
50 × 6 × \$.065 = \$19.50

Second Part

Preview

a. First reading:
Since Skip collects \$.60 per week from each customer, find the amount he collects each week. What profit does he make?

Question

a. Second reading
b. Questions:
How much does he collect altogether?
What is his profit?

Read

a. Third reading
b. Facts:
Collects 60¢ each week from each customer

Reflect

a. Fourth reading
b. What are the unknown quantities?

1. The total amount collected (must multiply $.60 by 50)
2. Profit (must subtract cost from total amount collected)

Rewrite

a. Rewrite numerically, estimate answers:
   1. 50 × $.60 = $30.00
   2. $30.00 − $19.50 = $10.50

Review

a. Does answer come close to estimate?

Home Economics

Reading in home economics may be of three types. If the material is about the problems of family living, it would be similar to social studies, and the lesson procedure would be like that of social studies. If the material is about colors and lines and how they can be used in clothing, you could have activities in which students experiment with colors and lines for themselves. Then your lesson procedure is like that of science in which experiments are performed. If the reading selection is a set of directions for making a vest or following a recipe, then your procedure is the same as that for following directions.

Preparation

Read the directions completely for an overview. Review in basic steps what is to be done. Clarify concepts (vocabulary).

Silent reading

Comprehension

Rereading

Each step is read. The execution of each step is equivalent to Step III, *Comprehension*. Checking the step would be similar to rereading. Then these three steps (read, do, check) are followed for each step of the directions.

Follow-up

The directions are read in their entirety as a final check as well as to confirm the result.

Study Guides

Tutolo points out that:

> Students' poor comprehension of expository texts is a problem that concerns most content teachers. A contributing factor is the extensive concept load found in most content area texts. The reader simply does not know what ideas are important and what topics deserve concentrated study.

> The teacher can improve student learning by designing study guides which lead the learner to the important concepts explained in the textbook.[5]

The study guide helps students structure the information, proceed with study, and know what is important and what is not. Further, it is a way to monitor students through the steps of a study formula. As we have noted before, students need much practice in study procedure before they can apply it automatically, eventually becoming independent in studying.

Study guides can be as detailed as you think necessary for your students. A study guide may give the following types of direction:

Preparation for reading

Preview—List specific features for the student to note in the text.

Title—What is it about?

Topical headings—Change these to questions.

Specific maps, pictures, diagrams, charts, etc.—Ask a question about each.

New vocabulary—How does the text define each term?

Aids at the end of a chapter, such as summary—What are the main points? *Vocabulary*—Can the words be categorized or grouped? *Questions*—Can you find answers to these in the reading selection?

Silent reading—Give an overall question to keep in mind or direct the students to write their own.

Comprehension—List questions which would be grouped according to levels (literal, interpretive, and so on). You may also give direction on how to proceed in answering each type or level.

Rereading—The student may be guided to the main understandings. These could be listed and the students directed to write a summary, list the implications of each understanding, restate the understandings, or put them into an outline or logical sequence.

Follow-up—List possible research topics from which each student would choose one, or list practical applications and ask the students to tell how the information would be applied in each case, or list related readings and require students to read them and report on them in some manner. The possibilities are endless.

Study guides may take time to formulate. However, a given textbook is used for several years in most schools. Once the study guide is made, it can be used again with only slight alterations as needed for a specific class.

The Unit Plan

The unit procedure, which usually encompasses a long period of time—two to six weeks—also follows the basic structure we have been describing. The procedure has the following steps, shown with the corresponding steps of the reading-thinking plan:

---

5. Daniel J. Tutolo, "The Study Guide—Types, Purpose and Value," *Journal of Reading* 20, No. 7 (March 1977): 503.

1. Introducing the unit (Preparation for reading)
2. Developing the unit (Read)
3. Student-teacher planning for research (Developing comprehension)
4. Conducting research (Rereading)
5. Culminating research (Follow-up)

The introduction of the unit includes evolving the unit problem with the students, establishing the scope of the problem, surveying the areas to be included, and filling in needed background. Developing the unit is the investigation into the basic subject matter pertinent to the unit.

Student-teacher planning for research results in research projects developed from the basic subject matter. The information is studied and discussed leading toward the research problems. This is similar to developing comprehension of a separate selection. Then, conducting research includes much the same pattern as the rereading which is done for separate purposes, just as the research is done around a specific problem. Finally, culminating the unit—presenting the research—is equivalent to the follow-up step of a lesson procedure.

A suggested science unit of approximately one week follows:

UNIT IV. How Does Weather Affect Your Everyday Living?

Problem

What are the physical forces that produce the climate of a place?

What are some of the elements of climate?

Aims (These can also be stated in the form of behavioral objectives)

To show students that the same physical forces that control the weather produce the climate of that place.

To increase awareness of the great variety of climates on the earth.

To assist students in determining how climates modify the activities of people living in them.

Method

Discussion-demonstration.

Procedure

I. Readiness
   A. Review
      1. Types of climates discussed in previous lesson.
      2. Demostrations on condensation and evaporation (redo experiment if necessary).
   B. Source materials
      1. Read short stories or selections from Walt Disney's work pertaining to weather.
      2. Use films (if available) depicting occupations, recreation, houses, and clothing of people in various geographical regions. Discuss.
   C. Questions
      1. What type of climate do we live in?

2. Why do you think we have the three types of climate? Make a list of factors that cause climates to vary from one another. (Record list on board.)

II. Concept development—Understandings
   A. The normal run of weather conditions over a long period of time denotes climate.
   B. Physical forces that influence weather produce the climate of an area.
   C. The heat of the earth comes from the sun.
   D. Land and water absorb this heat.
   E. Weather and climate depend on the condition of the air.
   F. Living things are prepared to meet climatic conditions.

III. Vocabulary
   Evaporation
      relative humidity—moisture
      water vapor
      saturated
   Condensation
      dew
      fog
      frost
   Mountains
      altitude
   Wind
      adaptation

IV. Establishing purposes for reading (Solicit questions from students if possible.)
   A. What happens when warm moisture-filled air comes into contact with cool air?
   B. Why is the air cooler on a mountain than on a flat plain or valley?
   C. How does the moisture get into the air?
   D. How does the air lose its moisture?
   E. Skim page ____ to find in what region most people live. Why?

V. Silent reading (reading to find answers to specific questions in Part IV)

VI. Oral discussion (discussion of purpose questions)

VII. Rereading (silent or oral; for clarification or critical examination of questions and discussion)

VIII. Developing deeper comprehension—*Demonstration*
   Demonstration I-Condensation
   Problem: What causes water to change?

Materials: One jar and cover (top); water

Procedure: Pour a small amount of water, about one-fourth inch deep, into the jar. Place cover on jar. Set the jar in the sunshine. Let stand for one-half hour or more.

Results: A misty film inside, on the side of the jar. There are several large drops of water hanging down from the cover. What caused the misty film and the water drops to form on the surface?

Demonstration II

Problem: What happens when warm air comes into sudden contact with cool air?

Materials: clean dry glass; ice; water; colored ink

Procedure: Fill a clean dry glass with ice water and add a few drops of colored ink. Wait for several minutes after filling the glass with ice and water; examine the outside of the glass.

Results: The outside of the glass is not dry. Why? When air is cooled, does it hold more or less moisture?

Repeat same experiment on humid days and on dry days. What are your results? Does the moisture in the air differ on different days?

Demonstration III—Relative Humidity

Problem: Does temperature affect humidity?

Materials: Sponge; water; pan

Procedure: Place a dry sponge (a sponge that has been heated in the oven for some time so that it will have no dampness) in a pan of water. Wet the sponge only enough to hold the water without dripping.

Results: The soaked sponge has 100% (or all) the water it will hold. What happens if more water is added to the top of the sponge? Help the students to draw the following conclusion: At any given temperature the air will hold a certain amount of water and no more, just as a sponge reaches a point at which it will hold no more water without dripping.

IX. Related activities

A. Plan a bulletin board of science pictures and reports on weather and climate.

B. Help students to plan a science quiz by using various concepts and vocabulary words.

C. Encourage students to find out the average climatic conditions of their community and compare it with nearby communities.

X. Assignment

A. Have students pass in a list (with illustrations) of ways in which water gets into the air.

B. Some students might want to do other demonstrations showing the processes of condensation and evaporation (water coming out of the air and water going into the air).

C. With each experiment the teacher should write on the board, in familiar terms, step-by-step observations and results.

GENERAL GUIDELINES TO PROCEDURES

This chapter describes the basic steps of effective classroom procedure as well as some of the many adaptations. As important as the basic procedures themselves are the habits and attitudes we have. George Polya, a mathematician who says that mathematics is the "art of plausible reasoning" (a delightful phrase), notes ten commandments for teachers:

1. *Be interested in your subject.* Teachers must be enthusiastic about what they are teaching. High school students often remark that nothing is worse than a teacher who covers the subject in a diffident manner.
2. *Know your subject.* A teacher must read the material assigned to the students, even though he does not need it for background, in order to know the structure of the information and to pose appropriate questions.
3. *Know about the ways of learning.* Active learning, Polya notes, involves discovery. Help students to do this by using the Socratic method of questioning—ask the question and get the students to evolve the information and ideas.
4. *Try to read the faces of your students.* Try to see their expectations and difficulties; put yourself in their place. If the students do not know a technique of reading or study that they should know, teach it!
5. *Give them not only information, but know-how—the habit of methodical work.*
6. *Let them learn by guessing—reasonable guessing.* Polya states that reasonable guessing is based on observation, conjecture, judicious use of evidence, and analogy. Plausible reasoning is an important part of the scientific method.
7. *Let them learn by proving—demonstrative reasoning.* We can easily see the application of this to subjects such as math and science through experiments, and to industrial arts through projects. In social studies, demonstrative reasoning takes the form of the problem-solving approach.
8. *Help the students to see the application of language to the study of all subjects.* The chart of study formulas (pages 101–102) attempts to establish a general pattern.
9. *Do not give away your whole secret at once.* Let the students find out by themselves as much as is feasible. This can be accomplished gradually in two ways: by questioning to help students evolve their thoughts and by guiding them toward independence in study.
10. *Suggest information rather than imposing it.* Avoid saying, "You're wrong"; such a statement often turns off students. Rather, say, "That's an interesting point, but have you considered __________? Would that make a difference?" Or, "That's a good general statement; now can you be more specific—go a step further?" Help the students by asking a leading question that invites them to continue a thought or jogs their memory.[6]

---

6. George Polya, *Mathematical Discovery,* Vol. 2 (John Wiley & Sons, 1968), pp. 112-120.

SUMMARY

The teacher's primary goal in the classroom is to develop the students' ability to think. Acquisition of information and understandings and growth in the use of reading study skills are for the purpose of increasing the ability to think. Independence in learning is consonant with the broad aim of education—to have students become constructive members of society at all levels.

QUESTIONS AND PROBLEMS FOR YOUR OWN CLASSROOM

For readers who are training to be teachers:

1. Prepare cognitive and affective objectives for a specific lesson. Translate these into student purposes.
2. Select a topic and note the background the students must have in order to understand the factual data.
3. Select a topic and note the concepts the students must acquire. Determine your role as the teacher in helping the students.
4. Determine the amount and type of practice necessary for competence after instruction in a skill.
5. List ways you might help students achieve success in your classroom.
6. Plan a complete lesson using as your guide the five basic steps of the reading-thinking plan. Show how you would combine instruction in both skill and content.

For readers who are teaching:

1. Review your subject syllabus and your basic classroom procedures and determine ways to have the students become actively involved in their learning.
2. Plan lesson procedures that incorporate the amount and nature of background information your students will need. Determine when and how you will present this information to them.
3. Go through the reading assignment for your students and note the concepts students should already know and need for comprehension and the new concepts.
4. For each unit of study, compile a listing of supplementary reading.
5. Plan lesson procedure to show how and when you would give instruction and then practice in a reading skill. Fuse the instruction in subject matter and skill.
6. Plan a unit of study and show:
   a. What skills you should teach and when they should be taught.
   b. How you would provide for the steps of research reading.
   c. The supplementary materials you would find effective.
   d. The application of the principles of learning.

SELECTED REFERENCES

Polya, George. *Mathematical Discovery,* Vol. 2. New York: John Wiley & Sons, 1968.
Excellent guidelines for effective teaching procedure in all subjects.

Stauffer, Russell G. *Directing Reading Maturity As a Cognitive Process.* New York: Harper & Row, 1969.
Detailed analysis of classroom reading procedure.

CHAPTER 8

Individualizing Instruction

OVERVIEW

In each class, a teacher has students who have much in common but nevertheless are unique individuals. How does this situation influence class procedures for individualizing instruction? This question prompts a closer look at the teacher's role in education and understanding of the students.

Society expects teachers to impart a specific body of information and to develop in students a certain level of competence. Teachers also know that adolescents as a group share certain interests, problems, and attitudes. Yet within each class there are as many individuals as there are students. Because they differ in prior experiences and capacities, they bring to the classroom a range of background and different levels of competence in reading, writing, and study. Likewise, there are variations of interests, aptitudes, and personalities. Subject matter must be accommodated to the characteristics of each student, but how is this done? There are no foolproof methods; however, this chapter offers guidelines and suggestions that can be adapted to each class.

Questions

Consider these questions before you read further:

1. How much individualizing of instruction do you accomplish in your classes?
2. As you individualize, what do you hope to achieve with each student?

THE TEACHER'S DILEMMA

Every high school teacher faces a range of capabilities in each class. If the class is a heterogeneous group, the range of reading level may span eight or more years. If it is a homogeneous class, the span of reading level may be reduced two or three years, but a range of several years is not uncommon. The range of reading level is influenced by the teacher's effectiveness. Very competent students who can read material considered difficult for the enrolled grade will develop their reading skills even more under effective teaching. Students who are unable to read the material required by the enrolled grade and who may have less than average ability will fall further and further behind because they cannot achieve one year's progress in one year. Only as teachers adjust their teaching to the average group in the class does the range appear to narrow.

Education in a democracy is for all students, because as adults they will be expected to contribute to society as responsible citizens. Education for all students implies mass education—mastering the same level and body of content. However, another tenet of democracy is that each individual is unique. Although very few teachers deny the uniqueness of their students, and very few maintain that mass teaching is appropriate, many teachers do not individualize as much as they would like. A number of reasons may be given. One is the large number of students they meet each day in their classes (around 125 individuals). Another reason is the demands of a full and growing curriculum. Faced with these two conditions, teachers sometimes take the position that students should already be competent in reading and study skills when they come to high school, thereby enabling the curriculum to be fully implemented. Teachers, then, find themselves in a dilemma: they often subscribe to the ideal of individualized teaching, but they face certain limitations in the real day-to-day experience of teaching.

CONSIDERATIONS FOR INDIVIDUALIZING INSTRUCTION

1. The form of individualization in the classroom is determined by the goals to be accomplished. Whatever type of classroom organization you employ—from whole-class instruction to one-to-one individualization—it should be chosen because it will enable you to accomplish specific goals with the students. For example, if a small group of students is having difficulty mastering the basic vocabulary of the subject, these students may be organized temporarily into a group that will receive additional instruction in learning the vocabulary. Student needs change, and the teacher's own purposes may change in the course of a year's instruction. Consequently, there will be times when you are with the total class and times when you are with specific groups or individuals.
2. You need to know the students' strengths as well as their weaknesses, their best modality of learning, their interests, and specific pertinent information about each of them.
3. Diagnosis is essential for individualizing because it reveals the

specific needs of individual students. Indeed, the degree to which you individualize is determined by the extent of daily diagnosis—noting the student's performance in each class.

4. No one method of individualization is adequate. Ideally you should use various methods to accomplish the purposes of instruction in accordance with the needs of the student. For example, some students may be able to undertake individual study, while another group may need intensive work in a specific skill of reading. Or one student may respond well to programmed materials while another does best through the use of tapes and films.
5. Individualization requires self-direction and independence, since the teacher cannot be with all groups and individuals at the same time. Some teachers hesitate to allow students to exercise self-direction for fear of losing discipline and direction of the class. Student self-direction and independence is not always easy to achieve, especially if the students have not had the opportunity to exercise it. It can, however, be developed. First you must believe that self-direction is a valid goal of education. Second, you must have high expectations for the students' ability to mature into self-directing individuals. Third, you must look upon your students as partners in the learning process. Students should (*a*) know their strengths and weaknesses in the reading skills; (*b*) understand the relationship of the reading skills to the content; and (*c*) understand the goals, purposes, and relevance of your classroom procedures and the content of what they are studying. You might even conjecture with your students on how to accomplish certain goals. They probably will suggest some form of individualization, and teacher and students can plan together for success.
6. Individualization requires planning. When you plan with the students, you still must know what needs to be done so that as you incorporate student suggestions you are able to hold to your purpose. Cooperative planning fosters student self-direction and independence of study.

FORMS OF INDIVIDUALIZATION

Individualization can take many forms in a classroom. The combination of methods you choose will be determined in part by the physical conditions of instruction, such as materials available, furniture arrangement, and class size. Other factors are your philosophy and purposes. Foremost are the students' needs and characteristics and the mode of instruction that will be best for them.

Flexibility in form of individualization is often considered desirable. Consequently, you may become involved with techniques of differentiating assignments and directing various types of groups. Materials organized to encourage self-direction and self-help include printed learning programs as well as instructional media such as TV, audio tapes, films, teaching machines, and learning laboratories. Further, two or more teachers may incorporate individualization into their procedures by working together as a team. The truly skillful teacher uses whatever form of individualization seems appropriate to the purposes of the instruction and the characteristics and needs of the students.

Grouping

Students should be grouped only if such a form of classroom organization best achieves the desired educational objectives. At times, the class may require no subdivision into groupings. The whole class can participate in such activities as hearing and reading a literary selection, viewing a film, learning a basic concept, and discussing information. However, if you do decide to use grouping as a means of individualization, different purposes will dictate the types of grouping. For example, if you wish to use materials on different levels of difficulty, grouping will be on the basis of reading competence; each group will read material appropriate to the particular reading level of the group. Or, if you note specific needs of pupils either by observation in class or by more formal diagnosis, groups may be organized to give students help and practice in specific skills.

If you want the students to work together on research problems, the group will have as its purpose the investigation of the problem, probably culminating with a report. You may assign topics or allow students to choose the research group. Interest groups might be organized for research. For instance, in a unit on ecology a group of several students may wish to investigate the ecology of the sea. This would be a grouping around an interest as well as a grouping for the purposes of research.

Sometimes you may designate certain students to work together for the purpose of having their traits and abilities supplement each other. Guidance grouping takes place when you have a withdrawn student or an isolate in the class work with students who are outgoing, perhaps the popular leaders. Another type of grouping is called paired grouping, duos, or trios in which one student helps another in mastering a specific skill. The goal of pairing is for the helpers to benefit as well; explaining a skill or process to another helps students achieve complete mastery or get experience in extending themselves to less able students.

Finally, grouping can be completely individual, such as in independent study. Various self-help materials, tapes, and programmed materials encourage the student to develop at his own pace.

In summary, groupings may range from the total class as a unit to individual assignment. Groups can be organized for level, need, research, interest, and specific pairings of students. Bear in mind that groupings have their pros and cons, particularly because students are sensitive to being grouped on the basis of competence. One way to blunt any stigma which students may attach to a particular grouping is to regroup frequently for many different purposes. Table 8.1 displays several types of groupings and the benefits and problems of each type.

TABLE 8.1 Forms of Grouping

Group	*Purpose*	*Advantages*	*Disadvantages*
Reading Level	Study of content in books of differing levels so that each student can succeed.	Materials suited to students' instructional level. Students can acquire skills at level of competence.	Students may feel stigmatized if in low group.
Need	Follow-up to give specific instruction for an observed skill deficiency.	Adds to pertinence of instruction to fit student needs.	
Research	Investigation into aspects of subject to supplement basic textbook materials.	Gives practice and application in reading-study skills. Leads to independence of study.	
Interest	Expand student interest through opportunity to investigate additional information.	Gives practice and application in skills. Motivates by giving opportunity to develop own interest.	If used at all times may impede balanced acquaintance with a subject.
Social	Allow students to work on specific topics with peers of their choice.	Motivates the students.	May not give students opportunity to work with wide number of their peers.
Guidance	Allow disparate students to work together in order to foster greater social development and tolerance.	Brings about opportunity for experience in working with students of dissimilar interests, ability, and competence.	Depending upon student understanding such grouping may prove to be negative in results.
Duo or Triplet	Two or three students work on a problem to the mutual advantage of each.	Gives special help to student.	Student can be exploited if expected to "sub" for the teacher.
Tutorial	Student who needs intensive help because of lack of competence or a special skill need.	Gives intensive help to student.	Tremendously time-consuming if used constantly (as often is required).

Planning for Groups with Students

The success of grouping within a class depends in large measure on the planning you do with the students. The planning has two aspects. One is your own plan, geared to what you wish to teach and the needs of the students, individually and collectively. The other is the planning you do with the students so that they understand why the procedure is chosen and how it must be implemented. Any grouping requires students to work constructively without your direct supervision. For this to occur, students must understand what the objectives are and how they are to be accomplished.

When students are set into groups without adequate discussion of the purposes and techniques of operation, a chaotic situation can result. Some teachers do not group for this reason—they fear losing control. One teacher announced in the teacher's room before class, "I decided on the way to school today to group my class." After the period, she came out of her room and said with exasperation, "Well, that's that! It was a madhouse. I know now that grouping doesn't work. It's just another one of those new ideas in education!" What this teacher failed to do was to plan adequately so that both she and her students would have a clear idea of what to accomplish. Planning with the students gets them to work *with* you rather than merely *for* you. Though this may be difficult, the students' increased motivation and self-reliance are satisfying results.

Take the time to let the students understand the reasons for classroom procedure. In doing so you are not abdicating authority; rather, you and the students are working together. Specifically, you need to plan with the students the following:

1. the goals of the class—understandings and skill needs as shown by informal diagnostic measures
2. the ways the goals can be accomplished—types of groups, materials available
3. the responsibilities of everyone involved to implement the procedures successfully
4. evaluation of the procedure for further improvements.

As noted in Chapter 6, on diagnosis, the students can plan with the teacher with maturity if they know specific strengths and weaknesses. For example, one seventh grade teacher spent the first two weeks at the beginning of the school year diagnosing reading levels and skill needs in English. Each day she conducted a reading, vocabulary, or syntax exercise. She told the students the approximate level of the material, which varied (sixth grade level, eighth grade level, and so on). She also identified the skill she was diagnosing, such as main idea, organization, connotative use of words, and so on. For two weeks the teacher and the students kept a record of the students' competence at each level and skill. Finally she announced what had become obvious to all the students: some were stronger than others in certain skills and some could read difficult materials with more success than others. The teacher said she wished to group them at specific levels in order to fit classroom instruction to their needs. She asked the students to place themselves at the appropriate level within the framework she outlined. In this class of thirty-five students, all except two placed themselves exactly where she would have; the other two placed themselves higher. After two days, one requested more appropriate placement, and the other was able by intensive effort to remain in the group he had chosen. Though this was a reading level grouping, the teacher did not feel the students were sensitive about being grouped by competence. They had chosen the groupings themselves through informal but objective means.

A teacher of eleventh grade English tried three reading levels in her class. She planned meticulously but did not inform the students except to say one day, "Class, we have three literature anthologies, each at a different level. Therefore, I am going to place you in groups." At this point, one student asked, "Just why are you doing this? Do you think some of us are dumber than the others?" The teacher realized her oversight and cancelled her plan for the day. For the next three days she explained her plan and also conducted informal objective tests of skill and reading competence. Reading and skill levels were noted as well as expectations for the eleventh grade. The students became aware objectively of their reading status. When the teacher went back to grouping by reading levels, the class worked with her. They understood what was being done and why.

In both illustrations, the often-maligned grouping by reading level was successful, with little or no feeling of stigma among students in the lower groups. Neither their peers nor their teacher held such students in low esteem. They may have preferred to be in a grade-level group, but they also saw the wisdom of the plan. Both teachers showed sensitivity to the students' feelings, presenting facts in a nondemeaning manner.

With appropriate materials available, reading level groups can be organized in all content areas. If multilevel material is not available, however, some degree of grouping can be accomplished by using the regular text. Readers who find the textbook too hard can be helped by reading and discussing small sections of materials at one time, making full use of the graphic aids, learning the important vocabulary, and using supplementary materials such as models, records, tapes, films, and pictures. Better readers can take on larger assignments, giving more attention to the subtleties of the language. Students in reading level groups can be regrouped by need, bringing together those who need help in a particular skill (such as seeing the text's organization). If students are doing research, those having difficulty with taking notes could be instructed in this while the others continue with their research. Interest, social, and guidance groups can all be used when students work on research projects. In such groups, level of competence is not a criterion; the poorest and the best readers may be in the same group. Student pairing or individual tutorial assistance by the teacher can be accomplished as the other students are working.

Let's look in on a teacher of ninth grade social studies (American History) and see how she incorporated various plans of classroom management:

Mrs. F's class was grouped heterogeneously, with a range in reading level of about ten years. Students were reading from the fourth grade level up into the college level. She had one basic textbook. However, knowing the range of the class, she established a classroom library of basic references, trade books, and other textbooks of varying levels. These books were collected from many sources: loans from the school library, the public library, her own collection developed over the years, selections some of her students brought in, and new materials she obtained with monies from the PTA and the school contingency fund. She constantly added to her collection whenever she had the means to do so.

At the beginning of the year Mrs. F had assessed her students' strengths and weaknesses by an informal reading inventory. The purpose of this assessment was to determine just how well each student could use the assigned text; she already knew it was too difficult for many and too easy for others.

An important feature of Mrs. F's planning is that the students were informed of her procedures and of how they would work together with her. She solicited ideas from the students and, in a sense, created a consensus on how to proceed. Through questionnaires and discussions, the teacher and students jointly evaluated the procedures and made changes. There were two excellent results from this approach. Mrs. F gained the cooperation of the students—they did not "turn off," because she approached them as thinking individuals and respected their views. And as the school year developed, the students' ability to work independently soared. By April the class was fully independent; they knew how to proceed in both study and interaction. In one instance, Mrs. F was called for a conference that extended into the class period. She returned to the class the last five minutes of the period, and she found the students in their research groups working as efficiently as if she had been there the entire time.

After Mrs. F had established a classroom library, assessed her students, and made them partners in the process, she began to teach a unit making use of the wide range of competence in this class. She and the students decided first to read the entire unit in the single textbook and then to tackle research projects. The students felt that they needed some background in the content in order to choose wisely the research projects; also, Mrs. F would be able to teach basic comprehension and study skills to insure greater competence for the research.

With such a wide range of competence and a single text, how to manage? Mrs. F figured out a possible solution, but she chose to discuss the situation with the students. From the assessment they knew their strengths and weaknesses and approximate levels; their decision was to work in reading level groups. (With only one textbook?) Those students who had low reading levels would use the classroom library, because Mrs. F had some easy materials in the library. Mrs. F was to give intensive instruction to these students in how to preview the material and use graphic aids effectively. The superior readers also would use the classroom library for materials to supplement the basic text. In this way reading level groups were set up, ranging in size from two to ten students.

Though the students worked in reading level groups, Mrs. F periodically brought the class together to discuss essential understandings of the content and to give instruction in techniques of textbook reading (vocabulary, comprehension and study). Because of the grouping, all of the students could contribute.

Upon completion of the basic material, the students were ready to choose their research topics. Mrs. F allowed each student to choose a research problem. To insure the success of this phase of the unit, Mrs. F spent considerable time on the dynamics of group work. She explained to the students the roles of various members of the group, such as chairperson, recorder (secretary), and process observer. (The process observer was a participating member who took note of the interaction and participation of the group members. At the end of each group session, the observer informed the chairperson so that plans could be made to encourage equal participation by each member during the next group session.)

To further insure success in the research group, Mrs. F set up a definite structure for the students. It was stipulated that five minutes before the end of the class period, the group was to plan what they would do in their next group session and what the group members were to do to prepare for it. This practice helped to reduce floundering at the beginning of a group session. Also, each day the recorder gave Mrs. F a record noting how far the group planned to get in the next session. In this way she was able to monitor the progress of each group and to troubleshoot as needed.

As the students started on their group topics, Mrs. F realized that they needed to learn research techniques. She chose a class research problem; for which the entire class would go through each step of research. Then the groups were to follow this procedure in their group projects. If some groups had difficulty, Mrs. F worked with them to reteach; if more than one group seemed to be floundering, she organized a group of need and gave further instruction. Essentially, Mrs. F followed the procedure of *teach, do, reteach as necessary,* using the whole-class research group and the skill or need groups. This procedure was followed through all of the research steps.

When it came time to write the research reports and to present them to the class, there was instruction and discussion with the students as to how this would be done. Thus, the basic techniques for reading were applied to writing, presenting (speaking), and note taking (listening). Mrs. F explained to the students that the research information from the various groups was information that all should know. She pointed out that the subject was vast and that there was not time for all students to read and study all of the topics (problems) in depth. Therefore, each group would present one area in depth.

Mrs. F did not allow students to read their reports aloud, but they could refer to an outline when giving the report to the class. Further, the reports had to be well-organized so that students listening could take notes in outline form. For instance, the student presenting the report might say, "Our topic is ________. We have three major points. The first is ________." To note details, one might say, "And there are two conditions that contributed to ________." The students taking notes had to date the material and keep it in their notebooks.

After the report had been presented to the class, Mrs. F instituted another interesting feature—a *feedback*. The presenter called on a member of the class to recite the points of the presentation. Although this procedure might seem boring, the opposite was true. The students were interested in the feedback because it gave them a chance to check their notes. Also, this procedure served as an evaluation of the presentation. Reteaching was done at this point if necessary.

To further emphasize the importance of the research information for all students, Mrs. F allowed each group to submit two or three questions to her for inclusion on the unit test. When the unit was completed, Mrs. F administered a simple questionnaire which asked students to evaluate the procedures followed, and she discussed these results with the class.

You may ask, "How in the world did Mrs. F complete the entire course of study for the year if she did all of this?" At first, of course, the coverage of subject matter was slowed down. In fact, by Thanksgiving her colleagues were into the Constitutional period and she was still on colonization! However, her principal was intrigued and urged her to continue. By the end of the year, however, Mrs. F had completed the entire year's curriculum, whereas other classes did not. The apparent reason for this was that as the students became more skilled in using their textbook—in understanding it and being able to use references—they could proceed much faster.

The intensive instruction in the beginning of the school year does not have to be continued throughout the year. The class project was necessary only for the first unit. In each successive unit, instruction became more individualized for those students who still were unsure, and for all students it became a process of continuing refinement of technique. Progress in curriculum coverage is a serious concern of secondary school teachers. However, as students become more competent, their pace quickens. The final result is that the subject is covered more thoroughly and extensively.

Flexibility, diagnosis, preplanning, and objectivity are all key concepts to effective grouping. One final requirement is that students must apply instruction immediately—instruct; and then do.

Differentiated Assignments

Differentiating assignments is a means of fitting each assignment to the capabilities and reading levels of the students in the class. As Karlin has pointed out, "all students in the group might read the same selection but would not be expected to attain the same levels of understanding from it."[1] Another form is to assign differing amounts of material to read. In some instances the teacher designates who among the class is to work at a specific level. Direct assignment to the students can create problems since the poorer readers are singled out and sometimes the better readers question why they are given more work. The better procedure is to allow the individual students to choose which level of assignment they wish to do. Some teachers handle differentiation by having a basic minimum assignment with various possibilities of extension and enrichment.

This sometimes can be a variation of the study guide (page 202). For example, in such a situation, the assignment sheet given to the student may have activities, problems, and questions under such headings as "Required Study" and "Additional Optional Study" or "Basic Requirements" and "Suggested Extensions." Since the teacher should know the goals of each of the students, he can suggest assignment possibilities.

One basis for differentiating assignments as well as for grouping can be the informal reading inventory. When used for diagnostic teaching, as it should be, the inventory yields information about student competence in the

---

1. Robert Karlin, "Methods of Differentiating Instruction in the Senior High School," in *Developing High School Reading Programs,* compiled by Mildred A. Dawson (Newark, Del.: International Reading Association, 1967), p. 73.

reading skills. A typical graph of the results of an informal reading inventory (see Example 8.1) conveys the following information:

1. The skills in which virtually the entire class needs instruction—vocabulary and drawing conclusions.
2. A basis for differentiation of assignments—those students who need simpler supplementary material, those who can master the basic textbook with normal classroom guidance and explanation, and those who are able to read more difficult supplementary material and acquire more depth of understanding.
3. A basis for grouping in accordance with skill need—all students who need specific instruction in using library skills, or noting main ideas, or organization, and so on.
4. Further differentiation can be achieved by letting Thomas, Stephanie, Julia, and Ann undertake independent study.
5. Complete individualization or a group of two (Frank and Bill) in the skill of using graphic aids.
6. Research or interest groups comprised of students with different skill needs. Dan, who is weak in noting main ideas, could be in the same group as Stephanie and Tom, who are not weak in noting main ideas. In the process of coordinating their research into a group report, Dan would receive peer instruction while getting practice in the area of his weakness.

Various forms of grouping can feature differentiation. Even in groups doing research in which the students may span several reading levels, differentiation occurs. As the students meet in their committees and plan their work, each student works in accordance with his or her level and strengths. For instance, the most able students may do much of the organizing and synthesizing of information into a report, while those who are less able may be charged with researching specific parts of the topics, contributing illustrative materials, and participating in skit or role playing. Within the committee, the less competent student is able to work with peers and learn from the committee discussion.

Individualization

Complete individualization can be accomplished only when you know the strengths and weaknesses of each student. Individual or independent study can boost interest and initiative. However, if the teacher is not readily available, students may get bogged down in the reading. They must have material they can read successfully—material in which the vocabulary and comprehension skills required do not present insurmountable difficulties.

Certainly, the students' proficiency in the techniques of study and comprehension directly affects their success in independent study. Without adequate proficiency, this means of individualization is doomed to fail. On the other hand, if students are sufficiently prepared for it, they often find independent study a refreshing opportunity to pursue their interests on their

EXAMPLE 8.1

Social Studies Reading Inventory

Class and Individual Profile

Read horizontally to note individual student weaknesses.

(Checks denote weaknesses)

	Parts of Books	Library Skills	Graphic Aids	Vocabulary	Main Ideas	Details	Dr. Concl.	Organization
Cynthia		√		√			√	
Bill	√	√	√	√	√	√	√	√
Gloria					√	√	√	
Steve		√		√			√	
Stephanie							√	
William	√	√		√				√
Lauren			√	√	√	√	√	√
Jessica				√			√	
Bruce	√	√	√	√	√	√	√	√
Julia							√	
Jeff				√			√	
Mary	√	√		√	√	√	√	√
Dan				√	√		√	√
Isabel				√			√	
Ginny	√	√					√	
Gayle							√	
Mary Ann				√	√		√	√
Wendy				√	√			
Gavin		√		√			√	
Douglas	√	√		√	√		√	√
Thomas								
Frank			√	√	√		√	√
Stevic	√	√		√			√	
Gloria				√			√	
Ann		√						

Read vertically to note class pattern

These students need simpler supplementary material

These students are able to use more difficult material and to acquire more depth of understanding own time. One of the most beneficial aspects is the one-to-one contact with the teacher who is monitoring the study. It is wise to have a point of contact between the student and the teacher on the average of once per week to insure success.

Niles and Early describe an interesting form of individualization: the use of job sheets. Diagnosis is necessary so that the job sheets can be assigned appropriately to each student.

> Job sheets are particularly useful in developing the more mechanical skills, such as word analysis techniques, finding main ideas, and following the author's sequence. They are not so effective with higher reading skills, such as distinguishing between fact and opinion, where group discussion is essential to growth in skill.
>
> The preparatory steps (in preparing job sheets) are as follows:
>
> —Collect or construct exercises in the various skills. The series of exercises for each skill should represent varying degrees of difficulty.
>
> —Paste copies of the exercises on sheets of oak tag of uniform size. It is best to have two or three copies of each, so that more than one pupil may work on the same exercise at the same time.
>
> —Label each sheet as to type of exercise.
>
> —Number the sheets within each type in order of difficulty.
>
> —Provide answer keys on the back of each oak tag sheet.
>
> —Study each pupil's diagnostic test record.
>
> —List by name and number the exercises which each pupil is to do.
>
> —Give each pupil his own personal list.
>
> —Instruct the pupils in the filing system so that they can find the appropriate sheet.
>
> —Prepare a series of mastery tests which the student may take after he has done a given series of exercises.[2]

Still another means of individualizing is the contract, which is similar in some ways to both the job sheet and independent study. The contract is determined jointly by the teacher and the student and is based upon diagnosis, which enables both to plan in detail for the student's needs. Like the job sheet, it outlines specific graduated assignments; like independent study, it places responsibility for execution with the student. Depending upon the maturity of the student, the teacher may need to structure the contract by suggesting resources and dates for the completion of items. Also, the teacher must monitor the student's progress in order to provide whatever instruction in skills and procedures the student may need.

The contract has several advantages. First, it involves students in planning for their own learning. Second, it guides students in taking responsibility for learning. Third, it is paced to the individual; and fourth, it is geared to each individual student (no two students may have identical contracts).

---

2. Olive S. Niles and Margaret J. Early, "Adjusting to Individual Differences in English," in *Teaching Reading in High School: Selected Articles,* ed. Robert Karlin (New York: Bobbs-Merrill, 1969), p. 374.

Record Keeping

All teachers who individualize immediately note the need to record each student's strengths and weaknesses and general performance. With an average of 125 students per day to teach, no teacher can keep all pertinent information about each student in mind. Therefore, there must be an efficient yet time-saving method for recording and storing information to help in planning classroom instruction. Two types of records are essential in addition to the usual class grade record. One is the individual and class record, illustrated in Example 8.1, showing the results of the informal reading inventory. The other is the daily record of classroom participation. In addition you may have an interest inventory, a reading autobiography, and a time use chart for each student. It would then be wise to make a folder on each student.

MATERIALS THAT HELP YOU INDIVIDUALIZE

The versatile teacher uses materials of many different levels and types for effective grouping and individualization. Of course, to use a variety of materials, they must be available in the classroom and you must know how to use them.

Books

Books and printed matter are traditional school materials that can be easily applied to individualization. Each student can use them for her particular interests and they can be read in different ways in accordance with the reader's desire (for example, to obtain an overview or to study in depth). In comparison with many of the newer automated materials, they are still the cheapest form of instructional material. Oddly, there are still classrooms in which books are not in an adequate supply. Not only should there be textbooks on different levels of difficulty, but also each classroom needs a collection of supplementary materials. Many types of grouping depend upon an adequate supply of printed materials—for example, to help students at different competence levels and for research and special interest projects.

Self-help Materials

Many reading textbooks contain directions that explain procedures and skills in order to aid understanding. Other materials are packaged so that the reader is shown how to attack a reading assignment, and comprehension checks and answers are provided.

Self-help materials come in both printed and automated formats. Aimed at helping students chart their individual progress, these materials are based upon sound educational principles. First, students can progress through the material at their own rate. Second, the design is such that the students usually can see their errors as they proceed. Third, the students are informed of the nature of the skill being taught as well as the subject matter covered. Fourth, the students are put in charge of their own progress. Self-help materials invite active participation more directly than do teacher-directed assignments from printed materials.

But there are cautions. Students often need guidance when they meet an obstacle. They may not know why they have made an error, or they may need more intensive instruction in a skill before they can apply it—even through self-help material. Further, they may need more background for understanding than is provided. Obviously, the teacher cannot assume the *laissez-faire* approach that self-help material is self-teaching. The careful teacher uses such material appropriately to provide for a high degree of individualization but keeps track of students' progress with self-help material and provides additional instruction when necessary.

Programmed Materials

Programmed materials are based upon specific behavioral objectives in which the students are exposed to the subject in small, self-learning steps. One of the greatest values of these materials is the high degree of individualization which can be accomplished.

In programming, a subject is analyzed into its components which are then arranged in proper sequence and divided into the smallest possible bits of instruction. Understanding is tested at each step to minimize error and to reinforce correct responses. The advantages include the following:

1. The techniques of a master teacher are used.
2. The classroom teacher is released from drill work and is free to work individually with each student.
3. Each student progresses at his or her own pace.
4. Reinforcement (correction or reward) is given at each step of learning.
5. Automatic teachers are more patient than human teachers.
6. The student's errors are recorded.
7. Programs show records of progress.

On the other hand, you should also be aware of disadvantages:

1. Mature reading skills are complex, and there are a number of learning situations for which there are not, as yet, adequate programs.
2. Much more is needed to include the entire repertoire of reading behavior such as telling stories, undertaking and accomplishing research, and group discussions of ideas.
3. Programmed instruction does not take into account the sequence of child development and readiness to learn. The program is individual in that the students progress at their own pace, but it is not geared to the particular needs of a student.
4. Programmed instruction cannot answer a spontaneous question.
5. The skills of creative reading based upon the open-ended question cannot be programmed.

Tapes

Tapes and cassettes are especially useful for teaching the reluctant or disabled reader. Tapes can be used with an individual or in group situations. They can build the student's background of information and establish concepts and vocabulary; and they can enrich and supplement printed material. You can use blank tapes and cassettes for taping specific instructions to be given to a student or a group for an assignment while you are engaged with other students in the classroom.

General Criteria for Automatic Materials

Whatever type of material is used, keep in mind the following criteria in determining its effectiveness:

1. The automated devices are valuable adjuncts to instruction; but they are only aids; you must not abdicate your position in favor of them.
2. The automated devices should be designed and used to discover how students learn.
   a. Is the process of self-development fostered so that students can draw their own inferences and become thinking persons?
   b. Are the students able to proceed at their own rate?
   c. Are there opportunities for self-instruction, self-correction, and self-evaluation?
   d. Is the material meaningful and pertinent to the learner?
   e. Is there adequate reinforcement?
   f. Is the love of reading fostered?
   g. Is emphasis placed upon reading comprehension?

The basic purpose of the automated devices is to provide a more complete battery of instructional materials with which to accomplish the ends of education. The value of the materials rests with your use of them.

SUMMARY

To be effective, instruction must be relevant to each individual student. Though the subject content of the class may remain essentially the same for different classes, each group of students exhibits a range of learning strengths. Likewise, students may share similar interests, skill needs, and aptitudes. The perceptive teacher notes these and incorporates them into his planning. He diagnoses daily. He uses many different types of classroom organization, selecting those which best suit the educational purposes and the needs of the learners.

QUESTIONS AND PROBLEMS FOR YOUR OWN CLASSROOM

For readers who are training to be teachers:

1. In your subject, plan how you could incorporate the various forms of

grouping. On what bases would you organize them? How would you have more than one form operating with the same class?
2. Develop a differentiated assignment job sheet for your class.
3. Compile a file of reading skill activities pertinent to your subject which can be used individually and with groups of students.
4. Compile a bibliography and listing of books, self-help materials, programmed materials, tapes, film strips, films, and recordings pertinent to your subject.
5. Prepare an interest inventory as a means of determining the interests of your students.

For readers who are teaching:

1. Determine the goals of instruction for your class with a specific unit of study. Plan the forms of individualization you can employ to accomplish your goals.
2. Poll your students concerning their thoughts about the goals of the class, how the goals can be accomplished, their responsibilities and what they think your responsibilities are. Discuss your findings with them and evolve strategies.
3. Discuss with your class the duties of the group leader, the recorder, and the process observer.
4. If there is a negative attitude toward reading in your class, use discussion and diagnosis to find the cause of it and how you can counter it.

SELECTED REFERENCE

Lapp, Diane. *Making Reading Possible Through Effective Classroom Management.* Newark, Del.: IRA, 1980.
A detailed discussion of good classroom management techniques.

CHAPTER 9

Exceptional Students

OVERVIEW

As soon as they meet a class, teachers realize that they have a group quite diverse in their accomplishments and needs—indeed, in all aspects of their beings. Inherent in this realization is the fact that each student is different from others. However, some students have differences that are more pronounced than usually found; these students we call *exceptional*. They are the superior student and reader, the slow learning student, the severely disabled reader, the reluctant reader, the bilingual student or one who uses English as a second language, and those who speak a dialect of English. Although these students are in heterogeneous classes, they require instruction that fits their special characteristics and needs.

Questions

Consider these questions before you read further:

1. What problems can you forsee with types of exceptional students?
2. What do you think is a teacher's responsibility toward these students?
3. In what ways have you altered your classroom procedure to accommodate the needs of these students?

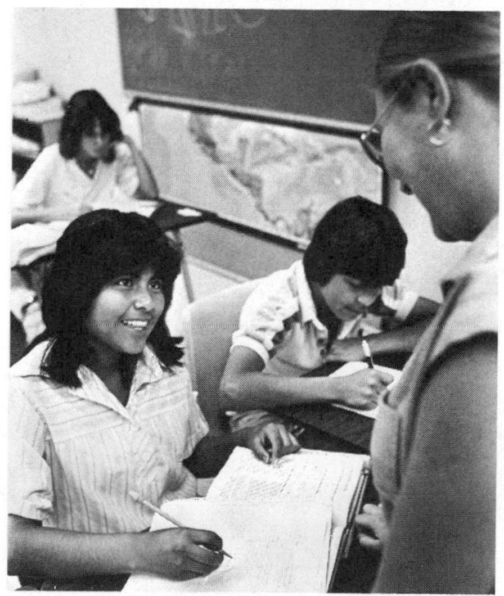

Democratic beliefs attest to the uniqueness of each individual, thereby supporting the idea that every student is exceptional in some manner. As teachers, we often are advised that we must know the strengths and weaknesses of our students, their levels of reading proficiency, their interests, attitudes and so on; in this way we discover the "exceptional" characteristics of each student. Of course, the movement toward increasing individualization also underscores this concept.

We also find groups of students in our classes who have prominent characteristics that place them outside of the norm. They may have many characteristics of their age group, but at the same time their presence in regular classes may mandate procedural adaptations. In order for them to learn, we must adapt to and accommodate their natures and abilities.

In all high school classrooms there is a range of reading levels and habits. Many schools today are *mainstreaming* students who heretofore have been in classes especially designed for their capabilities. Now, whenever possible, and by mandate in some school districts, these students are in classes with their age peers.

Society expects students to become productive, participating citizens, which means that they must acquire reading competence. Since we frown on segregation in society at large, segregation of "different" students should not be practiced in school. This philosophy and practice often places the teacher in a difficult position. The teacher's desire to individualize and to help each student often is stymied by inadequate materials, scheduling problems, the great number of students met in class each day, community attitudes and resources, the philosophy of a school board, lack of administrative leadership and support, emphases of instruction within a school district, as well as inadequate teaching methods. Despite such obstacles, there are measures an innovative and perceptive teacher can take.

SUPERIOR READERS

Superior readers usually are superior students who read above the enrolled grade level. They often are gifted students who learn rapidly and easily and often are avid readers. While such students give the teacher the joy of teaching subject matter with definite positive results, they can be challenging in asking penetrating questions and suggesting innovations. In one instance a ninth grade student gave the teacher a critique of the lesson after each class. At first, the teacher found that having a student come to him seriously and sincerely to suggest changes in some lessons or compliment other lessons was quite unnerving. After his initial reaction, however, the teacher came to welcome the comments. His lesson procedures did improve with the student's input and he observed, "I began to develop a clear rationale for my classroom teaching. It was a fantastic experience." When the teacher checked the cumulative folder and the guidance record he found that that student was a highly gifted one.

Characteristics

Your school may have identified gifted students through formal testing. But what can you note by observation that indicates such students? What are the usual characteristics? You would note that, in comparison with peers, they have a longer attention span; more persistence, curiosity, and initiative; a larger and more sophisticated vocabulary; are more articulate; they read more and can make logical associations easily (relationships, reasoning, generalizing, dealing with abstractions). In addition, they often have a wider range of interests, can work well independently, and respond quickly. They become impatient and bored with routine procedure, drill, and repetition, and their intellectual capacities in other subjects as well as in aspects of your subject can be uneven, like other students.

As a group, superior or gifted students often are physically more mature and healthier, are self-reliant, and choose older companions if other gifted peers are not on hand. However, gifted students seem to be more critical of themselves and others. They often receive more opportunities as student leaders. Yet socially, the gifted can be inadequate or adequate—similar to other students in the same age group. Bridges points out that:

> Both at school and at home gifted children may suffer as the result of an imbalance in their intellectual, social and physical developments. The commonest instance of this occurs when the intellectual development outstrips the social and physical so that we have the child with an adult level of thought who may still be very shy in company and who may still be smaller than many of his age-mates. The problems arising from this imbalance may easily be aggravated by adults who expect to find old heads on young shoulders or stress the discrepancies.[1]

Needs of the Gifted

You might suppose that superior students need no further help in the skills and techniques of reading and study. Yet, superior groups do have needs such as the following:

1. to develop more effective techniques of study
2. to develop the comprehension skills of interpretative and critical reading
3. to refine the precision and depth of their vocabulary
4. to increase their general speed of reading.

Further, superior students need to be freed as much as possible from a routine and dull curriculum. They seek involvement in worthwhile, creative projects. In fact, innovation and creativity often are viewed as hallmarks of giftedness.

As you work with superior students you will discover that they too can have serious problems, as far as they are concerned. However, not all have the

1. Sydney Bridges, *Problems of the Gifted Child IQ-150* (New York: Crane, Russak & Company, Inc., 1973), p. 25.

same problems, or to the same extent. You may note a reluctant reader or occasionally a disabled reader among the gifted. In fact, a gifted student who is reading or performing academically only as well as the average students can be regarded as having a problem or deficiency.

They may have feelings of inferiority and inadequacy, stemming from peer comments (peers may consider their perceptions as not "normal"). Also, the gifted strive for perfection; they see how things can and should be done. They can become bored with the activities of their peer group because they are usually more intellectual and bookish. As a result, gifted students can have unsatisfying relations with their peers.

Their varied interests can create a problem—they may be reluctant to choose and prepare for a single vocation. Some superior students thoroughly enjoy everything they do and imagine that the activity of the moment is their abiding interest. Then comes another involvement which they enjoy equally. Some do, however, have a deep and sustained interest in one area.

Another problem which may manifest itself is the difficulty to evolve a satisfying philosophy of life. Gifted students often perceive more cognitively than they can put into an emotional perspective. They simply have not yet lived long enough to mesh the two realms of experience. This can lead to despondency, cynicism, arrogance, or indifference.

As with all students, teachers must be aware of the mental health of superior students. Though they are capable of self-direction, we do need to guide and monitor their efforts. They should not be left to their own devices merely because they are extremely able.

Problems may also develop from school and parental pressure toward achievement. Many superior students who enroll in honors courses in high school become so overwhelmed by the heavy preparations required that they "burn out" or become disenchanted. We need to remember that such students need time to engage in their interests, many of which are creative in nature.

A dull curriculum is a serious problem for gifted students, and it can elicit such remarks as, "We have to spend two weeks on this novel. I've read it in three days, and one more to discuss it in class would be enough. I liked it, sure. It was interesting. But I don't need to have it dissected, as Mr. ______ will do." Another: "I don't agree with the teacher's interpretation, but I won't let her know what I think. Any interpretation but hers is wrong." These comments offer interesting guidelines for classroom procedures. In the second comment, imagine the levels of thinking and vocabulary development that the class and the student could have explored if the student's interpretation had been analyzed along with the "official" one.

Suggested Activities

1. Dramatizing stories
   a. Doing some of the things that the characters did to show insight into the mood and personality of each character.
   b. Rewriting the story as a play.
2. Making graphic representations of a story
   a. Showing a story in serial form; writing or telling what is happening in each scene.

   b. Making a picture to illustrate an event or a description from the story.
3. Oral and written presentations of stories
   a. Telling a story up to the point of climax.
   b. Rewriting an ending to a story.
   c. Writing about a story or book and showing why the student did or did not enjoy it.
4. Planning with the teacher for diagnosing the student's abilities in reading and developing those abilities.
5. Doing self-motivated independent research around an area of interest for practice in use of reference materials and library reference guides and finding information independently.
6. Working alone or with others in writing original stories and essays, analyzing authors' patterns of thought and organization, and determining new application of principles and of actual data.
7. Practice in the scientific method—the problem solving approach
   a. Discovering and clearly stating problems.
   b. Planning and executing ways of determining what is true.
   c. Checking with reliable sources and determining what is true.
   d. Applying what is learned to the environment.
   e. Making use of simple records.
8. Extensive reading of library materials for information, enjoyment, and enrichment
   a. Reading a wide variety of books.
   b. Scanning and classifying reading materials for the school library.
   c. Setting up displays of books to supplement and enrich classroom work.
9. Engaging in vocabulary study
   a. Noting special words pertinent to each content field.
   b. Determining general words with specialized meanings.
   c. Analyzing an author's connotative use of words.
   d. Becoming aware of an author's use of sensory words.
   e. Noting and defining figures of speech.
10. Classroom discussion. Superior students learn from each other by increasing their depth and scope of knowledge and by sharpening their vocabulary in the communicative process.
11. Organize projects in which the students will research and draw conclusions about the significance of an event, the influence of a historical figure, the impact on society of a scientific discovery, and so on.
12. Foster creativity whenever possible—through original writing, scientific experimentation, and independent study. One student became interested in writing essays conveying her views. She mentioned this to her English teacher and asked if he would be willing to go over her writing and make suggestions. The teacher readily assented, though the writing had no connection with the student's work in class. Another student proved very able in his mechanical drawing class. His teacher saw the student's talent immediately and paced him in the course. He had the student work on advanced drawing far beyond the curriculum. A social studies teacher had two very superior readers and gifted students in a

heterogeneous class. The students quickly mastered the essential information and simply passed the time while the remainder of the class progressed much more slowly. The teacher arranged for these gifted students to do library research on the next unit of study and to compile an annotated bibliography. This activity had two fundamental benefits: the gifted students were able to broaden and enrich their backgrounds, and the bibliography was mimeographed and given to the entire class at the start of the next unit, sparking wider reading for all of the students.

13. Organize a book discussion club in which classics or current books of interest can be reviewed or discussed.
14. Provide opportunities for the students to read more than textbooks and standard reference books. Have them read abridgements, book reviews, columns and editorials and analyze the effectiveness and point of view. Have them write rejoinders to columnists and editorials.
15. Seize upon students' special interests in a topic under study and guide them as necessary on in-depth research. One student became particularly interested in the clothing worn during the Middle Ages. The student researched the topic for presentation to the class. She accompanied her presentation with watercolors she had done of Middle Ages costumes and dolls dressed in period clothing which she had designed. Her artistic abilities also developed in working on this project.
16. Have the students make original mathematics puzzles, vocabulary puzzles (such as crosswords), and analogies involving key words in any subject which can then be used by the class. These projects could be located at a "fun" corner or table for the class members to use as they have time.
17. Organize language clubs in which students can learn a foreign language more thoroughly, read appropriate materials, investigate the history and customs of the people, compile idioms of the language, and so on. This would be an extracurricular activity. This type of club is excellent for bilingual students.
18. Have the students read a news account of some incident and have them rewrite it to show other points of view and slants by emphasizing specific aspects of the account or using certain words. The rewritten account must remain factually accurate.
19. Have the students write advertising copy for a school or class project in which they attempt to appeal to the reader.
20. Suggest that they write about scientific information or some other entirely factual and technical material in a manner suitable for a newspaper, a comic strip, or a cartoon.

A listing of activities appropriate for gifted students seems endless. There are three fundamental considerations you should always keep in mind. First, *free the students from the routine study* whenever possible, once you have ascertained that they know the essential information. Second, *monitor and guide the students* by giving instruction in technique and procedure when needed. Finally, *foster activities that are creative in nature* and in which the students can become personally involved.

EDITORIAL

The Verbally Gifted

Current interest in the education of verbally gifted students has arisen because of several factors. First, the number of students who have scored over 600 on the verbal section of the Scholastic Aptitude Achievement Examination has declined over the past decade. Second, our most prestigious colleges and universities have cited the inability of incoming freshmen to express themselves logically and coherently in written communication. Finally, the National Assessment of Educational Progress, while indicating growth in decoding skill among the country's nine-year-olds, also has noted the continuing inability of the nation's seventeen-year-olds to do well in inferential thinking. These three indices have verified a growing concern; our verbally gifted youngsters are not being offered the appropriate educational experiences that will guarantee them the basic skills in the art of language.

For some years now, the prevailing philosophy has been a romantic one; the verbally gifted will learn all they need, as long as there are sufficient resources available to them. These "children of promise" can read whatever they want. They will succeed no matter what the curriculum offers them. While gifted youngsters can, indeed, learn more quickly than average students, these special students must have training in specific cognitive skills.

Another myth that has complicated the development of educational programs for the verbally gifted is the assumption that students who score in the ninety-ninth percentile on standard achievement tests have acquired all the learning that can be expected. Recent studies of gifted youngsters in other disciplines indicate that there is little information about where these students actually are in the learning continuum.[1] Youngsters who constantly achieve 100s in their classrooms are not being adequately challenged. Appropriate testing procedures must be utilized for the verbally gifted to determine where they are in every aspect of reading and writing.[2]

1. Daniel Deating, *Intellectual Talent* (Baltimore: The Johns Hopkins Press, 1976).
2. Phyllis Mindell and Dorothy Stracher, *First the Fundamentals: Reading and Writing for the Gifted* (Pittsford: Well-Read Press, 1980).

Once such an assessment has been completed, teachers can develop unit themes that incorporate the reading of those works that comprise our cultural heritage. Included in such a package are specific skills needs for each individual gifted student. The youngster whose spelling still indicates an inability to recognize certain etymological patterns will receive that training; the student whose vocabulary is limited will be enriched by learning the meaning of affixes; the verbally gifted student whose paragraphs still do not incorporate transitional words will learn to use them in formal writing, and so on.

Within this framework, verbally gifted students are taught to develop their analytical abilities and then to synthesize their knowledge. They are encouraged to note the similar in the disparate, the dissimilar in the familiar. In this manner, the creativity of these youngsters is permitted to develop. Both the intellectual and the intuitive skills are united, and both expository and creative writings are assigned. Gifted students can then note the similarities and the differences between these two modes of expression.

Evaluation is the next step in this three-stage process. First, an assessment of individual student needs in the language area is completed. Then a program that offers a differentiated curriculum for the verbally gifted is developed. The final stage is evaluation, in which both teacher and student determine the growth achieved in every aspect of reading and writing. The evaluation also is the basis for the next year's planning.

Only by putting such a program into practice can appropriate education of the verbally gifted be assured. These students can and must receive curricula differentiated to fix their needs. As Nicholas Murray Butler stated:

> The education of the gifted child is from a very fundamental point of view the chief problem of democracy. The aristocracy of a democracy is not one of wealth, but it is one of excellence—excellence in whatever one may follow.

Verbally gifted students are most precious natural resource; it is our privilege and our responsibility to guide them towards the excellence inherent in their potential.

Dorothy A. Stracher, Ph.D.

Educational Consultant

SLOW-LEARNING STUDENTS

Teachers generally view slow-learning students as those who are below the average in achievement. They are identified through their inability to master basic content. Less than average mental capacity distinguishes slow learners from *disabled* students, who are capable but are not fulfilling their potential. In heterogeneous groups the slow learners comprise the few at the low side of the normal curve of ability within the population. They are the students who require intensive teaching with much practice and practical application.

Characteristics

Slow-learning students do not differ markedly from other students in most characteristics. They do not learn as rapidly as other students, and reading is often a laborious task for them. They may show a marked lack of interest in reading because of the difficulty they have with it; in fact, they may avoid it whenever possible. As a result of their lack of success in reading and academic achievement, they often show a negative self-concept which in itself can defeat their progress. For many, school means reading, and each day they are reminded of their deficient ability. We can understand why they may express attitudes such as, "I can't learn, I'm stupid, school has nothing for me." Many will seek to avoid an unpleasant situation in which they feel they cannot compete by dropping out of school.

However, slow-learning students are not likely to be slow in all that they do. They may be socially adept and show aptitude in physical activity and mechanical ability. They may also have talents in the arts. One student who was unable to read well and found academic pursuits difficult painted with oils. In a research group in his social studies class, his contribution was a series of oil paintings which portrayed the topic.

The major difference, then, is the inability to learn as rapidly as average students. Coupled with this often is a short attention span; there can be a tendency toward excitability. Further, slow learners want results quickly. They must see a direct and concrete application of what they are learning.

Needs of Slow Learners

Slow learners have the same basic physical, social, and emotional needs as other students. They need a sense of belonging and of affection. They need a balance between success and failure, and it is on this that we must focus. All too often the slow learner experiences more failure than success, especially in academic pursuits. Unless we can insure a positive mental attitude, we may see such behavior as indifference, apathy, insecurity, belligerence, and disruption.

Slow learners need to develop self-direction and the ability to manage their affairs. They are most susceptible to peer pressure. As a result, they are often caught up with fads and slogans and do not see beyond the face value of propaganda and advertising. In other words, they need concrete instruction in critical reading. Further, they usually require specific instruction in speaking and writing skills. They do not need academic exercises in "proper" language but rather instruction in how concreteness in language usage affects communication and life goals. We also want these students to be able to read newspapers, popular magazines, standard forms, and directions—all the media which society expects people to comprehend.

Suggested Activities

Procedures for teaching the slow learner are not markedly different from those used with any group. The major differences are the need for intensive practice and the need for concreteness. Concreteness includes first-hand experiences, tangibleness, and practical application. Activities have to be clear and specific as well as simple. Slow learners must see a definite relationship between an activity and how it can be used in a practical situation.

1. Instruct slow learners with material they are capable of reading successfully.
2. Give systematic instruction in tools of study and in the development of concepts. They are less able than average students to learn incidentally or to draw conclusions.
3. Show how the tools of learning and the information in various content subjects have a practical application. The more direct the application is to the content, the more motivated the slow learners will be. The practical application should encompass the basic goals of the students.
4. Go as slowly as necessary. The educational goal should not be curriculum coverage, but successful learning. Be concrete and even dramatic, if necessary, to tie the new material to the students' level of understanding and background of experience.
5. Try to understand slow learners by noting how they feel about themselves. Diagnose to find strengths and weaknesses. Be objective and truthful about level of competence; however, suggest ways they can work successfully.
6. Use procedures to build background and to provide for prereading activities.
7. Show specifically how to read and study in each content area. Give instruction in pertinent skills as necessary. For example, when the need for such skills is apparent, show how to break words into syllables, and how to get the meaning of a word from the context. This must be done for all basic skills.
8. Urge slow learners to communicate with each other. Let them talk. They need to become increasingly fluent with words. Meanings can be sharpened and new words introduced in discussion sessions.
9. Use newspapers, magazines, commercial brochures and other current printed matter as sources of reading material. Use the materials of daily life (e.g., driver manuals, job directions, business forms, and directions).

10. Use a wide variety of audiovisual aids to widen the students' background and provide alternative modes of learning which may be more appropriate for slow learners.
11. Differentiate assignments in the class in any of the various ways described in Chapter 8.
12. Present principles of grammar only as they facilitate everyday speaking and writing. Avoid technical analysis; instead, emphasize clarity of expression.
13. Read to the students to increase their appreciation and background as well as to stimulate their thinking.
14. Help the students to write business and social correspondence correctly and clearly. Refrain from trying to develop techniques of essay and story writing unless the aptitude and motivation seem to be present.
15. Keep coverage of subject matter units short and snappy. Long, abstract analyses of literature and social studies readings will lose slow learners. Yet factual details which make the subject more concrete hold their interest.
16. Allow some time for class study so that you can be free to give individual or small-group instruction as necessary.
17. Whenever possible, as in science and many of the vocational subjects, use demonstrations with guide questions of what to watch for and discussion of the results.
18. Stimulate thinking and concrete application by assigning first-hand experiences (from which you can build a lesson or unit of study): field trips, examination of a specimen, or school project. Only a few practical activities are listed here; to list specific activities for each unit of study in the secondary school would fill the remainder of this book!

    a. Learning or drawing maps of routes, road maps, and of sources and destinations of both things and people.
    b. Computing mileage, time, and speeds.
    c. Learning safety rules for travel–as much as possible from student experience.
    d. Writing letters to request information and brochures, to arrange visits, and so on.
    e. Investigating a local government problem to determine what the problem is, how it affects them and others, why the problem exists and what should be done.
    f. Keeping daily records of various sorts for specific purposes, such as weather, diet, health habits, and so on.
    g. Preparing campaigns to foster a needed school development. These could involve posters, letters to officials, radio talks and interviews, editorials, and so on.

As you reflect on each activity, the required skills are readily apparent. For instance, note the understanding of graphic aids in *a,* development of the ability to organize thoughts and express them correctly in *d,* and the purposeful reading required in *e.*

DISABLED READERS

Disabled readers are those students who can do the usual level of work for the grade but cannot achieve adequately because of disability in reading competence. The causes of reading disability can be many; two or more causes usually act in conjunction to create a "total cause" that the student cannot surmount. In some instances there is a single possible cause, such as emotional problems. For some students an emotional problem seems not to affect learning, while other students are "shattered" and unable to concentrate. We must always consider individual differences.

In order to understand students better, teachers should know the many causes of reading disability. These can stem from anything that has posed a problem for the students in their academic progress and development. Visual defects, auditory defects, possible neurological deficiencies or endocrine imbalance, and low intelligence can be causes. Causes also include social reactions by peers, emotional difficulties, inept teaching, and inadequate school resources. Further, a generally meager or different background may contribute. Many times the original causes bring about additional ones, such as anxiety, parental concern, or a negative self-concept.

Merely knowing why students are disabled in reading does not bring about improvement, but investigating all possible causes can give us direction in teaching. For example, if we find that a student comprehends poorly because of limited background, then we must attempt to build continuously the general fund of information needed to comprehend. If the student is unable to recognize words, then our presentation of vocabulary in class must use the techniques of analyzing the word (how to break it down into syllables) and applying its meaning concretely to the student's background of experience.

High school students with reading disability probably have a history of reading failure that may have started in kindergarten and first grade. Now, at a point of decision for a vocation, they are still fledglings, but they need to be able to study and acquire knowledge independently. Such students should have the basic skills of word recognition and a sizable store of vocabulary and concepts. Without these, students feel inadequate.

Students manifest feelings of inadequacy in many ways. First there are attempts to compensate or cover up. No one wants to feel inadequate; our self-respect demands that we view ourselves as being able to cope. So, students may give attention to areas such as sports or art where they can perform successfully, gain the approval of friends and family, and acquire the security of positive relationships and the sense of belonging. They may choose other defenses: withdrawal, so that attention is not focused on inadequacy; belligerent or disruptive behavior; or indifference and apathy, showing that they *could* succeed but really *don't* care to. Teachers find these reactions maddening because they are unconstructive and they only add to the problem. Consequently, in dealing with these students, it is vital that your classroom procedure enable them to succeed immediately.

Needs of Disabled Readers

What, then, are the needs of high school disabled readers? Obviously they need to read better in order to successfully study your subject. Next, they need a positive self-concept—they should feel that they can perform. Further, they need an objective analysis of their problems and a program of corrective action that includes continual monitoring. Finally, these students need your encouraging but realistic support. Your confidence in and expectations for them should be high though obtainable.

Many schools have remedial classes for these students, especially if they are delayed two or more years in reading level. While these students do need the extra help of the remedial classes, they also need help from their content teachers in how to read material in each discipline. Improvement as a result of remedial classes usually is gradual and therefore does not enable students to improve in content reading immediately. Further, the remedial teacher usually does not give specific practice in each of the content fields, but instead attacks the reading skills from a variety of materials. You cannot assume that students automatically will transfer learning from one class to another. Disabled readers often are not aware that reading skills need to be applied to each content area; their full attention is on the content. Also, a skill should be applied immediately where it is needed for the best results. For example, the intensive reading needed for mathematics problems is best practiced and applied in the mathematics class. The ideal program for disabled readers coordinates the efforts of all teachers in order to provide comprehensive help.

Suggested Activities

1. Identify writing patterns in each of the content fields to help students see how authors in each field structure their information.
2. Establish readiness for reading material in each content class. Investigate and expand the students' background for the topic, preview the material, clarify basic conceptual terms, and help them see specific purposes for reading.
3. Give specific instruction in study techniques when they are needed and then have students apply them immediately.
4. Make sure that materials at all reading levels are available.
5. Differentiate assignments to take into account levels of competence and skill needs of the students. Also use various modes of classroom organization to meet specific needs.
6. Evaluate the students' work with them to enlist cooperation in attacking reading problems.
7. Use audiovisual materials to help students increase the depth and scope of their background of information.
8. Apply different skills to increase reading competence, particularly writing. For example, have students apply their knowledge of paragraph patterns by writing their own paragraphs.

9. Alert students to the use of structure words.
10. Give consistent help in developing word meanings, in classifying information, and thinking precisely.
11. Using classroom procedures that employ simple and clear-cut directions and carefully posed questions that will foster logical thinking and concentration.
12. Give intensive instruction in the use of graphic aids found in textbooks. Many concepts and ideas are presented via these aids, which in turn build background for understanding the written exposition.

A detailed and more specific list of activities which can be adapted to classroom procedure is found in Chapter 10.

Reluctant Readers

Reluctant readers may be either disabled readers who have weaknesses in reading skills or adequate readers who do not read voluntarily. Students who do not read with ease and fluency will turn to a more satisfying means of recreation. Individuals have different preferences and, with some, reading may not be one of them. However, you should attempt to foster wide reading as a means of pleasure as well as for extending background. The goal should not be to develop all students into avid readers, but to be sure that they do have the skill they need to read for pleasure.

When you find reluctance to read, interest may be encouraged by identifying the students' interests and then providing related books at their reading level. And though the teacher may note a wide range of skill needs, the goal of *developing student interest in reading* must be kept in sight. Share and discuss the information in books. Enjoy an author's use of language. Analyze the author's line of reasoning. In short, discuss and evaluate the ideas of the author. You will find it valuable to read to your students occasionally and to provide time in class for them to read. And, of course, your enthusiasm as well as an adequate supply of books are essential ingredients.

Culturally Different and Bilingual Students

Bilingual and culturally different students often are puzzling to the teacher. Within a group of students with different interests, desires, strengths and weaknesses, you find these students who speak a different language and have a different cultural background, which may include a different set of values. Even within this group there are individual differences. Some students may know no English at all, whereas others may be minimally competent at least in spoken English. Some may be fluent in their native language and able to read it, but others may be illiterate in their native language as well as in English. However, these students, like all adolescents, have basic motivations, feelings, and concerns. The dramatic difference to teachers is that the language is different from standard English which you speak and which is used in most textbooks. Viewed from the position of academic requirements, such students will likely have many weaknesses and therefore need intensive remedial instruction.

Bilingual education is being adopted by many schools; in fact, it is often mandated. The reasons for this are valid. Obviously we need to start with the students where we find them. Therefore, using the language they know would seem to be a good place to begin. However, many question the efficacy of such programs. The overall aim is for the students to become competent in English, since English is the major language of the country.

Emotions can color our thought about bilingual education. On the one hand, teachers are concerned about having students acquire the academic content and may not understand the language and cultural differences of these students. On the other hand there are teachers who do not deny the need to learn English but also believe that culturally different students must be respected for their native culture and language. Indeed, in our modern world brought so close together by technological advances in communication, we should view these students' competence in another language as an asset; we should not ask them in effect to forget their native language and culture.

Bilingual students often view the school as an alien environment in which they are looked down upon and in which they do not seem to be able to succeed. Therefore, compounding the problem of language difference often is the problem of attitude. Depending upon the attitudes in their home life and their experiences in school, these students' attitude toward learning—and even toward society—may range from complete negativism to full acceptance of the situation, expressed by striving to achieve. Culturally different students who have failed each year in school or have been humiliated by either overt or subtle discrimination may well look upon school as a highly distasteful place. Therefore, all teachers must be aware and tolerant of the differences in culture, language, and values.

The very act of trying to change culturally different students says to them that they are not adequate. All individuals tend to react negatively to such attempts, especially if they have the impression that their language usage or dialect is inferior. Linguists agree that dialects are "not inferior deviations from some inherently superior form."[2] In fact, change in language pattern is *not* the chief aim. Rather, *culturally different students must learn the generally accepted language pattern of standard English so that they can communicate in that pattern when they need to.*

The success of our efforts with bilingual students may depend largely upon our own attitude. Therefore, there are some considerations we should review. First, these students are individual human beings with the same motivations, desires, and concerns as other students. Second, in a pluralistic society such as ours, we must appreciate the benefits of diversity. Third, bear in mind the value of all languages in our world of today, and use these languages to effect greater communication. Fourth, in recognizing that these students must become competent in English, realize that this does take time. It does not happen overnight! At first bilingual students may need to translate from English to their native language in order to comprehend; eventually, it is hoped, they will be able to think in either language. Finally, we must never lose sight of the personal nature of language. The language we

---

2. Louis V. Zuck and Yetta M. Goodman, "On Dialects and Reading," *Journal of Reading* 15, No. 7 (April 1972): 500.

use helps clarify our identity—it is an inseparable and intrinsic part of us. Criticism of our language is a criticism of *us*.

We should emphasize the *practical* benefits of adjustment to the larger society—to get and hold a job, to function as a citizen (vote, get licenses, and so on). Remember also that just as students need time to read widely, bilingual students need time to acquire a second language. They also need various situations in which to practice the second language.

The basic principles of remedial teaching are of extreme importance when working with culturally different students: immediate success, direct practical application of the learning, objectivity with the individual, acceptance and genuine concern for the students' language and culture, and goals and strategies planned with students.

Suggested Activities

1. Organize class sessions in the psychological study of language. Determine with the students how people use language and are affected by it. For example, investigate and discuss the connotative use of words. Have the students suggest expressions to use for emotional impact. A possibility here may be a mini-course of only a few weeks.
2. Discuss the goals of the students with them. Map out strategies for accomplishing goals.
3. Provide wide opportunities for students to hear and use language. Emphasize all aspects of the language arts. Assist them in discovering the effects of various forms of usage.
4. Provide immediate application of what they are being taught. In planning on how to accomplish their goals, help them to see where in the overall strategy the specific learning occurs.
5. Spend much time and emphasis on concept development and vocabulary. Use audiovisual and actual experiences to build background.
6. Surround the students with books of their interests and levels of competence. Help them to become familiar with the library. Create a reading atmosphere. However, also use other modalities for learning to supplement the reading.
7. Continuously provide varied oral language activities to enable the students to hear and use language, so that standard English becomes familiar. Such activities might include conversation and discussion in the classroom, storytelling (selections from literature as well as cultural anecdotes), practice in telephoning, dramatization of social situations and unique cultural customs, reporting from research and interest, giving announcements to the class and the school, stating directions, and explaining the steps of a process. In short, every opportunity possible for the oral use of language must be used.
8. Set up a bulletin board using attractive book jackets and captions which excite interest. Have the books under the display.
9. Have a class discussion to identify favorite books, authors, book characters as well as favorite TV programs and comic strips.

10. Utilize hobby interests to create reading needs.
11. Use word games, listening centers, experience charts, crossword puzzles.
12. Read to the class selections of high interest.
13. Make a card file of magazine pictures that students can relate to. Have the students write a paragraph about the picture to show narration or description as a means of communicating with language.
14. Have the students write instructions for:
    a. changing a tire
    b. preparing breakfast
    c. making a bed
    d. preparing for work in the morning
    e. tying a shoe
15. Give the students a hypothetical $100.00 and a mail order catalog. Help them with a budget for their holiday shopping. Instruction would give them the opportunity to fill out an order blank, figure sales tax, postage fee, and so on.
16. Give each student a telephone directory. Explain the yellow classified pages and pose questions that require finding specific information.
17. Bring in an object and have the students think of all the words possible to describe the object. Categorize the words as to shape, size, texture, color, etc. It would be interesting also to have the students supply the equivalent words from their native language.
18. Have the students compile a picture dictionary. (Perhaps use an old mail order catalog.)
19. Play with sentences starting with kernel sentences of N V (noun verb). Expand them by adding adjectives, adverbs, objects (nouns), linking verbs (feel, taste). If possible, have the students illustrate and explain differences that may exist between the two languages.
20. Have students use their senses to perceive objects new to them. Have them think of appropriate adjectives to label the sense they experience.
21. Start a continuing exhibit in your class of comparable idiomatic phrases between the native language and English.
22. Use the cloze procedure to emphasize key conceptual terms, specific word function of adjectives, adverbs, verbs, and so on.
23. Use a variation of the language experience approach in which the students recount an experience in English. Then have them practice reading the account.
24. Use *mimicry,* in which the students copy the teacher's intonation and stress.
25. Have students change the tense of verbs, plurals of nouns in sentences.
26. Work with the students on transformation—changing the sentence syntactically but keeping the meaning consistent.
27. Have fun with prepositional phrases. Elicit from the students what

the prepositions mean. This is an effective activity whenever directions are to be followed and in sentence instruction in English.

28. Play with adjectives. Determine what they do as they refer to size, color, shape, odor, and so on. This activity is particuarly effective in art and science as well as English.

Black English

Black English is a form of English, but it is not standard English. It is a *dialect.* All of us have a dialect, stemming from our geographical area, ethnic group, and educational background. Some speakers of black dialect are very close to standard English, while others are so different that for them standard English may be similar to a second language.

The terms *nonstandard* and *substandard* are demeaning and unfortunate. They invite an emotional distance between the users of standard English and those who use another form of English. Linguists have found that black dialect has rules similar to those that characterize all languages; it is a systematic and symbolic form of communication, as is all language. Our goal, then, is to teach *flexibility,* so that students can use the standard version of English when they need it and comprehend material written in standard English.

Since some forms of black dialect differ markedly from standard English, teachers should review and reflect upon their understanding and acceptance of it. The considerations of the personal nature of language, our attitude toward a language form as well as our respect for individual adolescents are the same as those noted in the discussion of bilingual students.

For students who have a pronounced dialect, incorporate the following guidelines into classroom procedures:

1. Whenever students read aloud in class, treat their natural dialect as acceptable. Refrain from stopping such students when their dialect causes them to say something that is considered faulty in standard English.
2. Emphasize the use of context to foster appropriate word identification as well as comprehension.
3. Focus your attention upon *comprehension* rather than recognition of words and syntax in accordance with standard English.
4. Discuss with the students how language develops; how it changes; levels of language usage (such as casual, business, formal, and oral versus written) and the need to be able to use the various levels; and how expressions and word usage can affect our interaction with people. Focus on language in general, not the language of the individual student.
5. In accordance with the premise of this book, teach the skills needed for reading in each of the content areas. Assess specific needs with an informal reading inventory. Then, teach students how to apply the skills to their study. Organize your classes around specific skill needs in which instruction is given in how to apply the technique.

Suggested Activities

1. Discuss major dialect areas in this country. This is an interesting English class project which could involve research.
2. Read to your students to increase background as well as understanding. Also, this serves as a model.
3. Teach new vocabulary every day.
4. Analyze sentences—play with them—with the focus on clarity of meaning. This can be done in any content class as a means also of increasing comprehension.
5. Investigate the role that punctuation plays in clarity of meaning. Again, play with sentences punctuated in different ways, and note the changes in meaning.
6. Have a lot of oral communication in class. Investigate the effect of stress on certain words, intonation, pitch at various parts of a sentence, pauses within the sentence.
7. Provide *practice* in punctuation, spelling, and syntactical forms.
8. Be sure that adequate preparation is given before you assign silent reading. (See lesson procedures in Chapter 7.)
9. Use variations of the experience story procedure in which the students dictate, individually or in a group, their version of the information covered in class.
10. Use creative activities where appropriate, such as writing skits, TV programs, dramatizations, news articles, or letters to friends about what they are learning. These could be done in both standard English and in the dialect. The students would have fun doing such activities and would also get practice in using standard English. This is a delightful way to develop flexibility.

SUMMARY

Understanding the various types of exceptional students and their characteristics is important for planning effectively. Our focus is not on the differences per se but rather on how we can foster success in working to potential and in becoming competent in all academic tasks. We are also concerned with the affective mode in that we try to provide these students with positive school experiences. Like all students, exceptional students are potential contributors to our society.

QUESTIONS AND PROBLEMS FOR YOUR OWN CLASSROOM

For readers who are training to be teachers:

1. Compile a list of activities in your content area that you could use with superior students, slow learners, disabled readers, reluctant readers, bilingual students, and students who speak a pronounced dialect.
2. Prepare a bibliography of materials which you could use with each type of exceptional student.

For readers who are already teaching:

1. For your class develop specific activities for superior readers, reluctant readers, slow learners, disabled readers, and culturally different students.
2. If you have bilingual students, discuss with them their goals and observations about the school. Help them form a committee that will suggest ways to incorporate their cultural patterns into your curriculum as appropriate.
3. Review a unit of study and describe the approach you might use successfully with:
   a. superior readers
   b. slow learners
   c. disabled readers
   d. reluctant readers
   e. culturally different and bilingual readers

SELECTED REFERENCES

Horn, Thomas D., ed. *Reading for the Disadvantaged.* Newark, Del.: IRA, 1970.

Many suggestions are given for teaching the disadvantaged.

Laffey, James L., and Shuy, Roger. *Language Differences: Do They Interfere?* Newark, Del.: IRA, 1973.

Practical insights are noted about language differences.

O'Brien, Carmen. *Teaching the Language Different Child to Read.* Columbus: Charles E. Merrill, 1973.

Excellent suggestions are given for classroom strategies.

Passaw, A. Harry, ed. *The Gifted and the Talented: Their Education and Development.* Chicago: University of Chicago Press, 1979.

A thorough discussion about the education of the gifted.

CHAPTER 10 Remediation

OVERVIEW

It is a well-known fact that there are high school students who need remedial instruction in reading. This chapter addresses the question of what constitutes a productive remedial reading program. Also discussed is the issue of basic reading competency. Fundamentally, teachers who have remedial students in their classrooms are concerned with providing adequate instruction for them.

Questions

Consider these questions before you read further:

1. How do you view your responsibility toward the remedial students in your classroom? How do you presently help such students?
2. What basic competencies do you think are related to the content of your subject?

All high schools have students who need instruction and guidance in reading techniques in order to meet the demands of study. Such students likely have a history of reading difficulty, often resulting in attitude and motivation problems. The deficiency can range from a severe general disability in reading (as in the case of a tenth grade student reading on a second or third grade level) to a pronounced deficiency in only one particular skill or in reading certain subject material.

IDENTIFICATION OF REMEDIAL READERS

Identification of students who need remediation can be through both structured and unstructured means. Many secondary reading programs have a formal or structured testing procedure that is designd to determine if there is a disparity between a student's potential and his or her performance. The first testing obtains a survey of the student's reading status and some measure of his potential. Reading personnel use the results to determine what further assessment is required to ascertain how much help the student needs and how best to provide that help.

Informal methods often are used in conjunction with formal testing to identify candidates for remediation. The two most common informal means are the school history and performance in class. Students who have a reading difficulty probably will have manifested it before the secondary school years; therefore, this difficulty would be noted in their school record. And, an alert content teacher will readily note those students who are not performing well in class. Inadequate accomplishment may be due to a number of reasons, such as having an extracurricular job commitment that is too demanding of the student's time. However, one of the main areas to investigate is reading proficiency.

Students assigned for remedial instruction usually are reading at a level two or more years below what is considered to be their potential capability. That is, in practice, they are students who are two or more years behind their enrolled grade in their ability to read. They cannot master the regular curriculum of the school without help in reading. As you consider the difference between performance and potential, it is very possible that gifted students reading just at grade level may be two or more years below their potential, and thus they could be candidates for remedial help. Other students who may show some slight difficulty but who are less than two years below their potential are termed *corrective*. These students should be able to get whatever corrective help is needed from their regular classroom teachers.

REMEDIAL READING PROGRAMS

In reviewing types of remedial programs in the secondary schools, we find little standardization and several inadequacies. Remedial classes usually have a small number of students. The range is from individual tutoring to classes of around fifteen, sometimes (unfortunately) more. The number depends upon school resources (such as personnel and budget), state and federal mandates, and—most important—the educational concern of the community. In some programs, students are assigned; in others, the student is urged but not compelled to attend (the rationale being that students who are compelled not only will be unmotivated but will actually be hostile, resulting in little or no progress).

One very unfortunate situation in many schools is that the remedial class and its curriculum is isolated from the rest of the curriculum. It is a "subject," just like social studies or mathematics. We must always remember a basic fact: *reading is a process, not a subject. Reading is part of all subjects offered by the school.* Therefore, the best results come from a coordinated effort by all personnel involved with the students.

One type of program organized in many schools is the reading *laboratory* or *multilearning center.* Such a room usually is equipped with tapes, recorders, and computers designed to enable the supervising teacher to prescribe an individual curriculum of correction for each student. Other materials include various self-help and self-monitoring practice materials and *books.* The materials are attractive, modern, and very much in step with today's technology.

The ideas of individualization of instruction and of students taking responsibility for their own learning (knowing what to work on, monitoring their progress, and pacing themselves) are excellent educational precepts. But this set-up is doomed to fail, for a number of reasons. First, the *material* does not teach; at best, it only reinforces what has been taught. The author has visited several reading labs and has found students making the same mistake over and over. They did not know what they were doing wrong, and sometimes they did not even know what skill was involved. This is an example of inadequate instruction—if it can be called instruction at all. Therefore, the teacher must monitor each student's practice even after the prescription has been planned. Then the teacher must provide the necessary instruction. Second, very few students are able to help themselves completely—they need instructions and guidance. It would seem that this is one reason for having teachers! Finally, the approach in many labs is mechanical. There is no place for the discussion of ideas with peers or even with the teacher. The emphasis is completely on skills, and this can be a sterile approach. When a teacher is concerned with interest, motivation, and the enrichment of background, ideas must be investigated.

Many secondary school remedial programs are in need of great improvement. Whether or not such classes are necessary and accomplish the goal of helping high school students often is brought into question. Some educators think that all help possible should be given; others seem to think that remediation should begin earlier in the student's educational career—high school is too late! In my opinion, it would seem that a school's function is to extend as much help as is possible within the resources of the school.

As educators, we need to be aware of the plight of all high school students who have difficulty reading. Shuman aptly states:

> The process of teaching a teenager to read is a long and often frustrating one—but the teacher must remember that it seems even longer and more

> frustrating to the youngster who has to live with this disability and who has suffered the defeats which all non-readers must endure in our society.[1]

Therefore remedial classes *should* be set up, but they must be well-designed in organization and procedure.

Guidelines for a Remedial Program

Whether the school has a lavishly equipped reading-learning center with both hardware (machines) and software (books), or just a regular classroom, meagerly equipped, there are guidelines and cautions for insuring teaching effectiveness. Many of these have been implied throughout this book, and they may seem idealistic given the practical school situation. However, they must be incorporated for students to benefit from the program.

1. Reading classes must not be isolated from the rest of the high school curriculum. Students attending a remedial reading class also are taking regular subjects with texts written at the high school level. The reading teacher should have copies of their textbooks and should know the types of assignments given. Likewise, subject teachers should know from the reading teacher the students' instructional level and needs as well as the skills the reading teacher is trying to develop. These skills, then, should be applied and reinforced in each content area. In addition, students need to learn ways to transfer learning from the reading class to each content subject.
2. There must be a coordination of effort between the reading teacher and the content teachers. The teachers involved will probably want to do this, but scheduling to allow time for teacher consultation is important. Some schools are providing time for reading teachers to work with classroom teachers—a healthy trend.
3. Teachers must be aware of the students' *attitude* toward reading instruction, which can affect the amount and rate of progress. Often we see students acting in ways that serve as defenses against the disability in reading (behavior which as teachers we may deplore). Yet there are few high school students who do not want to be able to read. What, then, are some of the techniques to counter negative attitudes?
   a. The instruction must be *encouraging*. Students must experience success from the very beginning.
   b. The instruction must be *meaningful*. Students should be guided to use the reading instruction in other classes and therefore realize its benefits to them.
   c. The teacher should be *honest and objective* with students. Let them know their strengths and weaknesses in reading. Incorporate their ideas into the planning for improvement; help them to map out a

---

1. R. Baird Shuman, "Of Course He Can Read—He's in High School!" *Journal of Reading* 19 (October 1975): 42.

program, thereby helping them realize the organization and progression of instruction.
d. As necessary, *explain the process of reading* to the students. Give them information about the science of reading. For instance, the analogy of the warm-up before a game to the preparation for reading a selection is one that almost all students can understand.
e. Give specific techniques which immediately help them in a subject that is of concern to them—for example, how to break a word into syllables, how to get information from a map, or how to use topical headings effectively.
4. The instruction must be *highly individualized.* Whatever materials are used, students should be allowed to pace themselves. Provide continuous guidance to help students overcome possible difficulties.
5. Base instruction on *diagnosis* to discover instructional needs.
6. The class must be *interesting.* Do not just assign a series of humdrum drills on skills in an isolated fashion. Though some such instruction is necessary to provide the students with know-how and to clinch their grasp of it, *discuss ideas.* Then through the discussion of the ideas, apply the skills.
7. Help students plot their progress. This may be done by giving short exercises once a week from which they can graph their achievements. Also, let the students know the level of material they are using and when they have progressed to the next level.

REMEDIATION IN THE CONTENT AREA CLASSROOM

The attack on remedial reading problems should be a team effort between the reading teacher and the content area teachers. Content teachers who have remedial readers in their classes will have to teach and reinforce reading skills. You will also need to employ sound procedures consonant with effective remediation.

Suggested Techniques

These suggestions are applicable to *all* content subjects. Many of them have been mentioned elsewhere in this text in the discussion of teaching subject matter and reading. Indeed, much that is done in a well-planned classroom can be applied to remediation.

1. Encourage students to share experiences pertinent to a topic. This is one way to increase students' background of experience.
2. Let students cooperate on some assignments in small groups or a buddy-type organization. Students do learn from each other!
3. Involve students in rewriting a textbook in their own words after discussion of a topic. This activity provides invaluable opportunities for noting organization, such as outlining the information, listing the relation of main ideas to details, and charting the use of

vocabulary terms. A variation is to write daily "news bulletins" of the essential points covered in class.

4. Collect a classroom library of materials consisting of one to two copies each of other textbooks on differing levels, trade books, and novels. Include periodical material. One teacher organized a collection of articles interesting to teenagers from past issues of a student science magazine. These articles also served as enrichment of the information she taught. Each folder of articles contained ten articles, and some folders were designated as advanced or easy. Each student was expected to read and react to a folder of articles during one marking period (nine weeks). Books for a classroom library may be obtained from the school library, public library, and from the students. Purchase inexpensive paperbacks.
5. Use a variety of classroom organization to accomplish your goal of individualization. (See Chapter 7).
6. Plan with the student an individual contract or job sheet which considers the student's level, ability, and needs. This also helps the student set realistic goals.
7. Give your class time to read for both study and recreation. Two goals can be accomplished with this technique: (*a*) you have an opportunity to work with individuals, and (*b*) you will likely foster the student's enjoyment of reading.
8. Use effective instructional procedure. Basic needs include: adequate *preparation* to read the selection, appropriate *instruction* in how to read the selection, necessary *reinforcement* through application and practice, and frequent *review* to develop familiarity with the information and terminology as well as proficiency in the skill.
9. Analyze the patterns of writing in the assigned reading materials. Show the students how the information is organized. Lead them toward independence in this skill.
10. Give instruction in study techniques. Review with them how to attack a specific assignment, how to take notes from their reading, how to use specific aids in the textbook, and so on. (See Chapter 5).
11. Ask clearly stated questions and give enough time for the students to formulate answers. Do not always expect a rapid, immediate answer to a question. Sometimes by a slow series of questions you may lead the students to an answer—and success.
12. Give thorough instruction in the graphic aids within the reading material. Reinforce graphics constantly by using them whenever possible.
13. Collect and use all media you can to teach the concepts and information: television, films, records, cassettes, pictures, models, and techniques such as role playing.
14. Use tapes of key paragraphs from the textbook. Students should follow in the textbook as the tape plays. In fact, Carol Chomsky recommends a "memorization" technique which she used in the primary grades with stories. Students listen to the tape often enough so that they casually "memorize" the selection and finally can read it

without the tape. Listening and absorbing is supplemented by writing activities and language games.[2]

15. Help students with word recognition techniques in the content classes, especially that of syllabication. Constantly review their knowledge of syllabication; reinforce it by breaking words into prefixes-roots-suffixes as appropriate. When introducing a new word, write it on the blackboard and show the syllabication by broken underlining.
16. Develop vocabulary meaning as much as possible from the students' background of experience. Evolve the meanings from them if possible. This is one way of helping the students to relate the new contextual meaning to what they already know. Further, alert them to and give practice in the contextual meaning of a new word as it is introduced within the textbook.
17. Help students to see the overview of the material, how it is organized. For instance, in an account of an historical event, conjecture with them what kinds of information will be included (the causes, what happened, people involved, and the effects). Have them check their textbook to see if the author follows such a basic order of presenting the information. In other words, help them to *anticipate* the kinds of information that will be included.
18. Assist students in establishing specific purposes for reading. What do they wish to find out? Give them specific purposes and evolve purposeful questions with them. With remedial readers, have purpose embrace only a page or a couple of paragraphs at first, and make the purposes as concrete as possible. Further, give practice and instruction in formulating questions from topical headings.
19. Structure the assignment for remedial readers. For instance, inform them that they will find two main ideas in the assignment, and each main idea has three details. Conjecture with them where the main ideas and details will be found. Alert them to *signal words* (such as *first, next,* and *finally*).
20. Ask open-ended questions which lead the students to relate their own experiences and values to the information. Ask questions: "How do you think we can use this information?" "What would you have done if ________?" "What is your reaction to this point of view?"
21. Lead remedial students toward independent study as quickly as possible by teaching them how to use the text. Help them acquire the ability to know how to use the Table of Contents, the index, chapter titles, headings, summaries, introductions, glossary, appendices and various study aids contained in the book.
22. Similar to analyzing the patterns of writing and overall organization, analyze in detail the organization of key paragraphs. Help students to see how each sentence relates to the others in the paragraph. One way of doing this is to review the information during discussion and then check how the author organized it in the paragraph. The purpose of various function or structure words should become apparent. Also, this technique reinforces key ideas.

---

2. Carol Chomsky, "After Decoding: What?" *Language Arts* 53 (March 1976): 288.

23. Give instruction in following directions. Check understanding of common words—for example, *place, set, to the right of, perpendicular to, horizontal,* and so on. Also, ask such questions as "What do you do after you have done ______?" "What do you do before you ______?"
24. Emphasize precision in the meaning of terms referring to space and time. Note which terms are more or less definite. For example, "at ten o'clock in the morning" is definite; "mid-morning" is less definite, "on the morning of ______" is even more indefinite. In regard to space, one also finds degrees of definiteness in space terms: "turn to the right and go six blocks," "turn right and go about one half to three quarters of a mile," "go right a short distance." Have students give directions using different degrees of definiteness, and analyze which are easier to follow.
25. As appropriate to the subject area, expose students to the various forms and applications that a person should be able to complete. Help the students understand the kind of information asked for, such as "no. of dependents," "physical disabilities," "committed any felonies or violations," and so on. This activity is very pertinent in mathematics (tax forms, checks, loan applications, and so on); all vocational subjects (job applications, various bookkeeping forms); and driver training (license application).
26. Help students learn to classify ideas by classifying the key vocabulary terms under appropriate headings (such as *process, events, places, people,* and so on). A variation is to place the words in a type of outline to show the fundamental concept and the other terms which relate to it. For instance, a key conceptual term may be *government,* and the other terms may be types of government (such as *democracy, monarchy, theocracy*). Or *atmosphere* may be the key conceptual term, with the other terms labelling parts of the atmosphere (such as stratosphere).
27. Help students state information in their own words by having them transpose key sentences from the text. Brainstorm with them to see how the sentence may be stated in different ways: made into a question, from active to passive, and from positive to negative.
28. Set up as many learning centers in your room as possible. Organize them around various topics in your subject to give enrichment and to allow students to work in areas of interest and to gain experience in independence. These centers can also be organized around skill areas. Steurer lists many learning center activities applicable to the various content subjects.[3] For example, in driver education, students could learn the rules of the road by answering the questions on the test for a driver's permit. In language arts, they could focus on the skill of following directions by writing a formal letter and then checking it against a listing of important elements of a letter. In science, students could sharpen searching skills by noting page numbers on which the answers to certain questions appear.

---

3. Stephen J. Steurer, "Learning Centers in the Secondary School," *Journal of Reading* 22, No. 2 (November 1978): 138-39.

EDITORIAL

The Remedial Reader and Content Reading

Mainstreaming has emphasized the need for adapting instruction to make content accessible to students regardless of their learning characteristics. However, conventional instructional approaches are ineffective with those students who exhibit reading and language deficiencies. For various reasons, the manner in which they process information results in inadequate acquisition and retention of content. Therefore, instruction should be adapted to promote effective processing, including accessing, storage, and retrieval of information.

Activities in the teaching of reading in the content area include specific procedures for alleviating deficiencies in processing that can be applied to various subject matter areas. The selection of the appropriate activities is influenced by the manner in which the remedial student approaches processing.

Many students who possess average and above average intelligence are appearing in mainstream classes with increasing frequency. Since their learning pattern tends to be holistic and simultaneous, they may not adequately process receptive language which is sequential in nature. Difficulties in differentiating between and focusing on details result in a slipshod grasp of new information. In addition, these students are frequently disorganized; consequently, the relationship and relative importance of ideas remain elusive to them. Since the information is neither received nor stored in an orderly way, the retrieval is laborious and memory is described as poor. Inadequate verbal and written responses are often considered to be the product of slow learners in need of special education programs. Actually, the failure and frustration can be alleviated through the application of reading strategies which are concerned with the process of presenting content.

The teaching of reading through the content areas exerts a global effect on the reception, storage, and retrieval of content. Several strategies are more versatile in terms of both the students' processing needs and the number of subjects to which they may be applied. These include strategies that:

1. Associate new information with the students' informa-

tion base using familiar syntax, content, and reality situations.

2. Provide organization for orderly reception and storage through the use of preorganizers, which include flow charts and grids.
3. Utilize questions as a means of accessing and retrieving information.
4. Include opportunities for multiple categorization.
5. Develop understanding of the author's pattern or schema to alleviate the distraction caused by focusing on details.
6. Provide for frequent repetition or echoing of content.

These strategies and others inherent in the teaching of reading offer a means of penetrating the barrier between the student with processing deficiencies and the learning of content.

The teaching of reading in the content area is not a new concept. However, in the world of today where computers set a model for learning theory and learning disorders are thought of as problems in information processing, and because content reading is process-oriented, it achieves a new stature in the remediation of students with reading and language disabilities who are faced with the acquisition and retention of content.

Margaret Carvo

High School Reading Consultant

BASIC COMPETENCY

A number of state departments of education are requiring that secondary school students have a basic competency in reading, social studies, and mathematics, as well as in some other areas. The principal concern is for students to be able to function as citizens in society. It is well-known that the level of literacy (the point at which a person is self-sufficient in using the graphic form of language) has been rising, chiefly in response to the increasing complexity of technology. One has to be able to read directions and manuals. No manual is necessary for the use of a shovel, but one is necessary in the use and upkeep of a ditch-digging machine. Mastering directions, signs, forms, labels, manuals, and a basic knowledge of the workings of government, measurements, and simple arithmetic are fundamental in our society. In brief, basic competency means the ability to read well enough to gain and apply information.

Tests of basic competency attempt to determine whether or not the individual knows information and can apply such skills as the following:

1. Read road signs.
2. Understand cartoons.
3. Read and understand labels on all commercial products.
4. Use a telephone directory.
5. Read directions on how to fill out a form.
6. Apply directions for the construction of some equipment or toy.
7. Write a simple sentence.
8. Use basic grammar: constructions, capitalization, punctuation.
9. Read and comprehend a simple sentence or paragraph.
10. Do simple arithmetic: addition, subtraction, multiplication, division, fractions, percent.
11. Understand and read measurements and distances.
12. Understand correspondence between words and arabic numerals.
13. Find area.
14. Know basic shapes.
15. Read and interpret simple graphs.
16. Obtain information from maps, such as distances and directions on a road map.
17. Do simple problems; e.g., if a pound/kilo of apples costs $.70, how much would 2½ pounds/kilos cost?
18. Interpret advertisements.
19. Understand an election ballot.
20. Understand the basic concepts of insurance contracts, and withholdings.

A sampling of the types of concepts often considered necessary for being a competent member of society readily shows those areas of concern today: safety; general health; disease and injury; the metric system; ecology and pollution; temperature and humidity; functions of government: taxes, census, structure, political parties; constitutional rights; economy, inflation; voting; and duties of various public officers.

Basic student competency lies largely in the ability to use the graphic form of language. Words in common usage have to be known (*installment, buying, employer, consumer, area, deposit, ballot, sum*)—in short, all of the general words in the various disciplines which have been suggested in earlier chapters of this book.

Part of basic competency is understanding questions that often are multiple choice. For example:

1. Which level of government is responsible for the minting of coins?

   A. local C. city
   B. state D. federal

   The technical ideas (concepts) and words which students must know are *level of government, minting of coins, local* (government), *state* (government), *city* (government), *federal* (government). The nontechnical word, *responsible,* is also one they must know as it is used in the question.
2. In a period of economic depression, what would you most likely see happen?

   A. raises in wages C. unemployment
   B. more factories built D. higher prices

   The concepts the students must understand are *period of, economic depression, raises in wages, unemployment, higher prices.*
3. The term *ecology* is best defined as the study of:

   A. conservation C. pollution
   B. the balance of nature D. our relation to nature

   The technical concepts the students must understand are *ecology, conservation, balance of nature, pollution, our relation to nature.* Nontechnical concepts are *term, best defined, study of.*
4. A football team won 70% of its games. If the team played 20 games, how many games were won?

   A. 14 C. 12
   B. 6 D. 16

   Students must be able to read and solve verbal problems and apply the concept of percent.
5. If a rectangle has a width of 3 feet/centimeters and a length of 5 feet/centimeters, what is the number of feet/centimeters in th distance around the rectangle?

   A. 7 C. 16
   B. 11 D. 18

   Students must know and *be able to visualize* the following concepts: *rectangle, width, length, distance around.*

In the content classes, give practical daily living assignments when appropriate to the topic under study. Most students benefit from such instruction. There are students who need little such instruction, others who need only a review of the basic competencies and still others who need much basic instruction and application. Use materials the students already use or might use in the future, such as television guides; the telephone directory; the yellow pages of the phone book; mail-order catalogs; and labels on cans, clothing, and boxes. Ask them to write how-to directions for a project, a description of the best route to take to school, and basic business letters. Have them analyze advertisements and interpret signs. The understandings needed for basic competency can be found in nearly all of the disciplines.

Basic competency seems to mean survival skills for functioning adequately in our society, but what is really involved? If desired literacy is at the twelfth grade level of reading proficiency, are mere survival skills enough? Should the competency needed for high school graduation include more than survival skills? In fact, there seems to be a trend toward higher competency requirements for graduation from high school.

Guidelines for Competency-based Programs

There are, as you can see, fundamental questions we need to answer. Cassidy helps us by suggesting ten guidelines for developing competency-based programs.[4]

1. *Multilevel competencies.* Students should be evaluated at various points during their school career, beginning at the end of the primary level. They should not find themselves in the position of nearly completing their schooling, then being judged incompetent.
2. *Insurance of due process.* Certainly, students must receive instruction as soon as they are found to be incompetent in certain areas.
3. *Adequate remediation.* Cassidy firmly believes that it is the school's responsibility to help students acquire the needed competencies.
4. *Flexibility of time.* Since students are different, they should not all be expected to achieve competency at the same time, and students should have more than one opportunity to show their competence.
5. *Minimum standards.* All students must pass these minimum standards for competency, but they do not constitute the entire curriculum.
6. *Certificates of competence.* These should be issued as an alternative to the traditional high school diploma.
7. *Uniformity of standards.* Cassidy thinks that this is vital from school district to school district, perhaps coming from the state level.
8. *Adequate performance indicators.* Valid and reliable assessment measures must be used.
9. *Dissemination of standards to all involved.* All participants—students, teachers, and parents—must know what the basic competencies are.
10. *Relevance.* The competencies must be relevant to functioning in adult society.

Teaching these basic competencies is not glamorous and is not particularly fascinating to the high school specialist in a specific subject area.

---

4. Jack Cassidy, "High School Graduation: Exit Competencies?" *Journal of Reading* 21, No. 5 (February 1978): 400-401.

Yet for two reasons we must not lose sight of them. One, the students need proficiency in background information and language usage so that they can acquire further learning; two, these are the understandings needed for independence and citizenship in a democratic society today. Further, Smith points out that "if students are to adapt to our present changing society and to our increasingly accelerated future, they must know how to adjust their thinking to different situations, how to evaluate changing conditions, and how to solve problems."[5]

SUMMARY

All content teachers have students who require remedial instruction in reading in their classroom. Therefore, the content teacher is as involved with their basic reading instruction as is a reading teacher. Content teachers must work collaboratively with the remedial reading teacher rather than in isolation. In this way, students learn to adapt reading skills to all content areas; reading is not seen as a subject unto itself.

QUESTIONS AND PROBLEMS FOR YOUR OWN CLASSROOM

For readers who are training to be teachers:

1. List those basic competencies which would develop from the content of your subject.
2. Consider how you will provide for the remedial student in your classroom: the focus of your teaching, types of classroom management and individualization, and the skills and reading techniques you may need to incorporate into your lesson planning.

For readers who are teaching:

1. Compile a list of the basic competencies in your subject which a student needs to master.
2. If students in your class also attend remedial reading classes, consult with the remedial teacher to coordinate ways to meet the needs of the student.

SELECTED REFERENCES

Bond, Guy L., Tinker, Miles A., and Wasson, Barbara B. *Reading Difficulties, Their Diagnosis and Correction.* 4th Ed. Englewood Cliffs, N.J.: Prentice Hall, 1979.

A comprehensive discussion is presented about remediation.

Klein, Howard A. *The Quest for Competency in Teaching Reading.* Newark, Del.: IRA, 1972.

Insight is given about the term competency.

Robinson, H. Alan, and Rauch, Sidney J. *Corrective Reading in the High School Classroom.* Perspectives No. 6. Newark, Del.: IRA, 1966.

Excellent suggestions are presented for classroom strategies.

---

5. Nila Banton Smith, "The Quest for Increased Reading Competency," in *The Quest for Competency in Teaching Reading,* ed. Howard A. Klein (Newark, Del.: IRA, 1972), p. 55.

CHAPTER 11

Adjusting Materials to the Student

OVERVIEW

All of us who teach must adjust materials to the reading proficiency of our students. Resourceful teachers can find several ways to do this. Perhaps one of the first steps is to judge the difficulty level of the materials you have so that you can note how the reading levels of your students match up with them. Then, employ teaching techniques that will help the students to use the textbook and other materials effectively. *Rewriting* sometimes is a possibility. And, of course, collecting supplementary materials for your classroom is essential.

Questions

Consider these questions before you read further:

1. How do you currently adjust reading materials to the students in your classes?
2. What criteria do you use to evaluate the textbooks you use?

"My students can't read their textbook! I can't tell them everything they should learn in my class. What do you do in situations like this? I don't know!" Content teachers in the high schools have voiced similar comments for a number of years. An obvious answer is to acquire some easier materials. However, though we know that a wide variety of material should be available in every classroom, in actual practice the teacher often has only one textbook. Also, the technical nature of the content in some subjects may preclude easier materials. Then, what is the teacher to do?

Studies of textbook difficulty often have discovered that textbooks in the content subjects are above the students' reading level. Since all teachers teach individuals with a range of reading levels, teachers need to think about the factors that determine the difficulty level of a book. These factors are many and they affect both cognitive understanding and the affective reaction. Once we review those factors that render the material difficult, we can begin to examine how to "work around" them.

FACTORS AFFECTING DIFFICULTY OF MATERIALS

The Affective Mode

What are your students' *interests* in the subject and, hence, what is their *motivation* to read? We have all seen students who, when keenly interested, can successfully tackle material that seems difficult. Related to this, do the students see the *relevance* of the information to themselves? Think about your own reading. Being interested in a subject makes reading about it easier; at least you are willing to put forth the effort. This is also true for students, and they must achieve success if the effort is to be sustained.

Obviously, *intelligence* is a factor. The *background of experience or knowledge* students bring to the subject quite markedly affects the difficulty level. The more one knows about a subject, the easier the reading material is to comprehend. Do you, then, prepare the students for reading an assignment in the textbook—filling in background, establishing the meanings of key words, previewing to see the overall organization, and setting definite purposes for reading? If your assignments are merely to read the next few pages and be ready to discuss it, the material certainly will prove difficult for many students. We must remember that high school students are not as independent as we are. *They need instruction and guidance in how to handle reading material successfully.*

Finally, there may be an *emotional reaction* to some topics. It has been established that subject matter which affects us emotionally in a negative manner tends to be forgotten quickly, and the understanding is less accurate. Therefore, should you use discussion, ask questions that clarify thinking, and use procedures such as problem solving to encourage objectivity?

The Textbook Format

Look at the book and note your reaction. Is it appealing, does it have an attractive format? Does it look difficult and forbidding or does it look manageable? Is the print readable? Are the illustrations and other graphics appropriate and close to the explanatory text? What study aids does the book provide? We know that textbooks vary in quality of format, but most have features which can assist the students. Make note of the positive features and how students can use them.

In one English class students were given a paperback text in which the print was small, the pages were crowded and had little "white space," and the overall impression was of oceans of print. One student said, "Oh, this is going to be hard! It looks boring." Wisely the teacher responded by suggesting that they read a paragraph or two to see if it *was* hard and boring. She read a paragraph to the class while they followed in their copies. They found it was very simply written. The teacher had successfully allayed the students' deepest fears, but the format itself could have affected the students' use of the book if the teacher had not interceded.

Organization

Note the *organization of information* in the textbook. Is it logical? Does it flow naturally? Can it be outlined easily? If you get affirmative answers to these questions, then in your classroom procedure work with the students in noting the organization of topical headings, anticipating the organization the author will likely use (before reading), basic patterns of the paragraphs, and so on. If you find that the book is not well-organized, then you might need to give the students study guides with suggestions such as: "On page 82 the following topic is discussed and the author gives three important factual details. On page 83 the author cites a cause and effect. See if you can note the cause and effect." (Note that the subject information is not given because you *do* want the students to read!)

Noting organization may well involve analysis of paragraph patterns. If the pattern, for instance, is mainly that of main ideas followed by detail, work with your students in identifying the pattern. Give guidance such as, "The main idea of this paragraph is ______. There are two important supporting details. Can you find them?" Or the opposite: "The two facts the author gives are ______ and ______. What do you think the main idea would be? Can you find such a sentence? Where is it located?" If you have a paragraph of definition, you may say, "Can you find the definition of ______ in this paragraph? Does the author qualify it, illustrate it, or support it in the remainder of the paragraph? Does he expand at all on the basic definition?"

There is a caution when you begin to analyze paragraphs. Some textbooks are not clearly written and sometimes paragraphs are garbled; this, of course, adds significantly to the difficulty level. Here, you will probably need to give students an accompanying study guide with suggestions. Further, you may encounter a disturbing practice: presumably to increase white space on a page or to make paragraphs look simple and readable, a rather long, well-constructed paragraph is arbitrarily divided into two or three short paragraphs. This makes it very difficult to teach proper organization, as the text itself does not portray it. The result is very confusing to the student, who has to structure the information into a logical organization.

Writing Style

Allied closely to organization is the *author's style of writing.* Is it lucid, logical, free-flowing? Is the writing in the popular vein, with many anecdotes and realistic illustrations, or is it technical? Because of the nature of the subject matter, many textbooks are technical—for example, mathematics and the sciences, bookkeeping, economics, musical theory, and industrial arts manuals. If your material is written technically, then the student needs instruction in how to read such material. Incidentally, it is with this type of material that we are unable to find easier texts. Much of this material is in an abbreviated style of writing, a shorthand language, in which complete ideas are expressed: equations, theorems, formulas, tables, and various graphic illustrations (such as maps and graphs). These technical subjects also have specialized vocabulary and expressions for comparing information; showing relationships, trends, patterns, and calculations; and noting quantities. Indeed, careful and meticulous reading is required. Help the students to translate the abbreviated language to "normal" language in their own words, show them the logical structure of the information (perhaps a study guide showing this would help), and be sure they understand the vocabulary and special symbols used.

Examples

Next note the *number of examples*—practical illustrations—given in the text. This can indicate a ratio of concreteness to abstraction. It is well-established that abstractions are more difficult to comprehend than concrete examples. In fact, this may be one reason why a single textbook with a number of illustrations can have a range of four to five years in the level of difficulty of passages. When a textbook author is presenting a principle or process and explaining factual information, the language tends to be more formal. The new vocabulary often is presented at this point. Examples and illustrations of the ideas tend to be in more casual syntax and simpler vocabulary.

Good verbal illustrations can be of great help to students who find a textbook difficult. They may well be at a frustration level when reading sentences and paragraphs that are abstract. But illustrations or anecdotes in simpler language help students understand the abstractions, relieving their feelings of frustration.

READABILITY

Research is endeavoring to identify the factors that make language readable. Upon reflection, you can conclude what some of these factors are: familiarity with the vocabulary, understanding of the grammatical structure, and the ratio of concreteness to abstraction. In the area of vocabulary, where there are multiple meanings of a word, students may know one or more of the definitions but not the meaning used in the reading selection. Long words are considered more difficult than short ones, though this can vary. (Even in first grade we find many children who can remember how to read *rhinoceros* but have continual difficulty with such a small word as *but.*) The complexity of a word may also be a barrier, as when prefixes, suffixes, or various inflectional endings are added to a root word.

Another assumption is that sentence length plays a role in the difficulty of a passage. Simple, direct statements are considered easiest to read, with compound sentences (two simple statements connected by a conjunction) next in ease of understanding. The complex sentence (a qualifying clause subordinate to the main clause) is much more difficult because a relationship is present and must be discerned by the reader. The complex-compound sentence is considered the hardest because it is the longest and there is a relationship among the clauses. However, we cannot always say that the passage composed only of simple statements is easiest to understand. For example, two simple statements—*The boys went to the movies* and *The boys played soccer*—do not show the relationship of time, while the following, longer sentence does: *After the boys went to the movies they played soccer*. It can also be argued that the second, longer sentence is more difficult to comprehend since it contains a referent for *boys*—*they*—and the reader has to comprehend this. The farther away a referent or modifier is from what is being referred to or modified, the more difficult the sentence. Apparently, readers have trouble keeping in mind what is being referred to or modified if the distance is too long.

Readability Formulas

The attempt to find factors that cause difficulty has lead to the continual development of formulas. These formulas, of which there are now between thirty and forty, are designed to measure the readability of an article or a book. They are objective measurements, usually expressed in grade level. Teachers can use these formulas to ascertain whether the material fits the students' level of proficiency in reading.

The formulas measure not the complexity of content but rather aspects of the author's style: word difficulty, as noted by either word length or familiarity; and sentence difficulty, noted usually by length. The most widely used formulas rely on these two aspects, though they measure them differently. Other formulas attempt to bring in other factors, and the formulas vary in the complexity and amount of time involved in doing the calculation. Some are designed for specific levels of materials (as for just primary materials); others measure the difficulty of materials beginning at fourth or fifth grade and extending through college.

Since most of the formulas measure only two factors, there is a general consensus that they are highly inaccurate. But, it is also generally agreed that they are useful guides to teachers in fitting the students to the book. In a discussion of readability formulas, Standal presents a sensible view:

> [The] brief consideration of readability formulas suggest two things. The first is that readability formulas are best thought of as guides for general indicators of a possible range of materials suited to any given child. They are not absolutes. If they are regarded as general indicators, they can be quite useful.

The second point is that a teacher who regards the formulas as guides and who is aware of the experiences, interests, and aspirations of the children in her/his charge almost automatically overcomes the . . . deficits of readability formulas. The various formulas cannot take interest and previous experience into consideration. But the teacher can—and should.[1]

Campbell further notes the need for teacher assistance to the students as they read the text:

Indeed, one of the considerations when assessing readability of texts should be the amount of teacher assistance which will be available. A difficult text can be made comprehensible by preteaching the essential concepts and unfamiliar vocabulary. Ongoing comprehension can be facilitated by discussion that directs a student's learning. Well designed questions can reinforce newly learned concepts, build up expectations, and focus attention on major points. . . . There is no need for teachers to discard texts because they are difficult. There is a need for teachers to be aware of possible difficulties.[2]

It would be impossible to cite all of the formulas with enough detailed description of their use here. Some of the most widely used ones will be named and briefly commented upon. For the detail you will require as you plan to use any of them, see the selected references at the end of this chapter. Table 11.1 shows four widely used formulas with brief comments about the nature and use of each.

In using any of the formulas, it is important to follow the directions strictly. Passages must be selected carefully; they can vary in difficulty within one book because of the particular subject matter covered, the ratio of concreteness to abstraction, and the style of an author when there are two or more authors. Passages should be an equal number of pages apart, varying the number of pages counted only if the page is a blank or is used completely for a graphic presentation (such as a picture, map, and so on). The greater the number of evenly spaced passages we analyze, the more accurate our measure of the book will be.

Teachers often do not use readability formulas because of the time involved in doing a thorough readability of a book, added to possible mathematical calculation time. Various devices and tables have been constructed to make it easier and less time-consuming to arrive at readability. One is the "Readability Estimator," put out by Charles E. Merrill Publishing Company. It is based on the Fry readability formula. The "Estimator" eliminates the graph of Fry's formula.

A departure from predicting readability is the cloze procedure for measuring readability. The cloze procedure, described in Chapter 6, measures reading comprehension of text materials. A comprehension score, not a grade level, is determined. The score obtained from the cloze procedure reflects intelligence, background of information, understanding of language usage and patterns, familiarity with styles of expository prose, and the

1. Timothy C. Standal, "Readability Formulas: What's Out, What's In?" *Journal of Reading* 31, No. 6 (March 1978): 646.

2. Anne Campbell, "How Readability Formulae Fall Short in Matching Student to Text in the Content Areas," *Journal of Reading* 22, No. 8 (May 1979): 685-87.

TABLE 11.1 Selected Widely Used Formulas

Dale-Chall	*Fry*
1. Uses a Dale list of 3,000 familiar words—user is to note words in passage not on the list.	1. Uses word syllable count.
2. Uses sentence length per 100-word sample.	2. Uses sentence length per 100-word sample.
3. Considered among the most accurate. Samples taken every tenth page.	3. Only three samples recommended.
4. Takes much time to apply. Some mathematical computation.	4. Relatively quick to apply. Graph supplants mathematical computation.
5. Good for grades 4 through college.	5. Can be used for grades 1 through college.
Flesch	*SMOG*
1. Uses word syllable count.	1. Word count of all words three or more syllables.
2. Uses sentence length per 100-word sample. Number of sentences determined by complete units of thought irrespective of punctuation.	2. Compute approximate square root of the number of polysyllabic words; add 3 for SMOG grade.
3. Twenty-five to thirty samples are recommended for each book.	3. Three ten-word samples: at beginning, middle, and end of book.
4. Can be time-consuming for the number of samples required.	4. Considered to be very quick.
5. Can be used for grade 5 through college.	5. Best used with grades 7 through college.

concept load of the material. Research is continuing in the application of the cloze to differing types of materials. There is some question, for instance, as to whether or not every fifth word should be deleted in some content materials, such as science; whether or not students should be expected to fill in the deletion with the exact word used by the author, and whether words for which there are no contextual clues should be deleted. Still, the cloze procedure does provide the discerning teacher with a measure of the students' comprehension of the reading material to be used. Further, it does call for more interaction between the reader and the selection than does the count of word frequency count and sentence length used by the predictive formulas.

TEXTBOOK EVALUATION

As implied earlier, you can judge the appropriateness of a textbook for your students. You can note the assets as well as the deficiencies of a text by reading and analyzing it. In this way, you will gain insights in how your classroom procedure may accommodate to the text. For example, if the text states the main ideas clearly and uses most often the paragraph pattern of a main idea followed by detail, you will certainly have your students become aware of such organization and provide practice in noting it. If, on the other hand, you find that main ideas are not clearly stated, then you may need to provide study guides, perhaps in the form of marginal notes, showing what and where the main ideas are. Irwin and Davis have compiled a "Readability Checklist" teachers can use to evaluate the readability of a textbook (see Table 11.2).[3]

TABLE 11.2 Readability Checklist

This checklist is designed to help you evaluate the readability of your classroom texts. It can best be used if you rate your text while you are thinking of a specific class. Be sure to compare the textbook to a fictional ideal rather than to another text. Your goal is to find out what aspects of the text are or are not less than ideal. Finally, consider supplementary workbooks as part of the textbook and rate them together. Have fun!

Rate the questions below using the following rating system:

5—Excellent
4—Good
3—Adequate
2—Poor
1—Unacceptable
NA—Not applicable

Further comments may be written in the space provided.

Textbook title: ______
Publisher ______
Copyright date: ______

Understandability

A. ____ Are the assumptions about students' vocabulary knowledge appropriate?
B. ____ Are the assumptions about students' prior knowledge of this content area appropriate?
C. ____ Are the assumptions about students' general experiential backgrounds appropriate?
D. ____ Does the teacher's manual provide the teacher with ways to develop and review the students' conceptual and experiential backgrounds?
E. ____ Are new concepts explicitly linked to the students' prior knowledge or to their experiential backgrounds?
F. ____ Does the text introduce abstract concepts by accompanying them with many concrete examples?
G. ____ Does the text introduce new concepts one at a time with a sufficient number of examples for each one?
H. ____ Are definitions understandable and at a lower level of abstraction than the conception being defined?
I. ____ Is the level of sentence complexity appropriate for the students?
J. ____ Are the main ideas of paragraphs, chapters, and subsections clearly stated?
K. ____ Does the text avoid irrelevant details?
L. ____ Does the text explicitly state important complex relationships (e.g., causality,

3. Judith Westphal Irwin and Carol A. Davis, "Assessing Readability: The Checklist Approach," *Journal of Reading* 24, No. 2 (November 1980): 129-30.

TABLE 11.2 *(cont'd)*

conditionality, etc.) rather than always expecting the reader to infer them from the context?

M. ____Does the teacher's manual provide lists of accessible resources containing alternative readings for the very poor or very advanced readers?

N. ____Is the readability level appropriate (according to a readability formula)?

Learnability

Organization

A. ____Is an introduction provided for in each chapter?

B. ____Is there a clear and simple organizational pattern relating the chapters to each other?

C. ____Does each chapter have a clear, explicit, and simple organizational structure?

D. ____Does the text include resources such as an index, glossary, and table of contents?

E. ____Do questions and activities draw attention to the organizational pattern of the material (e.g. chronological, cause and effect, spatial, topical, etc.)?

F. ____Do consumable materials interrelate well with the textbook?

Reinforcement

A. ____Does the text provide opportunities for students to practice using new concepts?

B. ____Are there summaries at appropriate intervals in the text?

C. ____Does the text provide adequate iconic aids such as maps, graphs, illustrations, etc. to reinforce concepts?

D. ____Are there adequate suggestions for usable supplementary activities?

E. ____Do these activities provide for a broad range of ability levels?

F. ____Are there literal recall questions provided for the students' self review?

G. ____Do some of the questions encourage the students to draw inferences?

H. ____Are there discussion questions which encourage creative thinking?

I. ____Are questions clearly worded?

Motivation

A. ____Does the teacher's manual provide introductory activities that will capture students' interest?

B. ____Are chapter titles and subheadings concrete, meaningful, or interesting?

C. ____Is the writing style of the text appealing to the students?

D. ____Are the activities motivating? Will they make the student want to pursue the topic further?

E. ____Does the book clearly show how the knowledge being learned might be used by the learner in the future?

F. ____Are the cover, format, print size, and picture appealing to the students?

G. Does the text provide positive and motivating models for both sexes as well as for other racial, ethnic, and socioeconomic groups?

Readability analysis

Weaknesses

1) On which items was the book rated the lowest?
2) Did these items tend to fall in certain categories?
3) Summarize the weaknesses of this text.
4) What can you do in class to compensate for the weaknesses of this text?

Assets

1) On which items was the book rated the highest?
2) Did these items fall in certain categories?
3) Summarize the assets of this text.
4) What can you do in class to take advantage of the assets of this text?

REWRITING

Another way to adjust materials to your students is to rewrite the text you have been assigned to use. Individual teachers have attempted to rewrite, though often committees of teachers have been assigned to do this. This activity can be quite time-consuming and costly, but it may be appropriate if easier materials simply are not available.

Rewriting on an easier level compels you to use all of your knowledge of language structure to make the material more comprehensible. Consider the following guidelines:

1. Keep the sentences short and direct. Use no more than ten or fifteen words per sentence. Avoid complex sentences in which there are modifications to the main clause.
2. Avoid punctuation that the students might find vague: semicolons, dashes, and so on. Mostly use the period and the comma.
3. If structure words are used, be sparing with them. As noted earlier, such words may be necessary to show a relationship. Be prepared to show the students what relationship these words show.
4. Each paragraph should be about one idea only. You will use extensively the pattern of main idea followed by detail.
5. Use a casual style. Bring in anecdotes to which the students can relate.
6. Provide detail and verbal illustrations so that the students can relate to the material. Too often, in the attempt to make a text simpler, the information is stripped of illustrative detail, thereby raising the ratio of abstraction to concreteness.
7. Be sure that a pronoun does not stray too far from its antecedent noun. It is no sin to repeat words—with moderation.

In short, in rewriting, remember that you are not writing a literary selection. You are writing simple, direct, expository prose that will meet the test of clarity and grammatical correctness.

Distantly related to rewriting is the use of tapes. With this procedure you transcribe the text material to a tape and the students listen to the tape as they follow along in the text. One positive feature of this method is that you can signal on tape to the students when you may wish to elaborate upon the text, explain further, and direct attention to a graphic aid. Also, this is not as time-consuming as rewriting.

A preferred alternative to rewriting is to have the students write their own text. Basically the procedure is as follows:

1. Short assignments are given to the students—usually a page or topical heading. A very specific purpose is cited to direct the attention of the students.
2. There is thorough preteaching, as required in the first step of a content reading lesson.
3. After the students have read for the assigned purpose, there is much discussion of the information. Many times the teacher may direct the students to specific paragraphs, sentences, and graphic aids in the text.

4. Evolving from the discussion, the students verbalize the information in their own words.
5. The student statements are written on the blackboard and the students copy them in their notebooks and date each page.

This procedure results, in effect, in a textbook written in the students' own words. The syntax and word usage are as complex as the students are able to comprehend. The value of such a procedure is apparent: it helps the students to become more able to use the standard text, and they use their own language to express information and concepts. It can be regarded as a variation of the language experience approach to reading (a procedure often used in the primary grades).

SUPPLEMENTARY MATERIALS

Another important way to adjust materials to the reading proficiencies of students is to compile a collection of supplementary materials and a classroom library (see Chapter 5). There should be materials on a variety of reading levels. The formulas of readability are a valid means of judging the approximate level of difficulty of supplementary materials. The materials should include all types of books: trade books and texts, fiction and references—all of which are pertinent to your subject and topics under study. Include also periodicals, and even comic books if appropriate. As specialists in a subject area, content teachers should know of such materials. Consult the catalogs of publishers from the file kept in most school or district offices for related material of high interest and low vocabulary load. Your school librarian can be of great assistance here; the librarian would know of specific bibliographies for you to consult and would welcome your suggestions about materials to obtain.

SUMMARY

As we discover more and more about the nature of language and its relation to reading comprehension, we are improving techniques for adjusting reading material to the students we teach. Adjusting materials requires that we know how our students presently use language and how they can improve in reading comprehension. While readability formulas are of some use in evaluating reading materials, our best tool for helping students is sound teaching procedure.

QUESTIONS AND PROBLEMS FOR YOUR OWN CLASSROOM

For readers who are training to be teachers:

1. Familiarize yourself with selected formulas for predicting readability and practice applying them.

2. Choose a passage from a textbook and practice rewriting it at a simpler level.
3. As you plan a hypothetical lesson, list techniques you would use to help the students use the textbook more effectively.
4. For your subject area, compile a bibliography of supplementary materials that would be appropriate for your classroom.

For readers who are teaching:

1. Use selected formulas for predicting readability (see the references below) and evaluate the textbook you use as well as supplementary material.
2. Practice rewriting important passages from the textbook at a simpler level.
3. Review your lesson procedures and list what you do to make the textbook more understandable to your students. List other techniques you could employ.
4. Begin building a classroom library by compiling a bibliography of appropriate materials.
5. Use the cloze procedure to evaluate your students' comprehension of the textbook.

SELECTED REFERENCES

Bormuth, John R. *Readability in 1968.* National Council of Teachers of English, 1968.

A detailed account of the cloze procedure for measuring students' comprehension with the reading material they are using.

Dale, Edgar, and Chall, Jeanne S. *A Formula for Predicting Readability.* Columbus: Bureau of Educational Research, The Ohio State University, 1948.

Instructional manual for the application of the Dale-Chall formula.

Flesch, Rudolf. *The Art of Readable Writing.* New York: Collier Macmillan Publishers, 1949.

A delightfully written analysis of the characteristics of clear and interesting writing. It also contains a description of the Flesch formula for predicting readability.

Fry, Edward. "Fry's Readability Graph: Clarification, Validity, and Extension to Level 7," *Journal of Reading* 21, No. 3 (December 1977).

Instructions for the use of the Fry formula.

Klare, George K. "Assessing Readability," *Reading Research Quarterly* 10, No. 1 (1974-1975).

An excellent summary of the characteristics of many readability formulas. Conclusions about their effectiveness are noted.

McLaughlin, G. Harry. "SMOG Grading—A New Readability Formula," *Journal of Reading* 12, No. 8 (May 1969).

CHAPTER 12

Applying Reading Skills to English, Social Studies, Science and Mathematics

OVERVIEW

The four subject areas in this chapter are often called the academic subjects of the secondary school. They are the core courses which all students take irrespective of their study emphasis—vocational or college-oriented. We think of each of these subjects as having a discrete body of reading skills because of the style of writing used. As students read for a variety of purposes in each subject, however, they find that the discreteness breaks down and that the specific subject contains writing identified with other subjects also.

Questions

Consider these questions before you read further:

1. What do you consider to be the reading skills students must have to read successfully in your subject?
2. How have you been fusing the teaching of reading skills and the content of your subject in your classroom procedure?
3. How do you view the time to teach reading skills as compared to coverage of the subject? What do you think is the relationship between the two?

English, social studies, science and mathematics are often called the academic courses in the secondary school. In each of the four areas we find distinctive styles of writing, yet the styles are not entirely pertinent to just one area. In *broad terms,* English materials tend to be mostly narrative and descriptive. They are probably the most similar to those materials the students learned and read in the elementary grades. In social studies, the students are introduced to factual prose, which may well contain anecdotal (narrative) passages. But, here they encounter chronology and cause-and-effect relationships. In science, the prose is dense with factual content that has much detail. Students must be able to classify information, categorize and organize it, and use a problem-solving approach. In mathematics, the reading is limited in quantity and what is presented is terse. It centers around word problems and the steps of a process.

Since all students take these courses, they will need instruction and guidance in how to read in each area effectively. They must perceive the style of writing used—the structure of language—in each subject area. The time to help them is as soon as they meet each specific style.

In helping your students make effective use of printed materials, keep in mind two fundamental points. The first is that the content of your subject is communicated to your students by language. You are a *teacher of the language of your subject;* therefore, change your focus from just teaching content to teaching the reading process. Tovey states that "language and content instruction are inseparable. . . . Effective language instruction cannot be isolated to a particular period of time in a school schedule. It should be an integral part of content instruction which extends throughout the day."[1] He notes also that in thinking and learning about a subject the students are dependent on the particular patterns that make the discipline's unique thoughts explicit.

The second realization is that there is a commonality of skills pertinent to all subject areas. For example, each subject area has a specific vocabulary and word usage which must be learned; each requires students to note the main ideas and the organization of ideas. There is also another aspect to this commonality: each subject area can have a style of writing which is often considered to be typical of another subject. Let's see how this works. When we consider English, literature is the type of reading material we associate most with that subject. However, if students read about the history of a period—such as the Elizabethan era when studying Shakespeare—or the social conditions of a period (when reading novels of protest), the reading material is like that of social studies. In teaching about language structure and the science of language, the reading material resembles scientific writing, possibly including experimentation. In social studies, historical writing is what we perceive as the basic style. But when students read a biographical account of a historical person, the material can be literature or literature-like. If students in social studies are assigned to read maps, charts, and graphs, the task resembles an aspect of mathematics. Similarly, classification of information and the steps of a scientific process are

1. Duane R. Tovey, "Inseparable Language and Content Instruction," *Journal of Reading* 22, No. 8 (May 1979): 724–25.

considered to be part of the scientific style. But again, the biography of an eminent scientist resembles literature, the social consequences or application of a scientific discovery would resemble social studies, and the reading of formulas is similar to mathematics reading. Even in mathematics there is an overlap. The terse materials showing the steps of a mathematical process would be labelled mathematical writing. But the biography of a famous mathematician is similar to literature, the impact of a specific mathematical theory on relativity or economics resembles social studies, and the explanation of a mathematical principle and following directions are similar to science.

Consideration of these overlaps compels all content teachers to be acquainted with styles of writing other than what is traditionally pertinent to their area. Though each content teacher may well emphasize the uniqueness of the writing style in the subject, this alone is not enough. Students must be guided to see the commonality of language and patterns in all subject areas.

APPLYING READING SKILLS TO THE ENGLISH CLASS

Lefevre states that English teachers are responsible for organizing and directing developmental learning experiences in language, literature, and rhetoric. They also must develop within students the arts and skills of communication: reading, writing, speaking, and listening, and also appreciation, creativity, criticism, and performance.[2] In essence, English teachers are primarily concerned with the formulation and expression of ideas.

The goals of the language arts are basically the same as those of education in general, since language and communication are intrinsic to all curricula. The goals may generally be listed as (*a*) cultivating within students the qualities needed for a satisfying life, (*b*) developing social sensitivity and effective participation in the activities of society, and (*c*) helping students toward vocational competence. To attain these goals students must learn to use language as an effective instrument of thought and communication, to gain insights from literature about the world, and to develop curiosity and the capacity for critical thinking.

The English curriculum includes utilitarian as well as literary uses of language. In the English class, knowledge of syntactical structure, composition organization and vocabulary usage are taught. These understandings are applicable to all parts of the school curriculum. However, it is not considered the province of the English teacher to teach the application of these understandings and skills to the other content areas. Therefore, the content area teachers must guide the students in this transfer as the students read the material of their subject.

Let us review briefly the basic skills taught in English classes. Vocabulary building is aimed toward improving oral and written communication, listening and reading comprehension, and precision of thought.

---

2. Carl A. Lefevre, *Linguistics, English and the Language Arts* (Boston: Allyn & Bacon, Inc., 1970), pp. 18-19.

EDITORIAL

Teaching Reading in the English Class

Teaching reading in the English class is essential if we, as educators, are to insure our students' vocational success, literacy, understanding of cultural, social and world issues, as well as esthetic and personal appreciation of literature. How is the teaching of literature and the language arts in the English classroom related to the teaching of reading? How does teaching reading in the English class enhance academic growth?

In the English class, students are called upon to interpret literature. They must find details that relate to the topic, theme, and thesis. To do this, students must be able to find topics, recognize paragraph patterns, sequence ideas, and summarize information. Moreover, before they can perceive details and information as important to understanding the topic, theme and thesis, students must be able to decode words, master sentence structure, and conceptualize the vocabulary. In short, the reading skills with which students must have proficiency include word analysis, oral reading for pronunciation and enunciation, using context, determining the author's meaning of a word, and conceptual understanding of denotative and connotative language. Now, what about interpretation and appreciation of literature, and how does mastery of the reading skills relate to both?

Before literature can be appreciated, the content must be interpreted. Interpretation or critical evaluation can occur only when the lowest level of comprehension or literal meaning is understood. The student's task then becomes to visualize descriptions, comprehend imagery and symbolism, draw conclusions from the logical organization of material, and make inferences. These are all reading skills. Only after these steps have been accomplished can the student even begin to appreciate and express emotional feelings in a creative medium. Thus, when the English teacher hopes to foster appreciation for language and literature and its incorporation into the students' own thoughts and experiences, the reading skills become the vehicles transporting readers to this destination.

In a February 22, 1979 editorial in the *New York Times* entitled, "What Makes Some Schools Work," three factors were cited as being directly accountable for successful school programs. One of these factors was "the emphasis on fundamental skills and the setting of high expectations for pupils and faculty." English teachers must become dedicated to their responsibility to do something about the reading skills of their students. They also must come to realize that they are teachers of language. Language comprehension is basically the same as reading comprehension. Reading and understanding the spoken language in its graphic representation—words—is essentially the same as understanding spoken language. It is the content area teacher's responsibility to make students aware of this. English teachers must be prepared with techniques and knowledge of organization of language to teach the content of literature.

Vocabulary and concepts relating to specific instruction must be emphasized as well as structure and organization of material. Reading many types of sentences and paragraph patterns, studying spelling and Greek and Latin roots, and instruction in composition all contribute to the student's understanding of the written language. Teaching reading through poetry, short stories, novels, and newspapers not only enhances conceptual growth but also makes skill learning more meaningful and applicable. Students must see the *relevance* of what is being discussed or studied. When students perceive relevance, they will be less resistant and will remember more of the material. For this reason, providing a background of information and relating it to personal experience is invaluable in increasing comprehension.

In teaching literature, as in teaching reading, the teacher must discover what the students know and what they do not know. Careful questioning elicits student interest and helps them discover the significance of the literature presented. Filmstrips, tapes, cassettes, records, pictures from magazines and articles that relate to the theme, characters, and conflict can be used as aids in clarifying concepts and expanding experience. The immediate goal is to get students involved in the literature to be studied; the English teacher's *ultimate* goal is to have students formulate and express ideas and enjoy and appreciate literature.

Though we want our students to read with understanding for enjoyment and appreciation, not all of our students can read at the same grade level. It is here that the teacher's knowledge of the reading/language process and the skills involved becomes essential. Attention must be paid to individual differences among our students. The successful English classroom depends on the English teacher's knowledge of specific techniques and skills involved in the reading of literature; familiarity with materials suitable to interest, maturity, and reading grade level; and expertise in evaluating levels of comprehension.

The teaching of reading skills in the English class is a must, as it is in all other content area classrooms. Administrators should be concerned with providing teachers with experience, opportunity, and support in developing a schoolwide reading program that encompasses the content areas. English teachers, like other content teachers, must be encouraged to take the responsibility for teaching the reading skills in the classroom if our educational institutions are to be successful.

Jane C. Bilello
Teacher of English

Understanding sentence and paragraph structure is essential if students are to perceive the author's structure and create their own language structure when writing. Locating information is an important research skill which should be taught generally in English class and then applied to other subjects by the teachers of the other disciplines. Likewise the reading-study process (SQ3R) can be taught in English class and then applied to each discipline. Interpretation and appreciation skills are fostered through the study of literature. Critical reading, especially of current selections, is important; students should be directed to find out to whom, by whom, when, where, and why specific ideas have been stated. Communication skills, particularly the oral use of language, are pertinent parts of the English curriculum. Denotative and connotative meanings of words and the structure of thoughts are investigated to show their effect upon the clarity and impact of the communication. Finally, voluntary reading is fostered so that it becomes a rewarding and enjoyable activitity.

Literature and the Reading Skills

Reading instruction and the study of literature are two very different processes. Reading instruction emphasizes specific skills of word recognition, word meaning, levels of comprehension, and is a means to an end. Skill instruction is usually best accomplished with nonliterary selections that can be analyzed to give specific guidance in the skills, which can then be practiced by application to literary selections.

Literature is usually considered to be the body of writing belonging to a people which includes their legends, myths, experiences, beliefs, values, and aspirations—expressed by an expert use of language. Literary writing is imaginative, descriptive, and narrative. Usually, factual data are not listed or explained, as in the writing of science and mathematics. In literature, there is little technical vocabulary, except as the craft of literary writing is investigated. Further, diagrams, maps, charts, and tables are not generally found in literary writing.

The basic comprehension skills, as pertinent to literature as they are to all prose writing, are the abilities to:

1. Read sentences of all types.
2. Develop scope and depth of vocabulary.
3. Note the main idea.
4. Be aware of sequence.
5. Read to note and recall details and see their relation to the main idea.
6. See the author's organization—recognize the plot structure.
7. Summarize the main points.

Specific activities which apply directly to literature are:

1. Develop word meanings by:
   a. investigating interesting word origins.
   b. noting words with multiple meanings.

c. examining word structure—prefixes, suffixes, roots, inflectional endings.
d. noting shifts in the meanings of words.
e. being aware of subject matter words.
f. noting words from other languages.
g. investigating idioms.
h. noting onomatopoeic words.
i. determining the differences in meaning between denotation and connotation.
j. recognizing words of classification.
k. noting abstract and concrete words.
l. thinking of antonyms, synonyms, homonyms.
m. investigating words not common in speech but used in writing.
n. recognizing slang.
o. noting strange words an author uses over and over.

2. Note main ideas and summarize by:
   a. giving in a sentence the events of a given scene or situation, the character or nature of the situation, the personality or general appearance of a character.
   b. selecting a revealing name for a character.
   c. choosing an alternative title.
3. Show sequence by:
   a. charting the main events or happenings, or story structure.
   b. using outlines or marginal-type explanations.
   c. listing the events in order.
4. Note details by:
   a. selecting a character whom the reader likes or dislikes and noting the details which substantiate the feeling.
   b. listing the details in the description of the setting or mood; noticing the things that give the description a mood of gloom, gaiety, impending doom, mystery.

The implementation of the skills through classroom procedure requires specific considerations:

1. *All students entering the secondary schools do not have the ability to read on their assigned grade level*. Therefore, it is unrealistic to expect all students in a grade, or even all students in a class, to be able to read a single literary selection with understanding, enjoyment, and appreciation. There must be differentiation, individualization, and flexibility in approach as well as in the selections. For example, students may be assigned by groups to literary selections of differing levels of difficulty. One teacher divided her class into two groups reading different stories. The stories were related in that they were both about lions. Though the stories were on different levels of difficulty, both were interesting to the students. One portrayed the lion very positively and the other negatively. After discussing the two stories individually with the two groups, the teacher brought them together so that they could share with each other. Students noted the

different impressions of the lion. The ensuing discussion centered upon the authors' points of view and their use of language and incident to present their positions. Finally, students were asked open-ended questions to encourage them to search their own knowledge about lions and support one or the other position, or both.

Increasingly, teachers are varying their selections and are finding materials to fit the reading levels of students. With paperbacks, the teacher can have at least a beginning toward a multitext approach. However, if for some reason the class as a whole is expected to read the same selection, then you can vary the procedure by (*a*) providing background and relevance, (*b*) having the students read only certain sections, (*c*) reading some sections to the students, (*d*) using films and recordings, and (*e*) using open-ended questions to stimulate the students to think about their reactions to the language, the characters, incidents, and the general mood.

2. *Secondary school teachers must cease to castigate the lower grades for a lack of student competence.* Teachers have the responsibility to maintain those skills acquired in the earlier grades, provide remediation and correction where necessary, and guide the students toward the acquisition and refinement of new skills. You are dealing with a process which needs continual instruction and practice for optimum development. Further, you know what is to be accomplished with each selection. For example, if students are to note the author's use of the setting to establish the mood of the story, then students should be given practice exercises prior to (and unrelated to) the story.
3. *Flexibility of literary selections is required.* To have the entire class read and analyze one literary selection is not consistent with our knowledge of individual interests and abilities. In one instance a teacher had her students select their own novel to read. She established only a specific general theme. Prior to reading she presented a diagram of the development of a plot. The assignment was to compare their novel with the standard plot presentation and development. After the students had completed their reading, class discussions were conducted in which all of the students told the class about their novel and how it compared to the standard plot. In the process, the students learned not only how a novel can be developed, but also many of the variations. They discovered possible reasons for the variations, such as the flashback technique, and noted the pertinence of the technique to the author's purpose.
4. *We cannot assume that growth will come automatically by exposure to literature.* Many of our secondary school students do not return to the literature they were exposed to. One point we must keep in mind: students must become *involved* with the story. They must be able to relate it to their own life experiences. Perhaps if we approached literary selections on the affective level—involving the students' feelings, hopes, and values—selections would bring about greater growth.
5. *We should not lament the onslaught of the mass media.* It is true that TV cuts into time that might be used for reading. Yet, we know that

such media can also build background and interest in reading for further information and enjoyment. Movies and plays on television are means of presenting selections of literature. You can guide the students' viewing, asking them to note which segment was the funniest or most exciting, or how the characters talked and dressed.

6. *We stimulate enjoyment of literature best by showing enthusiasm for it.* Your own background in literature and true enjoyment of it will do more than anything to stimulate the students' desire to read. If you say sometimes, "I read the most interesting story last night. It was about ________," or "I did not like the author's point of view, but he presented his points so well. Listen ________," the students will learn from you to enjoy reading and might even wish to share in class some of their outstanding reading. If, on the other hand, you teach literature merely because the curriculum requires it or "it's good for the students," then the program is doomed to failure.

7. *Growth in literature as in anything else comes over a period of time.* It does not come in one class period or even in one year alone. It comes as a result of a school-wide approach to literature through all the years of school.

   Student involvement (in the story, the action of one or more characters, or the author's handling of the story) seems to be one of the secrets of developing interest in literature.

   Questions such as the following may help to involve the students:

   What would you have done if ________?

   What would your reaction to such a character be? Why did he do what he did? Explain what you would have done. Discuss the character and his motivations.

   What would you have expected from such a description? How important is the description and setting?

   What is the crisis of the story? How is it resolved? How would you have solved the problem? What is your evaluation of the resolution?

   Why do you think the author wrote the selection? What is his theme? What is his approach to the subject? What reaction does he want from his readers?

   What techniques does the author use to foster his theme?

Selections chosen for high school students should be within the reach of their level of maturity and experience. Even then, the teacher sometimes needs to bridge the gap for them between their experience and the story. Their depth of appreciation is not likely to be the same as yours. But as they develop toward maturity and have a continuous positive contact with literature through the school years, their depth of perception and appreciation of literature will grow. Awareness of the universal themes of literature and their relevance, the author's purpose and techniques, and the ways language can be used to express ideas all contribute to increasing depth of appreciation.

Adapt your instruction to the students you have in class. For some, a cursory reading of the story may be all that is required, while other students may begin to interpret and evaluate characters, uses of language, setting, and so on. Ideally, the teacher will gently lead the students to deeper and deeper levels of appreciation, providing only as much challenge as they can meet at any one time.

Early lists a series of questions which each teacher may use as a basis for analyzing his own procedures:

> Do [you] frequently develop concepts and introduce vocabulary *before* students read an assignment?
> Do [you] help students to identify the reading tasks required by a particular assignment?
> Do [you] then demonstrate how to apply the necessary skills?
> Is attention paid not only to what a textbook says but to how it is said, that is, to the author's choice of words, his sentence structure, and his organization of ideas?
> Is the author's purpose examined?
> Are comparisons made among treatments of the same subject?
> Are students not only encouraged to make judgments but shown how?
> Are [you] aware of the different kinds of reading abilities students possess?
> Do [you] help them to make the best use of their various abilities by providing books and other reading materials on varing levels of difficulty?[3]

Skills and Student Involvement

For understanding literature, which is a prerequisite to appreciation, the basic comprehension skills must be applied. The students must understand the author's use of language; they must be able to identify and give meaning to the words and see their relationship to each other in the sentence.

The essence of literature for student readers is interpreting it and relating it to their own experiences and thoughts. It is the insights they get about their own life situations that are important and interesting. Interpretation involves both skills and attitudes. Those skills in which attitudes are most involved may be listed as:

1. recognizing the emotional reactions and motives of story characters
2. making inferences
3. forming and reacting to sensory images
4. anticipating outcomes
5. making judgments and drawing conclusions
6. perceiving relationships such as cause and effect, sequence, time, and place
7. interpreting figurative, idiomatic, or picturesque language
8. identifying and evaluating character traits
9. comparing and contrasting
10. identifying and reacting to mood or tone
11. identifying the author's purpose or viewpoint
12. evaluating and reacting to ideas in light of the author's purpose

---

3. Margaret J. Early, "Reading: In and Out of the English Curriculum" in *Teaching Reading Skills in Secondary Schools: Reading,* ed. Arthur V. Olson and Wilbur S. Ames (Scranton, Pa.: International Textbook Company, 1970), p. 249.

13. asking questions of critical evaluation
14. identifying techniques of propagandists
15. relating literature to personal experiences
16. contrasting form and style through the type of language used, repetition and rhythm, and person (first or third)
17. understanding the use of signs and symbols
18. sharing reactions to selections

General Guidelines for the Lesson

General classroom procedure can be varied depending upon your preference, the selection used and, perhaps most important, the needs of the students in the class. When teaching a selection of literature, one to several days may be required to complete all of the procedural steps. In teaching a novel or play, the time span may be even longer and may consist of a number of individual lessons as each new section is read.

The teacher will need to ascertain first the objectives to be accomplished. Many literature textbooks have a teacher's manual or guide book which can give help toward this end. The effective teacher will also adapt the content to the class. As he learns the capabilities of the students—their strengths and weaknesses shown by the diagnostic inventory—additional objectives, such as developing a greater vocabulary and practice in noting sequence or cause and effect, may emerge. Both cognitive and affective objectives pertinent to the selection should be determined—the cognitive objectives dealing with the skills to be applied as well as the ideas to be gained from the selection, the affective objectives dealing with student involvement and reaction to the selection. Lesson procedure for English classes basically follows the lesson procedure shown in Chapter 7, pages 174–176.

Free Reading

One valuable use of literature is to develop and foster the desire to read widely as a means of enjoyment. Usually, the more students read, the more they enjoy it. Consider the following stimuli to wide reading:

1. Use pop-rock lyrics to introduce students to poetry. These investigate many of the themes concerning young people in today's world. Nancy Larrick writes of this approach:

    > That's a very different approach to reading from the traditional one. It's a very different kind of reading material, too. But the pop/rock syndrome is tremendously significant in understanding our children and guiding them to pleasure from print. Here is the one great factor in our culture which is youth-centered. It screams out the importance of sound over sight, and it shows us that listening is the road to reading. It illustrates the power of first-person commentary in a rhythmical, conversational style. It exacts an emotional commitment that young people long for. It puts feeling above meaning and invites each listener to sing from his own senses.
    >
    > Pop/rock culture is not what many of us grew up with, and most of us still feel strange about a development which our children take for granted. But we can't turn back the wheels of time and make now into then. We can't recycle

the children to fit the old patterns, although some adults are making that foolish effort.

Our only choice—and it is actually an opportunity—is to become so immersed in the sounds of our children's language and in the sense of their feelings that we can sing and listen with them.[4]

2. Provide time in the school day for recreational reading for students and teachers alike. Richard M. Petre, in describing a total school-wide involvement, states that this approach depends upon four steps:

   Administration and faculty should schedule a daily thirty-five minute reading break for the total school.
   Students should select their own material to read during the reading break.
   Administrators and teachers must read during the break.
   A faculty-student reading committee should be appointed to select a variety of paperbacks to be placed throughout the school, conduct a monthly promotional idea, and evaluate the ongoing progress of the reading environment.[5]

   Petre noted also that students requested two things: more time for reading and an opportunity to discuss books with others who had read them.
3. Use paperbacks, which are less expensive than hardback books and often are less formidable in size and appearance. Most publishing houses publish paperbacks both as single titles and as collections around specific themes.
4. Let students read what they wish to read—what they think will be meaningful to them, what appeals to their interests.
5. Provide the students with opportunities to share the books they read, such as the following book-reporting activities:
   A. About a week before the book report is due, present a list of thought questions for class discussion. Each student then chooses two or three questions relevant to his particular book and uses them as the basis of a written report. Examples:
      What hardships or difficulties did the main character overcome?
      How does the setting affect the action?
      What part does coincidence play in the plot?
      Show how one character influences another.
      Show how responsibility changes a character.
      How is the main character typical of a boy (or girl) of his (her) age? How is he different from the boys (or girls) you know?
   B. Students can pretend that the book is to be filmed and:
      1. Select the cast for the leading roles, justifying their choices.
      2. Decide on possible locations for the shooting of various scenes.
      3. Decide which scenes would be suitable (or not) for inclusion in a movie and explain why.

---

4. Nancy Larrick, "Pop/Rock Lyrics, Poetry and Reading," *Journal of Reading* 15, No. 3 (December 1971): 189–90.

5. Richard M. Petre, "Reading Breaks Make It in Maryland," *Journal of Reading* 15, No. 3 (December 1971): 191–94.

4. Explain how they would change the ending to make it appropriate for a movie.

C. The class makes a project of compiling a useful outside reading book file. Cards list author, title, type of book, specific opinions and reasons for reading. The file is made available to the class for consultation. Cards may be distributed from time to time for discussion.

D. Students discuss how the author feels toward various characters.

E. Students write an imaginary conversation between two characters.

F. Students write a book review consisting of author and title, type of book, setting, identification of chief characters with one detail about each, a brief summary of two important incidents, and a few reasons for recommending (or not) the book. The class may be prepared for this activity by analyzing reviews in the daily or Sunday newspapers.

G. Students report on ideas gained through their reading.

H. Pupils choose a point of view for their reports from a series of suggested topic sentences: e.g., *This book made me see—wish—realize—decide—wonder—believe.*

I. Pupils compare their own neighborhoods or communities with localities described in the book.

J. Students describe their own reactions to various characters.

K. Students make oral reports to committees, and the members take notes.

Reading and Language Structure

Part of the English teacher's task is to teach English grammar and syntax. The goal is to help the students master language.

There are two considerations which should be investigated. First, the students must learn the structure of English so thoroughly that they do not have to concentrate on it as they read. Rather, attention should be on the *content* of the reading selection, with awareness and analysis of the structure operating at a subsidiary level. Second, instruction in grammar should emphasize the thought being expressed; the specific mechanics and rules should be learned and applied only as the thought is changed. Emphasis should be on the functions of grammar in the thinking process—that is, all of the various aspects of grammar would be approached from the point of view of how they affect thought. Students should be guided to note the effects of punctuation on the thought expressed in the sentence, and sentence patterns should be approached as ways of expressing ideas. Paragraph patterns should be analyzed as schemes of thought organization.

Linguistic research on Chomsky's ideas about *transformation* may, indeed, help the students to better understand the relationship between syntax and comprehension. Specifically, how can a sentence be expressed in different ways—transformed—and still convey the same meaning? One teacher asked students to restate an author's ideas in specific sentences. Her goal was to ferret out possible difficulties in comprehension and to help the students translate from an author's language into their own. At first students had some difficulty with this approach; they were used to "parroting" the words of the author. But during the year they became quite adept at transforming the author's sentences. The teacher found that their understanding increased, as well as their interest. It is interesting to note that a minimum of formal syntactical structure was taught, except as it was necessary to insure that the "sentence in your words" did indeed say what the author had stated. In substance, what this teacher did was to help students think through the medium of language.

The English teacher is charged with developing student competence in language. In this capacity he must relate the language arts to the student's complete knowledge, use, and appreciation of language. An understanding of the theory and structure of language is necessary. Further, masterful examples of written language serve to illustrate both effective communication and the beauty of language. Reading skills are essential for improving language development and appreciation. A major concern of skill instruction is to enable the students to receive the author's communication as fully as possible. Competence in a skill per se has no value; the emphasis must be toward the greater goal of communication.

APPLYING READING SKILLS TO SOCIAL STUDIES

Social studies draws its information from the various social sciences. The disciplines usually comprising the social studies curriculum are geography, history, economics, sociology, and civics. These subjects describe the interaction of human beings in small and large groups throughout the world. Social studies directs the students' attention toward the record of human activities and the study of current structures of government. The main thrust of social studies, therefore, is the chronicling and analysis of human interaction.

The objectives of social studies relate to the desires of society—what it wishes students to know, to achieve, and to become. They are pertinent to the times and to the mode of government and way of life society favors. Whatever the specific objectives may be, the teacher has a threefold responsibility: first, to impart a body of basic information which is considered important for the students to know; second, to help the students acquire specific skills which foster independence; and third, to inculcate certain attitides deemed necessary for the constructive working of society. In this chapter we are concerned with the second responsibility: providing tools for acquiring information and understanding which students will need throughout their lives as functioning members of society. The emphasis here is on the skills of effective reading.

The students' understanding in social studies depends upon their ability to use language. They must rely in large measure upon the ability to read in order to learn concepts. They must be able to discuss the information, listen intelligently in class, and express their thoughts in writing.

Problems in Reading Social Studies

Social studies material is often difficult for the students to read with understanding. Much of the reason for this is their lack of background and actual experience with social studies information and concepts. This consideration suggests that the teacher must use classroom procedures for providing the needed background.

Textbooks in the social studies sometimes are a barrier for students. Much of their reading instruction through the years has been in readers, which are comprised of story-type reading material. With the social studies the student is faced with factual prose jammed with data. Other problems typical of social studies materials are:

1. Condensing of many facts and ideas, thereby omitting much of the concrete factual and anecdotal material that would make the subject both more lively and more relevant to the students' own background.
2. Difficult ideas, which are largely outside the students' experience.
3. Sentence length—complex ideas often are expressed in complex sentences. Involved sentences add to the students' difficulty with the organization and treatment of ideas. Though many textbook authors strive to simplify the language, complex writing still persists. For instance, consider a sentence taken at random from a senior high school American history textbook: "Since the citizen puts up most of the money in the form of taxes, and since the money is supposed to be spent for the public good, each citizen has an important stake in the way government funds are spent." For competent readers who understand language structure and syntax, such a sentence is not difficult. For less competent readers, however, the main idea of the sentence may be unclear because the sentence has subordinate clauses. Further, they may not see that the subordinate clauses enhance the significance of the principal thought.
4. Organization may elude the students—they may find it difficult to note the sequential development of ideas, cause-and-effect relationships, and relevant versus irrelevant data.
5. Vocabulary is a basic difficulty. The words used are either general words used in a social studies context or technical words pertinent to the social studies. Students may know the meaning of the general words but may not know the meaning applied to the social studies. There are many such words in the social studies: for instance, *storm, grant, revolution.* Then there are the specialized social studies terms, such as *federalism, treaty,* and *capital*—abstract terms that represent whole concepts.
6. Students may not see the relevance of the information they are reading. They may not see the connection between the social studies information and what is happening in the world today.
7. Students may lack the skills necessary for thinking about and using the ideas within the subject.

Obviously, these difficulties, experienced by many students, require direct assistance through instruction by the teacher. With a richer background and broader base of experience, the teacher can help students to see the relevance of the information, define purpose, work with ideas, and acquire competence in the necessary study skills.

Social Studies Vocabulary

Only if students understand the concept which a word labels can they think about social studies ideas. A concept is a mental construct which the students develop, or rather evolve. It grows and is refined by experience and the acquisition of knowledge that bears upon the idea. Vocabulary in the social studies represents concepts by labelling them.

The meanings that students develop for words can be on two levels. The first, the superficial level, which is hardly adequate, is a memorized meaning of words. Whether the students know the idea the word represents is doubtful unless they have experience enough to make a concrete application of the term. Vocabulary study often is complicated by the glibness of high school students, who can use the correct words in the correct context because of their experience with language. But they may not be able to explain the ideas represented. In this case, vocabulary development is reduced to jargon.

The second level of vocabulary development, and the desired one, is when the students understand the concept labelled by the word and note the meaning as it is determined by the context of the sentence. It is at this level that they can think creatively and critically. Teaching the language of social studies, then, must involve the development of concepts. See Chapter 2, Vocabulary Development and Word Analysis, for further discussion of concept development.

Many words in the social studies vocabulary are abstract. They represent ideas rather than objects which can be experienced through the senses. For instance, the word *constitution* is concrete in that a written form of it can be seen, but the *idea* of what it is can be understood only as it applies to a structure of government. Obviously, the students' background of information and understanding will determine the degree of meaning they can extract. If background information and experiences are lacking, the teacher's role is to build them as part of concept development.

Suggested Activities

1. Write new words on the blackboard during a discussion to focus attention upon them. At the same time quickly review the syllabication of the word, its root, and its various forms. (If the word is *democracy,* note the two Greek roots and the meanings of each (*demos*—people; *fratein*—to rule) and the forms: *democratic, democrat, democratization,* etc.)
2. Have students identify and list names, places, and events related to the word to enrich its meaning.
3. Suggest that the students list the words peculiar to a period of history, such as *Whig, feudalism.*

4. Have students evaluate the definition of some figure of speech, slogan, or expression. Note its significance and impact. For instance: "What did Thomas Paine mean in the statement, 'These are the times that try men's souls?'"
5. Use films, recordings, tapes, drawings, dramatizations, models, and exhibits to add to the conceptual background of the words.
6. Have the students note the emotional use of words. Suggest that the students use other less emotional words and notice the difference in the impact of a selection.

Study and Comprehension Skills

The study skills enable the students to attack a reading assignment in accordance with a stated purpose, to locate information, and to determine the author's structure of thought. Of course, the social studies teacher gives guidance and instruction when needed. The study skills common to all content subjects are listed in Chapter 4, and the hierarchy of many of the study skills is discussed.

These specific principles of teaching will help the student become effective in use of the study skills:

1. Use material in the students' instructional materials (textbooks) when teaching the study skills. These skills are best developed as they apply to class materials.
2. Be aware of sequence in the study skills. If the students seem to have difficulty with getting the main idea of a paragraph when the idea is only implied, you will probably need to return to a simpler skill, such as determining the main idea of a paragraph in which it is stated. Then, through discussion of various clues, develop the skill to the implied main idea.
3. Teach the skill when the need for it arises. This practice usually brings about the best results. Motivation is highest when the students see the direct application of their learning.
4. Fuse the teaching of the skills with the teaching of content. Greater competence in the skill should bring about greater mastery of the content. The content is thus the body of information through which the skill is taught.

Suggested Activities

A. Developing purposes for reading
   1. Ask the students questions, or get them to formulate them, about the possible causes or results of a historical event.
   2. Help students to formulate questions of *why, what, where, when,* and *how* as guides in determining basic information.
   3. Have the students read the introduction to a chapter and note whether the author suggests questions to be answered.

4. Show the students how to formulate questions from the topical headings.
5. From the preview of a chapter or section, have the students speculate about the information or note what they do not know but would like to. Formulate questions accordingly.
6. Have the students list the facts they already know about the subject, and then have them formulate questions about information they still need to know.
7. Have the students evolve purposes and then find the paragraphs or sections in the textbook where they are answered. This can help them see the significance of the paragraph. A reverse of this is to have them read a selection to determine its main point or significance.

B. Using parts of a textbook
 1. Getting information from a table of contents
 From the perusal of a table of contents, have the students answer the following questions:
 a. How does the book seem to be organized?
 b. What are the major topics?
 c. Is the content organized by units or chapters? What is the significance of the organization when the chapters are grouped under unit topics?
 d. What is the scope of the book?
 2. Using an index
 a. How are the topics listed?
 b. What is the difference between a table of contents and an index?
 c. What is the purpose of the itemized sub-topics listed under a major topic?
 d. Give the students topics to look for in the index. Ask how they can find a topic when they have a question such as: "Why are the trade routes basically East-West in direction rather than North-South?" "What are the entry words to use to find pertinent page references?" (The key entry word is *trade* and the term is *trade routes*.)
 3. Using study aids in a textbook
 a. What is the purpose of an introduction to a unit and a chapter? What does the introduction tell the reader?
 Have the students find the sentence which may best express what information is to be covered.
 b. What is the purpose of a summary?
 c. How can the vocabulary list at the end of a chapter or unit be of help to a reader?
 d. What is the purpose of the questions following each chapter? (Determine the information the students are to acquire.)
 e. How does the textbook facilitate the reader's problems in discerning the important ideas in review?
 f. Have the students read the chapter headings, subheadings, and marginal headings, look at the pictures and other graphic aids, to get an overview of the material. Direct the students to express in a short paragraph the material to be covered.

4. Noting the importance of the foreword or preface
   a. What is the author's purpose in writing a preface?
   b. What reasons can we find that tell what the author hopes to accomplish with his books?
   c. What point of view can we note?
   d. How does the author think his book could be read and used?

C. Using graphic aids
   1. Whenever the students use a map have them note what it shows, or what the author's purpose is, the type, date, and parts of the map.
   2. Have students use maps to determine trade routes, ocean currents, climatic zones, etc.
   3. Have students compare types of maps such as one showing population distribution and the climatic zones. Note relationships.
   4. Suggest that the students maintain a bulletin board map showing the places where current events of note are taking place. Have them attach a ribbon from the place on the map to the newspaper clipping describing the event.
   5. Help students interpret cartoons. Note the symbolism, the hyperbole. Deduce the main point or inference.
   6. Discuss the impact of cartoons upon the reader.
   7. Discuss pictures and determine what the purpose of each is. Note the significance to the topic under study.
   8. Guide the students in using any key, symbol or scale accompanying a graphic aid.
   9. Have the students read the caption for a chart or picture. How does the caption relate to the information given by the chart or picture? How does it relate to the reading of the material?
   10. Suggest that the students write a summary of a topic using only pictures, maps, graphs, and other graphic aids as their sources of information.
   11. Have the students make a chart showing the comparisons and contrasts between two countries, two types of governments, etc.
   12. Have the students draw a time line showing the evolution of a condition or the progression of a period in history.

D. Locating information—library sources
   1. As a class project develop a topic with the students to review the use of:
      a. the library card file
      b. the *Reader's Guide to Periodical Literature*
      c. specific references such as encyclopedias, atlases, almanacs, biographical dictionaries and other available and needed references.
   2. Have the students determine the value of different types of source materials and the kinds of information found in each type.

E. Finding the main idea
   1. Have the students read the chapter headings and subheadings and determine the topic that is discussed under each heading. Have them express each topic in one sentence.

2. Ask the students to restate in their own words the author's main idea in each paragraph in a chapter or section of a chapter.
3. Have the students use the main ideas of the paragraphs in a chapter or chapter section to write a summary of the material.
4. Have the students read several paragraphs in their textbook to determine where the main-idea sentence is found in each paragraph. Have them note the function of the details included in each paragraph.
5. After the students have read a chapter in their textbook, have them think of a different but appropriate title for the material.
6. Select a series of paragraphs from the textbook and list four possible main ideas for each paragraph. Have the students choose the correct one. Discuss in class the reasons for the correct choices. This type of exercise can also be done with longer selections.
7. Collect a group of news articles and cut the headlines from them. See if the students can match the appropriate headline with the article. (This exercise increases in difficulty when all of the articles are about a single topic.)
8. Analyze paragraphs from the textbook to determine types. Have the students apply their knowledge of paragraph structure to determine the main idea and organization.
9. Determine the main ideas of several paragraphs. Draw a conclusion about the author's basic style of paragraph structure.

F. Recognizing important details
1. Have the students find paragraphs in which the main idea is explained by details.
2. Have the students note ways in which the author may indicate the relative importance of facts. Look for:
   a. more space to the discussion of one fact than to another;
   b. the use of introductory remarks, such as "above all," "preeminent," "the chief factor," "probably the most crucial";
   c. questions at the beginning of the chapter, or at its end, that indicate the most important facts;
   d. the use of italics.

G. Noting organization
1. Test the ability of the class to report an exciting event giving the main idea and the supporting details.
2. Have the students read about the organization of a type of government. Have them show how such a government would operate and how it would affect the lives of people under its jurisdiction.
3. Have the students use facts obtained from reading to list ways in which problems of the past have been solved or problems of the present are being solved.
4. Have the students write a term paper or an essay comparing one or more facets of a country with another, such as comparison of the governmental structure of one country with that of another.
5. Suggest that a committee of students gather data on local history and local problems. Have the committee organize the data and present a report to the rest of the class.

6. Have the students list the chain of events leading up to a historical crisis or incident. Point out words that suggest each step, such as: *second, finally, in response to this,* etc.
7. Have the students trace the growth of a group or a nation.
8. Have the students write a summary of the facts they have studied about some topic.
9. Suggest that some of the students describe a historical event in the style of writing used by newspapers of the time.
10. Have the students write a short biography of some historical figure.
11. Guide the students to prepare a forum, round-table discussion, or panel on a topic such as the causes of war or possible ways to prevent war.
12. Have the students classify topics under headings such as *Causes* and *Results*. Group historical figures in an event as they would be representative of specific countries or aspects of historical events; or in a discussion of the geography of a country make columns entitled: *Climate, Topography, History, Industry, Customs, Agriculture, Trade*. Comparisons can be made easily if such is done for several countries.
13. Give the students a partial outline with instructions for them to complete the subheadings. Example:

    I. Issues Facing the Continental Convention
        A.
        B.
        C.

    Outlines of increasing complexity or steps can be created to develop competence.
14. Have the students include two or three related points into a single sentence as a means of developing competence in summarizing.

H. Newspaper reading

Newspaper reading is an important source of information for social studies. Current information is available not from textbooks but from materials such as newspapers which are published daily. Gaining information from newspapers requires its own skills. The following outline highlights the skills and techniques needed:

1. Skimming

   First paragraph of a news story contains an account of "who, what, when, where, why, how."

   News articles have the "lead" paragraph which is the summary and "the body" which is the story in detail.
2. Newspaper makeup

   Use of the newspaper index
3. All of the basic skills:

   Previewing a reading selection
   Finding the main idea
   Reading for details
   Establishing purpose—change headlines into questions
   Noting key words and phrases
   Increasing vocabulary

4. Planning for newspaper reading (budget time)

Example:

Skimming	2 minutes
News	15
Financial pages	3
Sports	2
Drama, Music, Books	2
Radio, TV programs	1
Editorials	2
Columnists	1
Advertisements	1
Comics	1
Total time	30 minutes

5. Plan of attack
   A. Skim all headlines on the front page.
   B. Skim through entire paper. Make mental notes of what to read in more detail later.
   C. Read the news stories on the front page. Sometimes the first one or two paragraphs of an article will suffice.
   D. Read widely throughout the paper. Select the most informative, interesting articles.

Paragraph Patterns

Smith identifies several major patterns of social studies writing: picture and map, cause and effect, sequential events with dates, comparison, detailed statement of fact, and propaganda.[6]

The Picture and Map Pattern

The pictures and maps in a well-written social studies textbook supplement the printed material. As obvious as pictorial aids may be to competent readers, average students may get little from them. One student told his teacher, "I never look at the pictures and maps, but I like them in the book because the more pictures there are, the less reading." This student needed to realize that the pictures and maps could give much information, especially if one knew how to use them and had a purpose (information to find) for doing so. Teachers often find that students do not realize the relationship of the picture to its legend. With maps, the students may not understand types of projections, how to use the map key and scale, or know such basic map features as longitude and latitude. All students need to become adept in the use of pictorial aids. And, as many teachers have noted, poor readers especially can get much information from such sources.

The Cause and Effect Pattern

This pattern is a common and predominant one in social studies. Human interaction is characterized in large measure by a chain of causes and

---

6. Nila Banton Smith, "Patterns of Writing in Different Subject Areas, Part II," *Journal of Reading* 8 (November 1964): 97–102.

effects—sometimes with effects being the causes of further effects. An example of cause and effect within a single paragraph from a social studies text shows a cause with a number of effects (see Example 12.1).

EXAMPLE 12.1

___ Cause

=== Effect

> Increased Production, More Jobs. By 1923 the American economy had weathered the postwar depression. The automobile industry had grown rapidly, spurring prosperity in iron, steel, glass, and rubber manufacturing. Its development created all kinds of new jobs in the oil industry; road construction, as well as that of office buildings and dwellings, boomed and so did the demand for workers. In addition, other industries soon copied Henry Ford's assembly-line production techniques and his installment-plan sales procedures. As Americans purchased more goods, both necessities and luxuries, production increased and created new jobs and eventually still further demands for goods. Long before the political convention of 1924, general prosperity made the political outlook for the Republicans very good.

Reprinted by permission from T. Harry Williams and Hazel C. Wolf, *Our American Nation* (Columbus: Charles E. Merrill, 1966), p. 644.

Suggestions for classroom procedure:

1. Have the students list the factors that led up to a certain event.
2. After listing the factors that led up to an event, check each one to see how or if it may have been a cause.
3. Find similar situations in history. List the points that make them alike and those that make them different.
4. Suggest that students use facts as a basis for making predictions.

The Sequential Events with Dates Pattern

History evolves chronologically. One of the understandings students will need to acquire is the large movements of history and the overlap of historical movements. They must learn to appreciate the fluid nature of historical development and realize when they study a historical movement that it did not begin at a specified date or end with one. For instance, consider the Westward Movement in the United States: the movement did not occur *only* around the Gold Rush Period of 1849 (a time when this movement is described in many textbooks) but started with the first settlers and, according to current census reports, is still continuing.

Suggestions for classroom procedure:

1. Construct a time line showing the development of a historical period and the overlap with other periods.
2. Have the students note important dates relative to a period of history.
3. Make a chart of a historical period showing the chronology of events and persons involved. Use arrows to show relationships between persons, and between persons and dates.
4. On an outline map, record the place, names of persons, and date of historical events.

5. Direct the students to note the introduction of another step in a chain of events by such words as *then, finally, second, another, subsequently.*

The Comparison Pattern

Students use this pattern when likenesses and differences are to be noted on such topics as countries, theories of government, policies of different political leaders, and historical periods. Obviously, the purpose for reading should require looking for likenesses and differences as students read. Suggestions for classroom procedure:

1. Have the students compare and contrast the governmental structures of two or more countries.
2. Have the students compare the resources, economic conditions, and living standards of two or more countries.
3. Have the students compare two historical documents of different points of view or different countries during the same period.
4. Have the students compare living conditions of the present with a time in the past.
5. Compare means of travel today with a period in the past. An example of the comparison pattern is shown in Example 12.2.

Detailed Statement-of-Fact Pattern

This pattern of writing is designed to give information about some social studies phenomenon for the purpose of building background. Students use this information in large measure to arrive at comparisons, interpretations, and conclusions.

The procedures of this pattern are similar to those for noting the main idea, the pertinent details, and in seeing the organization of information. Have students tabulate or chart the information, as indicated in Example 12.3.

The Propaganda Pattern

Propaganda has been used throughout human history. The interaction of people involves points of view and the techniques of persuasion. This pattern calls for the skills of critical reading. Students will find propaganda in newspapers and in materials written by those who wish to convince readers of a point of view. Generally speaking, most school textbooks lack such a specific point of view.

Suggested classroom procedures:

1. Have the students decide what great powers control the strategic spots on the earth. What techniques of control are used?
2. Have the students evaluate the information used by the author to prove an important point. Direct them to note the words she uses to make an emotional impact or impression.

EXAMPLE 12.2

Comparison of Plymouth with Jamestown

Site, location

Site, drinking water

Difficulties of the First Years

Their choice of site was ill-advised, for they built Jamestown in a low, marshy, malarial spot without an adequate supply of drinking water. Then, because the promoters were demanding an immediate return on their investment, the Virginians feverishly searched for gold and prepared stocks of New World products such as lumber, pitch, tar, and iron ore to ship to England.

Food supply

The first settlers worked so diligently to accumulate money-making goods that they neglected to grow food to enable them to survive. The stores they had brought with them and the food they did grow were kept in a common storehouse and given out as needed. This system permitted "gentlemen" who labored only a little to draw the same rations as those men who worked hard. A great deal of resentment resulted, and dissension developed among the men. Not until Captain John Smith, a professional soldier employed by the company, silenced the wrangling by laying down some stiff rules did the colony begin to get on its feet.

Survival

In 1609 Smith had to return to England for treatment of a severe powder burn. During his absence about 440 of the 500 settlers died for lack of food. Those who survived this "starving time" decided to return to England in the spring of 1610. They turned back when ships arrived with supplies and new settlers.

Setting up the Colony

Site, drinking water

Site, location

Colonial Hardships. At Plymouth the Pilgrims had chosen a site with a supply of good drinking water, near hills of good timber and tracts of cleared land. In the bitter December cold, the whole group lived on the crowded Mayflower while the men built homes and a storehouse. When the meager supply of food brought from England ran out, obtaining more became a major problem. The sea could yield fish, but the colonists had no boats or fishing equipment. The woods were full of game, but the newcomers were not yet skillful hunters.

Food supply

Survival

The most heartbreaking experience of the winter was the epidemic that the colonists called the "general sickness." Its victims suffered from pneumonia as well as from scurvy brought on by a diet without fresh fruits and vegetables. Half the Mayflower passengers died during that first winter. Among the dead was the colony's first governor, John Carver. William Bradford succeeded to the office.

Reprinted by permission from T. Harry Williams and Hazel C. Wolf, *Our American Nation* (Columbus: Charles E. Merrill, 1966), pp. 45–46, 49–50.

EXAMPLE 12.3

Facts about Hoover

1. Wartime food administrator-directed work:
2. Secretary of Commerce—looking for business opportunities.
3. Kept close watch on other Cabinet departments—note opportunities to help business.
4. President—would suggest corrective legislation.

As a mining engineer whose work had taken him all over the world and brought him a small fortune, and as an ①efficient wartime food administrator in Europe as well as in his own country. Hoover was accustomed to directing the work of the offices he held. As ②Secretary of Commerce he had been determined to ferret out every kind of opportunity for American business. ③He had kept close watch on other Cabinet departments, alert for activities which might be correlated with those of his own department to the advantage of business. He tried, Coolidge had complained, to be undersecretary to every other Cabinet member. As ④President, he expected to be equally active. He would make his own studies of current issues and suggest his own corrective legislation.

The Farm Problem

1. Agricultural Marketing Act. (description of function)
2. Farmers responded.
3. Advice on how to increase production cancelled out limiting production by acreage.
4. Prices continued to decline.
5. Establishment of Grain and Cotton Stabilization Corporations. (description of function)

The Farm Problem

Since the farm problem seemed more pressing than any other, Hoover called a special session of Congress to consider it. When Congress assembled, he was ready with a program. Two months later, the lawmakers approved an ①*Agricultural Marketing Act* based on his suggestions. Farmers were urged to join voluntarily in marketing cooperatives which would be aided by the federal government. Supporters of the measure believed it would enable farmers to control production and distribution in much the same way that many manufacturers did. To aid the effort, the act created an eight-member Federal Farm Board with a half-billion dollar revolving fund for loans to cooperatives or to organizations which the board might set up to purchase, store, and market possible surpluses.

Farmers responded at once. ②During its first year of operation the board loaned over 165 million dollars. ③The advice it gave on limiting the production of crops already in oversupply, however, was to some extent canceled out by Agriculture Department and agricultural school advice on how to increase production. ④But cooperative marketing did not curtail the rapid decline of wheat and cotton prices. ⑤The board then exercised the second power which Congress had given it and established a Grain Stabilization Corporation and a Cotton Stabilization Corporation. In an effort to raise prices, each corporation purchased and stored the surplus of its particular commodity.

3. Have the students evaluate a historical figure of speech, showing its origin, application, and emotional appeal.
4. Suggest that students draw cartoons illustrating the effect of some historical event.
5. Have the students show how some country takes advantage of its geographical position.
6. Have the students describe the methods of leadership used by various historical leaders. Analyze the techniques of their leadership.
7. Have the students prove or disprove a statement with concrete factual information.
8. Have the students decide what the author's purpose is in writing propaganda and note her use of words to foster her purpose.
9. If an author presents two sides to a problem and draws a conclusion, have the students note the author's treatment of the facts for each side and have them determine the author's preference—if there is one—and the validity of her preference.

Noting Fact from Opinion

This is also a part of critical reading. Students need to note the author's use of words indicating conclusion and determine if it is founded on fact or conjecture. Then, a finer distinction is often required in which the students must judge conclusions based on fact, or statements presented as fact but based on accumulated circumstantial evidence. Such statements are often generally accepted ideas based upon common empirical knowledge about human activity throughout the ages.

Suggested procedures:

1. Have the students note statements in their textbooks which are based on fact and are therefore logical conclusions. Note the difference between these and statements of opinion which may not have factual support. For example: *The Continental Congress completed the Constitution in 1787 and voted to submit for ratification.* (fact) *All of the leaders in the congress were enthusiastic about the new Constitution.* (opinion, not based on fact) *Many of the leaders of the Congress had reservations about the new Constitution but submitted it for ratification since it represented the best solution to government they could devise.* (factual conclusion based on arguments during the writing of the Constitution)
2. Have the students be aware of the use of such words as *think, perhaps, in my opinion, maybe,* etc., which may indicate statements of opinion.

Time, Place, and Space Concepts

Understanding and appreciating human history and activity requires an awareness of *time* and its passage; of *place* and its characteristics (such as climate, topography, and importance); and of *space,* including an appreciation of distance. The chronology and sequence of history and, to some extent, cause and effect are understood with reference to time. Providing information about places and comparing them with the students' own environment also aids understanding. Distance can be determined by studying maps and understanding map scales. The concept of distance is critical in the interpretation of historical events, because we must remember the time it took to traverse distances—particularly as compared to today's rapid transportation. An understanding of time which includes a "feeling for it" helps students to see the continuous flow of human history. The *time line* is a device that conveys this movement of history. One technique which intrigues students is to note on a time line the space equivalent to their own life span. The contrast between the small segment on the time line that their life span occupies and the whole of human history dramatically shows the long period in time during which human history has evolved.

APPLYING READING SKILLS TO SCIENCE

The word *science,* deriving from the Latin *scire* (to know), means knowledge. The branches of science (botany, zoology, biology, physics, chemistry, and so on) are systematized bodies of knowledge based upon observable and provable data. Though there are hypotheses—suppositions—in science, they are tested against specific evidence and then become accepted generalization or fact or are discarded.

Scientists use all of the senses to gather evidence: they observe, feel, smell, listen, and taste. They also use language to evolve the problem and hypothesis, to think about the findings, and to read conclusions about the significance of the findings. They use language also to communicate discoveries to other scientists.

The science teacher helps students to learn scientific facts through their senses with such means as observation, films, experiments, field trips, models, pictures, and reading materials. The facts are not very important as isolated bits of information; rather, the significance of the facts is deduced, and generalizations are formed which incorporate scientific understandings. Of course, in the classroom there is neither the time nor the need to rediscover all the scientific facts noted throughout history. In fact, the students may only illustrate a principle, not prove it. They seldom hypothesize new understandings or prove new knowledge. Students acquire most scientific knowledge through reading. Therefore, language and reading are vital tools for the discovery and interpretation of scientific data and the formation of generalizations.

The science teacher can be guided by three related and sequential goals. The first is to endeavor to have the students obtain facts. Factual data is available through many sources, including written materials. This basic goal requires competence in the skills of gaining information from the printed page. The second goal is for students to understand the data. They should understand functional concepts, principles, and the procedure of the scientific method, and this requires many reading skills (vocabulary, interpretation, and evaluative reading). The final goal is for students to acquire scientific attitudes, appreciations, and interests. The goals for science are not too different from those of the reading process itself—to develop mature, effective, and interested readers who read with judgment and perceptiveness.

Problems in Reading Science

Scientific writing presents obstacles to many students. If their reading instruction has been largely from descriptive and narrative materials, they may be overwhelmed by the myriad of details and facts and their interrelationships. Students who may be able to read story-type materials well should not be expected to read scientific materials equally well, particularly if the science teacher does not provide instruction in reading science material.

Bamman lists the difficulties encountered in reading both science and mathematics:

1. Students have been accustomed to reading materials of narration, not the terse language of scientific writing.
2. There is little control over the number of concepts introduced on a page or within a chapter which require intensive and slow reading. Students must not only understand the concepts but also must see the interrelationships among them. The number of concepts introduced in a specified space affects the readability of the material.
3. Concepts are developed on an ascending scale of difficulty such that readers are required to use their previous knowledge. The lack of background and the lack of maturity and ability in using background are chief obstacles for the students.
4. Understanding science requires sensing relationships and thinking critically about what is already known and what is currently being read.
5. Critical reading is required, as students often must judge the relevance, authenticity, and value of data.
6. A mastery of study skills is needed. Not only are techniques of using textbooks and reference materials required, but in science the ability to interpret charts, tables, graphs, and formulas is also necessary.
7. The vocabulary of science can be formidable for students. Explosive growth in various fields of science adds to the sophistication of the materials with new and often complex vocabulary.
8. Materials used for wide reading are sometimes insufficient in quantity and highly varied in difficulty.[7]

Though these difficulties may seem insurmountable, there are procedures which can be employed to help students learn and achieve the objectives of the science course. Whatever the direction of science teaching—to teach how to obtain information from printed material in science or to teach some factual information—competence with the language of science is essential. Science teaching thus must be a balance between the

---

7. Henry A. Bamman, "Reading in Science and Mathematics," in *Reading Instruction in Secondary School: Perspectives in Reading #2* (Newark, Del.: International Reading Association, 1964), pp. 60–61. Reprinted with permission of Henry A. Bamman and the International Reading Association.

reading process and factual content, for the two are interwoven and dependent upon each other.

Required Reading Skills

There are three general types of science reading. One is the intensive study of textbooks and laboratory manuals. The writing in these sources tends to be technical and requires careful, slow, and analytical reading. Another type is the assigned collateral reading in scientific journals, popular science magazines, and books on scientific research. Books containing scientific research and many scientific journal materials are packed with small but important details; such materials also require analytical reading. Finally, the students read nontechnical scientific material—biographies of great scientists and newspaper and popular magazines reporting current happenings in the field. This is the easiest material to read and to understand. In organization and style it is most like literary and social studies writing.

The skills needed for reading science are essentially the same as those needed in the other disciplines:

1. Varying the rate of reading according to the purpose for reading and the nature of the material.
2. Using parts of a book.
3. Locating and using sources of information.
4. Using the vocabulary of science, which includes technical and nontechnical words and symbols.
5. Understanding and using formulas.
6. Gaining information from graphic aids such as charts, diagrams, and graphs.
7. Reading for exact meaning—noting main ideas and supporting details and seeing organization.
8. Reading directions accurately.
9. Evaluating science materials, drawing conclusions, making judgments, and discerning evidence.
10. Applying data from reading to practical problems.

Many science teachers want the students to learn through continual experimentation. Such a program is based on the concept of *discovery* and most often is individually paced. This technique not only makes the class more exciting but also prepares students to learn readily and apply the steps of the scientific process—all very positive objectives. However, teachers often find that many students are unable to work through a program of discovery through experimentation, for two major reasons. First, the students may not have an adequate conceptual background that would enable them to understand the significance and implications of experimental findings. Second, many students lack the skills to use the accompanying printed materials independently and efficiently. Therefore, instruction in both conceptual background and the appropriate reading skills is necessary. A class that concentrates just on skills, with the scientific understandings secondary, can be quite dull. Attempt to strike a balance between student discovery and instruction in the concepts and skills.

Varying the Rate of Reading

Since students read different types of material within science, they need guidance in how to attack each type. In science as in other disciplines, rate of reading is dependent upon two considerations. One is the *purpose* for reading; how complex this is will determine speed and concentration. For instance, if students are reading to find one isolated bit of information, they can skim by looking for the most essential word or number and then read slowly to check their information. On the other hand, if they are reading to see how an experiment is to be conducted or to understand the interrelationship of factors concerning some scientific phenomenon, they will need to read intensively and slowly. The other consideration is the nature of the material itself. Technical material that includes numbers and formulas requires slow, intensive reading. Material that describes the application of a scientific phenomenon or truth or that introduces a topic usually shows the relationship of major ideas to specific details. Reading such material will be faster and less intensive. Biographical material may be read as one reads a story—for enjoyment and for general information, but not necessarily with careful discernment and classification of detail. Background of information also contributes in determining the individual's rate in any subject. Examples 12.4, 12.5, and 12.6 show samples of different kinds of science writing. Also shown are guide questions for reading (purpose questions) and comments about the intensity of reading required.

Using Parts of the Book

Questions to guide reading, explanatory diagrams and pictures, review questions, word lists, and the outlined organization of the information as indicated by the headings in boldface print are aids for students. One of your responsibilities is to teach your students how to use the aids so that they understand them and use them independently. Example 12.7, from a physical science text, shows some of the various study aids labelled.

Locating and Using Information

Students must be competent in library research skills in order to search for additional information on a topic. Students probably will know general library skills from using them in other classes, but the science teacher should check the students' competence and be prepared to fill in any apparent gaps. Librarians will give valuable assistance in the library. Your particular responsibility is to alert the students to resource materials about scientific topics (trade books, textbooks, magazines and journals such as *Scientific American,* government publications, and bulletins published by various scientific organizations and foundations).

EXAMPLE 12.4

Wheels, the drive shaft, and pistons of a large steam locomotive work together to produce motion. *William Maddox*

Introduce Chapter 2 by having students describe the characteristics of moving objects. The descriptions should include characteristics such as speed, effort force, and distance. The concepts of force, work, and power are developed in this chapter. The six simple machines are discussed in detail.

Introduction to help students think about the topic

2 Force and Work

GOAL: You will gain an understanding of forces, work, simple machines, mechanical advantage, and power.

Preview—overview

Purposes:
How do forces and work relate?
What are the simple machines?
What is mechanical advantage?

Machinery is an important part of people's lives. Machines are used in a variety of ways for different purposes. Each machine has a particular use. For example, scissors are used for cutting. Vehicles on wheels are used to move passengers or goods.

The types of machines range from simple to very complex. However, each one has several things in common. These common features are explained by the concepts of force and work.

Relating to students' background

General questions of purpose

2:1 *Force*

How can you set an object in motion? Kick a can. Throw a ball. Pound a nail into a board. In each case an object is moved. It takes a force to put an object at rest into motion.

Definition

A **force** is a push or a pull. For example, a wagon can be pulled or pushed. In either case, a force moves the wagon. When the wagon moves, it is in motion.

What is force?

All sports involve forces and motion. Relate these principles to baseball, basketball, football, hockey, and other sports. Have students name the forces they experience in their home or school.

Relating to student experiences—the known

Does a force always produce motion? Push down on your desk top as hard as you can or push against the wall in your room. Only an unbalanced force produces motion. Unbalanced means the force you or something exerts must be greater than the force that opposes it. When this happens, motion occurs. **Resistance** (rih ZIS tuhnts) is a force which slows down or prevents motion. *Friction* is an example of resistance.

Two definitions

Figure 2-1. When a wagon is pulled or pushed, a force is exerted on the wagon.

Figure 2-2. A force only produces motion when it is greater than the opposing force.

PROBLEMS

1. What force is great enough to move your desk top? If not fixed in place, a student's arms.
2. What force moves your body parts? The forces of muscles on bones.
3. How could you exert a force to lift yourself? Sit on chair, place hands on chair, and push down

Questions of application

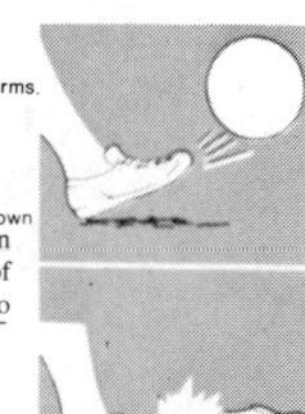

The unit of force in the English system is the pound (lb). Force in pounds can be measured with a spring scale. The metric unit of force is the newton (N). A *newton* is the unit of force required to accelerate a one kilogram mass at 1 m/sec².

Definition

Reprinted by permission from Charles H. Heimler and Jack Price, *Focus on Physical Science* (Columbus: Charles E. Merrill, 1977), pp. 20–21.

EXAMPLE 12.5

quadrivalence of carbon and the
linkage of carbon atoms
formulae
1. Ethyl chloride
2. Ethyl alcohol
3. acetic acid
4. acetamide
5. methyl formate
6. Methyl cyanide

General background information—biographical writing

Friedrich August Kekulé
(1829-1896)

General purpose for reading this section might be: For what is Kekule noted? (Answer underlined.)

German chemist Friedrich Kekulé was considered by many the most brilliant of his day for his ideas on the linking of atoms. <u>He was the first to speculate on the existence of bonds between atoms and he drew structural diagrams similar to those we use now.</u>

These ideas he developed while trying to elucidate the structure of carbon compounds. At this time he proposed that carbon was tetravalent. Kekulé explained that in substances containing several carbon atoms, it must be assumed that some of the bonds of each carbon atom are bonded to the atoms of other elements contained in the substance—and some are bonded to the other carbon atoms.

This concept led Kekulé to propose a ring structure as the logical arrangement for the atoms composing benzene. At this time, many felt that this was the "most brilliant piece of prediction in all of organic chemistry."

<u>Many of our present theories on the structures of compounds were formulated by Kekulé.</u> His teaching career was centered in Heidelberg, Ghent, and Bonn where personally trained investigators followed through with his theories after his death.

Reprinted by permission from Robert C. Smoot, Jack Price, and Richard L. Barrett, *Chemistry: A Modern Course* (Columbus: Charles E. Merrill, 1971), p. 189.

EXAMPLE 12.6

Use topical heading to determine purpose questions:
What determines the shape of molecules?

Use italicized terms as sources for purpose questions;
i.e., What is the bond axis?
What is the bond angle?
What is the van der Waals radius?

Further purpose:
What is the effect of the bond angle, the bond axis and the van der Waals radius upon molecule shape?

THE SHAPE OF ATOMS AND MOLECULES

9:1 The Shape of Molecules

When two or more atoms form a molecule, we say that the atoms are bonded together. The line joining the nuclei of two bonded atoms in a molecule is called the *bond axis.* Ordinarily, the orbitals formed by the bonding electrons are symmetrical about the bond axis. If one atom is bonded to each of two other atoms, the angle between the two bond axes is called the *bond angle.* The distance between nuclei along the bond axis is called the *bond length.* This length is not really fixed, because the bond acts much as if it were a stiff spring and the atoms vibrate as though the bond were alternately stretching and shrinking. Bonds also undergo a bending vibration which causes the bond angle to constantly change. However, the amplitudes of these vibrations are not large; and the bond lengths and bond angles which we measure are accurate, though average, values. We may think of them as the values for a molecule completely at rest. However, molecular vibration does not entirely cease, even at absolute zero.

When two atoms approach, they cannot come closer than a certain minimum distance. Electrons of one atom repel the electrons of other atoms and, therefore, two atoms or molecules can never occupy the same space at the same time. In effect, colliding free atoms and molecules act as if they had a rigid outer shell which limits the closeness with which they may approach other atoms or molecules. Since the molecular bond consists of shared electrons, bonded atoms come closer together than atoms which are not

10A

5A

4A

FIGURE 9-1. Balanced repulsive (electron-electron and nucleus-nucleus) forces and attractive (nucleus-electron) forces determine the van der Waals forces and the van der Waals radius (point of closest approach).

bonded. The radius of the imaginary rigid shell of an atom is called the *van der Waals radius.* (See Figure 9-1.) Figure 9-2 shows the relationship between the various dimensions which are needed to describe a water molecule. If we know these dimensions we can construct a physical model which represents a molecule to scale. The heavy circles represent the covalent radii of the oxygen and hydrogen atoms in the water molecule. The outer dashed line represents the approximate closest approach of the other non-

Reprinted by permission from Robert C. Smoot, Jack Price, and Richard L. Barrett, *Chemistry: A Modern Course* (Columbus: Charles E. Merrill, 1971), p. 191.

EXAMPLE 12.7

3:7 *Velocity* 1. Purpose: What is velocity?

The speed and direction of an airplane traveling north at 600 km/hr may be shown by a vector. This vector is drawn by using a scale of 100 km/hr = 1 cm. A line, 6 cm long, is drawn pointing to the top of paper (north). The vector which shows both speed and direction is called a velocity vector.

Word recognition

In physical science, speed refers to how fast a body is moving. **Velocity** (vuh LAHS uht ee) refers to how fast a body is moving and the direction in which it is moving.

100 km/hr

600 km/hr

R

1 cm = 100 km

Figure 3-28. Vectors can be drawn to show the speed and direction of an airplane. Plotting a course must include an allowance for wind speed and direction.

How can vectors be used to show velocity?

What is the difference between speed and velocity?

PROBLEM

Practical problems of application

19. A motorboat moves south across a river at 20 km/hr. The river current moves at 5 km/hr. Use vectors to find the velocity of the motorboat. Scale: 1 cm = 5 km (See Teacher's Guide.)

Allan Roberts

Figure 3-29. Sailboat navigation takes wind speed and direction into account.

MAIN IDEAS

Summary—students advised to read this before studying chapter

3:1 **1.** Weight and mass are different. Weight is the amount of force the earth exerts on a body due to gravity. Mass is the amount of matter in a body.

3:1, 3:2 **2.** Motion starts and stops through the action of forces.

3:3 **3.** Speed is the distance covered per unit time. Velocity is speed in a given direction.

3:3 **4.** A force must be applied to vary speed or velocity.

3:4, 3:5 **5.** Acceleration and deceleration result from the action of forces.

3:6 **6.** The amount of force may be measured in newtons.

3:6 **7.** A vector represents both magnitude and direction.

3:6 **8.** Force vectors are used to find the resultant of two or more forces acting together.

3:7 **9.** Velocity vectors are used to find the speed and direction of a body in motion.

VOCABULARY

Vocabulary review
Can any of the terms be related?
(i.e., speed
acceleration
deceleration)

Write a sentence in which you correctly use each of the following words or terms.

acceleration	magnitude	speed
deceleration	mass	vector
equilibrium	resultant	velocity
force	scale	weight
gravity	scientific law	

Reprinted by permission from Charles H. Heimler and Jack Price, *Focus on Physical Science* (Columbus: Charles E. Merrill, 1977), p. 67.

Using Science Vocabulary Correctly

In science, students encounter four types of words which present difficulty: technical words peculiar to the subject, general words used in a scientific context, difficult general words used in a scientific context, and difficult general words with multiple meanings. Those who teach science readily assume the responsibility for the technical words and the general words used in a scientific context. However, teachers must be alert to the difficult general words as well. For instance, in a single chapter on energy, one might teach technical terms—*kinetic energy, heat of fusion;* general words used in a technical manner—*work, power,* and *heat;* and general terms—*substance, standard,* and *expands.*

The teacher can enlarge the student's vocabulary in many ways:

1. Show enthusiasm for the correct use of words. Develop a large vocabulary and use it in the classroom.
2. Search for ways to minimize differences between specialized words and those in everyday speech. When appropriate, a common term may be used as a translation or substitution for the technical term. For instance, the meaning of *density* in physical science is the mass per unit volume. In lay terms the words *body* and *thickness* may be used to give clues to the term. Fascinating vocabulary lessons can be taught by comparing the looseness of the everyday terms with the precision of scientific meanings.
3. Students should be guided to use the new words consistently in class discussion and in their writing.
4. Analyze the words with the students. Note acronyms (such as *laser*—light amplification by stimulated emission of radiation). Help the students to understand how many scientific words are directly related to roots—that a long word usually consists of strung-together word parts, each of which has a meaning, and that putting together the parts usually gives the meaning of the complete word. For example, the word *isotherm* consists of the prefix *iso* (meaning *equal*) and the root *therm* (meaning *heat*); *chlorophyll* consists of the root *chloro* (meaning *green*) and the root *phyll* (meaning *leaf*).
5. Strive for precision by encouraging students to say exactly what they mean. For example, would they be able to distinguish among the words *spherical, globular,* and *round?*
6. Alert students to structure words which indicate the relationship between facts and ideas. Such structure words may indicate time order (*after, before, while, during*), cause and effect (*since, because, for, for this reason, therefore*), likenesses and differences (*unlike, different, same,* and comparative and superlative forms), and order of importance (*least, most, essential*).
7. Alert the students to multiple meanings; for instance, *cell* as used in biology and in electricity.
8. Classify words listed at the end of a chapter or unit in accordance with the interrelationships of the concepts they represent. For

instance, in a chapter entitled "The Atmosphere," the vocabulary listing at the end is presented alphabetically:

atmosphere	hydrosphere	stratosphere
barometer	ionosphere	temperate zones
climate	marine climate	transpiration
conduction	mesosphere	tropics
convection	nitrogen	troposphere

These words can be rearranged in an outline of the chapter done by topical headings. This is also a way of categorizing the terms. Thus, if the topical heading is *Air Pressure,* the term listed below would be *barometer.*

9. Note whether there are any pictures, diagrams, or charts that illustrate the meaning.
10. Note italicized words or words in boldface print (usually new technical words) and determine the meaning as given in the textbook.
11. Encourage students to keep a list of new words in a notebook, each with its definition.

Understanding and Using Formulas

Formulas and the symbols used in them may be considered an extension of vocabulary, as they represent ideas by a symbolic code which can also be labelled by words. The formula is a type of shorthand that represents a thought. If students understand the thought, the only additional skill needed is translation. Perhaps the formula can be presented as a type of language with its own vocabulary. For example, the formula for computing the size of a centripetal force is

$$F = \frac{MV^2}{R}$$

(Vocabulary)

F = force measured in newtons, dynes, pounds
M = mass measured in kilograms
V = velocity measured in minutes per second or feet per second
R = radius of the curve measured in milligrams

Expressed as a sentence, the formula reads: "Centripetal force is equal to the mass times the velocity squared divided by the radius of the circle."

Gaining Information from Graphic Aids

Most science textbooks are filled with graphic aids that supplement many of the ideas presented. They are of value to all students, but particularly to those who have difficulty reading and understanding the words. However, students may not realize the relationship between the graphic aids and the language of the text—how they supplement each other. Example 12.8 shows pictorially the amount of work required to move a force in different directions (straight up, inclined up, sidewards). The formula is stated in the paragraph below with definitions and directions for working an example. Example 12.9 shows the relationship of frequency to wave length. Example 12.10 displays the food chain; other relationships also may be noted. In Example 12.11, the diagram (labelled as Figure 13.11) and the accompanying text show pictorially the relationship of time, velocity, and distance. In this way, students are assisted in understanding the relationships in the formula. In Example 12.12, the diagram requires a sense

EXAMPLE 12.8

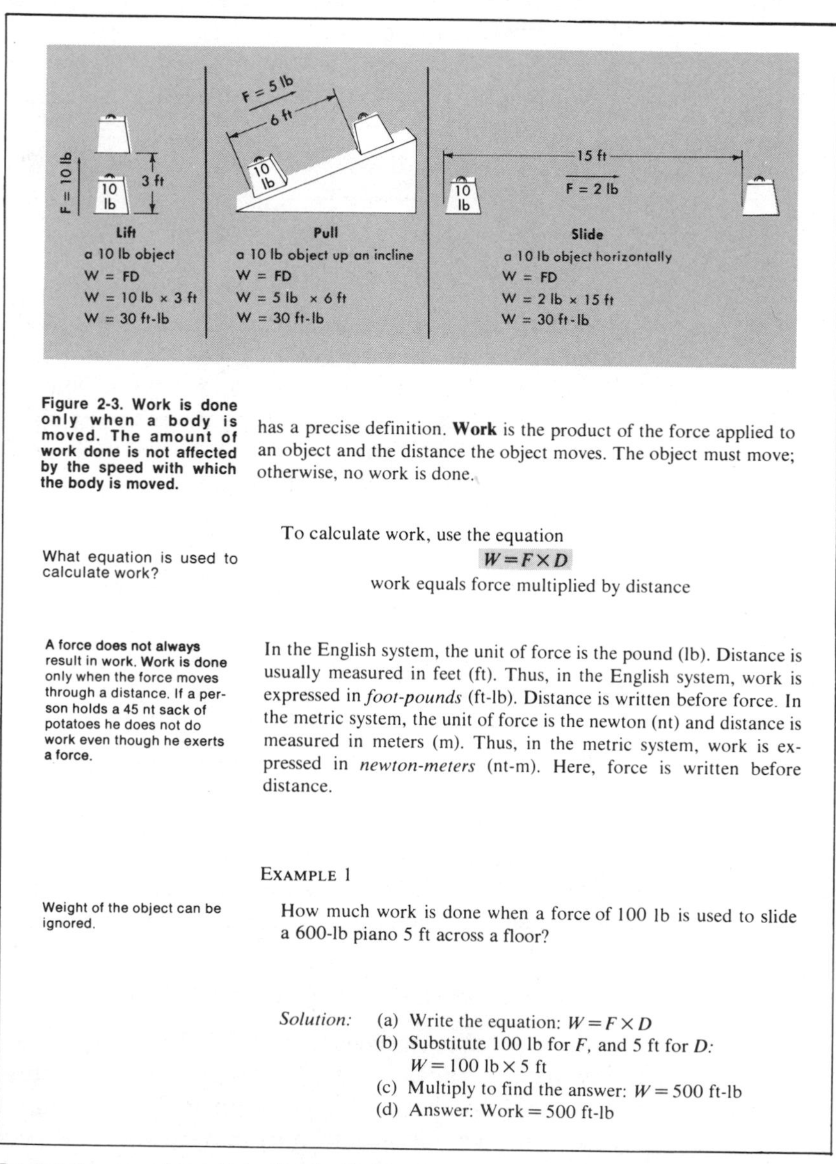

Figure 2-3. Work is done only when a body is moved. The amount of work done is not affected by the speed with which the body is moved.

has a precise definition. **Work** is the product of the force applied to an object and the distance the object moves. The object must move; otherwise, no work is done.

What equation is used to calculate work?

To calculate work, use the equation

$$W = F \times D$$

work equals force multiplied by distance

A force does not always result in work. Work is done only when the force moves through a distance. If a person holds a 45 nt sack of potatoes he does not do work even though he exerts a force.

In the English system, the unit of force is the pound (lb). Distance is usually measured in feet (ft). Thus, in the English system, work is expressed in *foot-pounds* (ft-lb). Distance is written before force. In the metric system, the unit of force is the newton (nt) and distance is measured in meters (m). Thus, in the metric system, work is expressed in *newton-meters* (nt-m). Here, force is written before distance.

EXAMPLE 1

Weight of the object can be ignored.

How much work is done when a force of 100 lb is used to slide a 600-lb piano 5 ft across a floor?

Solution:
(a) Write the equation: $W = F \times D$
(b) Substitute 100 lb for F, and 5 ft for D: $W = 100 \text{ lb} \times 5 \text{ ft}$
(c) Multiply to find the answer: $W = 500$ ft-lb
(d) Answer: Work = 500 ft-lb

of spatial relations; it shows why the total area surface increases. In Example 12.13 no computation is necessary. The students merely note the arrows pointing in all directions and the legend states the idea. Example 12.14 shows diagrammatically the classification of matter.

EXAMPLE 12.9

In the diagram, no mathematical computation is necessary. However, using the information in the paragraph, inferential questions could be posed:

(1) Do low tones or high tones have the longer wave length?
(2) What is the relationship between the frequencies of high tones and low tones?

Notes made by a piano show the relationship between frequency and wavelength. Sound waves of different frequencies have different wavelengths. As frequency increases, wavelength decreases. When you strike the extreme right key of a piano, you produce sound waves of high frequency. Their wavelengths are about 7.7 cm long. Strike the extreme left key and you produce waves of low frequency. Their wavelengths are about 12.2 m.

Wave A and wave B have the same amplitude.

Figure 3-16. Wave B has a wavelength one-half that of wave A. The frequency of wave B is twice the frequency of wave A.

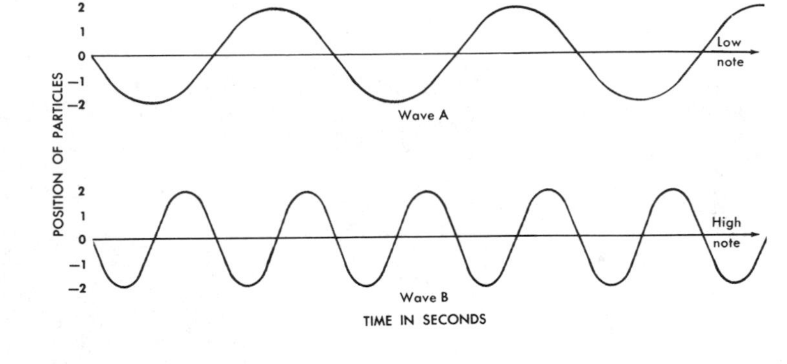

Reprinted by permission from Charles H. Heimler and Jack Price, *Focus on Physical Science* (Columbus: Charles E. Merrill, 1977), p. 341.

EXAMPLE 12.10

Main relationship →

Other relationships noted by inference:
(1) What is the relationship of animals and plants in the food chain?
(2) What is the basic source of all energy?
(3) Why do plants need light?

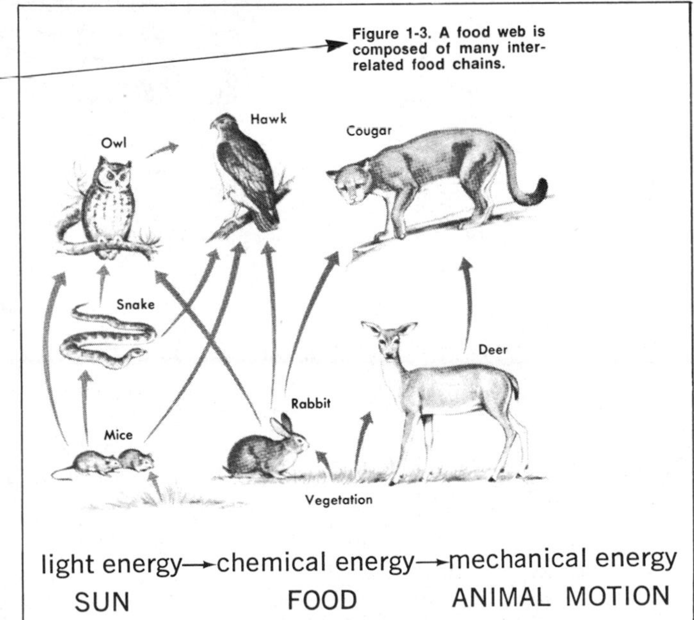

Figure 1-3. A food web is composed of many interrelated food chains.

Reprinted by permission from Charles H. Heimler and J. David Lockard, *Focus on Life Science* (Columbus: Charles E. Merrill, 1977), p. 421.

EXAMPLE 12.11

3:3 *Speed*

Definition: basis for formula

A force can set a body in motion. A body in motion moves a certain distance in a certain unit of time such as a second, a minute, or an hour. **Speed** is defined as the distance a body travels per unit of time. Speed = distance/time.

An automobile speedometer indicates speed in mi/hr or km/hr. Automobiles on a highway may move at a constant speed. Constant speed means that the speed does not vary. For example, a car travels at a constant speed of 50 km/hr. The car travels 50 km in the first

Gary Walker

Relating to student background

Figure 3-10. Speed limit signs indicate the speeds at which it is safe to travel.

Figure 3-11. To find the average speed between San Francisco and New York, divide the distance (4800 km) by the total hours of time.

Diagram showing relationship of time, velocity, and distance

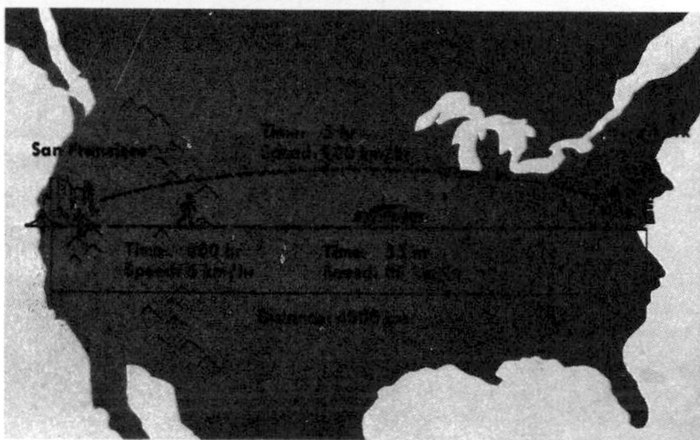

hour and 50 km in the second hour. Thus, it travels a total of 100 km in two hours. When it goes 50 km every hour, it maintains this constant speed.

You can calculate speed, distance, or period of time in motion for a moving body. Use the equation below.

What equation is used to calculate speed?

$$v = \frac{d}{t}$$

speed equals distance divided by time

Application

Have students consult Appendix A. Explain the tables listed and how they may be used as an aid in solving problems.

EXAMPLE 1

What is the speed of a truck which travels 10 km in 10 min at constant speed?

Solution: (a) Write the equation: $v = \frac{d}{t}$

(b) Substitute 10 km for d and 10 min for t:

$$v = \frac{10 \text{ km}}{10 \text{ min}}$$

(c) Divide to find the answer: $v = 1$ km/min

Reprinted by permission from Charles H. Heimler and Jack Price, *Focus on Physical Science* (Columbus: Charles E. Merrill, 1977), pp. 51–52.

EXAMPLE 12.12

Inference: why does the area increase?

Diagram shows the content of one paragraph (about 1/3 page in length) and why the area increases

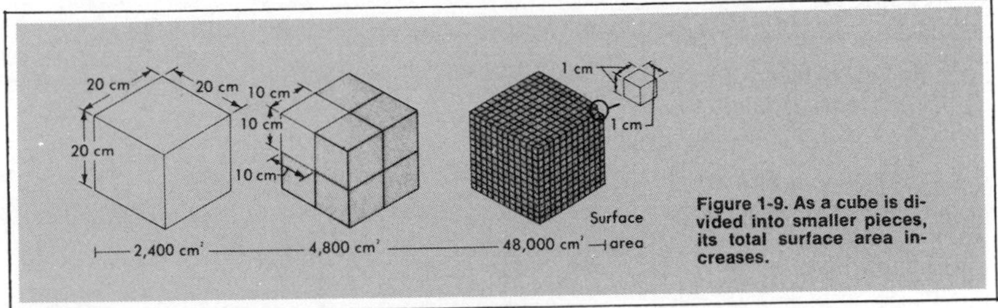

Figure 1-9. As a cube is divided into smaller pieces, its total surface area increases.

Reprinted by permission from Charles H. Heimler and Jack Price, *Focus on Physical Science* (Columbus: Charles E. Merrill, 1977), p. 231.

EXAMPLE 12.13

Pictured concept

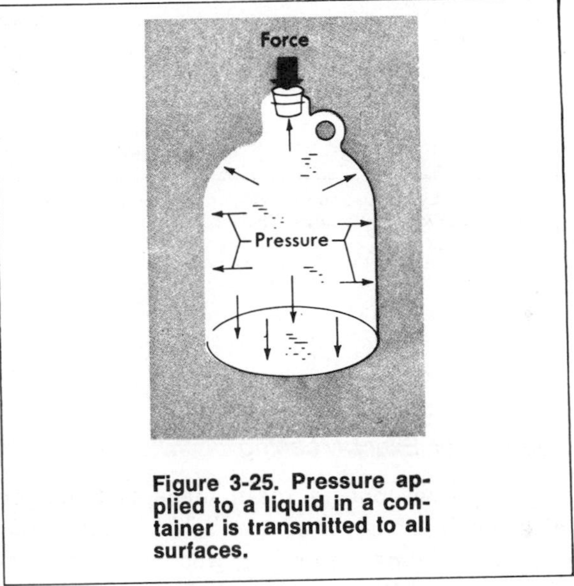

Figure 3-25. Pressure applied to a liquid in a container is transmitted to all surfaces.

Reprinted by permission from Charles H. Heimler and Jack Price, *Focus on Physical Science* (Columbus: Charles E. Merrill, 1977), p. 149.

EXAMPLE 12.14

Diagrammatic representation of the classification of matter

Students should be able to outline the classification which is also described in the printed text.

- Matter
  - Substance
    - Element
      - Atom
    - Compound
      - Molecule
  - Mixture
    - Homogeneous mixture
      - Solution
    - Heterogeneous mixture
      - Mixture
  - Concept also shown regarding the relationship of
    - order ↔ disorder,
    - specific ↔ general

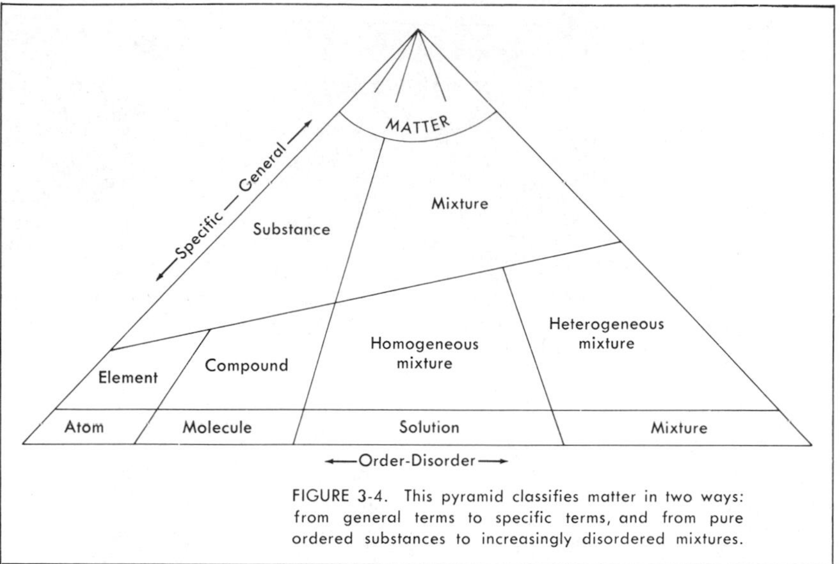

FIGURE 3-4. This pyramid classifies matter in two ways: from general terms to specific terms, and from pure ordered substances to increasingly disordered mixtures.

Reprinted by permission from Robert C. Smoot, Jack Price, and Richard L. Barrett, *Chemistry, A Modern Course* (Columbus: Charles E. Merrill, 1971), p. 46.

Reading for Exact Meaning

This involves noting main ideas and supporting details and seeing organization. It is basic to comprehension and is a prerequisite to the skills of forming conclusions, inferring, and weighing evidence. One approach to teaching these skills requires that the student be able to recognize and analyze types of scientific writing. Nila Banton Smith suggests that these types include classification, problem solving, statement of fact and information, and cause and effect.[8] These are basic patterns, and much scientific writing does not clearly follow the patterns. They may be used in combination and the student may be confused when they try to fit the pattern to the content. Consequently, the basic techniques we must help the science students to acquire are:

1. To develop the basic vocabulary and the concepts it represents.
2. To be alert to the author's organization through the use of topical headings.
3. To read for specific purposes.
4. To know how to apply the steps of problem-solving.

8. Nila Banton Smith, "Reading in Subject Matter Fields," *Educational Leadership* 22 (March 1965): 382–85.

5. To know how to use graphic aids.
6. To note the interrelationships of items of information—reading for the main idea, for sequence or outline, and for details.

Examples 12.15, 12.16, and 12.17 illustrate typical paragraph patterns in science and the techniques students must apply.

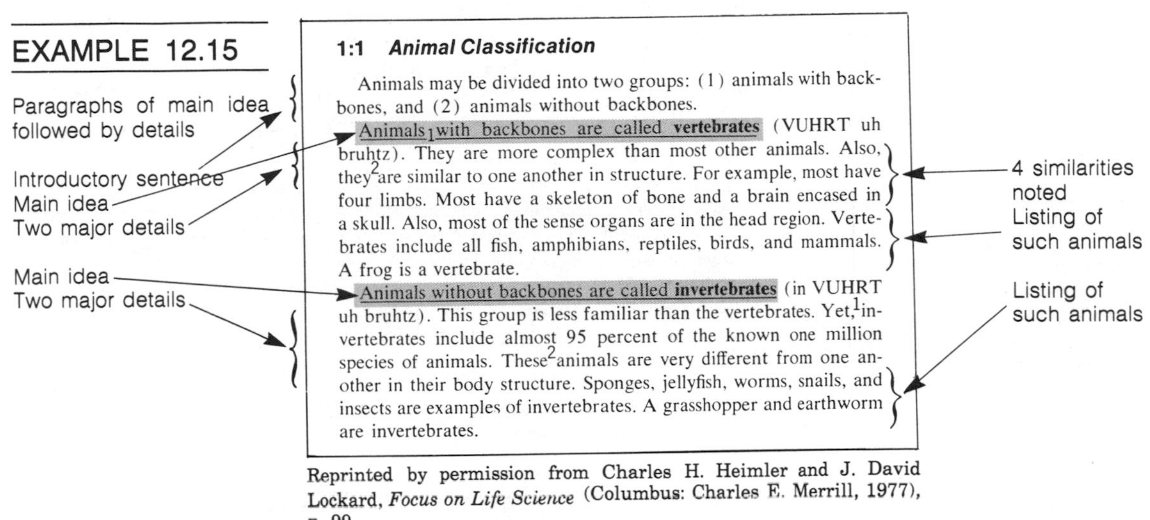

EXAMPLE 12.15
Paragraphs of main idea followed by details
Introductory sentence
Main idea
Two major details
Main idea
Two major details
1:1 Animal Classification
Animals may be divided into two groups: (1) animals with backbones, and (2) animals without backbones.
Animals with backbones are called vertebrates (VUHRT uh bruhtz). They are more complex than most other animals. Also, they are similar to one another in structure. For example, most have four limbs. Most have a skeleton of bone and a brain encased in a skull. Also, most of the sense organs are in the head region. Vertebrates include all fish, amphibians, reptiles, birds, and mammals. A frog is a vertebrate.
Animals without backbones are called invertebrates (in VUHRT uh bruhtz). This group is less familiar than the vertebrates. Yet, invertebrates include almost 95 percent of the known one million species of animals. These animals are very different from one another in their body structure. Sponges, jellyfish, worms, snails, and insects are examples of invertebrates. A grasshopper and earthworm are invertebrates.
4 similarities noted
Listing of such animals
Listing of such animals

Reprinted by permission from Charles H. Heimler and J. David Lockard, *Focus on Life Science* (Columbus: Charles E. Merrill, 1977), p. 99.

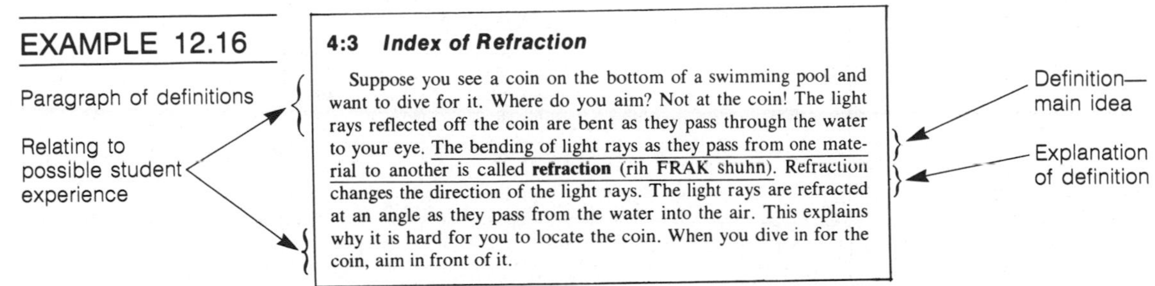

EXAMPLE 12.16
Paragraph of definitions
Relating to possible student experience
4:3 Index of Refraction
Suppose you see a coin on the bottom of a swimming pool and want to dive for it. Where do you aim? Not at the coin! The light rays reflected off the coin are bent as they pass through the water to your eye. The bending of light rays as they pass from one material to another is called refraction (rih FRAK shuhn). Refraction changes the direction of the light rays. The light rays are refracted at an angle as they pass from the water into the air. This explains why it is hard for you to locate the coin. When you dive in for the coin, aim in front of it.
Definition—main idea
Explanation of definition

Reprinted by permission from Charles H. Heimler and Jack Price, *Focus on Physical Science* (Columbus: Charles E. Merrill, 1977), p. 362.

EXAMPLE 12.17

Chemistry example

Introductory paragraph

Reference made to objects in students' experiential background

Paragraph of concept development—definition: homogeneous materials phase substances

Graphic aid: diagram to show classification

Paragraph of classification Definitions: elements compounds

Restatement of earlier concepts: Substances Elements Compounds

3 MATTER

The world around us is filled with objects of many kinds: people, chairs, books, trees, quartz crystals, lumps of sugar, ice cubes, drinking glasses, door knobs, and an endless number of other familiar objects. Each of these objects may be characterized by its size, shape, use, color, and texture; by its physical attributes. Many diverse objects have certain important things in common. For example, a tree and a chair are both made of wood. Millions of other objects with different shapes and different purposes may also be made of wood. The word *material* is used in referring to a specific kind of matter (such as wood). Materials which are familiar to us in the everyday world are wood, steel, copper, sugar, salt, nickel, marble, concrete, milk, etc.

CLASSIFICATION

3:1 Homogeneous Materials

A homogeneous material is one which is the same throughout. If you break it up into smaller pieces each small piece has the same properties as every other small piece. If you examine one of the pieces under a microscope, it is impossible to distinguish one part as being a different material from any other part. Examples of homogeneous materials are: sugar, salt, sea water, quartz, window glass, etc. Any sample of homogeneous material is referred to as a *phase*. Every sample of a homogeneous material is a single phase. Sometimes we can actually distinguish between different phases of the same homogeneous material, for example, ice and water. Some homogeneous materials like pure salt, pure sugar, pure water, or pure sulfur always have the same composition. Such materials are referred to as *substances*.

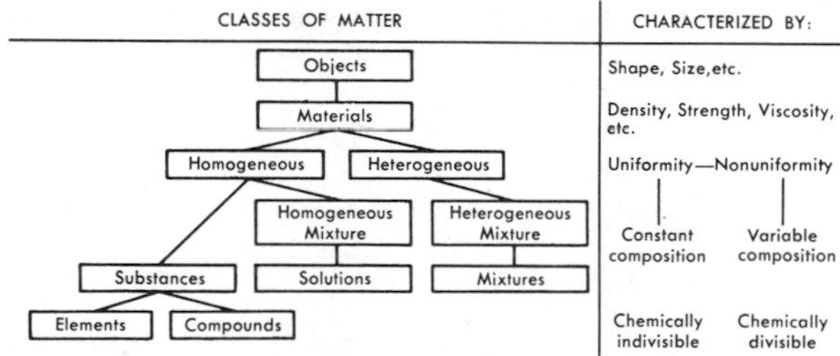

FIGURE 3–1. Both heterogeneous materials and solutions are mixtures of substances.

According to the atomic theory, matter is composed of minute particles called atoms. Substances may be divided into two classes. Substances composed of only one kind of atom are called *elements*. Examples are: sulfur, oxygen, hydrogen, nitrogen, copper, gold, and chlorine. If the particles of a substance are composed of more than one kind of atom, the substance is called a *compound*. The atoms in the particles of compounds are always bound together in definite ratios. Chemistry is a study of substances. The composition of the particles in a compound may be determined by a process called chemical analysis. Chemistry is sometimes defined as the science of substances and of the processes by which substances may be transformed into still other substances. Homogeneous materials which always have the same composition are called substances.

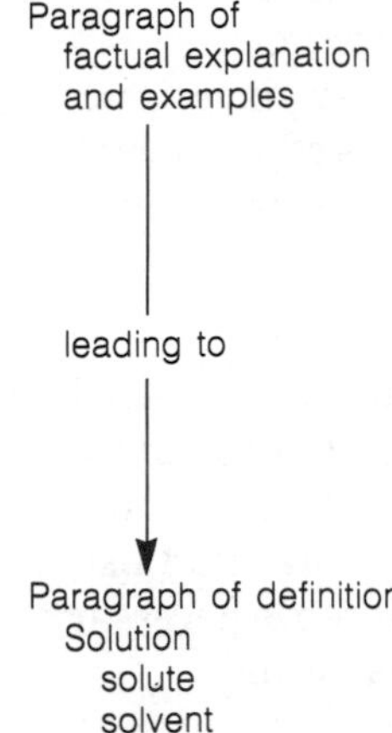

Other homogeneous materials such as sea water, window glass, and gold-silver alloys, have a variable composition. If we put a small quantity of pure salt into pure water and let it stand, we get a homogeneous material. If we add a larger quantity of pure salt to the same amount of pure water we again get a homogeneous material but the composition of this material is different from the first. The second material is homogeneous but it contains more salt in an equal volume of water. Such a homogeneous material is called a *solution*. For example, we may add 5, 10, or 15 grams of salt to 100 grams of water and in all cases the resulting material is homogeneous. A solution may be defined as a single phase which may have a variable composition. Solutions are not necessarily liquid. Air is a homogeneous material composed of nitrogen, oxygen, and smaller quantities of other gases. Window glass and silver-gold alloy may also have a variety of compositions, yet each sample is homogeneous. All of these materials are examples of solutions.

A solution is generally thought of as consisting of a *solute*, or dissolved material, in a *solvent*, or dissolving material. The solute is dispersed throughout the solvent in such small particles (of molecular or smaller size) that the solution appears uniform even under the most powerful optical microscope. Since the dispersion of particles appears to be completely uniform, solutions are classified as homogeneous materials.

3:2 Heterogeneous Materials

Most of the materials which we can see around us can be distinguished either with the naked eye or the microscope as consisting of two or more materials which are distinct from each other. Such non-uniform materials are said to be *heterogeneous*. Wood, granite, concrete, and milk, are examples. It is usually possible with the naked eye to see that granite is composed of at least three minerals: quartz, biotite, and feldspar. If a specimen of granite is crushed so that the particles are the size of fine sand, it is possible to pick out the quartz and separate it mechanically from the biotite and feldspar. Milk normally appears to be homogeneous but under the microscope particles of various kinds can be seen suspended in water. Milk is not a solution; it is a heterogeneous mixture. One type of particle (in this instance, globules of fat), can be separated from the other particles of milk by a device called a centrifuge or cream separator.

Activities to help students develop these comprehension skills include:

1. *Reading for the main idea*
   A. Express the purpose of an experiment in one or two compact sentences.
   B. Express the finding of an experiment in one sentence.
   C. Express the utility of this finding in one sentence.
   D. Find the author's statement of the purpose of an experiment.
   E. Find the main idea in a number of different kinds of paragraphs.
   F. Write a paragraph containing a main idea. Give the paragraph to another person who must find the main idea.
2. *Reading for sequence or outline*
   A. Note the purpose of the experiment, and as you read, anticipate what will be done; see how the steps are related to the purpose.
   B. Note the steps you must take to carry out an experiment. Translate the author's words carefully into your own in a list of things to be done. Read your list to see why each step is necessary, noting especially the order in which the steps occur.
   C. List the chain of events leading to a scientific discovery.
   D. Number the steps in the life cycle of an insect or animal. Try to see the relationship of one step to another. If a title for each of these stages is not given, write in the margin a title for each. Underline or write the important characteristics of each state. Close the book and try to enumerate the states; open the book and compare; repeat if necessary.
3. *Reading for details*
   A. In scientific definitions and laws, notice the qualifying words: the descriptive words, the phrases that narrow the application of the law or the scope of the thing defined. Read the definition carefully for the general meaning and look up any words that trouble you. Put the definition into your own words.
   B. Read additional material that describes the function of the thing referred to and tells its good and bad uses. Make some special note of the definition, underlining it, writing the word and its definition in the margin, putting the word with a statement of its characteristics and its functions into a vocabulary notebook.
   C. Read through the explanation of the derivation of the formula. See whether you can follow the reasoning that leads to its final form. Note the examples and read the text to find out when the formula is appropriate. Work a problem through to experience the effectiveness of the formula. Notice what precautions must be taken in the use of the formula.
   D. In reading an experiment, notice the kinds of words that suggest the introduction of a new step: *then, to this, add,* etc.
   E. Number the steps as they are given.
   F. Underline or write down the important words of each step. Reread each step underlined and try to visualize it or draw a

diagram of it. Try to see the relationship of each step to the next and of each to the purpose of the experiment. Ask yourself "Why do we do this?" and "Why does this step come here instead of sooner or later?"

G. Close the book and try to enumerate the steps and their details; open the book and compare.

H. In reading about the lives of scientists, be sure you know the time in which they lived, their country, the field to which they contributed. Try to recall in what connection you have heard of them. Note the words (*then, chief contribution,* etc.), or the forms (new paragraph) that introduce new steps in their lives. Underline or write the important events in their lives. Number them. In the margin give a name to each discovery or event.

I. Note the methods that they used in their studies, if those methods are important. For each discovery notice what the author has to say about its value or significance to scientific thought and to our lives. Try to think of ways in which the scientists' discoveries have affected your thinking or your life.

J. Close the book and enumerate the events or discoveries and give the important details of each; open the book and compare.

K. In material that has too many facts for you to remember, decide how many things you can remember. Notice the ways in which the author indicates the relative importance of facts. For example:
   1. By giving more space to the discussion of one fact than to another.
   2. By the use of introductory remarks; *above all, preeminent, the chief factor,* or *probably the most crucial.*
   3. By organization, such as paragraphs in which a big fact is illustrated or supported by a lot of little facts, or using marginal headings to point out the big facts.
   4. By questions at the beginning or end of the chapter to call attention to the most important facts.
   5. By a list of important words at the end of the chapter.
   6. By a summary at the end of the chapter or section.
   7. By the use of italics.
   8. By pictures or other illustrative material.

Otherwise, note for yourself the relationships among the facts and choose the key facts among these. Compare the facts in the text with the kind the teacher usually requires in questions in class, in tests, and in assignments.

Reading Directions Accurately

In reading directions the students need to know the meaning of all of the words and be able to distinguish one step from another. They may need to be alerted to structure words such as *next, after, first,* and so on, which indicate the steps. In reading directions the following procedure is suggested:

1. Read the entire set of directions to get an overview of the procedure. At this time the students should obtain clarification of any words they do not know.
2. Read the directions to identify the equipment needed and collect it.
3. Read each step of the directions and proceed as indicated.
4. Read the step again to check whether the procedure was carried out correctly.
5. Repeat items 3 and 4 as many times as there are steps to be followed.
6. Upon completion of the directions, look them over once again as a final check. (See Example 12.18.)

EXAMPLE 12.18

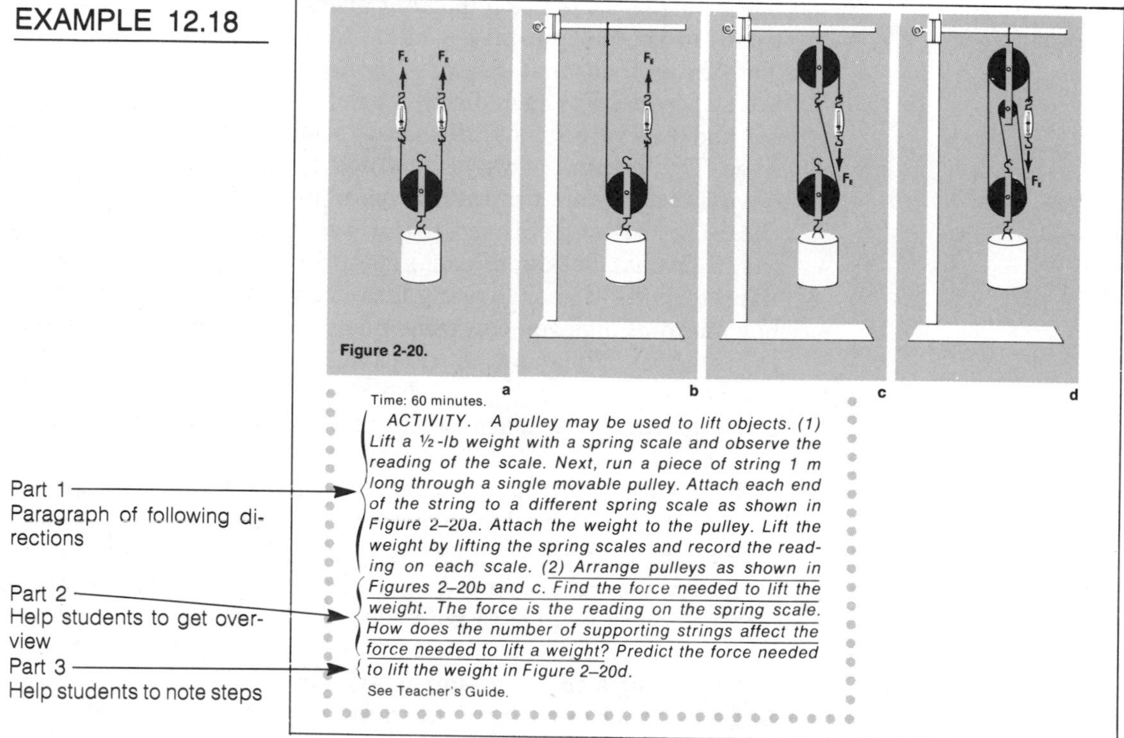

Time: 60 minutes.

ACTIVITY. A pulley may be used to lift objects. (1) Lift a ½-lb weight with a spring scale and observe the reading of the scale. Next, run a piece of string 1 m long through a single movable pulley. Attach each end of the string to a different spring scale as shown in Figure 2–20a. Attach the weight to the pulley. Lift the weight by lifting the spring scales and record the reading on each scale. (2) Arrange pulleys as shown in Figures 2–20b and c. Find the force needed to lift the weight. The force is the reading on the spring scale. How does the number of supporting strings affect the force needed to lift a weight? Predict the force needed to lift the weight in Figure 2–20d.

See Teacher's Guide.

Reprinted by permission from Charles H. Heimler and Jack Price, *Focus on Physical Science* (Columbus: Charles E. Merrill, 1977), p. 31.

Evaluating, Drawing Conclusions, Making Judgments

Though there is much factual data students must acquire in science, they must go beyond mere acquisition to make judgments about it and draw conclusions from evidence. For example:

1. Have the students note the structures of various living organisms and the characteristics of their environments. Show the indication of *cause and effect:* environmental conditions as the cause of the structural characteristics.
2. Have the students *compare and contrast* characteristics of two or more kinds of living organisms or inanimates.

3. Have the students speculate as to the effects of specific conditions, either real or fanciful. In an experiment the students may be asked to *make a judgment* of what will happen under a specific set of conditions. The experiment can then be conducted to show the validity of the judgment. Or the students may be asked to predict what would happen if the polar ice caps were to melt in the next 50 years.
4. Develop in students the ability to *suspend judgment.* For example, if an experimental finding appears to be contrary to a belief of long standing and apparent logic, have the students plan to gain further evidence (from reading from authoritative sources and by conducting the experiment again).

Applying Data from Reading to Practical Problems

One of the goals of reading instruction is the ability to read creatively, which means, in part, applying information from books to practical problems and life situations. Techniques to encourage this application might include:

1. Relate an experience you have had with a principle or an object discussed either in your science text or in class.
2. Apply the results of an experiment to various areas of life. Show how a specific occupation or people in general are affected by the results.
3. From descriptions of various plants and animals, determine their major characteristics—where they live, what they eat, what their role is in the ecosystem.
4. As you read about the conditions needed for life, relate the information to plants and animals and determine if all of the conditions are needed for each species.
5. Whenever a scientific law or principle is cited in your science text, think of at least two applications.

Fusing Reading Skills with Steps of Scientific Method

Shepherd has listed the steps of the scientific method and the reading skills pertinent to each:

> The first step of the scientific method is to define the problem to show that it has limits, is specific, and can be investigated. The basic reading skill needed here would relate directly to the vocabulary of science. An adequate background in scientific vocabulary as well as precision in the use of such terms are both requirements to be met if the student is to state his problem with accuracy and definiteness.
>
> The next step is collecting evidence that bears upon the problem. The skills of reading that are related to his step of problem solving are (a) those needed for locating information in printed sources (using various parts of a book and many different sources), and (b) those needed for getting the literal understanding of the reading material (understanding scientific vocabulary, symbols, and formulas; interpreting graphic aids; reading directions accurately; noting main ideas, their supporting details, and the sequence or organization of main topics).
>
> Setting up hypotheses is the third step. In setting up possible solutions to the problem, the pertinency and relative importance of the individual data that have

> been collected must be determined. Basic relationships between the data must be perceived. (Steps 3, 4, and 5 of the scientific method involve critical thinking and critical reading. They require an interpretation of the facts. The validity of the interpretation depends upon the ability to evaluate science materials and to draw conclusions.)
>
> The fourth step is selecting the most likely hypothesis and testing it. Selecting and testing the most likely hypothesis involves substantiating all data, organizing the data into the logical sequence, and determining the adequacy of the selected hypothesis by relating it to the problem.
>
> The fifth step, drawing conclusions, requires the students to compare the consistency of the conclusion with the data and the problem. Judging the significance of a finding and seeing the relationships of it to various phenomena point up the use of such interpretative reading skills in science.
>
> Finally, the sixth step is applying scientific data to practical situations. Even though "applying scientific data to practical situations" is not a step of the scientific method, the ability to think of practical applications is of such importance that instruction in the skill is generally included in any problem solving unit.[9]

In each of the steps of the scientific method, the students must ask questions. This is akin to, and in some cases the same as, formulating questions before reading—purpose questions pinpointing information which must be found: What is to be found or proven? What outcomes are to be anticipated? What facts are known? What other facts are needed? How will the solution be derived? What are the steps? What equipment is needed? What numerical quantities are or can be used to solve the problems? What do the findings imply? Are they reasonable? How can they be applied? What other problems have been discerned? What conclusions can be made? Do these coincide with the tentative solutions suggested at the time that the problem was defined?

The Science Project

Science projects provide students with the opportunity to use their imagination to find out information of interest to them. Projects are of value in many ways. First, they enable students to seek further information and understandings. Second, they can develop student interest. Third, they provide a practical application of the scientific process, thereby showing the process as a means of investigating a problem. Fourth, they call for applying reading skills to scientific information. In planning a science project, students must consider all of the steps from the beginning to its final completion. Perhaps they will find a listing of do's and don't's helpful as guidelines.

Certainly you will know the reading study skills students must use to research printed sources. You must provide whatever instruction is needed in science reading and research reading.

---

9. David L. Shepherd, "Reading and Science: Problems Peculiar to the Area," in *Fusing Reading Skills and Content,* ed. H. Alan Robinson and Ellen Lamar Thomas (Newark, Del.: International Reading Association, 1969), pp. 152–53.

APPLYING READING SKILLS TO MATHEMATICS

Mathematics comprises two languages. One is the language of *words*—the technical vocabulary of the discipline as well as the peculiar usage of common words. The other is the language of *symbols,* which also are technical. Distinct mathematics symbols represent words or even phrases that indicate relationship or process. Symbolization in mathematics may be simple or highly complex. For instance, = means "is equal to" and embodies the idea of equality. A more complex symbol is $\frac{(\sqrt{2} - 3)^2}{(\sqrt{2} + 3)^2}$ which, if written in words, would be "the quantity, the square root of 2 minus 3, squared divided by the quantity, the square root of 2 plus 3, squared." In mathematics, both words and symbols label concepts and ideas.

To read mathematics, students must be able to read two languages and translate from one to the other. Lerch has pointed out that words are used in explanations, giving directions, descriptions, and word problems. Mathematical signs are also used, he says, in much the same way in explanations, illustrations, examples, and descriptions. Competence in both languages is needed if the objectives of mathematics are to be achieved.[10]

The Objectives of Mathematics

There are three major objectives of the various fields of mathematics. Each relies upon understanding the language of mathematics, and each involves the various uses of language: speaking, listening, reading, and writing.

The first objective is to enable students to understand mathematical concepts, ideas and meanings. Accomplishment of this objective depends upon the mastery of vocabulary—both the words and the mathematics symbols. In mathematics, students explore, hear, discuss, experiment with, talk about, and explain as they develop the concepts.

This leads us to the next major objective: students should learn to *reason*—a skill which can be developed only after the concepts are grasped. Word problems require reasoning. *Reasoning* is the rearrangement of known facts to derive a new relationship. Students need to be able to recognize the essential characteristics of a problem situation as well as to test a hypothesis and evaluate conclusions. Reasoning involves using what is known in a problem to find what is unknown.

The third major objective relies upon the ability to reason: students must know how to compute and estimate. Students should become competent in the following:

1. Performing the fundamental operations with integers and fractions and generalizing to signed numbers and literal numbers.

---

10. Harold H. Lerch, "Improving Reading in the Language of Mathematics—Grades 7-12," in *Improving Reading in Secondary Schools: Selected Readings,* ed. Lawrence E. Hafner (New York: The Macmillan Company, 1974), pp. 325–26.

2. Using computational tables.
3. Making and interpreting measurements.
4. Working with approximate data.
5. Constructing and interpreting simple statistical and functional graphs.
6. Making geometric constructions and simple scale drawings.
7. Using simple formulas and equations.

The Nature of Mathematical Writing

Reading material in mathematics is concise, to the point, and specific. It requires analysis—recognizing ideas and the relationships among them. Of special concern is the vocabulary of mathematical reading, in which precision of meaning is required. Concepts are built sequentially, one upon the other. Another concern is the use of symbols, which in a sense constitute another form of vocabulary. Strategies for reading mathematics are determined by the nature of the material and the students' purpose.

There are three types of writing in mathematics textbooks today: explanation of concepts for understanding, steps in the explanation of a process, and word problems. Examples 12.19 (pp. 308–9), 12.20 (p. 311), and 12.21 (pp. 312–13) show these types of writing.

Students need training in the following aspects of language use that are basic to mathematics ability:

1. Solving problems—they must know what they have and know how to use the results.
2. Checking answers and verifying results.
3. Making intelligent estimations.
4. Interpreting quantitative data.
5. Recognizing and interpreting relationships.
6. Understanding and making generalizations.
7. Thinking in symbolic language.

At all grade levels, mathematics instruction must focus on comprehension of basic concepts, determination and analysis relationships, efficiency in solving problems and in making sound applications, confidence in shaping intelligent and independent interpretations, as well as progress in developing an appreciation of the role mathematics plays in our society. The fundamental reading skills and mathematical skills are aimed toward these emphases.

Relevant Reading Skills

The fundamental charge of mathematics teachers is twofold: to teach students how to read mathematical materials as well as teaching the concepts and their applications. In order to teach the reading of mathematics, teachers must first know the basic concepts and generalizations of the subject. Second, they must be familiar with the skills of reading as they relate to mathematics. Finally, they must know how to relate skills instruction to the mathematics content—how to fuse the subject matter and the skills.

The reading skills that apply to mathematics are:

1. Careful reading of the succinct language of mathematics material.
2. Understanding the vocabulary, which includes technical terms, words labelling processes, general words with a mathematical meaning, and general words.
3. Interpreting mathematical symbols, which are extensions or a shorthand of mathematical terms.
4. Reading equations and formulas, which are mathematical sentences.
5. Analyzing statistical reports such as tax and financial data.
6. Solving word problems by using the necessary analytical and computational steps.
7. Analyzing and interpreting pictorial and graphic representations.
8. Relating information already learned to what is currently being read.
9. Following directions.

Reading for a Purpose

Mathematics requires methodical, slow, word-by-word reading. Often, as with word problems, it is necessary to read several times, each time for a different purpose. Your responsibility is to assist the students in making a habit of establishing purposes. Purposes tend to be more specific in mathematics than in narrative and expository material. The purposes in problem reading relate to each step of problem solving or to the sequence of a process in explanatory passages.

Vocabulary

There is a heavy load of vocabulary in mathematics. Often, a lack of vocabulary is the major barrier to students in communicating and thinking about mathematical processes and understandings. Two aspects of mathematical vocabulary must be explained to the students. One is the conceptual foundation of the terms; acquiring the conceptual background is essential if students are to understand and not learn by rote. This is particularly true because mathematical understandings are *cumulative*—they build on the concepts which preceded them. The second aspect is word recognition, which may involve assistance in syllabication and structural analysis of prefixes, roots, and suffixes.

In mathematics there are four kinds of vocabulary words, any of which can cause difficulty. The first type is the technical word peculiar to some area of the mathematics—for example, *sine* and *cosine* in trigonometry; *polynomials, linear equations* in algebra; and *isosceles, arc,* and *polyhedron* in geometry. The second type is the general word in our language which has a mathematical meaning, such as *prime, natural, radical, exponent,* and *square.* The third type is the word which signals a mathematical process; this includes such words as *subtract, times, multiply, difference, column.* Many of

EXAMPLE 12.19

Teacher's edition

(Marginal notes are suggestions to teachers)

EXPLANATION OF A CONCEPT

8:3 MONOMIAL FACTORS See T.G.

Let us turn our attention from numbers to algebraic expressions that represent numbers. You have found many *products* in earlier chapters. You will recall that the basis for multiplication of polynomials is the Distributive Property of Numbers. Stress

Note difference between multiplication and factoring →

$$a(b + c) \underset{\text{Factoring}}{\overset{\text{Multiplication}}{\rightleftarrows}} ab + ac$$

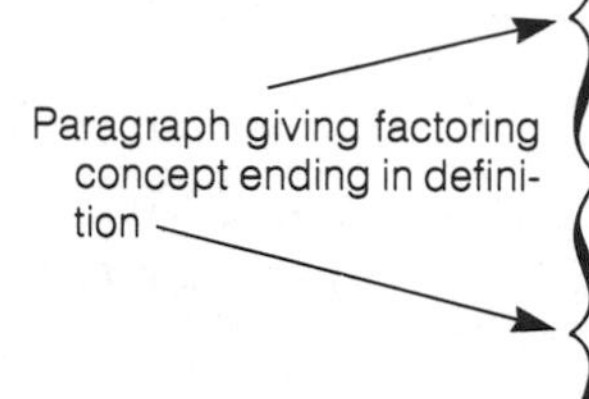

Paragraph giving factoring concept ending in definition

The arrows indicate that the property is reversible, that is, the Symmetry Property applies. If we are given an expression in the form of the left member, we can carry out the operation of multiplication according to the Distributive Property and express the product as two terms. We sometimes call this operation "removing parentheses." It is also possible to use the Distributive Property when we are given an expression in the form of the right member. In this case there must be a common factor, that is, an exact divisor, in each term. If the equation is read from right to left we can remove, or "factor," the common factor, and express the result as a product. Factoring is a process of renaming a number or algebraic expression as the product of two or more numbers or expressions. In the expression $a(b + c)$, a is a factor and so is $(b + c)$. Note: This is the meaning of factoring.

Review—with most students such review should be directed by the teacher in class.

A review of multiplication and division of polynomials (Sections 4:4, 4:5) is desirable at this time. This will help you develop speed and accuracy in performing these operations. The Laws of Exponents will also be required. In this list of exercises you should do as much of the work mentally as you can. Stress

Former concepts used.
Teacher will need to insure student understanding of them.

Reprinted by permission from Glen D. Vannatta, A. Wilson Goodwin, and F. Joe Crosswhite, *Algebra One: Teacher's Guide and Solutions Manual* (Columbus: Charles E. Merrill, 1970), pp. 275, 277.

these also have other meanings in general language usage. For instance, one mathematics textbook used the word *gross* in the context *a gross of eggs* and on the next page used the term *gross profit*. Finally, the fourth type is the nontechnical word that is considered to be general and simple. Many signal a relationship, such as *than*. Most students can recognize these words with ease, but often their understanding of the meaning is not as precise as the mathematical usage requires. Table 12.1 (p. 310) lists many of the nontechnical words that also are used in mathematics.

In developing the concepts of the vocabulary, start with concrete objects or situations that the students know. For example, draw a diagram on the chalkboard to show the ratio of the sine to the hypotenuse of a right triangle

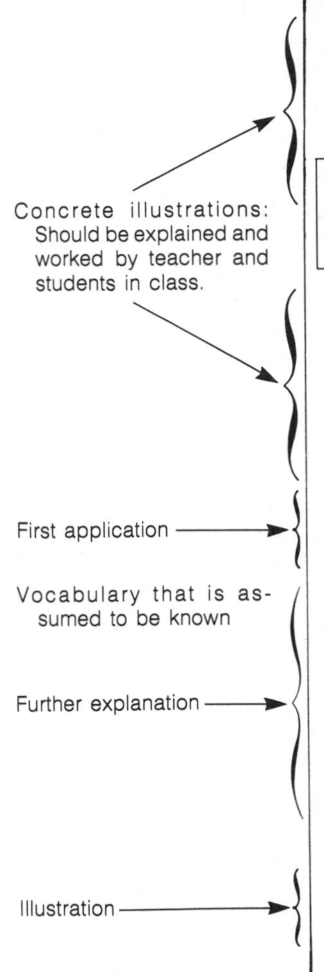

As we have shown, the Distributive Property enables us to factor certain algebraic expressions. Monomials are usually considered factored because the single term involves only products. For example, $10ax^2$ is the product of 10, a, and x^2, each of which is a factor. If a prime factorization is desired, we can write $10ax^2$ in the form $2 \cdot 5 \cdot a \cdot x \cdot x$. This is not ordinarily needed, however.

Factoring is clearly related to division. If one number or algebraic expression, N, is divided by another number or algebraic expression, D, it gives a quotient, Q. Then, according to the definition of division, we have the relation

$$\frac{N}{D} = Q, \text{ if and only if } N = D \cdot Q$$

which means $\frac{N}{D} = Q$ implies $N = D \cdot Q$ and $N = D \cdot Q$ implies $\frac{N}{D} = Q$. We say that D and Q are factors of N.

Suppose that N is the binomial $8x^2 - 12x$. Let us divide this expression by the common factor 2.

$$\frac{8x^2 - 12x}{2} = 4x^2 - 6x$$

Therefore, $8x^2 - 12x = 2(4x^2 - 6x)$, where 2 and $(4x^2 - 6x)$ are factors of $8x^2 - 12x$.

Can $8x^2 - 12x$ be factored in other ways? Check these factorizations by using the Distributive Property.

Ask the students to do this.

$$4(2x^2 + 3x); \quad x(8x - 12); \quad 2x(4x - 6); \quad 4x(2x - 3)$$

We say that a polynomial has been completely factored if each of the factors is *prime.* The binomial $2x - 3$ is prime if we restrict ourselves to integers as coefficients. No polynomial would be prime, however, unless we place such a restriction upon the factors. For instance, we could factor $2x - 3$ into $2(x - \frac{3}{2})$ or $\frac{1}{3}(6x - 9)$, and so on indefinitely. It is understood that in complete factoring the greatest common factor is to be removed, even if it is not a prime number. In the example $8x^2 - 12x$, complete factoring gives us $4x(2x - 3)$. Although x might be replaced by a real number that would enable us to factor further, we consider the expression $4x(2x - 3)$ as a prime factorization.

Note: This is sometimes called G.C.F. and is defined to be the product of all prime common factors of two or more numbers or polynomials.

▶EXAMPLE: Factor completely $12a^3 - 18a^2 + 3a$.

Solution: The number 3 is the only common factor of the coefficients, and a^1 is the highest power of a that occurs in *each* term. Therefore the expression can be divided by $3a$ and written in factored form.

$$3a(4a^2 - 6a + 1)$$

and the ratio of the cosine to the hypotenuse of a right triangle so that the students can *picture* them:

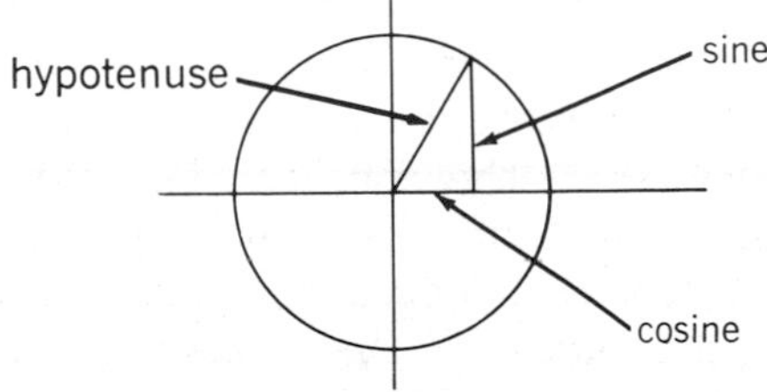

Use a practical problem to show the use of the functions of sine and cosine. With *polynomial,* break the word into its parts: *poly*—many, and *nomial*—pertaining to number. Then illustrate algebraically what the

TABLE 12.1 Nontechnical Vocabulary—Mathematics

above	more than (higher than; over; on top of)
about	nearly; near to
across	crossed; from one side to the other
after	lower in rank or order; later; next
all	the whole quantity or extent of
allow	to permit; to provide or keep (as an extra quantity) so as to have enough
before	ahead; in advance; in front
compare	to examine in order to observe similarities or differences (often followed by *with*)
cost	price; the amount of money, time, labor, etc., required to get a thing
each	apiece; an item separately
fare	the charge for transportation
increase	to become greater in size, amount, etc., usually signifies addition
large, larger	big, great—of greater extent or amount
least	smallest in size, amount, degree, importance
left, leftover	remaining unused; remainder
lower	to reduce in height, amount, etc. (lower prices)
next	nearest; immediately preceding or following as of time, place, rank, degree
over	more than
step	any of a series of acts, processes; arrange in a series of degrees
require	demand; to ask or insist upon as by need, authority
same	identical; alike in kind or quantity; unchanged
table	a compact systematic list of details; compact orderly arrangement of facts, figures, etc., usually in rows and columns
than	to introduce the second element of comparison; compared to
wages	money paid to an employee for work done, usually on an hourly, daily or piecework basis
whole	complete, not divided up; in a single unit, not a fraction

polynomial is. Or with the word *arc,* show how a flashlight would make an arc of light. Draw a diagram showing it as part of a circle. In short, present the words through actual nonmathematical experiences the students would know, investigate the derivations of the terms and note how the root meaning applies, show the concept diagrammatically, or relate the term to the students' mathematics knowledge. You may think that such procedures are too elementary, but students gain independence only as all are able to relate new information to their existing fund of knowledge.

Students should talk about the situations which illustrate the concepts so that they can appreciate the relationships and significance of concepts. Next, introduce the appropriate symbols used in mathematics to represent the concept. Finally, give students the opportunity to apply the concept to both practical and hypothetical situations. Provide enough practice for the students to feel completely comfortable with the concept.

EXAMPLE 12.20

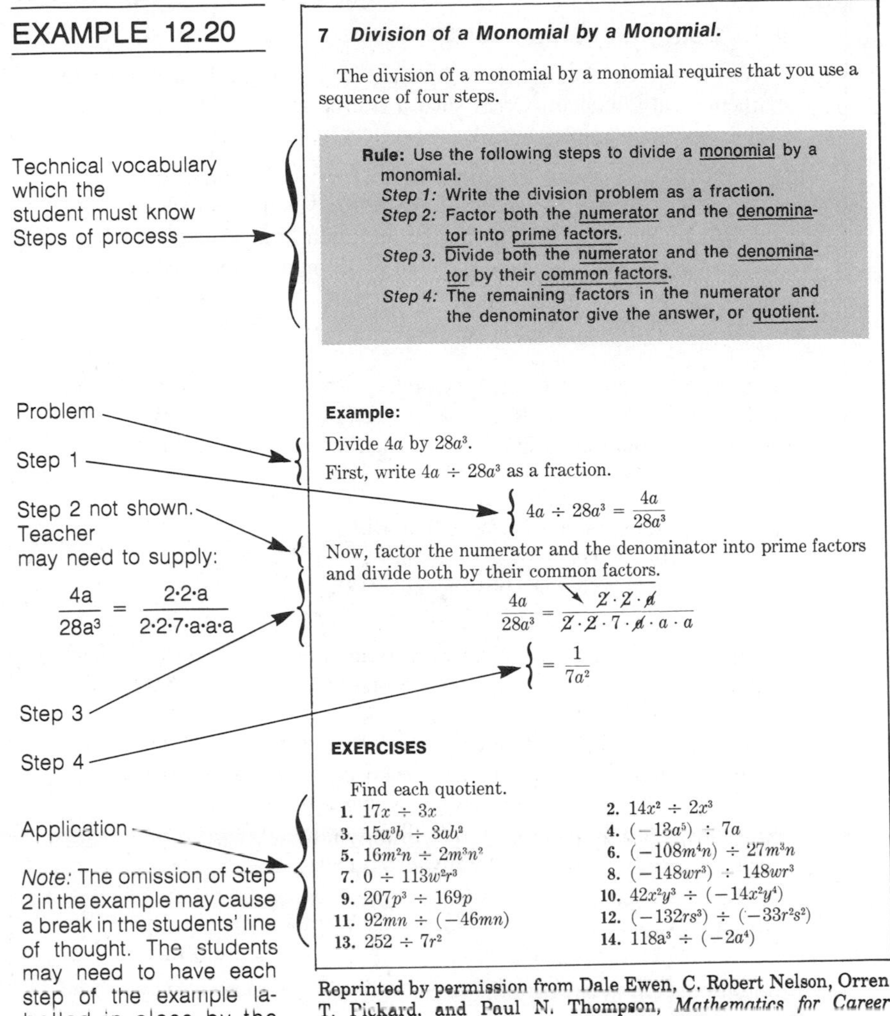
Technical vocabulary which the student must know
Steps of process
Problem
Step 1
Step 2 not shown. Teacher may need to supply:
$\frac{4a}{28a^3} = \frac{2 \cdot 2 \cdot a}{2 \cdot 2 \cdot 7 \cdot a \cdot a \cdot a}$
Step 3
Step 4
Application
Note: The omission of Step 2 in the example may cause a break in the students' line of thought. The students may need to have each step of the example labelled in class by the teacher.

7 *Division of a Monomial by a Monomial.*

The division of a monomial by a monomial requires that you use a sequence of four steps.

Rule: Use the following steps to divide a monomial by a monomial.
Step 1: Write the division problem as a fraction.
Step 2: Factor both the numerator and the denominator into prime factors.
Step 3. Divide both the numerator and the denominator by their common factors.
Step 4: The remaining factors in the numerator and the denominator give the answer, or quotient.

Example:

Divide $4a$ by $28a^3$.

First, write $4a \div 28a^3$ as a fraction.

$$4a \div 28a^3 = \frac{4a}{28a^3}$$

Now, factor the numerator and the denominator into prime factors and divide both by their common factors.

$$\frac{4a}{28a^3} = \frac{\not{2} \cdot \not{2} \cdot \not{a}}{\not{2} \cdot \not{2} \cdot 7 \cdot \not{a} \cdot a \cdot a}$$

$$= \frac{1}{7a^2}$$

EXERCISES

Find each quotient.

1. $17x \div 3x$
2. $14x^2 \div 2x^3$
3. $15a^3b \div 3ab^2$
4. $(-13a^5) \div 7a$
5. $16m^2n \div 2m^3n^2$
6. $(-108m^4n) \div 27m^3n$
7. $0 \div 113w^2r^3$
8. $(-148wr^3) \div 148wr^3$
9. $207p^3 \div 169p$
10. $42x^2y^3 \div (-14x^2y^4)$
11. $92mn \div (-46mn)$
12. $(-132rs^3) \div (-33r^2s^2)$
13. $252 \div 7r^2$
14. $118a^3 \div (-2a^4)$

Reprinted by permission from Dale Ewen, C. Robert Nelson, Orren T. Pickard, and Paul N. Thompson, *Mathematics for Career Education* (Columbus: Charles E. Merrill, 1972), p. 363.

Interpreting Symbols

Symbols and signs in mathematics are a type of vocabulary. They should be developed sequentially and meaningfully, usually at the time when the concept related to them is developed. Do not assume that the students know the symbol. Whenever they work an example, question students about the meaning and use of the symbols and clarify for them if necessary. In this way you can note and correct gaps in understanding or misinformation.

Analyzing Statistical Reports (Tables, Formulas, Equations)

This material is often tabular and may include statistical equations and formulas. The steps listed on p. 313, undertaken by both teacher and students, can aid in understanding.

EXAMPLE 12.21

WORD PROBLEMS
Directions to students of procedure in solving problems.

Problem must be read several times.

1st reading
Overview

2nd reading
What is given

3rd reading
What is asked

General vocabulary indicating direction in process.

Solving the problem.

May involve additional reading of problem.

4:4 Using Mathematical Sentences

We have seen that we may translate many English sentences to mathematical sentences. Often such a translation is helpful in solving problems. For example, consider the following problem:

> Bill and Frank drove to the beach for some surfing. Frank was certain that he had \$4.20 with him when he left home. Bill forgot the exact amount he had with him. Frank spent \$.60 more than Bill, who spent all of his money, and together the boys spent \$6.00. How much money did Bill take with him? How much money did Frank have left after the trip?

Here we have several English sentences which can be translated to mathematical sentences. Read the paragraph carefully. Pick out the sentences or phrases which include mathematical information.

> Frank was certain that he had \$4.20 with him . . .
> Frank spent \$.60 more than Bill . . .
> Bill . . . spent all of his money.
> . . . together the boys spent \$6.00.

There are two questions to answer. What are they? Consider them one at a time. Let us try to answer the first one: How much money did Bill take with him?

Let x represent the amount of money which Bill took with him. Since Bill had no money left when he returned home, he must have spent x dollars or the same amount of money which he took with him.

Frank spent \$.60 *more* than Bill. This implies *addition.* Frank spent $x + \$.60$. They spent \$6.00 altogether. Thus,

Bills' money	+	Frank's money	=	Amount spent by both boys
x	+	$(x + .60)$	=	6.00

Simplify the left member of the equation:

$$x + x + .60 = 6.00$$
$$2x + .60 = 6.00$$

Eliminate the quantity .60 from the left member by subtracting .60 from both members:

$$2x + .60 - .60 = 6.00 - .60$$
$$2x = 5.40$$

Divide each member by 2:

$$\frac{(2x)}{2} = \frac{(5.40)}{2}$$
$$x = 2.70$$

Reprinted by permission from Eugene P. Smith et al., *Discoveries in Modern Mathematics, Course 2* (Columbus: Charles E. Merrill, 1968), pp. 124–25.

Since x represented the amount of money which Bill took with him, we know that Bill had \$2.70.

Let us consider the second question: How much money did Frank have left after the trip?

Frank spent \$.60 more than Bill, and Bill spent \$2.70. Therefore, Frank spent \$2.70 + \$.60. How much did he have with him when he left home? \$4.20 How much did he have left after the trip? \$ .90

Encourage students to write out these sentences to clearly identify what the variable represents.

Exercises

Translate the following English sentences to mathematical sentences and determine the solution set for each.

Vocabulary indicates relationship and process:
older than—relationship
sum —addition
difference—subtraction
twice —multiplication

1. Charles is 4 years older than his brother Dave. The sum of their ages is 24. How old is Dave? (*Hint:* Let x represent Dave's age. Then Charles' age is x + ?4.) x + x + 4 = 24; x = 10

2. The difference in age between Keith and his younger brother Robert is 10 years. The sum of their ages is 18 years. How old is Robert? (*Hint:* Represent Keith's age by x. Then Robert's age is x − ?10)

3. Richard is now 14. Four years from now he will be twice as old as his sister. How old is Richard's sister now? (*Hint:* Let x represent the age of Richard's sister now.) 2 (x + 4) = 18; x = 5

1. Read and understand the statement that tells what the table represents.
2. Study each vertical column of items and read the headings for them to see what they represent.
3. Study the vertical columns thoroughly to compare or draw conclusions.

(See Examples 12.22 and 12.23 on pp. 314, 315.)

In order to deal with formulas and equations, students must realize that each formula and equation is a sentence in mathematical shorthand. In fact, some textbooks call equations in algebra *algebraic sentences*. Therefore, a first step might be to have the students write the formula and equation in a sentence, or state it orally in class. The operational symbols (+, =, −, ÷, and ×) represent verbs. Next, have the students retranslate the formula or equation into mathematical symbols. Or, if the formula is given in a sentence in the text, as in word problems, have the students start by translating it into its mathematical equivalent. The following formula was written in a textbook:

EXAMPLE 12.22

3 *Table of Trigonometric Ratios.*

In the previous examples and exercises, the final step was not completed. To complete this last step, you must be able to find values for the trigonometric ratios in a table. Use Table 7 in the Appendix to find decimal values of the trigonometric ratios of angles from 0° to 90°. The following is a portion of Table 7.

Deg.	Sin	Tan		Cos	
40.0	0.6428	0.8391	1.1918	0.7660	50.0
.1	.6441	.8421	1.1875	.7649	49.9
.2	.6455	.8451	1.1833	.7638	.8
.3	.6468	.8481	1.1792	.7627	.7
.4	.6481	.8511	1.1750	.7615	.6
40.5	0.6494	0.8541	1.1708	0.7604	49.5
	Cos		Tan	Sin	Deg.

Directions for reading the table

Notice that angle measure (in degrees and tenths of a degree) is given in both the right and left columns. Use the angle readings in the *left* column with the trigonometric ratios labeled at the *top* of each inside column. Use the readings in the *right* column with the trigonometric ratios labeled at the *bottom* of each inside column. That is, angle measures from 0° to 45° are read in the left column using the names of ratios at the top of the page, and angles measures from 45° to 90° are read in the right column using names of ratios at the bottom of the page.

Example 1:

Application

Student must know abbreviations:
Deg.
Sin.
Tan.
Cos.

Find the value for each trigonometric ratio using the table on page 432.

a. sin 40.2° = .6455
b. tan 40.4° = .8511
c. cos 49.6° = .6481
d. tan 49.9° = 1.1875

Reprinted by permission from Dale Ewen, C. Robert Nelson, Orren T. Pickard, and Paul N. Thompson, *Mathematics for Career Education* (Columbus: Charles E. Merrill, 1972), pp. 432–33.

$(a + b)^2$ =
The square of the sum of two numbers equals
verb

a^2 + $2ab$
the square of the first number plus twice the product of the numbers,
structure word

+ b^2
plus the square of the second number.
structure word

Algebraic form: $(a + b)^2 = a^2 + 2ab + b^2$

In such intensive detailed reading you can help your students by analying the written version of the formula as shown, indicating to the students the basic parts of the sentence and the function of the process and structure words. Then have them place all known number values for the letters. At this point, the students are ready to solve the formula or equation mathematically.

EXAMPLE 12.23

Students must be aware of the order of degrees as explained in text

TABLE 7 (Continued)

Deg.	Sin	Tan		Cos	
34–	.55919	.67451	1.4826	.82904	**56–**
.1	.56064	.67705	1.4770	.82806	.9
.2	.56208	.67960	1.4715	.82708	.8
.3	.56353	.68215	1.4659	.82610	.7
.4	.56497	.68471	1.4605	.82511	.6
.5	.56641	.68728	1.4550	.82413	.5
.6	.56784	.68985	1.4496	.82314	.4
.7	.56928	.69243	1.4442	.82214	.3
.8	.57071	.69502	1.4388	.82115	.2
.9	.57215	.69761	1.4335	.82015	.1
35–	.57358	.70021	1.4281	.81915	**55–**
.1	.57501	.70281	1.4229	.81815	.9
.2	.57643	.70542	1.4176	.81714	.8
.3	.57786	.70804	1.4124	.81614	.7
.4	.57928	.71066	1.4071	.81513	.6
.5	.58070	.71329	1.4019	.81412	.5
.6	.58212	.71593	1.3968	.81310	.4
.7	.58354	.71857	1.3916	.81208	.3
.8	.58496	.72122	1.3865	.81106	.2
.9	.58637	.72388	1.3814	.81004	.1
36–	.58779	.72654	1.3764	.80902	**54–**
.1	.58920	.72921	1.3713	.80799	.9
.2	.59061	.73189	1.3663	.80696	.8
.3	.59201	.73457	1.3613	.80593	.7
.4	.59342	.73726	1.3564	.80489	.6
.5	.59482	.73996	1.3514	.80386	.5
.6	.59622	.74267	1.3465	.80282	.4
.7	.59763	.74538	1.3416	.80178	.3
.8	.59902	.74810	1.3367	.80073	.2
.9	.60042	.75082	1.3319	.79968	.1
37–	.60182	.75355	1.3270	.79864	**53–**
.1	.60321	.75629	1.3222	.79758	.9
.2	.60460	.75904	1.3175	.79653	.8
.3	.60599	.76180	1.3127	.79547	.7
.4	.60738	.76456	1.3079	.79441	.6
.5	.60876	.76733	1.3032	.79335	.5
.6	.61015	.77010	1.2985	.79229	.4
.7	.61153	.77289	1.2938	.79122	.3
.8	.61291	.77568	1.2892	.79016	.2
.9	.61429	.77848	1.2846	.78908	.1
38–	.61566	.78129	1.2799	.78801	**52–**
.1	.61704	.78410	1.2753	.78694	.9
.2	.61841	.78692	1.2708	.78586	.8
.3	.61978	.78975	1.2662	.78478	.7
.4	.62115	.79259	1.2617	.78369	.6
.5	.62251	.79544	1.2572	.78261	.5
.6	.62388	.79829	1.2527	.78152	.4
.7	.62524	.80115	1.2482	.78043	.3
.8	.62660	.80402	1.2437	.77934	.2
.9	.62796	.80690	1.2393	.77824	.1
39–	.62932	.80978	1.2349	.77715	**51–**
.1	.63068	.81268	1.2305	.77605	.9
.2	.63203	.81558	1.2261	.77494	.8
.3	.63338	.81849	1.2218	.77384	.7
.4	.63473	.82141	1.2174	.77273	.6
39.5	.63608	.82434	1.2131	.77162	**50.5**
	Cos		Tan	Sin	Deg.

Deg.	Sin	Tan		Cos	
39.5	.63608	.82434	1.2131	.77162	**50.5**
.6	.63742	.82727	1.2088	.77051	.4
.7	.63877	.83022	1.2045	.76940	.3
.8	.64011	.83317	1.2002	.76828	.2
.9	.64145	.83613	1.1960	.76717	.1
40–	.64279	.83910	1.1918	.76604	**50–**
.1	.64412	.84208	1.1875	.76492	.9
.2	.64546	.84507	1.1833	.76380	.8
.3	.64679	.84806	1.1792	.76267	.7
.4	.64812	.85107	1.1750	.76154	.6
.5	.64945	.85408	1.1708	.76041	.5
.6	.65077	.85710	1.1667	.75927	.4
.7	.65210	.86014	1.1626	.75813	.3
.8	.65342	.86318	1.1585	.75700	.2
.9	.65474	.86623	1.1544	.75585	.1
41–	.65606	.86929	1.1504	.75471	**49–**
.1	.65738	.87236	1.1463	.75356	.9
.2	.65869	.87543	1.1423	.75241	.8
.3	.66000	.87852	1.1383	.75126	.7
.4	.66131	.88162	1.1343	.75011	.6
.5	.66262	.88473	1.1303	.74896	.5
.6	.66393	.88784	1.1263	.74780	.4
.7	.66523	.89097	1.1224	.74664	.3
.8	.66653	.89410	1.1184	.74548	.2
.9	.66783	.89725	1.1145	.74431	.1
42–	.66913	.90040	1.1106	.74314	**48–**
.1	.67043	.90357	1.1067	.74198	.9
.2	.67172	.90674	1.1028	.74080	.8
.3	.67301	.90993	1.0990	.73963	.7
.4	.67430	.91313	1.0951	.73846	.6
.5	.67559	.91633	1.0913	.73728	.5
.6	.67688	.91955	1.0875	.73610	.4
.7	.67816	.92277	1.0837	.73491	.3
.8	.67944	.92601	1.0799	.73373	.2
.9	.68072	.92926	1.0761	.73254	.1
43–	.68200	.93252	1.0724	.73135	**47–**
.1	.68327	.93578	1.0686	.73016	.9
.2	.68455	.93906	1.0649	.72897	.8
.3	.68582	.94235	1.0612	.72777	.7
.4	.68709	.94565	1.0575	.72657	.6
.5	.68835	.94896	1.0538	.72537	.5
.6	.68962	.95229	1.0501	.72417	.4
.7	.69088	.95562	1.0464	.72297	.3
.8	.69214	.95897	1.0428	.72176	.2
.9	.69340	.96232	1.0392	.72055	.1
44–	.69466	.96569	1.0355	.71934	**46–**
.1	.69591	.96907	1.0319	.71813	.9
.2	.69717	.97246	1.0283	.71691	.8
.3	.69842	.97586	1.0247	.71569	.7
.4	.69966	.97927	1.0212	.71447	.6
.5	.70091	.98270	1.0176	.71325	.5
.6	.70215	.98613	1.0141	.71203	.4
.7	.70339	.98958	1.0105	.71080	.3
.8	.70463	.99304	1.0070	.70957	.2
.9	.70587	.99652	1.0035	.70834	.1
45–	.70711	1.00000	1.0000	.70711	**45–**
	Cos		Tan	Sin	Deg.

Reprinted by permission from Dale Ewen, C. Robert Nelson, Orren T. Pickard, and Paul N. Thompson, *Mathematics for Career Education* (Columbus: Charles E. Merrill, 1972), p. 509.

Solving Word Problems

The students' grasp of concepts and their understanding of how to read mathematics become very apparent when they read written problems. The following steps are necessary for the reasoning and purposeful reading of a problem:

1. *Read* it slowly and carefully. Picture the scene or situation in your mind. Note any unfamiliar words or phrases. Clarify these in your mind.
2. *Question.* Reread the last sentence or part of the problem. Decide what is asked.
3. *Reread* the entire problem to determine the facts.
4. *Determine* the process to use—the mathematical operations. Note key words such as *more than, how much, find the price per* ______, *find the amount,* etc.
5. *Estimate* the answer. Judge the reasonableness of the estimate.
6. Compute the problem.

For example, these steps would be followed for the following problem:

> Mr. Stone bought a new sewing machine for his family. The store asked him to make a down payment of 20%. If the cost of the machine was $160.00, how much was the down payment?

1. The situation: Mr. Stone is buying a sewing machine and he must make a specified down payment.
2. What is asked: How much is the down payment?
   How much is a key term. Does it indicate process?
3. Facts given: The sewing machine cost—$160.00
   Down payment must be 20%.
   Underlined terms may be ones on which students will need specific clarification.
4. Process: Multiplication to compute the size of the down payment.
5. Estimate: A little more than $30.00
   (20% of 100 is 20.00; 20% of 50 is 10.00
6. Compute the problem: 20% of 160

Some suggestions for overcoming difficulties in reading problems are:

1. Have many exercises in vocabulary study:
   a. Finding meanings
   b. Matching words with objects
   c. Grouping words that relate to the same process, e.g., *plus, sum, and, longer than* relate to addition
   d. Classifying and identifying words and concepts, e.g., *radius, diameter, circumference, arc* refer to circle
   e. Dramatizing concepts such as buying and selling
2. Have students determine unfamiliar words or expressions in a problem.
3. Begin with an easy problem and have students state what the numbers in the problem stand for.
4. Help the students to visualize the problem situation. Can they describe the situation presented in the problem without using the quantities cited?

5. Have the students read many different types of problems:
   a. One-step problems—If 18 inches of ribbon are needed to tie one diploma, how many inches will be needed to tie all the diplomas for a graduating class of 106?
   b. Two-step problems—Martin's Department Store was having a 98¢ sale. Dan's mother bought three tee shirts at 98¢ each, five pairs of socks at 98¢ a pair, and six face towels at 98¢ each. How much did she spend altogether (not including tax)?
      1. Find total cost of each type of item.
      2. Find total cost of all items together.
   c. Problems with hidden questions—A telephone pole 57 feet long fell straight across a road. If 2⅓ feet were on one side of the road and 14¾ feet were on the other side of the road, how wide was the road? Hidden question: How many feet of the pole were not on the road? (A two-step problem)
   d. Problems without numbers—What unit of measure would you use to measure the area of this page in your book? The area of New York City? The area of your classroom floor?
   e. Problems with irrelevant facts—Tim liked to sit at the street corner and count cars. During *a half hour period* 38 station wagons, 97 sedans, 18 convertibles, and 46 sports cars passed by. How many cars were there in all? (A one-step problem)[11]
6. Have the students in class discussion *talk through* the problem to determine everything the problem does and why.
7. Have the students solve problems orally and use, when possible, classroom situations.
8. Have students make up and read problems related to their own activities.
9. Have the students keep a chart throughout the year on which they record all of the words used to indicate a specific symbol or process. For instance, for the symbol = such words as *equals, is equal to, the same as,* would be noted. The chart would look similar to this:

=	×	+	÷	−
is	times	add	divide	minus
equal	multiply	plus	ratio	less than

Interpreting Pictorial and Graphic Representations

Students are taught in mathematics to construct graphs to show visually the results of division, mathematical growth, gain, and so on. Graphs of various types—bar, line, circle—enable readers to see results quickly from which conclusions can be drawn. The students should be guided to read graphs by:

11. Eugene P. Smith, George A. Calder, William G. Mehl, and Dean S. Rasmussen, *Discoveries in Modern Mathematics, Book I* (Columbus, Ohio: Charles E. Merrill Publishing Company, 1968), pp. 57, 63, 75, 191, 361.

1. Reading the phrase beneath the graph so that they will know what is supposed to be pictured.
2. Reading the numbers at the left of the graph so that they can analyze and note what is being measured.
3. Reading the letters at the bottom so that they can analyze and note the quantity or units of measurement.
4. Noting the name and amount of the fractional part of each section. If the graph is a pictograph, they will need to be able to use the key to translate each picture into numbers.

Examples 12.24 through 12.29 show sample graphs.

EXAMPLE 12.24

Enrich concept of plotting on a coordinate grid by a comparison to plotting on a map—a place or ship's position using longitude and latitude as coordinates.

Here is a coordinate grid that has each quarter section or *quadrant* labeled by a Roman numeral. Notice that the quadrants are numbered in counterclockwise order.

Vocabulary that should be known.

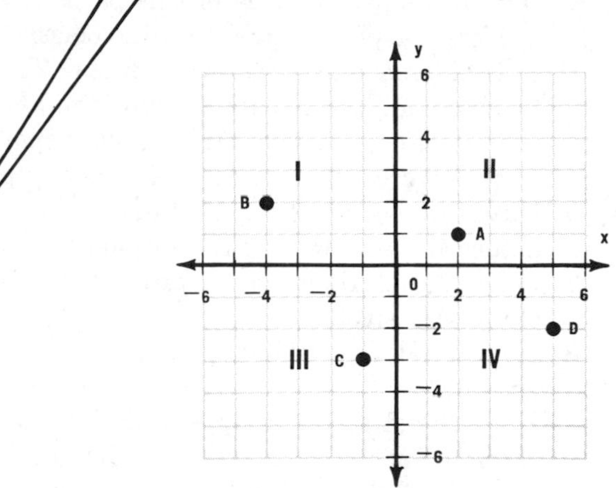

Observe point A in quadrant I. How many units is it to the right of the y-axis? How far is it above the x-axis? The distance from the y-axis is always described first or before the distance from the x-axis. Thus we would say that point A represents $x = 2$, $y = 1$, or the *coordinates* of A are $(2, 1)$. Similarly, the coordinates of point B are $(^-4, 2)$. What are the coordinates of point C? What are the coordinates of point D? The process of locating a point on a coordinate plane is called **plotting** the point.

Exercises

Draw a pair of coordinate axes and locate the following points. Label each point with its coordinates.

1. $(3, 3)$ **3.** $(^-2, 1)$ **5.** $(4, ^-2)$ **7.** $(^-3, ^-1)$ **9.** $(5, 2)$
2. $(4, 5)$ **4.** $(1, ^-3)$ **6.** $(^-5, ^-2)$ **8.** $(^-3, 6)$ **10.** $(^-1, ^-4)$

Reprinted by permission from Eugene P. Smith, George A. Calder, William G. Mehl, and Dean S. Rasmussen, *Discoveries in Modern Mathematics* (Columbus: Charles E. Merrill, 1968), p. 140.

EXAMPLE 12.25

Pictograph

Key
(Check its use with students)

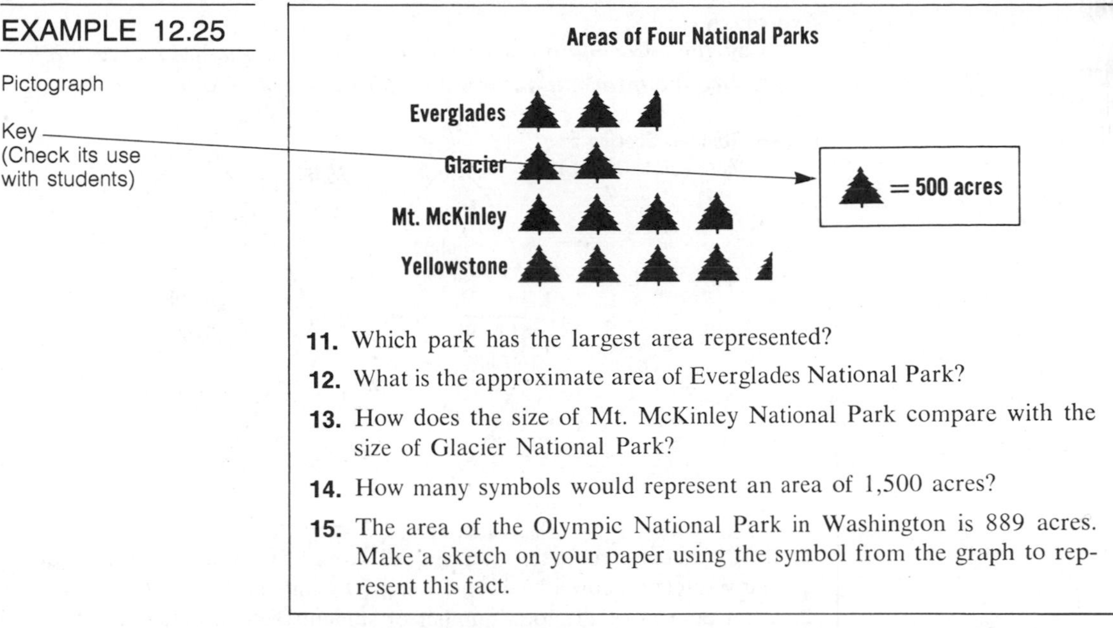

11. Which park has the largest area represented?
12. What is the approximate area of Everglades National Park?
13. How does the size of Mt. McKinley National Park compare with the size of Glacier National Park?
14. How many symbols would represent an area of 1,500 acres?
15. The area of the Olympic National Park in Washington is 889 acres. Make a sketch on your paper using the symbol from the graph to represent this fact.

Reprinted by permission from Eugene P. Smith, George A. Calder, William G. Mehl, and Dean S. Rasmussen, *Discoveries in Modern Mathematics* (Columbus: Charles E. Merrill, 1968), p. 442.

EXAMPLE 12.26

Students must know values and relationships of units→tens→hundreds→thousands

Record the reading on each electric meter.

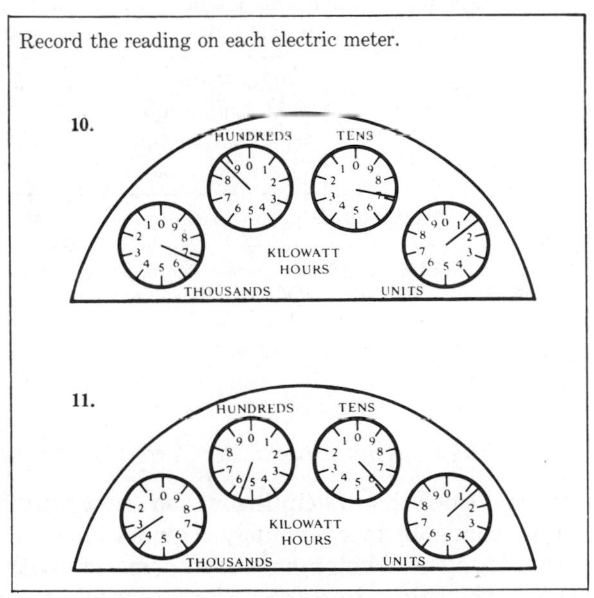

Reprinted by permission from Dale Ewen, C. Robert Nelson, Orren T. Pickard, and Paul N. Thompson, *Mathematics for Career Education* (Columbus: Charles E. Merrill, 1972), p. 244.

EXAMPLE 12.27

Pictorial representation of amounts in percent

Exercises

Study the information which is presented in the following circle graph. Use the information in the graph to answer Exercises 1-6.

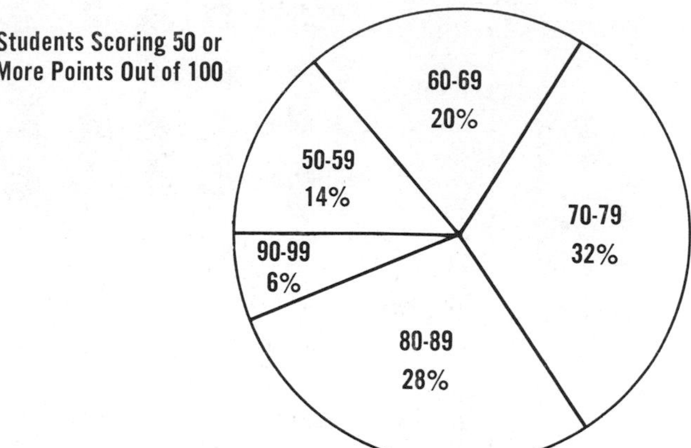

1. If 120 students took the test, and all scored 50 or more points, how many students scored between 59 and 70 points on the test?
2. What percent of the total number of students scored below 80?
3. Does the graph show that anyone received a score of 100%?
4. According to the appearance of the graph, which two score ranges included approximately the same number of students?
5. How many students scored better than 69 points, but less than 90 points?
6. Which two groups together have the same percentage as the 60-69 group?
7. David stood at a busy highway intersection and counted the number of automobiles which were painted white, red, blue, and green for a period of one hour. His research provided him with the following data:

White Automobiles	270
Red Automobiles	45
Blue Automobiles	108
Green Automobiles	27

Construct a circle graph to show the results of David's research.

Reprinted by permission from Eugene P. Smith, George A. Calder, William G. Mehl, and Dean S. Rasmussen, *Discoveries in Modern Mathematics* (Columbus: Charles E. Merrill, 1968), p. 432.

Relating Previous Information to Current Reading

In perhaps no other discipline is it so important for students to be able to relate new concepts to previously learned ones. You should always help students realize the development of information within the subject. This can be started at the beginning of the school year when the overview of the course is presented. Many textbooks include a review of essential concepts in the first chapters. This must also be done throughout the year as new concepts are

EXAMPLE 12.28

12:8 Broken Line Graphs

Broken line graphs are useful for pointing out changes in data over a period of time or changes brought on by varying conditions. In a broken line graph, line segments are used to connect the points which represent the given data. In some line graphs, these line segments are drawn only to guide the eye and to indicate the rate of change. In other line graphs, the connecting lines can be used to guess information which was not given.

The broken line graph below records the number of rainy days for each month of the school year in a particular city. The dots represent the number of rainy days in a given month. The lines help to show the amount of increase or decrease in rainy days from month to month. Note that there are two scales on a line graph: one on the horizontal axis and one on the vertical axis.

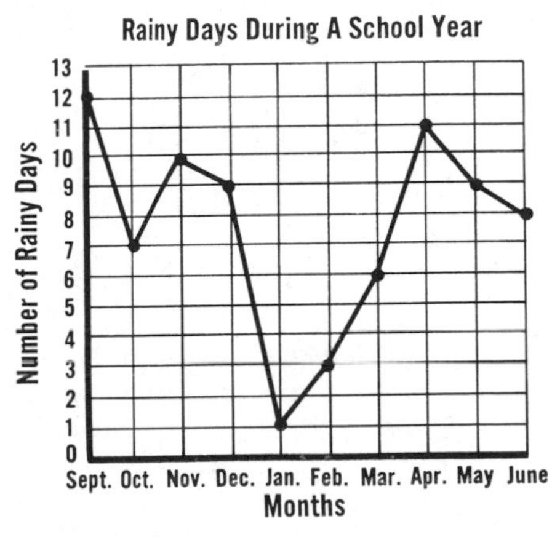

—— General

~~~ Explanation to student

--- Specific

Reprinted by permission from Eugene P. Smith, George A. Calder, William G. Mehl, and Dean S. Rasmussen, *Discoveries in Modern Mathematics* (Columbus: Charles E. Merrill, 1968), p. 433.

introduced so you can assure that students fully understand the earlier ones. Ask the students themselves to determine the previous understandings when they meet a new concept. Another effective practice is to have students see the order of development within a chapter. For example, the preview section of a chapter entitled "Operations with Polynomials" (see Example 12.30) indicates understandings students should have acquired before beginning the chapter. Knowing that they will be dealing with *operations,* students may be able to anticipate some of the major sections of the chapter. The following headings would be listed:

Addition of polynomials
Subtraction of polynomials
Multiplication of polynomials
Division of polynomials
Sentences with polynomials
Sentences with fractions
~~~

EXAMPLE 12.29

Explanation

New vocabulary

12:10 Histograms

At the beginning of this chapter you organized data to find measures of central tendency. Sometimes it is useful to know how frequently a particular score, weight, height, or other kind of numerical event occurs within a set of data. One way of presenting such data is by a frequency table or frequency distribution. A tally or count is kept of the number of times each "score" appears in the data.

Example: Mr. Kelley's mathematics students made the following scores on a test: 90, 85, 85, 95, 85, 80, 75, 65, 80, 75, 85, 95, 100, 85, 90, 80, 80, 65, 75, 90, 85, 100, 85, 95, 90, 80, 75, 80, 85, 90, 80, 75.

Mr. Kelley recorded the information on a distribution table, marking a tally mark in the appropriate line for each score.

Score	Tally	Frequency
100	//	2
95	///	3
90	~~////~~	5
85	~~////~~ ///	8
80	~~////~~ //	7
75	~~////~~	5
70		0
65	//	2

Reprinted by permission from Eugene P. Smith, George A. Calder, William G. Mehl, and Dean S. Rasmussen, *Discoveries in Modern Mathematics* (Columbus: Charles E. Merrill, 1968), p. 439.

Following Directions

Following directions is as important in mathematics as it is in science. Directions require intensive reading, and students will need to follow these steps:

1. Read the directions completely and carefully to get an overview.
2. Read just one direction at a time very carefully (if need be, word by word).
3. Think about each direction and be sure that it is understood exactly. If not, reread the direction.
4. Carry out the directions.

Inadequate Readers in the Mathematics Class

The concept load and the intensity of mathematical writing can spell defeat for less able readers. It is desirable, of course, for such readers to get

EXAMPLE 12.30

#1. Earlier knowledge

a

b

c

New material to be learned

#2. Earlier knowledge

Introductory statement

New material to be learned

Operations with Polynomials 4

4:1 PREVIEW

Before you could solve practical problems in arithmetic, you had to be able to perform the fundamental operations with numbers. You needed to know the addition combinations before you could find the total cost of a number of items. You needed to know how to multiply accurately before you could find the cost of several pounds of a commodity at a given price per pound. Before you could work problems containing fractions and decimals, you had to learn the operations with those special types of numbers.

In algebra, we shall be dealing largely with polynomials. You must learn to perform the basic operations with polynomials before you can use them in practical applications. You already have an understanding of the properties of the set of rational numbers and the operations with monomials. This knowledge should help you in learning to handle polynomials. Check yourself to be sure that you remember and can use the rules of operations with rational numbers and the laws of exponents. You must know these principles in order to combine monomials by addition, subtraction, multiplication, and division.

Remember that a polynomial is an algebraic expression made up of sums and products of variables and constants. A polynomial in one variable is an expression like $3x^2 - 2x + 1$, $4x + 3$, or $3x^4$. The general form is $ax^n + bx^{n-1} + \cdots + k$, where $a, b, \cdots k$ are constants and n is a non-negative integer. You will learn how to add and subtract polynomials with two or more terms by combining like terms. Later in this chapter you will multiply and divide polynomials by procedures similar to those used in arithmetic. When you have mastered the basic operations with polynomials, you will use your knowledge to solve algebraic sentences and other problems in algebra.

Reprinted by permission from Glen D. Vannatta, A. Wilson Goodwin, and F. Joe Crosswhite, *Algebra One* (Columbus: Charles E. Merrill, 1970), pp. 138–39.

assistance in remedial reading classes, and many do. However, these students still are in the regular math class while receiving remedial help. Therefore, teachers must vary their instructional techniques and procedures in order to insure success for less competent readers.

One of the most important measures you can employ is to build background by a program of readiness before introducing each new concept. In the readiness period, you may do the following:

1. Inventory the students' mastery of skills to determine the gaps and specific points of difficulty that need to be corrected. Then teach to these.
2. Use a sequential question-and-answer technique to lead the students to the concept or process. Guide their reasoning in small steps.
3. As each new understanding is evolved, and as each old one is

reviewed, write the appropriate word or term on the blackboard. Focus attention upon it. Underline the word to indicate the syllables.
4. Use discussion to elicit questions from the students as well as experiences they have had which involve the concept or process. Guide the students in the use of the words.
5. Review frequently—refresh their memories—and show the interrelationship of understandings.
6. Use concrete materials and illustrations wherever possible.
7. Review the use and meaning of mathematical symbols as they are required.
8. Find easier materials if possible.
9. Rewrite explanations and problems. One technique is to explain a concept and then have the students evolve an explanation in their own words which can then be typed and presented to them as a supplement to their textbook.

Lesson Procedures

As applied to mathematics, the Directed Reading Activity class procedure includes the following steps:

1. Readiness—this beginning step of the lesson is designed to enable the students to accomplish the objective of the lesson. The teacher will:
   a. Explore and supplement where necessary the background necessary for the lesson.
   b. Introduce the new terms and vocabulary, which may consist of both general words and technical ones.
   c. Set purposes with the students for the tasks to be accomplished.
2. Guided silent reading pertinent to the purposes or problems of the lesson.
3. Discussion of the reading material (either explanation of a process or a problem) to probe and aid understanding. You may use different types of questions (fact, vocabulary, inference, step of problem solving, relationship) to assist the students in their logical thought and understanding. Specific mathematical problems and exercises may be used to apply the conceptual and explanatory material.
4. Rereading, which may be silent or oral and is done as the need arises to determine a specific fact or consideration. Such need may arise from the problems and exercises, and it indicates the students' grasp of the material.
5. Application—the students practice, independently or with teacher help, by applying the process to specific problems.

When students have been taught the theoretical concepts and the lesson is now concerned with application through the computation of verbal problems, an effective procedure is a union of the standard steps of a reading lesson and the steps of problem solving:

1. The preparation for reading and understanding would have been completed in the explanation and discussion of the conceptual processes.

2. Have the students read the problem. For example, "The perimeter of a triangle is 62 inches. The second side is 4 inches longer than the first and the remaining side is 6 inches less than the second. Find the lengths of the three sides."
3. Develop comprehension. Have the students visualize the problem. Clarify vocabulary as necessary. In this instance, clarify the words *perimeter, than, less than* (note that *than* means "as compared to").
4. Rereading—read to find what is asked for and what is given. Determine the process—in this case, the mathematical equation or sentence:
$$X + (X + 4) + (X + 4 - 6) = 62.$$
5. Compute the problem. Check it against the facts given in the problem.
6. Follow-up. Application of procedure to other problems, following steps 2-5.

The discipline of mathematics has a dual language. Students must be able to understand both language and mathematical symbols. These symbols which label the mathematical concepts are best taught by the mathematics teacher, since he is the one who is expert in the discipline. For the students to become independent in the study and reading of mathematics materials, they must become competent in the language of mathematics.

SUMMARY

The goal of fusing the process skills of reading and subject content is to foster student competence and independence. We work toward achieving this goal by teaching students how to read the printed materials of each discipline as they use them in class.

QUESTIONS AND PROBLEMS FOR YOUR OWN CLASSROOM

English

For readers who are training to be teachers:

1. Plan how you will provide for different needs and reading levels in your literature program.
2. Compile approaches that will foster student interest in literature.
3. Identify the reading skills you wish to apply to each selection of literature. Work these into your lesson procedure.
4. Plan a teaching unit in English and make provision for developing appreciation, teaching the pertinent language arts skills, and differentiating the study to the competence level of each student.
5. Set up a classroom library. Compile bibliographies of books related to each theme for your students to read.

For readers who are teaching:

1. Review the goals of your language arts curriculum. Note the areas in which both cognitive and affective objectives would be included.
2. Review the content of your language arts curriculum. Note where instruction in reading, writing, speaking, and listening would be included. Determine the skills you would include in each area.
3. Review the literature selections you will be teaching and plan questions and activities to stimulate students to relate them to their own life experiences.
4. Through the results of a diagnostic informal reading inventory or in conjunction with the guidance office, determine the reading levels of your students. Plan how you will provide for these levels in your literature program.
5. For each unit in your curriculum, compile a bibliography of the appropriate and available books in your school library.

Social Studies

For readers who are training to be teachers:

1. Analyze the material of a social studies textbook to determine the difficulties you think students might have in reading it. Then, plan how you could help the students with the difficulties.
2. Analyze materials in a social studies textbook and note the various patterns of paragraphs.
3. Compile a bibliography of materials for each unit topic.
4. Identify the reading skills you consider pertinent to social studies. Use a selection and compose two questions requiring the use of each skill.

For readers who are teaching:

1. Discuss with your students the difficulties they experience in reading social studies materials. Evolve with them some corrective procedures.
2. In each reading assignment, note the various patterns of information as a means of planning the emphasis of the subsequent lesson.
3. Plan a unit of study by coordinating the requirements of the subject and the skill and informational needs of the students.
4. Identify the concepts you want students to learn and link them with the reading skills required. List discussion questions for developing these concepts by using the appropriate reading skills.

Science

For readers who are training to be teachers:

1. Select paragraphs from science textbooks and analyze them to determine their structure and use of structure words.

2. Devise or use behavioral objectives for your lesson procedures. Either cite the reading skill needed for each behavioral objective in science or state the skills as behavioral objectives.
3. Develop a tentative list of do's and don't's for a science project.
4. Plan in your lesson procedures how you will provide time and opportunity to foster wide reading.

For readers who are teaching:

1. Review your textbooks thoroughly and note the study aids for your students. Plan to alert them to these aids and to teach their uses.
2. In the next reading assignment, determine how the students can best organize their notes from the material: outline, chart, table, comparison and contrasting columns, diagrams, graphs, etc.
3. Consult with your school librarian and compile a bibliography of reference material for your science class. For each major unit prepare a bibliography of extended readings.
4. Throughout the school year make a list of the Greek and Latin roots used in your science vocabulary.
5. Evolve with your students a tenative list of do's and don't's for a science project.

Mathematics

For readers who are training to be teachers:

1. Review a mathematics textbook and list:
   a. the technical vocabulary
   b. the general words used with mathematical meaning
   c. words that indicate process
   d. general words that indicate relationship or degree
2. Before you plan to teach a formula, analyze its verbal form. Note the meaning units and words indicating process and relationship.
3. For each major topic in a specific mathematics class, determine practical applications to help students realize the relevance.
4. For each topic, determine the prior knowledge the students should have in order to realize the cumulative nature of mathematics.
5. Consult with the school librarian and prepare a bibliography of related mathematics materials for supplementary and enrichment use.
6. Analyze verbal problems for words that indicate process and relationship.

For readers who are teaching:

1. Analyze the printed material in your mathematics textbook and note for each assignment the vocabulary that is technical, general words used with a specialized mathematical meaning, and words indicating process.
2. Use a class assignment and determine how you can help your students realize the practical application of information.

3. Poll your students for reasons why they think verbal problems are difficult. List the reasons and evolve with them appropriate techniques for overcoming the difficulties.
4. Analyze the mathematics textbook with your students to determine the patterns of writing.
5. As you plan to teach a new mathematical concept, determine the steps you would employ to introduce and to clarify the concept.

SELECTED REFERENCES

Aukerman, Robert C. *Reading in the Secondary School Classroom.* New York: McGraw-Hill, 1972.

Lamberg, Walter J., and Lamb, Charles E. *Reading Instruction in the Content Areas.* Chicago: Rand McNally College Publishing Company, 1980.

Roe, Betty D.; Stoodt, Barbara D.; and Burns, Paul C. *Reading Instruction in the Secondary School.* Chicago: Rand McNally College Publishing Company, 1978.

All of these references provide lesson illustrations and suggestions.

CHAPTER 13

Applying Reading Skills to Business Education, Industrial Arts, and Home Economics

OVERVIEW

A major premise of this book is that the reading skills have a specific application to each content area. This chapter describes how the reading skills apply to business education, industrial arts, and home economics.

Questions

Consider these questions before you read further:

1. Survey the reading material of your subject and list the reading skills that the students must have.
2. If your subject is one in which the students are actively involved in project assignments—a "hands-on" approach—how does reading instruction fit in?

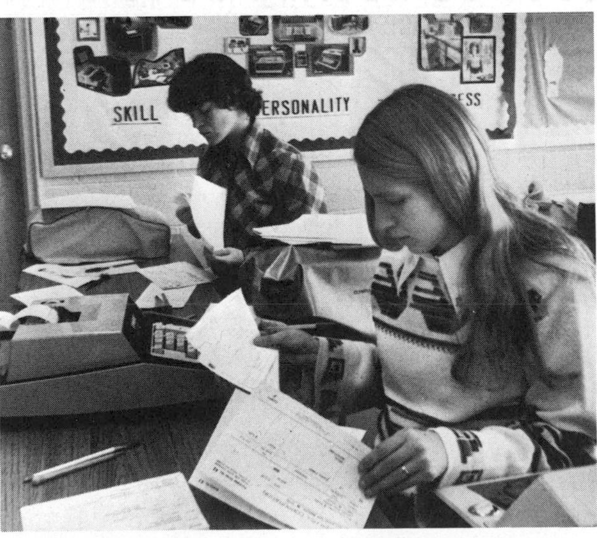

APPLYING READING SKILLS TO BUSINESS EDUCATION

Business education attracts a cross-section of the student body, and it makes use of all of the reading skills found in the other disciplines. The students who enroll in business courses range from the potential dropout to the college-bound—from unmotivated students who are disabled readers to the most motivated and competent students. Many business education classes, therefore, have a wide range of reading levels, sometimes from a third grade level to the college level (an eight- to ten-year spread). Business education courses range from social studies types, such as business law, to those of a mathematical nature, such as bookkeeping and accounting.

In one comprehensive suburban-urban high school, a chart was made of the courses in the business department. The nature of each course was identified with one of the four major disciplines (English, mathematics, social studies, and science), and the reading skills pertinent to each course were listed. The chart clearly showed the reading tasks required for each course as well as for the department in general (see Table 13.1).

A quick glance at Table 13.1 suggests that the courses offered in the department of business education relate in type, and hence in pertinent skills, to various other disciplines. A closer look shows that each course in the department has its own requirements. Business education courses deal with material similar to that found in course work in English, social studies, science, and mathematics. Therefore, the business education teacher must be quite flexible in order to help the students with the various courses offered.

Suggestions for Specific Areas

Mathematics

The business subjects most similar to mathematics are bookkeeping, business arithmetic, and record keeping and retailing. The writing style is spartan and concise, with a heavy vocabulary load. Usually there is little anecdotal writing; the style requires meticulous reading for all details. In addition to learning the vocabulary, students must see clearly the organization of information.

Vocabulary. Certainly there are many technical words you expect to teach—for example, *assessed value, cashier's check, unearned premium,* and *round lot*. Then there are also general words that have a technical meaning in the subject. Such words can present comprehension problems. Students may pronounce a word readily and know its general common meaning, and therefore not consider it "new" and give it close attention. In business education there are many words with multiple meanings (for example, *savings, paycheck, liability, claim,* and *interest*). Finally, there are common words that the students recognize and define in a general way but do not define precisely enough. Both teacher and students may regard such words (for example, *data, concrete, expire,* and *quart*) as elementary, but it is important for students—particularly less able readers—to get the precise meaning.

TABLE 13.1 Business Courses and Pertinent Reading Skills

RELATED SUBJECT TYPE	SUBJECT	Proof and Copy Reading	Reading Verbal Problems	Relationships: Formulas	Reading Pictures, Graphs	Applying Theory	Following Directions	Researching	Dr. Concl., Crit. Rdng	Seeing Organization	Supporting Details	Noting Main Idea	Vocabulary: Special Symbols	Vocabulary: General	Vocabulary: Technical	Using Parts of Book	Reading-Study Technique	Reading for Purpose
Mathematics	Bookkeeping I		√	√	√	√	√	√	√	√	√	√	√	√	√	√	√	√
Mathematics	Bookkeeping II		√	√	√	√	√	√	√	√	√	√	√	√	√	√	√	√
Mathematics	Business Arithmetic		√	√	√	√	√		√	√	√	√	√	√	√	√	√	√
Mathematics	Clerical Mathematics		√	√	√	√	√		√	√	√	√	√	√	√	√	√	√
English/Science	Clerical Typing	√				√	√				√			√	√			
Science, gen'l.	Everyday Business		√		√	√	√	√	√	√	√	√		√	√	√	√	√
Science, gen'l.	Introduction to Business		√		√	√	√	√	√	√	√	√		√	√	√	√	√
Mathematics	Nurses' Mathematics		√	√	√	√	√	√	√	√	√	√	√	√	√	√	√	√
Science	Office Machines					√		√		√		√			√		√	√
Science	Office Practice I					√		√		√	√	√			√		√	√
Science	Office Practice II					√		√		√	√	√			√		√	√
Soc. Studies	Personal Law				√	√		√	√	√	√	√		√	√	√	√	√
Science/Math.	Record Keeping				√	√	√			√	√	√	√		√	√	√	√
Soc. St./Math.	Retailing I			√	√	√	√	√	√	√	√	√	√	√	√	√	√	√
Soc. St./Math.	Retailing II			√	√	√	√	√	√	√	√	√	√	√	√	√	√	√
Science	Secretarial Practice			√		√	√	√	√	√	√	√		√	√	√	√	√
English	Shorthand I				√	√	√						√	√	√	√	√	√
English	Shorthand II and Transcription				√	√	√						√	√	√	√	√	√
English	Stenoscript				√	√	√						√	√	√	√	√	√
English/Science	Typewriting I						√			√	√	√		√	√	√	√	√
English/Science	Typewriting—personal						√			√	√	√		√	√	√	√	√
Soc. Studies	Business law				√	√	√	√	√	√	√	√		√	√	√	√	√

Cultivate vocabulary consciousness in class. Of particular value are vocabulary charts, posted in the classroom, that evolve throughout the year. As new words are read in context, they should be discussed and related to the students' background. For instance, with the word *balance,* what does it mean in "Often, the balance on the bank statement is not the same as the balance in your checkbook"? Probe for student experiences. Ask the meanings of such common expressions as "You may have the balance of the candy" or "Now that I have completed the job, what will I do with the balance of my time?" The word could be added to a chart in the proper category. All words relating to a common concept would be put on one chart; different words with the same meaning, or which can be used interchangeably, could be put on another chart. If you wish, students could also keep such word lists in their notebooks.

Comprehension skills. The comprehension skills required for reading business mathematics include:

1. noting definitions
2. determining the main idea and the appropriate details for each main idea
3. seeing the organization of information
4. following directions
5. solving problems

In most business mathematical textbooks, paragraphs of definition are predominant (see Example 13.1). Such paragraphs can also be analyzed for main idea and detail, another rather common paragraph pattern.

EXAMPLE 13.1

Definition and main idea

Three details

Terms the students must know:
- principal
- account
- savings account
- interest
- simple interest

Adding interest to principal to earn more interest is called compounding interest. All savings accounts pay compound interest. In fact, this is one way people try to increase their savings. (1) The interest is computed several times a year. (2) Each time it is figured by the bank, the interest is added to the principal, thereby increasing the amount in the savings account. When the interest is figured again, the new amount in the account will be used. (3) The only time compound interest is not computed is the first time interest is paid on the account. Then it is the same as simple interest.

Some of the paragraphs may incorporate more than one pattern. Often such is the case in business arithmetic—following directions and the steps of problem solving. For instance, note the following:

Problem: Find the number of board-feet in 10 pieces of ponderosa pine 1 inch thick and 2 inches wide, cut in 6-foot lengths.

Directions: 1. Find the total length.
$10 \times 6 = 60$ feet
2. Find the width in feet.
2 inches = $\frac{2}{12}$ foot = $\frac{1}{6}$ foot
3. Multiply.
$60 \times \frac{1}{6} \times 1 = 10$
4. 10 is then the number of board-feet.

The student must know the concepts of *board* and *feet,* as well as basic units of measurement, how to multiply fractions, and how to reduce fractions. With this very simple problem, the practice problem for the students may be stated similarly or put in a more social context: Mr. Quintero wishes to build a railing around his patio. He figures that in addition to 12 posts, he will need eighteen pieces of oak 2 inches thick and 4 inches wide, cut in 10-foot lengths. How many board feet of oak will he need?

The steps of problem solving would include:

1. Read to visualize the situation.
2. Read to find what is asked for.
3. Read to determine the facts.
4. Determine the process to use.
5. Estimate the answer.
6. Compute the problem.

Using any textbook effectively requires involving students with its overall organization. For instance, if the chapter to be studied is about taxes, speculate with the students about what will be included. They may list the types of taxes, such as income taxes (federal and state), property taxes, and sales taxes. They may suggest that the chapter will define each type, point out its characteristics, and describe how it is computed. It is likely that they can devise a preliminary outline for the chapter just from their common general knowledge. In soliciting their ideas in this way, you help students review what they already know, organize their information in a logical manner, and thereby anticipate what they will be studying. They will note organization by checking their own outline against that of the textbook.

In bookkeeping classes, students meet problems of a mathematical nature and must understand the various forms used in business record keeping. The forms are an intrinsic part of the subject matter; consequently, students learn and practice setting up and keeping records. The ability to make and use business records depends not only on meticulous attention to detail and a general mathematical ability but also on understanding the vocabulary. For instance, students must understand what a *journal* is and the types of journals (cash receipts, cash payments, and so on) as well as what a *ledger* is and the various types of ledgers (accounts receivable, creditor's, customer's, and so on). The pages of most ledgers and journals are devoid of any printed headings, showing only horizontal and vertical lines to facilitate orderly recording. Bookkeepers label the columns in accordance with the needs of the business. The students may need to label columns as assets, liabilities, balance sheet, debit amount, credit amount, accounts payable, accounts receivable, and so on.

Science

The patterns of writing in many areas of business education—general business, office practice, record keeping, typing, and secretarial practice—resemble those found in scientific content. These subjects are full of data and details that students must understand and arrange logically. There is little anecdotal writing; much of the material is explanation of procedures and forms. The technical vocabulary may present a formidable barrier to students. For instance, in a standard general business textbook, a unit on insurance may use all of the terms shown in Table 13.2. (Note that these terms have been categorized.)

TABLE 13.2 Terms in a Unit on Insurance

Insurance	*Automobile insurance*
economic risk	bodily injury liability
policy	collision
policy holder	comprehensive physical damage
premium	medical payments
	property damage liability
Property and liability insurance	*Life insurance*
homeowners policy	straight life policy
extended coverage	convertible
depreciation	endowment
inventory	family income policy
personal property	term policy
real property	beneficiary
fire	annuity
	cash surrender value
	group insurance
Health insurance	*Pensions and Social Security*
basic health coverage	unemployment insurance
general medical expense insurance	estate planning
hospital expense insurance	medicare
major medical expense insurance	social security account number
surgical expense insurance	social security taxes
workmen's compensation	
total disability insurance	

Simple arithmetic shows that if there are only ten units to be covered in a ten-month school year, students might have to master approximately thirty to forty words each month. A rather formidable assignment, particularly when we wish them to know not only just a rote definition but also the concept that each term represents. You will further note that there are terms or parts of terms, labelled as technical, which have a general meaning; they have meanings that depend upon the context. Such words from the list in Table 13.2 are *policy, depreciation, inventory, beneficiary, real, straight, extended,* and so on.

Pattern of writing. The typical general business textbook often has paragraphs of main idea followed by details and definition, with further details expanding the definition (see Example 13.2). Another pattern is showing steps of a process (see Example 13.3). Many textbooks also include problems for student practice. Such problems resemble those of mathematics, and the procedure which the student should follow is similar to that of solving mathematical problems.

In a typewriting manual, the predominant pattern of writing is directions. The writing is succinct, and students must read slowly and thoroughly and then do each step. Usually, clues labelling each step (such as

EXAMPLE 13.2

Main idea definition

3 details expanding the definition—the reasons for a house to depreciate (or not to)

Depreciation. The decrease in the value of property caused by use and time is depreciation. (1) If a good house is kept in good condition, the depreciation may amount to very little. (2) In fact, if a house is in a neighborhood that is favorably located and in which the property is well kept up, it may actually increase in value over the years. (3) But if a house is in a neighborhood that is unfavorably located and in which the property is not well maintained, it may decrease in value rapidly.

Reprinted by permission from Ernest H. Crabbe, S. Joseph DeBrum, Peter G. Gaines, and Dean J. Malsbury, *General Business for Economic Understanding* (New Rochelle: Southwestern, 1966), p. 318.

EXAMPLE 13.3

Steps for making deposits in a savings account—*A* and *B*

Underlined sentence shows 3-step process for opening a savings account.

How to open a savings account. The steps to be taken in opening a savings account in a bank are similar to those followed in opening a checking account. (1) A person fills out a signature card, (2) makes a deposit, and (3) receives a savings passbook. When the depositor makes a deposit, (A) he fills out a deposit ticket much like that used in making a deposit in a checking account. (B) He then presents this ticket, the savings passbook, and the deposit to the bank clerk, who enters the deposit in the passbook. If the depositor forgets his passbook, the clerk accepts his deposit and gives him a receipt for it. The entry is then made in the book by the bank clerk upon the presentation of the book and the receipt at a later date.

The savings passbook shows the deposits and the withdrawals made by the depositor, the interest earned, and the balance of the account.

Reprinted by permission from Ernest H. Crabbe, S. Joseph DeBrum, Peter G. Gaines, and Dean J. Malsbury, *General Business for Economic Understanding* (New Rochelle: Southwestern, 1966), p. 298.

first, second, (1), (2), *A, B*) are within the paragraph or are in list form. You may need to alert students to these aids for understanding the structure of the paragraphs. Often, pictures accompany the paragraph. Though in typewriting the students are aided by concrete application—practicing each step in class—their ability to read the directions depends upon knowing precisely such common words as *set, release, slide, press back, shift, approximate, thirds, circular,* and so on.

Social studies. Business law is the course which most resembles the social studies pattern of writing. The vocabulary load is large, consisting mostly of technical legal terminology which will likely be unfamiliar to the student. Further, much of the writing is similar to that of a general business course which contains many of the same units (for example, insurance). The application of legal principles, usually is covered by the pattern of main idea/definition followed by details. Next, a concrete illustration and an ensuing paragraph analyzing the legal principles involved are presented, similar to a problem-solving pattern. Students will need to use basically a mathematical type of problem solving—what is the problem, what are the facts, what is the question—and read accordingly. Then, they must follow the ideas brought out in the analysis of the situation, much as they would consider steps of an argument in legal application. Steps of an argument include perceiving the situation, noting the governing legal principles, and then coming to a solution. For instance:

> If you unknowingly purchase a stolen diamond ring from someone who had stolen it, do you obtain a valid title?
>
> Step I — Students perceive the situation and express it in their own words; they can visualize the problem, cite the facts, and note the question.
>
> Step II — They note legal principles (steps of the argument) which would be imbedded in the discussion of the situation:
> A. A person cannot sell what he or she does not own.
> B. The title to stolen goods has never left the true owner.
>
> Step III — Solution: You would not obtain a valid title.

English. Shorthand, typewriting, and business English require a knowledge of the sounds of English as well as fundamentals of syntax and organization of ideas. An efficient business organization relies on effective communication in order to sell a product or service. All aspects of the language arts are used, with emphasis on speaking and writing.

Business students not only must read the communications of other business people, they also must be able to write and speak in order to get their ideas across clearly. Therefore, they will study the parts of speech and how to use them in constructing sentences. They will study how context and punctuation affect meaning. Knowing the appropriate words (antonyms, synonyms, and homonyms) and the function of phrases and clauses is important. Finally, understanding paragraph structure is necessary for composing memoranda, reports, and business letters of various kinds.

As you work with sentence structure, have the students experiment with linguistic transformation—restating the sentence in different ways and still retaining the same meaning. Investigate the effect of different words in a communication—are some more accurate and appealing than others? Ask students to react to communications stated in different ways: which is best according to the purpose?

Typing class, in which the goal is to learn to type quickly and accurately, involves specific reading skills. An analysis of the Table of Contents of the typical typing text will give clues to many of the reading skills required. The skill of following directions is necessary for manipulating the typewriter as well as for typing different kinds of copy. In addition, students must learn to read the various types of copy: correspondence, forms, tabulations, and manuscripts of all kinds.

Shorthand requires the ability to organize information and to hear the sounds of the language. Here the students are faced with a situation similar to mathematics and some sciences. In math and science there are specific symbols, formulas, and equations that represent words or phrases. Like the letters of our alphabet, shorthand is a code—another form of written language.

Since shorthand is tied so closely to the sounds of language, students must be able to hear the sounds correctly and also must know the traditional alphabetic symbols for spelling words correctly. Skills in this area may well include a review of phonetic principles. Much use of spoken language is important to give students practice in hearing language sounds and to distinguish them. Obviously, the listening skills are important.

Reading comprehension skills also are important in shorthand courses using expository material. The essential reading comprehension skills in shorthand are:

1. finding the main idea of a paragraph
2. noting related details
3. seeing the organization (outline) of information
4. using "signal" words
5. noting comparison and contrast pattern
6. noting definitions and examples

Since shorthand also involves the ability to write up shorthand notes, the writing skills are essential, and they parallel those of reading.

Guidelines for Classroom Procedure

Business teachers should be capable of developing their own skills in teaching students how to read the books and other materials in their courses. Anderson notes that teachers can do this by *(a)* recalling the processes that they went through in learning a specific concept, *(b)* analyzing the reading materials carefully, and *(c)* analyzing how students read and study the materials.[1] These three suggestions can be implemented by the following classroom practices:

1. Bernice Anderson, "Business Teacher: Are You Prepared to Teach Reading?" *Business Education Forum* 26, No. 1 (October 1971): 3–4.

1. Conduct a diagnostic analysis of possible learning difficulties in the reading of business materials.
2. Be alert to the trouble spots and vocabulary difficulties of students, and make efforts to clarify the difficulties for them.
3. Prepare the students for the study and reading of the material:
   a. Preview the material in the textbook by looking at headings, pictorial materials, introductory paragraphs, specific study aids in the material.
   b. Determine with the students how the information is organized. Show them how to read and study.
   c. Relate the material to the students' background. Find out what they know about the information, what experiences they have had.
   d. Note students' questions about the information. For example, in studying insurance, what do they know about it? What experience have they had with it? What questions do they have?
   e. Establish basic conceptual terms prior to reading. For example, an assignment to read about insurance would require explaining the basic idea of what insurance is. Audiovisual aids, demonstrations, and concrete illustrations may be used to present the new concept prior to reading about it in the abstract.
   f. Establish purposes or reasons—information to find out—for reading. Again, if the topic is insurance, one purpose could be to find out about the different kinds of insurance. Depending upon the material and the level of the class, the purposes may be quite specific or more subtle and general.
4. In discussion of the material, explain and clarify specific understandings. But also note if there are any skill deficiencies, such as not observing a main idea. Be prepared to give instruction in paragraph analysis using paragraphs from the reading material.
5. Provide as much reinforcement as is necessary. An effective procedure is to have the students read and then do the task or apply the information to a practical problem. A reading skill also can be reinforced—for example, by assigning students to find the main idea of paragraphs which contain content you want the students to know.
6. Applying new information to practical situations or problems is necessary to show students the relevance of their learning.
7. Provide for supervised study, during which you can assist individuals and small groups with specific difficulties.

Vocabulary Development

You are concerned with two kinds of vocabulary: technical words and common words with special meanings. For example, *bulk sale, forged indorsement,* and *warranty deed* would be classified as technical while *credit, statement,* and *capital* are common words with special meaning in business. Students learn words best when they can associate them with experiences. You may need to probe for student experiences or provide relevant experiences. It would be wise to analyze the reading material for both technical words and special common words and insure that the students learn their spelling and meaning. Be consistent in vocabulary usage. Alert students to the synonymous meaning of two or more terms, such as *charge sales* and *sales on credit*. Study guides are helpful for alerting students to new words and their application.

Using the Textbook

Students may also need help in reading and using their textbook. The teacher can provide suggestions on how to study a textbook by following the basic SQ3R study formula discussed in Chapter 4:

I. Survey
   A. Ask yourself these questions after you have looked at the chapter title:
      1. What do I know about this?
      2. What do I want to know about this?
      Your answers will help you establish purposes for reading the lesson.
   B. Look over the headings (boldface print) to see what main ideas are being discussed. Some people write down these topics as main headings of an outline, leaving space between these points to fill in details to be read later.
   C. Look at any pictures, graphs, or tables. These aids are included by the author to emphasize important points.
   D. Read the introductory paragraph and summary paragraph if included in the chapter.
   E. Glance over any key words or questions that might be at the end of the chapter.
   F. Ask yourself: "What do I know about this lesson at this point?'

II. Question
   Go back to the beginning of the chapter and *turn the first heading into a question.* For example, if the first heading was "Remedies for Breach of Contract," your question might be: "What are the remedies for breach of contract?"
   This step will arouse your curiosity, help you bring to mind information already known, and aid you in seeing important points being made, thereby making it easier and quicker to understand what you read.

III. Read
   Read to the end of the first section to answer the question you have just asked.

IV. Recite
   A. Look away from the book, *after reading the first section,* and try briefly to recite, in your own words, the answer to your question. A good way to do this reciting from memory is to jot down brief phrases in outline form; or you can fill in the outline you might have started in the Survey step.
   B. Glance over the section again if you cannot recite the correct information.

Repeat steps II, III, and IV on each succeeding section heading. Turn the next heading into a question, read to answer that question, and recite the answer by saying it out loud or by jotting down brief phrases in outline form.

V. Review
   A. Look over your notes or main headings of the chapter after you have finished the lesson. Try to get an overview of the points and their relationships. Check your memory of the content by reciting the major subpoints under each heading.
   B. Review 24 hours after you have read the lesson. Just refresh your memory of main points and subpoints, since people often forget much after 24 hours. After studying something, this review is very important.
   C. Review a week later.
   D. Review periodically.

In the beginning of the school year go through these steps with the students several times to insure their independence in following the formula. Refer to the steps constantly thereafter during the school year; adapt them to your own lesson procedures.

Wide Reading

Courses in business offer numerous opportunities for wide reading. As such, they broaden background, reinforce vocabulary and other reading skills, and stimulate interest. If the textbook does not include a bibliography of related materials for students (and many do not), you can compile one with the assistance of the school librarian. The bibliography can include materials on careers in business as well as the current news and periodical journals related to your subject. Wide reading in such materials helps students appreciate the relevance of their business studies.

APPLYING READING SKILLS TO INDUSTRIAL ARTS

Reading material in the industrial arts is generally technical, terse, and factual. Much of the content is directions and explanations. It employs a vocabulary peculiar to the tools, equipment, and processes and it closely resembles aspects of scientific and mathematical writing.

The vocational subjects require a wide range of reading skills. Students in vocational classes display a range in reading competence, from severely disabled to superior. Many have reading levels commensurate with the intermediate elementary grades. Therefore, in reviewing the reading levels of students and the nature of the reading material in the vocational subjects, the teacher has a twofold responsibility: one, to teach the processes and manipulative skills of the course and two, to teach the skills required for successful reading of the material.

Johnston states an important reason for students in vocational subjects (such as industrial arts) to be able to read and use the reading material of the courses effectively. She maintains that the course design must not only

> encompass the current prerequisites for a job; but it must also provide students with the capability to continuously upgrade their skills after leaving the

classroom so they may remain competitive in their profession. In our technological world, that means being able to "read how" as well as "to do."[2]

Relevant Reading Skills

1. *Mastering the vocabulary.* The vocabulary includes technical terms; abbreviations and symbols; names of tools, patterns, plans, equipment, and materials; and general words used with a technical meaning pertinent to the subject.
2. *Following directions.* Many of these are minute, complex and must be followed exactly. The directions may include safety instructions, recipes, the use of tools and equipment, and the steps of constructing a project or completing a job.
3. *Reading diagrams, charts, pictures, patterns, cutaways, drawings, and plans.* Parts of this ability will include the recognition and understanding of symbols and the interpretation of the legend or the scale.
4. *Understanding and interpreting technical magazines, catalogs, and journals.* This is an important skill since technology is constantly changing and students must be able to acquire new and related information on their own. In addition to being able to use the index and the Table of Contents, the students must understand the ratios of quantity and quality; to note the pertinent clues to agencies which underwrite, approve, or rate materials and products; to use order forms; and to interpret the analysis of specification descriptions with prices.
5. *Ability to read for main ideas and specific details and then see the interrelationship of the information.*
6. *Ability to read occupational material for information about careers, individual or avocational interests.*
7. *Ability to apply information, such as following a job sheet, planning for a production job, and understanding safety signs.*

Industrial arts and home economics classroom procedures lend themselves well to providing readiness for reading. Student readiness, which is the first step of a content-directed reading lesson, is an intrinsic step in vocational instruction. Tools are demonstrated and materials are handled before the students embark upon their projects. Vocabulary is introduced at these times; diagrams, patterns, and illustrations are studied; and the labelled parts are identified. Processes are guided sequentially so that students develop concepts and skills gradually.

Vocabulary

The vocabulary terms pertinent to the industrial arts are similar to those found in other disciplines. There are basically two types: technical terms peculiar to the field or to a part of it, and common terms with a special

2. Joyce D. Johnston, "The Reading Teacher in the Vocational Classroom," *Journal of Reading* 18, No. 1 (October 1974): 27.

meaning appropriate to the field. Technical terms are most often taught, since such terms probably would be new to students. These terms usually designate materials, equipment, and operations. However, common terms often are not taught because students usually can pronounce them fluently. For instance, students may know the general meaning of *edge, rim, face, cut, file, trim, set, tap, draw, turn, center line,* and many other terms, but they may not know the meaning that pertains to a specific process. Example 13.4, from a textbook on industrial arts drawing and blueprint reading, illustrates common words used technically.

EXAMPLE 13.4

Diagrams show pictorially the technical usage of general terms

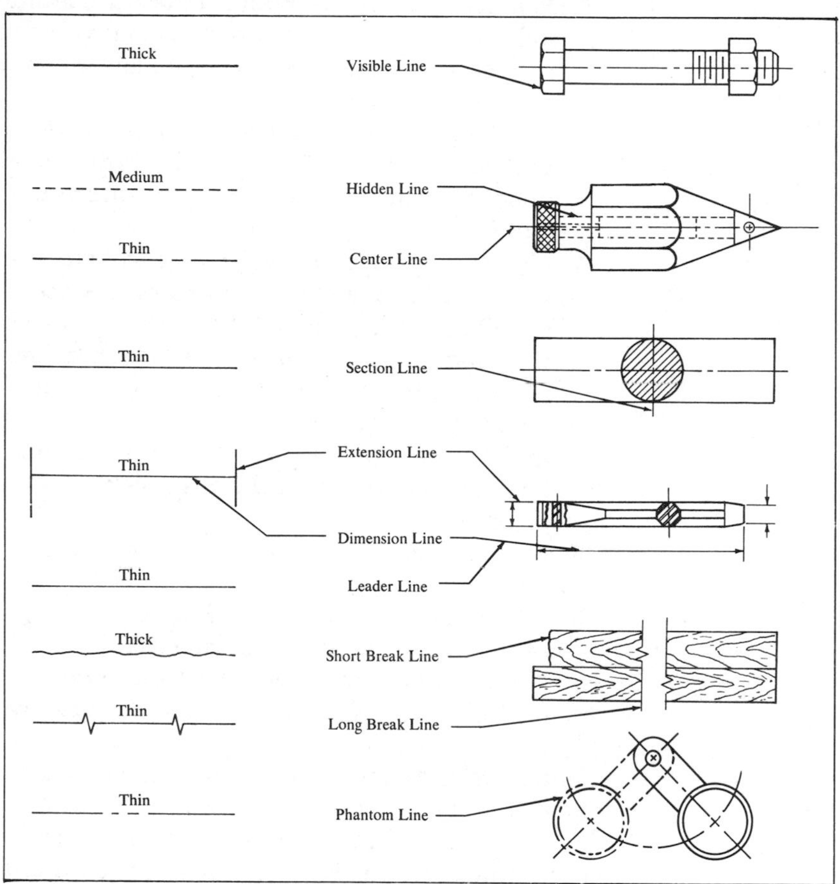

Reprinted from *Industrial Arts Drawing and Blueprint Reading,* p. 17, by Shriver L. Coover, copyright 1961, with permission of Webster/McGraw-Hill (New York).

Suggested techniques for building vocabulary are:

1. As words are needed for specific concepts, teach them as part of the lesson procedure when they can be illustrated with material, tools, equipment, and operation.
2. Show explanatory pictures, properly labelled, of equipment and its parts as well as a schematic drawing to show the process.

3. Label tools and equipment in their appropriate storage places.
4. Construct a class dictionary which a committee of students can update continually as new words are introduced. This may be in addition to each student's individual notebook.
5. Incorporate the vocabulary in student projects. After introducing the term, its concept, and use for an immediate purpose, students should reinforce it as the project is constructed, demonstrated and explained.
6. Use whatever textbook aids are available to help students learn the term: glossary, context, diagrammatic illustrations.
7. Point out the relationships between technical vocabulary and the students' background. For example:

   Toughness (steel)—resiliency of a young tree to withstand pushing with the feet while pulling with the hands
   Hardness (of steel)—similar in nature to the brittleness of glass
   Method of striking (arc welder)—described as to tickle it.
8. Use direct experiences such as films, field trips, patterns, and models.
9. Use comparison charts, such as one showing similar types of cuts (a *chamfer* and a *bevel*).
10. Use oral questioning and specific reading assignments for reinforcement.
11. Organize terms into categories.

Comprehension

Comprehension in industrial arts is similar to comprehension in mathematics and science in that the material is highly factual and new knowledge depends on what has been studied before. Students face several different organizational patterns in the writing on vocational subjects. The patterns occurring in the greatest frequency, either singly or in combination, are *(a)* explanation of a process, *(b)* vocabulary, *(c)* combination of verbal text and diagram, and *(d)* directions. In explanation of a process, the pattern is very similar to a main idea followed by details. The main idea is the process and essential nature; the details usually describe steps of the process, state exceptions and cautions, and give application. The ability to outline or list sequentially is of value here. Structure words indicating sequence or order of importance may be used. In the vocabulary pattern, the meaning is provided along with possible application. Diagrams may accompany the definition. Students must be able to read the diagrams and to note the definition in context. The combination of verbal text and diagrams requires slow, intensive reading. Students must constantly shift their attention between the verbal text and the diagram. Such reading often is required in the explanation of a process. In following directions, the procedures already outlined for doing so would apply. Understanding vocabulary and reading diagrams are components of this skill. See Examples 13.5 through 13.9.

EXAMPLE 13.5

Students must apply the skills in following directions and reading diagrams. Students must know vocabulary:

— General words indicating action.

= Technical words (It is likely that students will know many of these words; however, the teacher should check them with the students.)

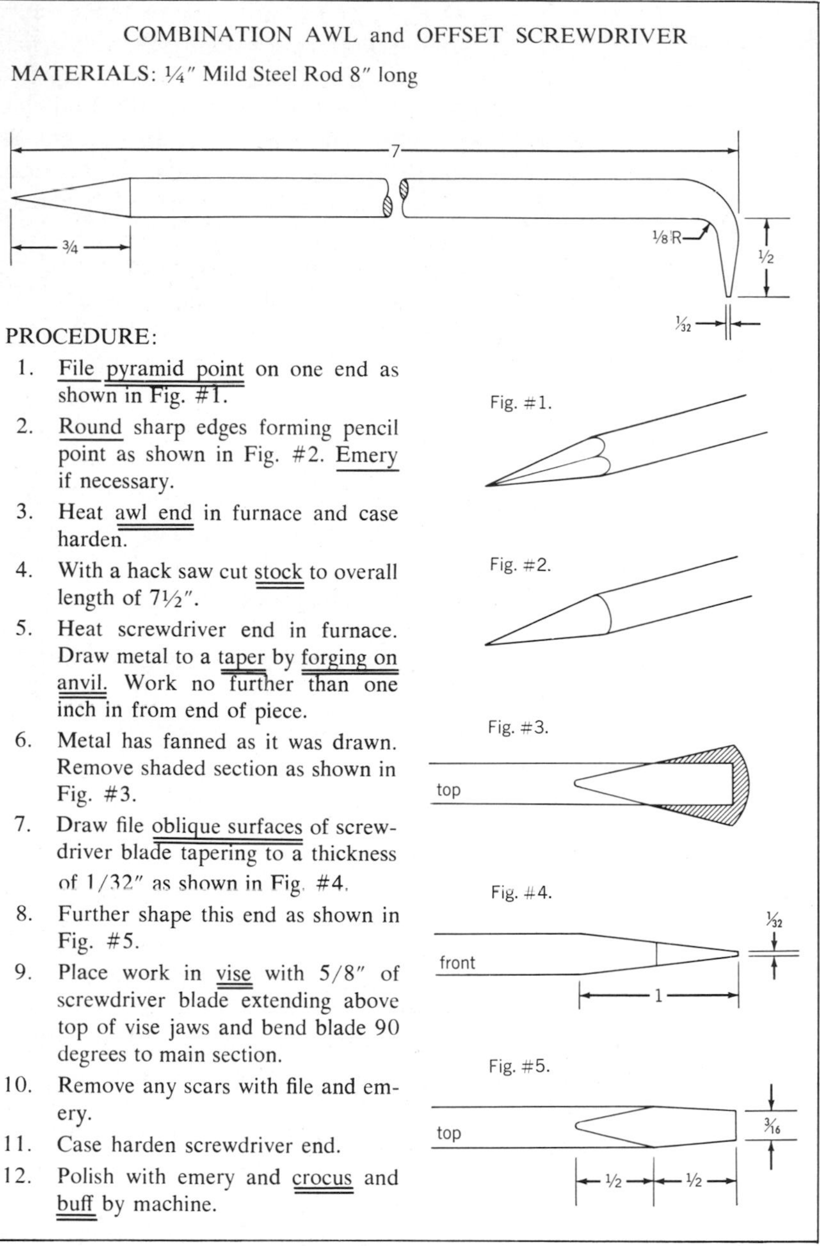

COMBINATION AWL and OFFSET SCREWDRIVER

MATERIALS: ¼″ Mild Steel Rod 8″ long

PROCEDURE:

1. File pyramid point on one end as shown in Fig. #1.
2. Round sharp edges forming pencil point as shown in Fig. #2. Emery if necessary.
3. Heat awl end in furnace and case harden.
4. With a hack saw cut stock to overall length of 7½″.
5. Heat screwdriver end in furnace. Draw metal to a taper by forging on anvil. Work no further than one inch in from end of piece.
6. Metal has fanned as it was drawn. Remove shaded section as shown in Fig. #3.
7. Draw file oblique surfaces of screwdriver blade tapering to a thickness of 1/32″ as shown in Fig. #4.
8. Further shape this end as shown in Fig. #5.
9. Place work in vise with 5/8″ of screwdriver blade extending above top of vise jaws and bend blade 90 degrees to main section.
10. Remove any scars with file and emery.
11. Case harden screwdriver end.
12. Polish with emery and crocus and buff by machine.

Suggested techniques for developing comprehension are:

1. Teach comprehension skills directly as they are needed.
2. Use repeated questioning to elicit specific information.
3. Have students verify information when possible in projects by inspecting, measuring, and testing (evaluate schematic diagrams, patterns and plans found in hobby magazines for accuracy and appropriateness of design, for advanced levels).

EXAMPLE 13.6

Dado Joints:
Types: dado and butt; dado and rabbet. The dado is the cut, or groove, across the grain.
Nature: the dado helps in assembly. Glue is effective. Nails and screws are also used. The depth of the dado should be from 1/3 to 1/2 the thickness of the stock.

Lap Joints:
Types: half lap; cross lap; end lap; middle lap; scarf.
Nature: when the joints are flush, as shown in Fig. 4-3, the lap is cut halfway through each piece. Glue alone is adequate for fastening, assuming that the parts fit well.

Technical vocabulary

Construction (for both lap and dado joints):

1. Mark out the joint accurately, using a knife and try-square.
2. Hold the piece in a vise; clamp on a guide block for the back saw.
3. Make the end cuts first.
4. Using as wide a wood chisel as possible, clean out the waste.
5. For a machined joint, use the dado head on a circular saw.

Diagram pictures types of joints

Fig. 4–2. Dado joints. *Fig. 4–3. Lap joints.*

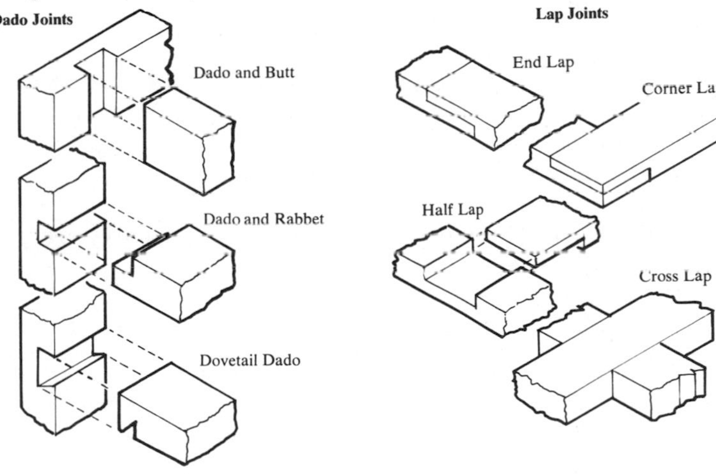

Reprinted by permission from Delmar W. Olson, *Woods and Woodworking for Industrial Arts,* 2nd ed. (Englewood Cliffs, N.J.: Prentice-Hall, 1965), p. 78

4. Alert student to and have them use aids from the organization of the textbook.
5. Use "job sheets" with specific instructions. Discuss with the students to see if they can visualize the process—have them explain it.
6. Have students assemble simple machinery according to printed directions.
7. Have students draw up plans, exchange them, and see if they are clear for other students to follow.

EXAMPLE 13.7

Definition of buffing and polishing compositions with details of the consistency and functions of the parts of the compositions

Basic definition

What the compositions consist of

Contextual definition

Functions of the bonding agent

— Key vocabulary terms

Buffing and Polishing Compositions. Buffing and polishing compositions are gritty substances (mild abrasives) in cake form. They usually consist of a mixture of a bonding agent such as tallow or oil, chemicals, and the grit, which is the cutting agent or abrasive. Many different cutting agents are used, such as emery, crocus, lime, tripoli, and others. ①The bond holds the abrasive in cake form, making it possible for the composition to stick to a revolving buffing wheel. ②At the same time, the material acts as a lubricant during polishing.

Reprinted by permission from Roland R. Fraser and Earl L. Bedell, *General Metal: Principles, Procedures, and Projects,* 2nd ed. (Englewood Cliffs, N.J.: Prentice-Hall, 1962), p. 88.

EXAMPLE 13.8

Precision of meaning required

~~~~ terms—general

—— vocabulary

How to Sketch a Circle

First, lay out the vertical and horizontal center lines as shown in 11–**10**. Sketch in two more lines at 45 degrees. These lines will divide the space into eight equal parts (11–**11**). Place a mark on each line, making the distance the length of the desired radius (11–**12**). Sketch arcs through these points as shown in 11–**13**. Darken the circle (11–**14**).

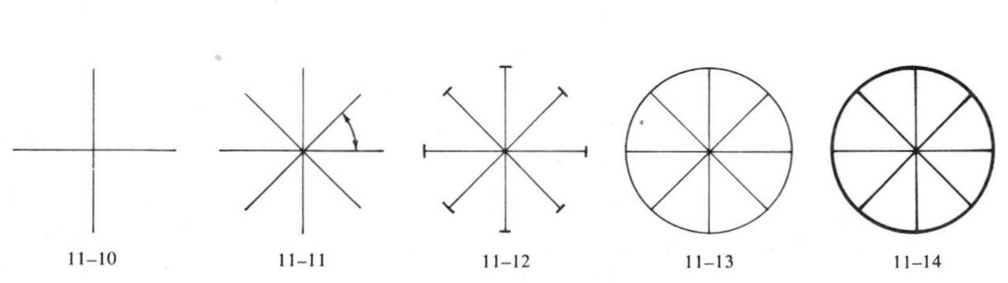

Reprinted from *Industrial Arts Drawing and Blueprint Reading,* pp. 31–32, by Shriver L. Coover, copyright 1961, with permission of Webster/McGraw-Hill (New York).

Guidelines for Classroom Procedure

Even with a large vocabulary load and intensive detailed writing, material in the industrial arts tends to be concrete. Information can be seen, handled, demonstrated, and directly applied. To insure the greatest effectiveness of your lesson, be sure to:

1. Relate the new information to previous learning and experience. Help the students to see the progression of the information and how the ability to apply a new technique is often based on previously acquired skills.
~~~~

EXAMPLE 13.9

Introduction

Type of clamps

Technical vocabulary

Directions

General words as terms
Students must know how to do what each word suggests ——
Other general words ~~~~

CLAMPS AND CLAMPING

Clamps are very handy devices in woodworking. They are used to hold work that cannot be held in a vise. They can supply the necessary pressure for hard gluing. They are used when setting up a project to test the fitting for the pieces before the final assembly. There are many types of clamps, but those used most often are "C" clamps, hand screws, and bar clamps.

"C" Clamps. Shaped like the letter "C," these clamps are used when holding wood face-to-face. Sizes are given as inches of opening.

Hand Screw Clamps. These clamps have wooden jaws capable of applying pressure over a large area. They can hold work when the surfaces are not parallel. Common sizes have openings which range from 6″ to 14″.

Bar Clamps. Bar clamps are for holding large work, especially for gluing stock edge to edge, as in a table top. They are especially helpful in the assembly of furniture. Sizes are given in feet, referring to the maximum opening.

How to Use Clamps for Gluing:

1. Select the best clamps for the job.
2. Get some scrap blocks to place between the clamp jaws and the work, to prevent damage.
3. Assemble the work with the clamps to get the proper adjustments. Then disassemble it, laying the clamps in a convenient order.
4. Apply the glue. Get a buddy to help you assemble and clamp the pieces.
5. Apply enough pressure to draw the parts snugly together but not enough to distort or damage the parts.
6. Wipe off any excess adhesive immediately with a damp cloth. This can save hours of work later on. Let the glue dry at least as long as the directions recommend, before removing the clamps.
7. Apply the adhesive to only as many parts as you can quickly clamp together. Modern adhesives set rapidly and if clamping is delayed, maximum strength will not be obtained.

Reprinted by permission from Delmar W. Olson, *Woods & Woodworking for Industrial Arts,* 2nd ed. (Englewood Cliffs, N.J.: Prentice-Hall, 1965), pp. 29-30.

2. Provide motivation and interest for reading. Student motivation depends largely on being able to read the material competently and seeing the direct application of learning. Fortunately, in industrial arts, the learning leads concretely to application in projects.
3. Provide students with the opportunity to discover how tools and processes work under specific conditions. Student projects provide for discovery, since the students actually do what they have read about and have seen demonstrated. You may also say on occasion, "See how this would work if you did ______" or "Why do you think this direction is included at this point in your project directions?"
4. Study the difficult words and concepts. Be sure the students know the vocabulary before they embark upon their projects and before they are expected to read. Be aware of both technical words and common words used technically.
5. Provide clear and definite directions. Review as necessary how to read directions.
6. Discuss and question for understanding, both before the students read and after they have finished the project. Question their understanding of directions and job sheets before they go ahead. For example: "Why is it necessary to put a double hem on your piece of sheet metal?" Or, in using a power saw, you might ask for the reason for a safety rule, such as "Always stand to one side of the blade and never in line with it" or "Keep the floor around a power saw clean of sawdust."

Wide Reading

There are many opportunities for students to read widely in each field. Catalogs, journals, advertisements, guides, instructional manuals, consumer guides—all require careful reading and at the same time do much to enrich background. Each vocational class should have available a library of related materials. The library is valuable in stimulating interest and in allowing the opportunity to practice the skills of reference reading. Reading reports from consumer guides or about a new process or a new development in equipment introduces a vibrant feeling in class; the material comes alive because it is relevant.

APPLYING READING SKILLS TO HOME ECONOMICS

Home economics is similar to and yet different from the industrial arts, though both would be categorized as vocational subjects. Home economics contains printed material very similar to the industrial arts; students read succinct directions in following a recipe and specific directions for using a dress pattern. Yet in other areas of home economics the printed material resembles social studies or science. Social studies type of material includes such areas as relationships with others (family, friends), citizenship, understanding oneself and career planning, and the history of clothing design. Science-oriented material includes nutrition (which may involve chemistry, depending on the level of the course), consumer education, aspects of health education, child care, grooming, as well as units on clothing and food preparation.

Relevant Reading Skills

1. *Mastering the vocabulary, both technical terminology and common words used technically.* Examples of technical terms are *emulsion, albumen, hydrogenated, bonded knits, interfacing, tricot.* Common terms include *hem, dart, trim, clip, patch, fiber, cotton, detergent, suds.*
2. *Following directions.* Students will need to follow directions especially when using a dress pattern (see Example 13.10) or following a recipe (see Example 13.11).

EXAMPLE 13.10

Technical vocabulary:
- facings
- stay stitching
- seams
- hem

UNIT 4
front and back neck facings

STAY-STITCHING

a.

BACK

FRONT

a–Stitch shoulder seams of facings.
Stitch 1/4" from long unnotched edge.
Press under edge along stitching and stitch.
Clip neck edge to stay-stitching.

b–With RIGHT sides together, pin facing to neck edge, matching centers and seams.
(Facing extends 5/8" beyond center back opening edges.)
Stitch neck edge.
Trim seam; clip curves.

b.

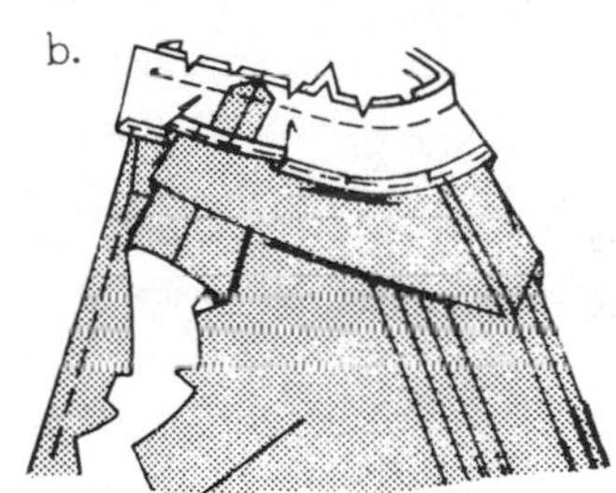

General vocabulary that students must understand is underlined

Following directions
- Steps numbered
- Help students to recognize each individual step

c–Press facing out;
press seam toward facing.

Facing side up, understitch close to seam line thru facing and seam.

c.

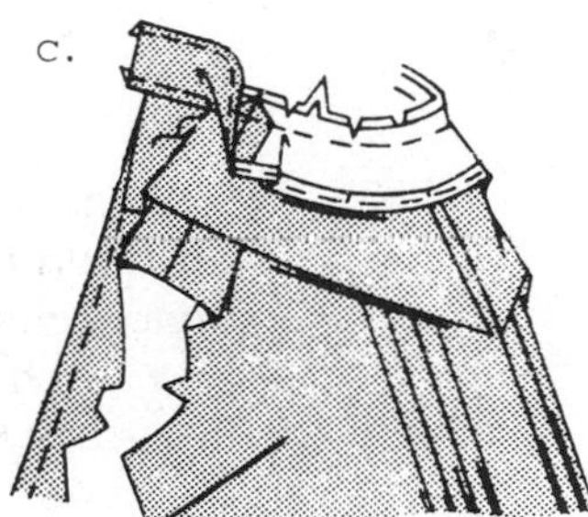

Skills required:
- vocabulary
- following directions
- relating diagrams to directions
- reading diagram

Reprinted by permission from Pattern #8294 *Sewing Direction Sheet* (New York: Simplicity Pattern Co., 1970).

EXAMPLE 13.11

How low?

How slowly?

How many steps are there in this recipe? Have students read the entire recipe to get an overview, then collect equipment and ingredients. Then, do the recipe step by step.

Underlined words are technical terms (all are general words with technical meanings).

Great-Grandma's Devils Food Cake

2½ sq. baking chocolate (unsweetened)
½ c. milk
5 Tbsp. granulated sugar
Cook over low heat, stirring slowly until chocolate is melted and mixture bubbles and thickens. Remove from heat and allow to cool.

1½ c. sugar
½ c. butter or margarine
½ c. milk
½ c. sifted cake flour
3 eggs separated
1½ c. sifted cake flour
2 tsp. baking powder
Cream butter until soft. Add sugar gradually; continue creaming until light and fluffy. Add 3 egg yolks and stir until blended. Add cooled chocolate mixture, stirring until blended. Add milk and ½ c. flour alternately, blending after each addition, beginning and ending with flour. Add 1½ c. flour sifted with baking powder. Stir until blended. Beat egg whites until stiff but not dry. Fold these into the batter. Pour into two greased and floured 9″ layers or one greased and floured 9″ × 13″ baking pan. Bake at 375° (about 25 minutes for layers; 40 minutes for loaf) until centers spring back when touched lightly and cake begins to separate from side of pan. Layers: Let stand on cooling rack in pans for 10 minutes. Then turn out onto racks to finish cooling.
Loaf: Let stand on rack in pan until cool.
Ice with your favorite cold or cooked icing, chocolate or vanilla.

3. *Reading diagrams, charts, patterns, and pictures.* Food value charts, nutrition charts, and spot and stain removal charts are among the myriad charts students need to be able to use. A chart is a categorized way of showing vital information in a succinct form. It may be necessary to review the organization of the chart so that the students see its flow and the ease with which information can be obtained. See the chart "Kinds of Poultry" shown in Example 13.12.

Note how charts are likely to be organized. A chart on spot and stain removal would likely include columns for washable fabrics, and dry cleanable fabrics. Then, within the respective column might be types of stains or spots with directions for removal—candle wax, grass, grease, chewing gum, etc. Or, on a nutrition chart there may be such headings (categories) as the nutrients (carbohydrates, proteins, fats), food sources, body needs, results of shortage upon the body.

4. *Interpreting information from technical magazines, catalogs, and journals.* This involves knowledge of how a book is usually organized, the function of its various parts, how to get information from it, and the logic of its organization. For instance, a book on child care might include categories of information on what a child is, the infant, the child years, discipline, schooling, play, clothing, etc. Students may need instruction in how to use the Table of Contents, index, appendices, study guides within the book, and the general organization of each chapter.
5. *Reading for main ideas and specific details and seeing the relationship between the two.* In this area we come to the style of the expository prose. We are concerned about the pattern of the writing; refer to Examples 13.13 through 13.16.
6. *Reading trade materials for information about careers, individual or avocational interests.* This enables and requires students to do wider reading of supplementary material, a very important habit for

EXAMPLE 13.12

Categorized by type of poultry

KINDS OF POULTRY

TYPE	DESCRIPTION	AGE	WEIGHT	COOKING METHOD
Chicken				
Broiler or Fryer	Very young, either sex, smooth thin skin, tender, small amount of fat	9–12 wks	1½–2½ lb (0.68–1.1 kg)	Broil Fry
Roaster	Fully developed, either sex, young, tender, smooth skin with layer of fat	3–5 mos	2½–4½ lb (1.1–2.04 kg)	Roast
Capon	Young, desexed male bird, very meaty, juicy flesh	less than 8 mos	4–8 lb (1.8–3.6 kg)	Roast
Stewing chicken or Fowl	Mature bird, coarse skin, less tender, well-developed muscle	more than 10 mos	4–6 lb (1.8–2.7 kg)	Braise Simmer Stew
Turkey				
Fryer or Roaster	Young, tender	15–17 wks	4–6 lb (1.8–2.7 kg)	Broil Fry Roast
Roaster	Young, tender	5–6 mos	hen 6–14 lb (2.7–6.4 kg) Tom 9–24 lb (4–10.9 kg)	Roast

From *The World of Food, Third Edition* by Eva Medved, © Copyright, 1981, by Ginn and Company (Xerox Corporation). Used with permission.

EXAMPLE 13.13

Main idea

Why saving buttons is wise

Directions for sewing on buttons

Two items of important information in this paragraph: *(a)* why you should keep a button box and *(b)* directions for sewing on a button

A button box comes in handy. When you throw clothes away or wear them out, save the buttons. Put them in a button box. You will be surprised how often you will have something in the button box you can use. You may even be able to use these buttons when you make something new. These are the steps in sewing on buttons.

1. Choose buttons which are the correct size and color.
2. Use thread to match the button. Use heavy button thread on coats and suits when possible.
3. Stitch several times to attach the button firmly.

From *Living, Learning, and Caring* by Martha Davis Dunn and M. Yvonne Peeler, © Copyright, 1976, by Ginn and Company (Xerox Corporation), and *Lessons in Living* by the same authors, © Copyright, 1970, by Ginn and Company (Xerox Corporation). Used with permission.

enrichment of the skills you have been teaching. Every home economics classroom should have a classroom library of commercial and trade materials available to students. Assignments should incorporate these materials as a way of widening background and providing information toward possible careers. Some textbooks in the field suggest supplementary materials at the end of chapters; these materials should be obtained for the school or classroom library.

7. *Applying the information from labels, pattern guides, and recipes.* Often, current newspaper articles provide supplementary reading of a practical nature. For instance, how to read the labels in the meat case may be a news story. Skill in arithmetic may also be needed. For instance, "A pint of vegetable oil sells for $.79, while a quart of vegetable oil sells for $1.90. Which is the better buy?" If unit price labels are not available, students would need to know how many pints (or better yet, ounces) are in a quart. Such measurements will have to be taught and applied. Vocabularly skills are also necessary because the students will need to know the concept of unit price.

Guidelines for Classroom Procedure

Depending on the type of material, the lesson procedure will vary. The guidelines noted for industrial arts are pertinent in home economics, especially for following recipe and dress pattern directions. But suppose you are going to teach a lesson on buying food. The textbook has about twelve pages devoted to this topic you would like your students to read. How would you proceed? Note these guidelines:

1. Prepare and motivate the students toward the reading by:
   a. Previewing the material. Note what is included by going over the topical headings—such topics as why food costs differ, how to manage a food budget and buy wisely, how to interpret labels, how to judge quality in types of food (fruit, vegetables, meat, etc.). Note how the material is organized.

EXAMPLE 13.14

Main idea

Main idea followed by details

Directions

Note vocabulary

Replace Zippers

When zippers break, you usually have to sew in a different one. To replace a zipper, either buy a new one or use one you have on hand. You can save zippers, as you do buttons. When clothes wear out and the zipper is still good, remove it to use again. Whether you choose a new or used zipper, follow these steps.

1. Remove the broken zipper carefully. Cut the threads with a small pair of scissors or a safety razor blade. Work slowly and carefully so that you do not cut the material or yourself. Note how the zipper was put in. This can help you to figure out how to put the new one in.
2. Press the garment, especially the seam from which the zipper was removed.
3. If the garment is a skirt, slacks, or shorts, you will also have to take out some of the stitching in the waistband.
4. If you are using a new zipper, read the instructions that come with the zipper. Follow the instructions carefully.
5. Follow the old stitching lines for a guide. Use a needle or pin to work the zipper ends under the band at the top. Then, baste the zipper. Next, sew the zipper following the old line of stitching. Finish by pressing carefully.

Lapped Application

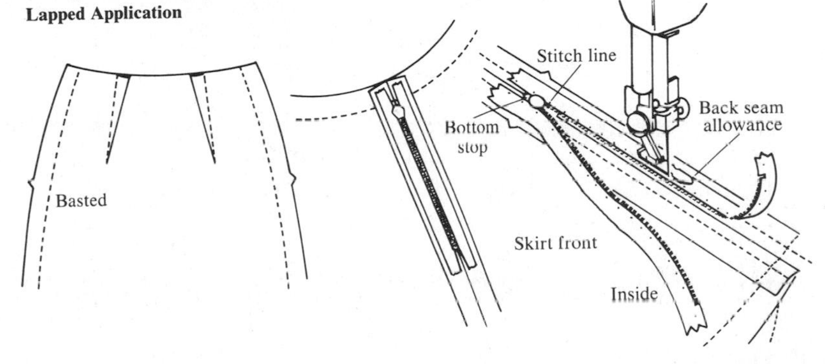

From *Living, Learning, and Caring* by Martha Davis Dunn and M. Yvonne Peeler, © Copyright, 1976, by Ginn and Company (Xerox Corporation), and *Lessons in Living* by the same authors, © Copyright, 1970, by Ginn and Company (Xerox Corporation). Used with permission.

b. Soliciting experiences students have had in judging the quality of food and in reading labels (some secondary students do the family grocery shopping). Help students to relate their experiences to the material of the reading.

c. Pointing out specific vocabulary terms that need to be clarified: grades of meat *(USDA Prime, Choice, Good)* or of eggs (*Grades AA or A, B,* etc). Add to the students' background as necessary. Use pictures or audiovisual aids you have on hand.

d. Developing the information they are to look for as they read. Use questions to guide their reading: Why do food costs differ? What information can you expect to find on a can label? What do you consider when buying meat, poultry, fish, fresh produce?

EXAMPLE 13.15

Paragraph of definition

What is etiquette? There are certain accepted practices for behavior in nearly all situations. These guidelines or rules for behavior can be called etiquette. Some formal situations which call for proper etiquette are weddings, receptions, and graduations. Entertaining guests, attending formal parties, and traveling are easier when there are guides to follow.

Good manners are a part of etiquette. Manners are based on thoughtfulness and consideration for others.

EXAMPLE 13.16

Main idea followed by details

Main idea

Your family history goes back many generations. ①One generation is made up of people who were born at about the same time and are about the same age. [a]You and your friends are one generation, [b]your parents another, and [c]your grandparents still another generation. These people belong to three different generations. ②Your family history involves many places and people, too. [a]Some of these you know from the family stories you hear. [b]Others you know because they are a part of your own life.

2. **Have the students read to find the answers to such questions.**
3. **In discussion of the questions, conjecture with the students the answers to the purpose questions. Ask other questions to underscore the concepts you wish to teach. If there is confusion on a question, you may need to go back to the textbook to note the overall organization (as in the preview) or specific paragraphs. Perhaps a subtopical heading, such as seasons of the year, would be one apparent reason for the differences in produce cost. Students can note such reasons topically by scanning. Alert the students to the author's outline. Or, if there is confusion about why the season could affect the cost, you may need to go back to the paragraph in question and note the reasons given therein.**
4. **Reinforce the printed material by assigning a practical project in which students plan a grocery list for their family. Have them describe how they chose the specific foods in various categories; that**

is, what criteria did they use in buying canned goods, meat, produce, bread, and so on? How did they figure the unit price on each of the various items? A practical application of a lesson incorporates all that has been read and discussed. The student has the opportunity to practice a fundamental routine human activity—buying groceries. Such a project usually clinches the students' grasp of the concepts.

SUMMARY

An industrial arts department head once observed, "Many people do not think that we need to be concerned with how well a student reads because they think that all the student does is work on projects. This is wrong! Our students must be competent in reading manuals and directions and in understanding the appropriate scientific principles. We are teaching students to be independent in obtaining and understanding the information they need."

QUESTIONS AND PROBLEMS FOR YOUR OWN CLASSROOM

For readers who are training to be teachers:

1. In your subject, determine for each lesson the technical vocabulary words the students must know. List also the general words used in a technical sense.
2. Compile a bibliography of references and trade books pertinent to your subject which you can have the students read for enjoyment and enrichment.
3. In your subject, prepare diagrams and other graphic aids and plan how you would help your students in using them effectively.

For readers who are teaching:

1. Have your students write a set of directions for doing some project. Discuss and evaluate the clarity of the directions.
2. Discuss with your students how they think reading applies to your subject. Make a list of the skills with them.
3. Have your students compile a pictorial dictionary of technical terms they must know for your subject.
4. Review the vocabulary of a unit of study in your field, and group the terms in categories.
5. Review your planned curriculum for a year's time and note what you hope to teach and accomplish. Then determine where the various aspects of the language arts—listening, speaking, reading, and writing—will be emphasized. Also, show the specific reading skills and determine where each skill would be emphasized. A suggested format might include topic headings such as *month, area, basic understanding, language arts aspects,* and *reading skills.*

SELECTED REFERENCES

Lamberg, Walter J., and Lamb, Charles E. *Reading Instruction in the Content Areas.* Chicago: Rand McNally, 1980.

Roe, Betty D.; Stoodt, Barbara D.; and Burns, Paul C. *Reading Instruction in the Secondary School.* Chicago: Rand McNally, 1978.

Thomas, Ellen Lamar, and Robinson, H. Alan. *Improving Reading in Every Class.* Boston: Allyn & Bacon, 1972.

These references all provide classroom procedures and activities.

CHAPTER 14

Applying Reading Skills to Foreign Languages, Art, Music, and Physical Education

OVERVIEW

Reading instruction should permeate the secondary school curriculum, for each subject requires an understanding of language structure and usage. Many reading techniques and skills are common to all of the subject areas. Thus, we should help students appreciate the value of language mastery in all subjects. Also, students need to read widely in materials related to each subject for reinforcement, enrichment of background, and career information. In courses where students mostly are involved in projects and activities—in *doing* rather than just reading—we must approach the teaching of reading with caution. Students come to such courses to *do;* thus, we must not force reading upon the students. Reading and doing must be complementary aspects of the learning process.

This chapter discusses the application of reading instruction in foreign languages, art, music, and physical education.

Questions

Consider these questions before you read further:

1. What importance do you place on reading instruction as it relates to your subject? What do you see as your responsibility?
2. How do you incorporate reading instruction into your subject area?

APPLYING READING SKILLS TO FOREIGN LANGUAGES

Reading skills in foreign languages largely are those skills required in English classes. Not only do the students read to get ideas and understandings, but they also have the added dimension of learning to decode another language. There is a greater emphasis on the sounds of the new language as well as on the acquisition of a new vocabulary. Therefore, a prerequisite to both understanding content and thinking in a foreign language is learning a different phonetic system.

If students are learning one of the Western languages such as German, French, Spanish, or Italian, the graphemes are similar to those of English, though pronunciations will likely differ. However, in Russian, many of the eastern European languages, and Oriental languages, students must learn an entirely new alphabet. High school students of these languages are in a position similar to that of first graders learning to read English; even first graders would be able to use some English words in both speaking and listening.

In addition to the skills and techniques needed to decode and comprehend English, several other skills apply, including: *(a)* to read and memorize the vocabulary of a foreign language, which requires associating a foreign word or phrase with its English equivalent; *(b)* to read (that is, translate) a selection in a foreign language; *(c)* to comprehend and appreciate the common idiomatic expressions in a foreign language; *(d)* to comprehend and apply explanations and examples related to the grammar and the construction of a foreign language; *(e)* to read with comprehension English descriptions that deal with the people and the history of the country; and *(f)* to think in a foreign language while reading, writing, speaking or hearing it. (This last skill is especially fostered by language laboratory programs in the schools.)

Since the skills required in reading a foreign language are much the same as those for reading English, the scope of the students' *vocabulary* is of fundamental importance. The various techniques of recognizing the meaning of the word are used—wide related reading, contextual usage, dictionary, and structural analysis.

Suggestions for Vocabulary Study

Using context to note the meaning of a word is as important in a foreign language as it is in English. We know that the relationship of a word to the remainder of a sentence (indeed sometimes to an entire paragraph) can determine its whole meaning or the application of a meaning. We know also that students' experiences with the word govern the meaning they recognize. For example, idioms and proverbs can cause difficulty in translation, because they seldom translate literally. In English, if we say that someone is *hung up,* we do not mean that the person is literally hanging somewhere, but rather that he or she is presently at the frustrating point of being unable to complete a task. Thus, we have expressions that if translated literally would be quite awkward and even nonsensical. Each language has a number of these expressions.

Each student should keep a notebook dictionary of new words from reading as well as of troublesome words which he or she finds difficult to remember. The notebook dictionary should list the word, its contextual meaning, and other dictionary meanings. Memorizing vocabulary, using words in both oral and written sentences, and repeating the meanings and examples of usage from memory are time-honored and valuable techniques.

One of the best features of most lanugage programs today is the emphasis on *dialogue*. Nearly every textbook starts a new chapter with dialogue that students are to learn. Records and language laboratories particularly bolster the oral use of foreign languages. When secondary students begin to learn a foreign language, the effort involved is tantamount to that of primary children beginning to read. We know that primary children must have the opportunity to listen to and use the oral form of English in order to become familiar with the sounds of English. They must learn to note the similarities and differences among the sounds: such is also the case with a foreign language; as every language teacher knows, direct instruction is necessary with some of the sounds that differ from those in English.

Students should note both similarities and differences between English and the language under study. The similarities can center upon common roots, similar sounds (phonemes), and common or similar spelling (graphemes). Note also any words used in English that have come from the language, such as *blitz* (German) or *gazpacho* (Spanish). Investigation of common roots stemming from either Latin or Greek and a comparison of prefixes, suffixes, and inflectional endings also can be helpful.

Flash cards are useful for developing quick recognition. Usually the English word is on one side and the new word is on the other, sometimes accompanied by a picture to help students arrive at its meaning.

An interesting activity for vocabulary study is to use the cloze procedure. Give the students a passage with the new words deleted. List the words randomly beside the passage. This exercise encourages students to rely on the context.

Suggestions for Improving Comprehension

Dealing with the sounds of a language involves a concern with the surface structure. But learning a language also requires mastering its grammar, which in turn leads to *meaning*—the deeper structure. You can create, with the help of the class, a comparative chart showing similarities and differences between English and the foreign language. The chart can be updated throughout the year as different aspects of the language are studied.

Have students experiment with forming sentences and seeing the syntactic structure. Start with a simple noun–verb pattern and have them expand upon it. Both English and the foreign language use this basic structure; however, as sentences expand using various modifiers, note that the order of words may differ from English. Advanced students may even experiment with transformations—different ways, to express the same idea.

Comprehension skills and techniques for foreign languages are the same as those for English. Similarly, we are concerned with understanding. Point out to students that they will be involved with the same basic skills, with the organization of the information, and with relating to the information. One interesting procedure is to have the students compare and contrast the culture of their country and the country whose language they are studying. Discussions can be sparked by speculating about why certain similarities and differences have developed. Students may begin to understand that to know a language is to learn about a people.

Lesson procedure when reading a foreign language follows the same steps as in English. However, the lesson procedure may differ markedly, certainly in the beginning, because of the emphasis needed upon oral usage, vocabulary, and syntax. For instance, the lesson may begin with a dialogue. If the dialogue contains ideas about customs of the country, it will be necessary to establish such background. Discussing the American version of such customs would give additional background. New vocabulary should be pointed out, as well as forms of the word in accordance with its syntactical placement in the sentence. Emphasize speaking and listening first, then written exercises. Finally, lead the students to devise their own dialogue pertinent to the information.

Later, when the students do not need basic vocabulary and syntax, they can read for reinforcement of the skills and for general meaning. Of particular importance is preparing the students for reading the selection—background pertaining to the setting, history, and so on essential for a complete understanding and appreciation of the selection. Students reading a selection in a foreign language also need to know their purpose for reading and to preview.

APPLYING READING SKILLS IN ART

The reading skills relate to art instruction in three ways. Students need to *(a)* acquire the meanings of technical terms, *(b)* read and follow directions accurately for performing technical operations such as mixing paints and other processes, and *(c)* read biographies and materials on the description, history, and criticism of works of art. The first two skills and the type of subject content are similar to those found in science and the vocational subjects, such as industrial arts. The third skill and type of content relate closely to social studies.

Most art classes are characterized by hands-on activity rather than passive reading. The teacher demonstrates, showing the process, and then works individually with the students as they develop their own work. Many art classes do not have textbooks or other printed materials. The amount of reading required in these courses also depends upon the goals set forth in the curriculum guide. If the only goal to have students experience working in various art media and processes, then little reading is required. On the other hand, if the goal is to guide students toward independence in using various media and executing different processes, reading will be required.

Students in art classes have a broad range of capabilities. Superior students often elect to take art because they are interested in developing a pleasurable activity. Poor readers often choose art because they can be successful without having to read well. (Indeed, achieving success is critical in developing a positive self-concept.) The alert and innovative teacher can do much to foster growth as well as interest in reading. The art teacher can capture interest and lead students into supplementary reading about various art media. Rather than teaching them directly, the teacher may introduce skills and techniques as necessary as means to an end. Further, the art teacher operates in the affective mode. As students discover that their understanding and expertise in art are growing, their attitude toward reading will likely become more positive.

Suggested Activities

1. Build a classroom library of art books on art techniques, biography, and history. Since these books can be expensive, used book stores are a good place to shop first. Art sections from magazines and material from museums and similar sources will provide good supplements. One art teacher was able to interest students in the art process of batik. They wanted to know where the process originated, what materials had been used, and what some of the early designs were like. Fortunately, she had references available that provided this information. Even some of her poor readers were interested and often reached for the materials.
2. Teach students how to follow directions. One art teacher found it helpful to demonstrate and then brainstorm with the students about how to write directions for a process, and she then recorded it on the blackboard. Another teacher found that if she gave only the principal steps of a process, the students would be required to consult materials for the details. For example, the teacher could demonstrate how to use a potter's wheel but not explain the speed of turning or the pressure of the hands. Students then could consult references in the classroom as well as experiment to develop their own technique.
3. Have the students evaluate their work in various ways. One teacher asked the students to write advertising copy which an art store might use. Another teacher had the students mount an exhibit in the school and provide explanatory brochures, such as museums do, to accompany the exhibits. In fact, one innovative teacher had her students mount an exhibit in which the works were for sale. The proceeds from the sale were used to buy art books for the classroom library. These activities made demanding use of reading skills. Advertising, which required close attention to word usage and to the effect (connotation) of certain words, was an excellent lesson in vocabulary. Mounting exhibits with accompanying brochures led the students into accuracy of description, history of a technique, and the significance of the technique in art. Students had to read to get this information. In the exhibit of works for sale, the teacher noted that one of the best pieces was by a poor reader. His work sold well and she noted a heartening improvement in his self-concept. More directly, she observed, "He began to consult my art books more and more, reading from many which I thought were too difficult for him."
4. Give individual help to the student in reading. Since the art class is largely one where students are actively involved, the teacher is free to go about the class and give individual help on a technique. This can be

done for reading if a student consulting an art reference needs clarification of terms and discussion of the meaning to insure comprehension. Even paragraph analysis can be used: ask what the student thinks the main point of a paragraph is and then say, "O.K., now there are three specific details mentioned. What are they?"

5. Find out the students' reading levels so that you can direct them to appropriate materials. The guidance department or the reading consultant for your school may supply these levels.
6. Have the students keep a notebook of technical terms, showing the syllabication of the term, its meaning, and its application to a process if appropriate.

Patterns of Writing

In classes of art history and appreciation, we find material which is like social studies. Material often is historical, showing movements and the reasons for them and requiring background for complete understanding. Questions, problems, and activities in art books also are similar to those in social studies materials. For example, review questions tend to be factual, asking *what, who, why,* and *how*. Example 14.1 is an example from an art book that contains writing similar to that of social studies.

EXAMPLE 14.1

Introduction to Chapter

Transition sentence recalling subject of prior chapter

Causes of change

Remainder of paragraph states effects of change on art and artists

Neither paragraph has stated main idea

Topic of current chapter

Revolution and Revivals

When religion and kingship ceased to command the allegiance of Western peoples, the end was near for the Renaissance-Baroque era. Political revolutions in America and France soon launched a new age of rapid and violent change, eventually producing our own modern world of science, mass industry, giant cities, and faster-than-sound travel. The ideas and feelings that shaped Renaissance-Baroque art have little strength today, so little that almost every important painter or sculptor has abandoned Renaissance habits of representation. The picture surface has ceased to be a window into space. Painted and sculptured images have ceased to be convincing likenesses of the people and things in the world around us. Artists have cast off the framework of traditional authority; they choose their own messages and invent their own styles. No limits are imposed upon them. This utter freedom exhilarates them—but it frightens them, too.

In our time, stylistic changes come so fast that what is new today is old tomorrow. Styles by the dozen, old and new, exist together. During the first century of the modern era, change came more slowly. There was a great clashing of styles, each with its set of dedicated champions. The styles were not exactly new, for eighteenth-century style was continued and earlier styles were revived (revival of past style was an important characteristic of the earlier modern period). But they were not the same old styles, either, for they were filled with the new spirit we call Romanticism.

Reprinted by permission from H. W Janson, *History of Art for Young People*. Harry N. Abrams, Inc., Publisher (New York: American Book Company, 1971), p. 277.

APPLYING READING SKILLS TO MUSIC

Music, as a subject, divides into five areas that pertain to clusters of reading skills. The first involves the ability to read musical notation and to interpret music symbols. Usually, at the high school level little is taught in this area except to recognize various symbols and to distinguish one from the other. For instance, the students are taught the difference between a whole note and a half note and they are taught such musical symbols as the clef sign, key signature, rests, and so on. However, little is done to help them read music as they would read print—for meaning. That is, students are not taught how to imagine the melody from the printed representation of the music. In practice, then, the first area of music instruction resembles the symbolic aspect of mathematical vocabulary—the recognition of the parts and symbols that comprise a musical score.

Reading music, similar to learning mathematics, is like learning a new language code. Whereas in mathematics there are symbols such as ⧁, ⧀, as well as the arabic numbers themselves, in music there are numerous symbols such as < >, 𝄞

and time signatures of 6/8, 3/4, 2/4, and so on. The ability to read a musical score depends largely upon understanding such symbols. Involved here also is a specific technical vocabulary of words, such as *octave, clef,* and *diatonic scale*. However, there are a number of common words used technically, such as *note, rest,* and *scale* (on an elementary level), and *major chord, minor chord, augmented fifth* (on a more advanced level).

Further, the style of writing describing and explaining musical notation and its scientific basis is terse and succinct, such as is found in mathematics and physics. Numerous diagrams usually accompany the text. For comprehension, students not only need to read carefully and intensively for specific information (guided by questions you assign) and to be able to interpret the diagrams, but they also need a demonstration of the information to add concreteness. Some students may be able to demonstrate on an instrument.

The second area of music encompasses a technical vocabulary, usually consisting of words from Italian (such as *andante, allegro, forte,* and *panissimo*). Knowledge of this technical vocabulary also helps students to interpret a music score in both vocal and instrumental music. Other technical words may include various forms of music, such as *sonata, ragtime, folk music, secular music,* and so on. Names of instruments are included in the technical category, such as *marimba, bassoon,* and *glockenspiel.* Musical vocabulary can be categorized easily. For example:

Woodwind Section	*Forms of Music*	*Types of Bands*	*Types of Chords*
flutes	sonata	concert	tonic
clarinets	symphony	jazz	dominant
oboes	oratorio	swing	arpeggio

EXAMPLE 14.2

Category

The important types of compositions in this period were:

(1) *the Suite*	a series of dance movements.
(2) *the Fugue*	a procedure in which a theme is presented, generally in three or four voices successively, and developed through the principle of imitative writing.
(3) *the Mass*	a large composition which uses a Biblical text and is written for chorus, soloists, and accompaniment.
(4) *the Oratorio*	combined vocal and instrumental music, based upon a serious text and offering opportunities for vocal soloists.
(5) *the Concerto grosso*	a work featuring a group of instrumental soloists (generally three), contrasted against a larger mass of orchestral instruments.
(6) *the Orchestral overture* . .	The *French overture* consists of a slow, richly harmonic section, followed by a lively section, and concluded with a return to the material of the opening section. The *Italian overture* reverses the order of movements—fast, slow, and fast.

The categories can be numerous, and they help students to note the structure of the information. Example 14.2 presents a categorization of musical terms from a textbook.

Musical theory is the third area. Usually, only a small number of students who wish to specialize in it embark on this more advanced level of music. This aspect of musical instruction is not taught in all high schools but is taught in some large city and suburban schools. We have already noted music's similarity to mathematics and to physics. The whole science of sound involves understanding sound waves, vibrations, semitones, and harmonics. Many of the features can be demonstrated and even experimented with, just as in science and mathematics. For example, you can demonstrate how to make a note high or low by adjusting the tautness of a string. Also, music textbook diagrams often are similar to those in physical science (see Example 14.3).

Phrase, idea, theme—three important concepts in music—are words much used in English classes. Similarities between English and music can be noted on a comparative chart. Ideas from linguistics can be applied also as they relate to function *(rests)*, stress *(forte, pianissimo)*, and intonation *(pitch)*. Linguistics applies to the speaking voice; similar ideas apply to the singing voice and the playing of musical instruments. For instance,

EXAMPLE 14.3

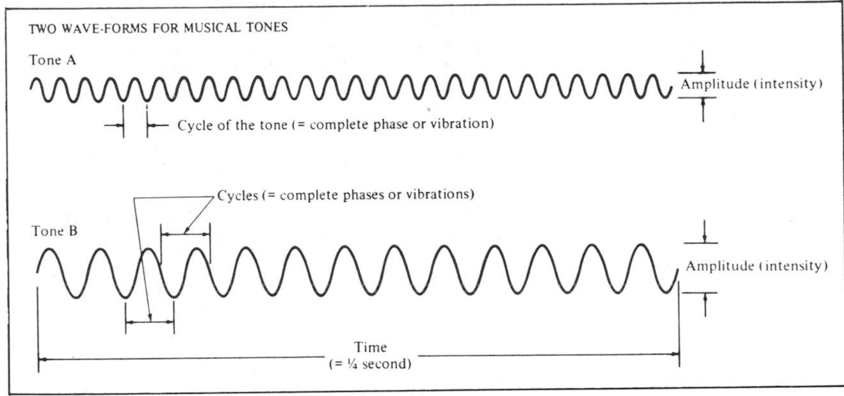

Reprinted by permission from William Thomson, *Introduction to Music as Structure* (Reading, Mass.: Addison-Wesley, 1971), p. 112.

appropriate speed and rhythm are as important to an instrumentalist or a vocalist as to a reader. Likewise, there are phrase and thought units in music just as there are in written and oral language.

The fourth area of music as a subject includes the type of reading required in English and the social studies: reading for background and enrichment to investigate musical history and the lives of composers. Historical content, biographical material, and description of musical forms typify the writing in this area. The purpose of this type of information is to increase the students' overall appreciation of music. The skills needed to read such material include noting *(a)* chronology, *(b)* cause and effect (why certain types of music were written in various periods of history, or why a composer composed a particular type of music), *(c)* types of music and musical forms, and *(d)* descriptions of a historical period. Much of this can be seen in Example 14.4.

The fifth area involves musical criticism. Current newspaper writing about musical events includes comments by music editors and critics. Obviously such material is written with a specific point of view. Readers must evaluate the criticism just as they would read critically in any subject. They will need to check out the qualifications and point of view of the writer, the use of words to present a specific impression, as well as the writer's grasp of the subject.

Lesson procedure in music classes to guide students' reading of printed material follows the same guidelines as other content areas:

1. Establish the background of information and knowledge of fundamental terms before students read.
2. Relate the new material to the students' background of experience and information.
3. Establish clear purposes of what they are to get from their reading.
4. Show students the relationship of the material to the other disciplines so they can see the similarities in material type and skill application.
5. When necessary, analyze the reading material with the students to help them see the author's organization of information.
6. Urge the students to read widely through special projects, your enthusiasm, and a classroom library of related materials.

EXAMPLE 14.4

General description of Baroque music

The Baroque gave equal importance to vocal and instrumental forms. The music of this period is characterized by melodies which were elaborately ornamented and expanded to great heights in a continuous flow. Because of the new attention paid to instrumental music, the (1) rhythm of the Baroque is dynamic, accented, and driving. Although the polyphonic technique of writing was still employed, (2) the importance of a single melody and the movement of strong harmonies came into being. (3) The levels of volume did not change within a particular portion of the music; a passage was uniformly loud or soft, giving sharp contrast to the music. (4) The instrumental style did not include subtle blending of instrumental color; it allowed for only one group of instruments to be involved in a particular portion of the music at a time.

Introductory sentence
Main idea
4 details

Purposes to listen for

Goal: to increase knowledge, resulting in greater application

As you listen to the fugue, try to fix the initial theme in your mind; follow the several entrances of it and then notice how skillfully Bach develops the material. Also, notice the rhythmic structure of the theme: two short notes followed by three notes which are twice the duration of the first two.

Fugue II

Biographical information

George Frideric Handel (1685–1759) is another musical giant of the Baroque period. Born in Halle, Germany, and started on a brilliant career in law, he turned to music, his first real love. Unlike Bach, Handel traveled a great deal, with the result that he became a rather well-known figure during his lifetime. He was a fine organist, choir director, and composer, and held positions as musician to the court and director of the opera. Handel did more to establish the oratorio as a major work than anyone in his time. *Messiah,* the most famous of his oratorios, was written in less than a month's time, and it is said that during its London performance the King of England was so moved by the "Hallelujah Chorus" that he stood on his feet, causing everyone in the audience to repeat the gesture. Rising during the singing of that chorus became a tradition which is still practiced today.

You will enjoy listening to the following parts:

Overture
"Comfort ye, my people"

APPLYING READING SKILLS TO PHYSICAL EDUCATION AND HEALTH

The physical education teacher also can be involved with the teaching of reading. Gentile lists the general reading skills that are pertinent in physical education classes:

1. Reading to follow a sequence of directions and relating these to diagrams and charts.
2. Understanding specific vocabulary and terms of multiple meaning.
3. Making inferences and assumptions based on diagrammed plays.
4. Reading to understand the history of a sport or game.
5. Reading sports articles in newspapers or magazines.[1]

You can readily note the similarity of these skills to those in social studies and science, particularly. Let's look more deeply into three areas in which physical education teachers are involved. First, if they teach classes in health, there is scientific writing in textbooks, pamphlets, and materials pertinent to current sociological and health problems. The content of a textbook on health education very closely parallels units on human development in a biology course: growth toward maturity, good food habits, sexual understanding, oral health, vision, and hearing. In addition, sociological problems dealing with alcohol, tobacco, and drug usage are usually investigated. Health texts are organized topically similar to science texts, with pictures, diagrams, and technical vocabularly terms (such as *allergies, cardiovascular, malocclusion*). Consult the chapter on reading in science for suggestions in helping the students read the material. Examples 14.5, 14.6, and 14.7 illustrate the similarity between health textbooks and textbooks in science, particularly biology.

Other reading material in physical education may include textbooks on playing games, with the bulk of the material containing terms, rules, and techniques of playing specific sports (see Examples 14.8–14.10). As in art, most classes have the students actually *playing* the game rather than reading about it—and this is what the students want to do! However, if students are to become independent, they need to know how to read succinct, specific directions. This kind of reading is very similar to the reading required in industrial arts and science. Games also involve a technical vocabulary that the students must be able to read and apply. For instance, in lacrosse, some technical terms are *center draw, cradling, goal,* and *crease*. Physical education teachers can chart the technical terms of the games they are describing and demonstrating. They can point to the term when they use it and write out the meaning succinctly or diagram it on a portable blackboard.

The physical education teacher usually has a strong rapport with students and knows them well as individuals, not just academically. A mutual feeling of trust and a broader knowledge of the students place the physical education teacher in a prime position to motivate, counsel, and direct students toward improvement in reading.

---

1. Lance M. Gentile, *Using Sports and Physical Education to Strengthen Reading Skills* (Newark, Del.: IRA, 1980), pp. 5, 8–65.

EXAMPLE 14.5

7-1 Caring for your skin

Objectives

General Describe basic skin care, including prevention and treatment of some common problems.

Specific 1. Describe the structure and functions of the skin.

2. Explain the causes of and ways to deal with dry and oily skin, acne, body odor, and some other common skin problems.

3. Explain how overexposure to the sun can harm skin and how such harm can be prevented.

Diagram

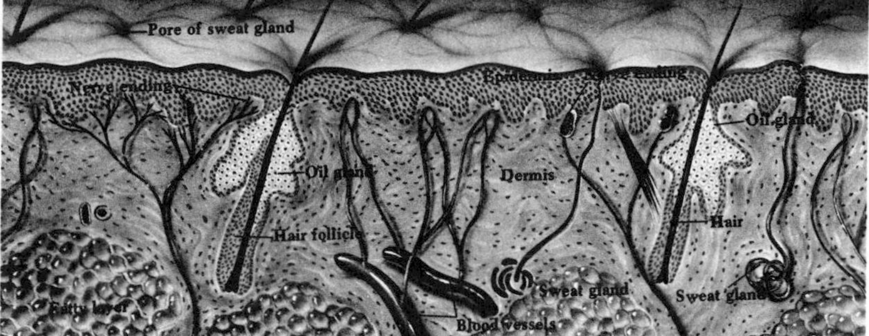

a

Paragraph pattern is mainly main idea followed by detail

Main ideas are underlined

Your skin is the covering of your body. Do you ever think about all the things your skin does for you? It protects body tissues from disease-causing organisms, from physical abuse, and from water loss. Your skin helps control body temperature and aids in removing wastes from your body. The skin contains nerve endings that receive sensations of pressure, pain, temperature, and texture. So your skin is something you want to take very good care of.

b

In two paragraphs a question is asked that implies the main idea (paragraph *a* and *b*)

Questions are used to stimulate students' thinking while reading.

Did you know your skin has two layers? The inner layer, called the *dermis,* is made of living cells. The health of this inner layer depends on oxygen and nutrients brought to it by circulating blood. The outer layer of skin is called the *epidermis.* Dead cells at the top of the epidermis are continually being scaled off and replaced by cells from below.

The health of the epidermis depends largely on cleanliness. A general rule for keeping the skin clean is to wash it at least once a day with soap and water. Yet there are times when this general routine is not enough. Sometimes special problems arise that require speciai care.

Dry skin and oily skin

The amount of moisture in your skin has a lot to do with how it looks and feels. Moisture is held in the skin by ***sebum,*** an oily substance produced by oil glands. Oil glands are located all over the body, except on the palms of the hands and the soles of the feet. Oil glands are most numerous on the face, scalp, chest, neck, shoulders, and upper back.

When the skin on your hands or other areas is too dry, it may feel tight, sore, rough, and flaky. Dry skin may even crack and bleed. Dry skin can be the result of exposure to wind, cold, or sun. It can also be caused by use of soaps or detergents, frequent

Point out that the pores are the openings for ducts that begin in the sweat glands. Pores are not oil-gland outlets, as many people believe.

Skin, Hair, and Nails **147**

EXAMPLE 14.6

Chart

Questions to stimulate students to relate the information to themselves

Discuss these with the student—why these items are helpful

activities require in order to gain weight.

You can lose weight if your intake of Calories is less than the Calories you use. Here are some ways to safely reduce and still maintain a balanced diet.

- Take smaller portions than you usually do.
- Eat more slowly. This allows time for your body to let you feel satisfied.
- Avoid taking second helpings.
- Eat four or five small meals rather than three large meals so you don't feel so hungry between meals.
- Leave out the extras. For instance, eat a baked potato without sour cream or ice cream without topping.
- Exercise regularly.
- Don't take over-the-counter reducing drugs.

You should realize that there are no pills or other special products that will control weight. You simply cannot buy weight control. You have to practice it. You need all six kinds of nutrients all the time, but your caloric intake must match your energy needs.

Questions to think about

1. How have your food needs changed in the last five years? What changes do you anticipate in the future?
2. Do you know anyone who has lost weight safely? How did that person do it?
3. Why do you think fad diets are so appealing to many people?
4. What advice would you give to a person who needed to gain weight?

for additional information. Students could make out sample menus following each diet and evaluate the nutrients each provides.

Nutrition and You **121**

EXAMPLE 14.7

Factual review

Chapter Review Test

True or false?

1. People often choose foods based on where they live, what they can afford, and what their grandparents ate.
2. Emotions usually have nothing to do with the foods people choose to eat.
3. Food is oxidized in the cells, giving off energy and heat.
4. Certain enzymes, proteins produced in the body, speed digestion of foods.
5. Pleasant surroundings at mealtime can aid digestion.
6. Some uses of food additives are to enhance flavor and color and to preserve freshness.
7. Calories are nutrients that promote growth.
8. Undernutrition affects only a person's physicial health.
9. A single food, such as milk, usually provides only one kind of nutrient.
10. Carbohydrates and fats regulate body functions.
11. Calcium and phosphorus are essential during periods of growth to build bones and teeth.
12. Vitamins and minerals provide fuel for energy.
13. Choosing a diet from the Basic Four Food Groups assures you all essential nutrients except water.
14. Digestive upsets are often caused by strong emotions.
15. Adults need more protein-rich foods than adolescents.

Choose the best answer.

16. Vitamin C is found in all the following except
    a. potatoes b. berries c. peppers d. meats
17. Which are complete proteins?
    a. fruit b. cereals c. meats d. fats
18. Which snack provides energy and protein?
    a. peanuts b. chocolate c. carrots d. apples
19. If you eat foods containing about as many Calories as you use, you will
    a. gain weight c. use stored fat
    b. maintain your weight d. lose weight
20. Most digestion takes place in the
    a. small intestine b. mouth c. stomach d. liver

1. true
2. false
3. true
4. true
5. true
6. true
7. false
8. false
9. false
10. false
11. true
12. false
13. false
14. true
15. false
16. d
17. c
18. a
19. b
20. a

EXAMPLE 14.8

Paragraphs showing a combination of definition and description of how to accomplish the types of plays

Definitions are underlined

Diagrams help to illustrate the plays

KICKING

A. Instep Kick

B. Inside Foot

C. Half Volley

D. Full Volley

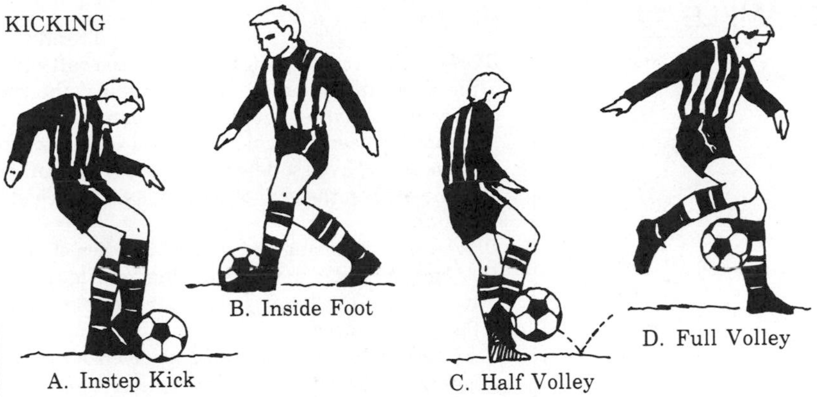

Fig. 2. Kicking: A, in-step kick; B, inside-foot; C, half volley; D, full volley

Heel Kick. Kicking with the heel is used for passing backwards. It is good only for short distances.

Volleying. Once you have a certain amount of power and accuracy in kicking a stationary ball and a moving ground ball, practice kicking the ball just as it rises from the ground (half volley) and also in the air (full volley) (Fig. 2C and D). The important things to remember on the half volley is to be over the ball, to keep your eye on the ball, and to kick at it with a short follow through. To become efficient with a full volley, keep your eye on the ball, meet the ball with a lot of surface of the instep, and don't kick too hard.

Punting. A punt is a kick that may be used only by the goal-keeper, since the ball must be caught and dropped to be kicked. The ball is held in both hands at arms length at about waist level, in front of the body. One or two steps may be taken preliminary to kicking. The kicking leg swings forward and upward with the knee bent and the toe pointing forward, so that the ball is kicked on the instep. The bent knee and straight ankle position will cause the ball to travel diagonally forward and upward. The ball is dropped just before the kicking leg starts the forward swing.

EXAMPLE 14.9

Vocabulary

References:
Provide practice in reading, enrichment, and further interest.

SOCCER TERMS

Blocking. Intercepting the progress of the ball with any part of the body, except the arms and hands if not held against the body (girls game).

Corner kick. Awarded the attacking team when the ball passes over the goal line except between the goal posts and is last touched by a defender.

Defense-kick. Given a defensive team if the ball goes over the goal line other than between the goal posts and is last touched by an offensive player (girls game).

Dribbling. Advancing the ball by a series of short kicks.

Free kick. Awarded to the defending team for fouls committed by the attacking team inside the penalty area and to either team for fouls committed outside the penalty area.

Goal kick. In boys game, same as defense-kick above.

Heading. Allowing the ball to come in contact with the head.

Kick in. Putting the ball in play after it is out of bounds over the side line.

Passing. Kicking the ball to a teammate.

Penalty kick. Awarded the offended team at the penalty kick mark if the defensive player fouls in his own penalty area.

Roll-in. Putting the ball in play after a foul by both teams, or after opponents have simultaneously kicked the ball out of bounds.

Tackling. Taking a ball from an opponent by use of the feet.

Trapping. Stopping and controlling a moving ball (with legs and feet only, in a girls game).

Volleying. Kicking the ball while it is in the air (boys game) or playing a ball which is in the air with the shoulder, hip, leg, or foot (girls game).

FOR MORE INFORMATION

Meyer, Margaret H., and Marguerite M. Schwarz. *Team Sports for Girls and Women.* 3rd Edition. Philadelphia: W. B. Saunders Co., 1957.

Miller, Donna Mae, and Katherine L. Ley. *Individual and Team Sports for Women.* Englewood Cliffs, N.J.: Prentice-Hall, 1955.

Mitchell, Elmer D., editor. *Sports for Recreation.* Revised Edition. New York: The Ronald Press, 1952.

Paterson, Ann, editor. *Team Sports for Girls,* New York: The Ronald Press, 1958.

Walters, Earl C., John R. Eiler, and A. E. Florio. *Soccer.* Revised Edition. Annapolis: U.S. Naval Institute, 1950.

Official NCAA Soccer Guide. Chicago: National Collegiate Athletic Association.

Soccer-Speedball Guide, current edition. Division for Girls and Women's Sports, AAHPER-NEA, 1201-16th St., N.W., Washington 6, D. C.

Selected Soccer-Speedball Articles. Division for Girls and Women's Sports, AAHPER-NEA, 1201-16th ST., N.W., Washington 6, D. C.

EXAMPLE 14.10

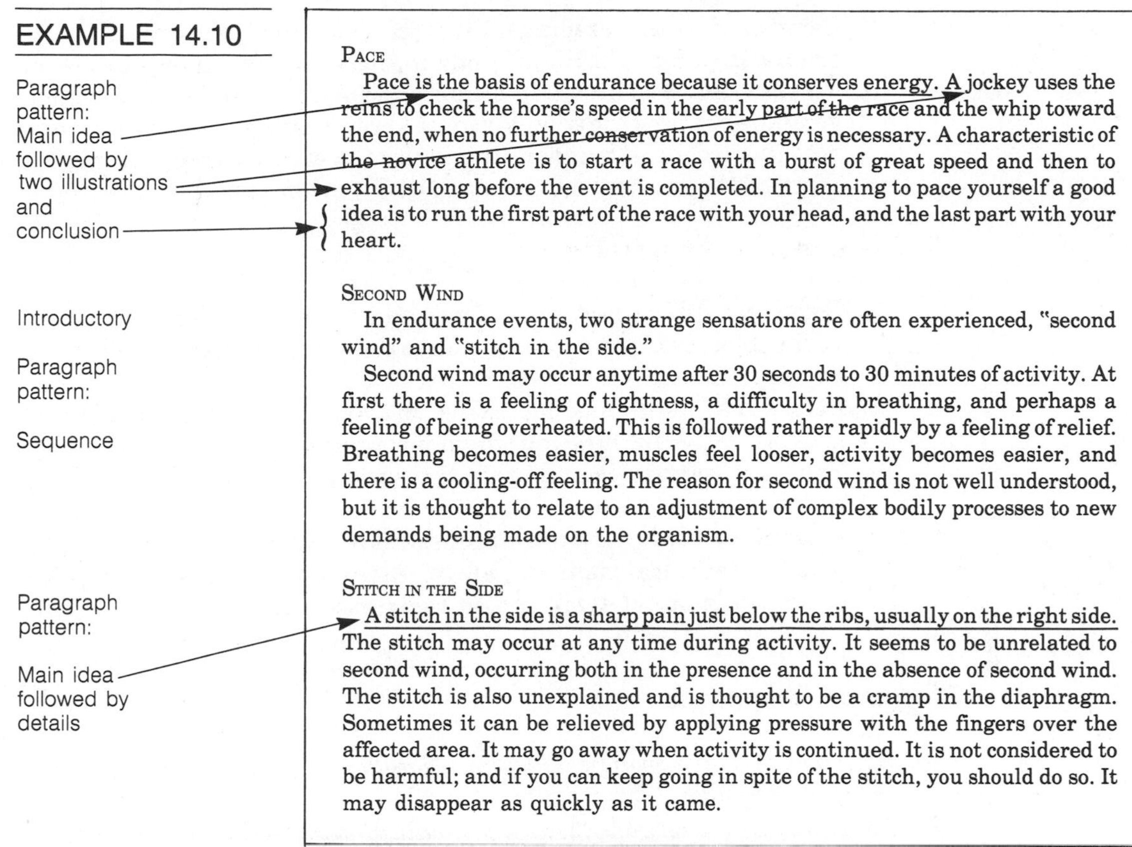

PACE

Pace is the basis of endurance because it conserves energy. A jockey uses the reins to check the horse's speed in the early part of the race and the whip toward the end, when no further conservation of energy is necessary. A characteristic of the novice athlete is to start a race with a burst of great speed and then to exhaust long before the event is completed. In planning to pace yourself a good idea is to run the first part of the race with your head, and the last part with your heart.

SECOND WIND

In endurance events, two strange sensations are often experienced, "second wind" and "stitch in the side."

Second wind may occur anytime after 30 seconds to 30 minutes of activity. At first there is a feeling of tightness, a difficulty in breathing, and perhaps a feeling of being overheated. This is followed rather rapidly by a feeling of relief. Breathing becomes easier, muscles feel looser, activity becomes easier, and there is a cooling-off feeling. The reason for second wind is not well understood, but it is thought to relate to an adjustment of complex bodily processes to new demands being made on the organism.

STITCH IN THE SIDE

A stitch in the side is a sharp pain just below the ribs, usually on the right side. The stitch may occur at any time during activity. It seems to be unrelated to second wind, occurring both in the presence and in the absence of second wind. The stitch is also unexplained and is thought to be a cramp in the diaphragm. Sometimes it can be relieved by applying pressure with the fingers over the affected area. It may go away when activity is continued. It is not considered to be harmful; and if you can keep going in spite of the stitch, you should do so. It may disappear as quickly as it came.

Interest in sports, an area where students can excel and maintain a positive self-concept, offers the coach and physical education teacher an enviable opportunity. They can serve as models. Thus, a coach's positive approach toward reading can guide reluctant readers toward improvement.

SUMMARY

There is not one subject in the curriculum that does not require students to use the reading skills in some way. There is not one subject that does not support reading profitably for enrichment. The moral is that reading instruction must include content. Reading cannot be taught in a vacuum or be relegated to one subject. Rather, it permeates the curriculum.

QUESTIONS AND PROBLEMS FOR YOUR OWN CLASSROOM

For readers who are training to be teachers:

1. Compile a bibliography of references and trade books pertinent to your subject field which you can have the students read for enjoyment and enrichment.

2. Determine those reading skills in your field that need to be emphasized. Show how you would incorporate them into your lesson.
3. In your subject area, determine for each lesson the technical vocabulary words the students must know. List also the general words used in a technical manner. Categorize the words. In music, compile a chart of the musical symbols and their meanings.

For readers who are teaching:

1. Compile a bibliography of references and trade books pertinent to your subject field which you can have the students read for enjoyment and enrichment.
2. Determine those reading skills in your field that need to be emphasized. Show how you would incorporate them into your lesson. You may want to compile this list with your students.
3. In your subject area, determine for each lesson the technical vocabulary words the students must know. List also the general words used in a technical manner. Categorize the words. In music, compile a list of the musical symbols and their meanings.

Selected References

Gentile, Lance M. *Using Sports and Physical Education to Strengthen Reading Skills.* Newark, Del.: IRA, 1980.

Lamberg, Walter J., and Lamb, Charles E. *Reading Instruction in the Content Areas.* Chicago: Rand McNally, 1980.

Thomas, Ellen Lamar, and Robinson, H. Alan. *Improving Reading in Every Classroom.* Boston: Allyn & Bacon, 1972.

All of the references provide practical suggestions to teachers of the subjects covered in this chapter.

CHAPTER 15

The Complete High School Reading Program

OVERVIEW

Reading instruction must pervade the entire high school curriculum —a point that is emphasized throughout this book. Language is the basic tool for learning. Instruction in language coupled with practice is needed in all subjects.

Instruction in reading language—in the recognition of graphic symbols and the acquisition of meaning from these symbols—is required for students to gain ideas independently through reading. They need help in learning to infer, conclude, evaluate and apply ideas. Competence in reading should be the prime consideration of all teachers.

Questions

Consider these questions before you read further:

1. What are the components of a complete high school reading program?
2. What do you see as the reading needs of the high school students in your school district?
3. What kind of program do you envision to meet the needs of the students in your school district?

PARTS OF A COMPLETE PROGRAM

In considering or planning a high school reading program, the following essential elements become apparent as the school philosophy is determined:

1. Reading instruction is provided in each of the subject fields as it applies.
2. The central library of the school provides opportunities to read for both research and pleasure.
3. Supplementary classroom libraries must be available to provide enrichment.
4. Elective courses are offered in the mechanics of reading for those students who wish to sharpen their reading study skills.
5. Remedial courses are available for those students who need help in addition to the content reading instruction in each classroom.

The five parts are interrelated. The school library is the nucleus of the program and should contribute to each of the other parts by providing materials for wide reading (and thereby practical application of the reading skills). Each teacher would teach the reading skills needed for research projects in the content disciplines, with the librarian assisting the students in applying them. Finally, the library offers enrichment to the various disciplines. The library can be a source of supplementary classroom materials by lending books on a specific topic under study. It contributes to interest in reading for the elective and remedial classes as well as in the content areas. Classroom libraries offer opportunities for developing interest and enrichment. They are particularly effective because the books are readily available to the students; this encourages wide reading.

Reading instruction in each content subject is fundamental and should be available to *all* students. Those who need extra help are assigned to remedial classes, often held in a reading laboratory or learning center. There must be coordination between the content teacher and the remedial teacher; each must know what the other is doing.

IMPLEMENTING A COMPLETE READING PROGRAM

The guidelines for successfully implementing a complete reading program are grouped under three areas: philosophy, practice, and personnel.

Philosophy

A philosophy of reading must be determined—is the program to be linguistically based? Eclectic in methodology? Will emphasis be on reading in the content fields or on remediation? Then, how is such a program to be coordinated? Who is to do what? What will be the responsibilities of the reading consultant, coordinator, teacher (whatever the title)?

1. Secondary school reading instruction should be an all-school program that involves all personnel. The program should be comprehensive, using all opportunities to teach reading skills. The program should have the unity that comes from all teachers and personnel being involved in upgrading the students' use of reading as a medium of learning. Adequate progress does not come as an isolated effort from a single teacher. Transfer and reinforcement are assured as teachers in all of the content fields work with the same skills, applying them to their particular discipline.
2. The school staff must know what their objectives are—they must think about what they are to accomplish. Essentially, the goals are derived from a simple question: "What do we want the students to be able to do and to become as a result of our instruction?" The answer to this question will determine the emphasis and scope of the program. If the answer is to have the students read their textbook materials, then the program will become largely remedial; the emphasis will be on those students who are not reading adequately (a large or a small number, depending on the school). If the answer is to have all of the students become independent in using reading as a means of attaining information as well as a means of recreational pleasure, then the program will encompass all disciplines and all students.
3. Reading must be linked to the other language arts. This idea goes back to the fundamental goal of instruction: facility in language use. Since all teachers are teachers of language, albeit the language of their discipline, all forms of language are employed—speaking, listening, reading, and writing—to help students learn. Each element is interwoven with the others. Skills of reading can be applied to speaking, listening, and writing, and this transfer of skills should be noted.
4. Teaching both reading skills and the goals of reading instruction must be continuous from grades K–12. As students learn and practice continuously, their competence in reading grows. Many factors affect the *extent* of growth, but the *capacity* to increase in competence is infinite.
5. The ultimate goal of reading instruction is *to increase the background of knowledge,* not only of those concepts and understandings that have evolved through the centuries but also of modern ideas. Learning the reading skills is fundamental to this basic goal. Faculty and students must be able to see the relationship between skill instruction and the acquisition of knowledge. Skill instruction as an entity in itself usually leads to little understanding of concepts or knowledge. If reading instruction is reduced to just teaching skills, the process is quite sterile.
6. Reading must be considered a *process* rather than a subject.
7. Instruction in reading must be systematic. There must be, as in all skills, a development in the application of the many skills of reading that starts simply and grows more and more complex as mastery increases. Students should be paced by their own development.

Further, the interrelationship of the skills must be made apparent to the students. For example, the skills of discerning main ideas and relating pertinent details to the main idea are the beginnings of the skill of noting organization—outlining.

8. Reading instruction must be geared to the students. Their social and personal development and capabilities must be considered in relation to reading progress. Positive conditions should be capitalized upon and negative conditions corrected. Teachers must know the students as individuals, not merely as names in the class grade book. Students have the right to expect an accurate and objective assessment of their strengths and weaknesses in reading. The plan evolved *between* the student and teacher must fit the student individually, and he or she must understand its goals and design. It must incorporate student goals, and its design must be realistic and acceptable to the students.

PRACTICE

1. An effective program provides for both instruction and application. Students need to be shown how to use the reading skills effectively with whatever material they are reading. Instruction in a skill, however, is not enough. Students must practice the skill with various materials. Much of the practice should be supervised. There should also be independent practice in applying the skills.
2. Emphasize meaning as the students read. The secondary teacher has the fundamental responsibility to help students gain meaning from the reading material. He will need to insure adequate background, vocabulary, and comprehension of the main idea, related details, and the organization of the material. Then the students will be likely to interpret and evaluate logically what they read.
3. All of the necessary skills are taught as their use is required. In addition to vocabulary and comprehension, students must receive instruction and guidance in how to study—how to attack an assignment, conduct library research, and understand syntax.
4. Instruction should be differentiated in the classroom. The skills emphasized in the classroom must be a balance between those required by the assignment and the content and those needed by the students. For example, if students are adept at noting main ideas, the teacher will not find it necessary to teach this skill. Or the teacher may find that a portion of the class does need such instruction. Procedure, then, must be flexible so that such students receive the necessary instruction.
5. Conduct continuous evaluation to measure competence in the skills. Use diagnostic teaching and informal inventories as well as standardized tests. The teacher should know at all times the strengths and weaknesses of each student, even when the total class load per day is large. Easy, effective and continual records must be kept.

6. Adequate materials are needed for effective teaching. Though the teacher is the key to teaching effectiveness, materials that fit both the levels of competence and special interests of the students are necessary. Students cannot read with understanding materials which are above their level; however, reading material below their level of competence dampens student interest and accomplishment. A variety of materials is needed in the classroom.
7. Use the fundamental steps of the directed activity. Adequate preparation for reading and instruction in and application of the skills are essential to planning.
8. Provide a stimulating classroom environment. The classroom should be filled with materials—exhibits, displays, books, models—appropriate to the discipline. The atmosphere that emanates from the physical environment as well as from the manner of the teacher should invite learning and the development of interests. Nothing is drearier than a barren classroom and an unenthusiastic teacher.
9. Effective classroom teaching incorporates the concept of *diagnostic teaching*—classroom instruction which relates to each individual, provides immediate reteaching when needed, and uses daily diagnosis.
10. The teacher needs to preplan the learning experiences on both a short-term and a long-term basis. Long-term planning includes the understandings, skills, and attitudes the teacher hopes to impart during the course. Short-term planning is a result of diagnostic teaching.

Personnel

A total school reading program is as effective as the involvement of all the professional school personnel in its administration and functioning. The responsibilities of the various personnel should be delineated as carefully as possible. Though these responsibilities are not static and change somewhat as the program evolves, a well-thought-out listing of duties and the interrelationships of the various personnel insures smooth implementation.

The *classroom teacher* is the person most important to the success of the school program. Each teacher's expertise with his discipline enables him to best teach the related reading skills. He can best differentiate instruction to special needs of the individuals within the class. He is therefore best qualified to give specific corrective help to students as the need arises.

The *school principal* sets the tone of the school and through his leadership can engender enthusiasm in the school teaching staff. Through administrative considerations of scheduling and budgeting he can govern the effectiveness of teachers. Proper facilities, materials, and time are necessary ingredients. His concern is to provide help for teachers: reading specialists, inservice courses for an understanding of the reading process, and support of the teachers in their efforts and explanations to the community. All of these contribute fundamentally to the success of the program.

The *curriculum coordinator* is the principal's delegate to plan and execute the program. He should be knowledgeable about reading and be able to give specific help to teachers.

The *reading consultant,* if he is a part of the school, should be a prominent member of the curriculum coordinator's team. Often the consultant in reading is the coordinator's delegate charged with specific planning and administration of the program. Some reading consultants also spend part of their time as reading teachers for remedial students.

The *reading teacher* most often gives additional help to the students in accordance with their level and needs. Sometimes he is assigned to teach general classes in reading—for those high school students who wish to refine their skills. There should be at all times a close liaison between the content teachers and the remedial teachers. Many times the lack of such coordination is a basic weakness. A unified approach, with everyone working for the same goals, is obviously more effective.

The *guidance counselor* is a resource to teachers in advising and alerting them to the problems, needs, strengths, weaknesses, and interests of the students. Special schedules may be arranged. Also, information about the students other than school information can be provided, which may give the teacher insights about the students as well as suggesting classroom approaches.

The *school nurse* can investigate the general physical condition of students. Vision and hearing problems which need correction can be noted and proper referral made.

The *librarian* obviously plays an important role—especially in the areas of the reading research skills and in fostering wide reading. One librarian organized a committee of students to assist in choosing new books for the library. This was an ongoing and active committee throughout the year. When the books were received she placed them on a table for students to browse. The librarian believed that student involvement was of prime importance in stimulating wide reading and interest in the library.

The *media specialist* helps classroom teachers with the use of materials—tapes, films, film strips, transparencies, and so on which can enhance understanding of the printed page. Materials which enliven, clarify, and dramatize classroom learning can be provided.

ORGANIZING THE READING PROGRAM

Organizing, enlarging, or adapting a high school program involves all school personnel. The leadership is usually channelled through a reading committee of teachers (usually one from each discipline and other interested personnel). It is particularly necessary to have teachers engaged in the structuring of the program since they will be responsible for its success or failure. Open lines of communication must be maintained between the committee and the educational staff.

The Reading Committee

A reading committee best grows out of a commonly felt need among the staff—and commitment to work together to solve a problem. Initiating the committee may come from several sources: concerned teachers, the principal, the curriculum coordinator, the school superintendent, or the reading consultant or teacher.

The program must be organized democratically, receiving input from all personnel who will be actively involved with formulating and executing it. Teachers *must* become involved, since only with their support and participation can the plan succeed. The classroom teacher is the one who will be implementing the program daily; it cannot be effected by the administrative staff or the committee.

Though teachers may not have extensive background in reading instruction, they do observe deficiencies in reading skills and techniques. Under the guidance of the reading personnel and with support from the administration, the teachers on the committee can acquire more understanding of the reading process. These teachers in turn can disseminate the information to their colleagues in the subject departments. This is the beginning of inservice education.

Working to improve high school students' reading proficiency may be stimulated by the characteristics of the school district or by the student body's level of reading proficiency. For example, schoolwide testing may show glaring deficiencies. Teachers may have classroom problems because students cannot read the textbooks. There may be serious concern about the number of students who cannot read at a desired competence level. The committee will do well to address itself to the concern or problem first and evolve a plan of action—the program—from the concern. At this point, qualified reading personnel can offer their expertise in directing the work of the committee and formulating the program.

The best results seem to occur when the teachers can see benefits *immediately*. Therefore, the committee should develop short-range goals as well as long-range ones. The short-range goals are specific; they often are suggestions to teachers of techniques and procedures that can be implemented immediately in the classroom. For example, suppose a teacher's concern is, "My students say that they cannot concentrate on their reading assignment." A newsletter or a general meeting may describe an appropriate technique and explain how teachers can make an assignment more effectively. (Instead of merely telling the students to read a specific number of pages, the following suggestions may be offered: preview the selection, determine meanings of new vocabulary, use graphic aids in the textbook, establish questions to keep in mind while reading, and change topical headings into questions.)

The long-range goals will be those that incorporate the complete plan for the program. The teachers may not be aware of this as yet; their concern is with what can they do with those students they meet daily who cannot perform adequately. In setting up the long-range goals, the committee will find that a complete program is implemented in steps. Again, using the example of students being unable to concentrate, we would start with remediation for students in the regular classroom. The next step probably would be examining reading as it applies to each content area, thereby benefiting all students—not just those who need remedial instruction. This step leads to the use of the school library and the setting up of classroom libraries. By this time there may be discussion of what can be done for remedial students (remedial classes) and what else can be done for adequate readers (elective courses).

Unless it is extremely narrow in concept, no program can be implemented in one year. Experience has shown that a comprehensive program takes five to seven years to implement and requires constant monitoring thereafter. In a sense, this "goes against our grain." It seems so slow! However, the committee must always be responsive to the teaching staff. Teachers are the implementers, and it takes time for them to understand the program, see its effectiveness, and thus support the program.

Administrative Support and Involvement

The administrative personnel of a school is where we look for leadership. Though superintendents or principals may delegate the task of creating program to personnel trained in the field, these administrators must acquire an understanding of the need for the program, its scope, and its characteristics. It is their responsibility to facilitate and give *support:* adjustments of schedules, budget allocations, and spokespersons to the Board of Education and the community. They also set the tone by showing their concern. Such a small gesture as attending the reading committee sessions or the sessions of an inservice program can mean much to the teachers involved.

Teacher Support and Involvement

We may consider this the key to the success of the program. In our discussion on leadership we noted the importance of getting teacher input, beginning with their expressed concerns, and then evolving the program. One visiting consultant said, "When a principal or superintendent calls me, I immediately ask him to poll his teachers to find out their problems in the area. Then I tailor my work to these problems. Often, if I am to give a course, I will tabulate and categorize the problems. Then I give them to the teachers along with a syllabus of the course, pointing out where each problem will be dealt with. It is amazing how this sparks interest in the group."

Another help for the reading committee is to survey the teachers to find out their views about teaching reading in the high school and in the content classes. The purpose here is to alert the committee to teachers' present views and to how much these thoughts and attitudes may need to be modified. Committee members then can plan ways to counter negative attitudes. In this vein, the committee should remember three points. First, objectivity is necessary—the teachers are not to be "put down" for their views and concerns. Second, practical help must be given immediately. Third, adequate follow-up and guidance must be given until the teacher feels secure in the new approaches.

Vaughan has devised "A Scale to Measure Attitudes Toward Teaching Reading in Content Classrooms."[1] There are fifteen items denoting viewpoints of classroom teachers. Such a scale can give a reading committee insight into teachers' attitudes, but this type of survey can pose a threat to some teachers. This, in turn, may pose problems for the implementation of the proposed program. If this survey is used, anonymity of respondents must be assured.

Adequate Budget

Usually, when a new program is being instituted within a school district, extra money is required. New materials have to be purchased. Additional personnel may be necessary, such as reading teachers or a consultant. If visiting consultants are brought in, money to pay their services has to be budgeted. The amount of additional monies depends, of course, upon the resources of the district. Likewise, funds determine the scope of the new program and affect how quickly it can be instituted. Since new programs require funding, many reading committees invite a Board of Education member to sit on the committee.

Teacher Inservice Training

Inservice teacher training can take a number of forms, some of which are more effective than others. It is arguable whether a course given by a visiting consultant or even by the reading personnel of a school district actually results in changes in the classroom. To effect changes, the course content should derive from the teacher's expressed needs; practical suggestions should be given which the teachers can use directly in their classrooms, and there should be follow-up with the teachers to assist them in implementing suggestions.

One school system conducted a successful inservice program by having first a course in reading which teachers attended voluntarily. Then a visiting consultant met with selected teachers, individually or in small groups, approximately ten times during the school year. The teachers were polled before the course to determine their concerns and the course addressed itself to these concerns. During the follow-up sessions with individual teachers, they were given specific assistance. Teacher assignments were reviewed and the consultant suggested how reading instruction could be incorporated into the assignment. Later, the consultant checked with the teachers about how well the suggestions had worked and offered alternatives and variations as necessary.

Of special note here is that the first group of teachers had already shown their interest by volunteering for the course. Also, the consultant worked with only a small group at any one time. Further, the vice principal of the high school, who was the curriculum coordinator, evolved a plan with the consultant which took five years to complete. The consultant worked with one department at a time, starting with social studies, then with science, and so

---

1. Joseph L. Vaughan, Jr., "A Scale to Measure Attitudes Toward Teaching Reading in Content Classrooms," *Journal of Reading* 20, No. 7 (April 1977): 605–9.

on. Though the program's implementation may seem slow, in five years every teacher in the school had received individual follow-up. The department chairpersons met with the consultant also so that they could provide effective leadership in the consultant's absence.

Selecting Materials to Fit Students' Needs

In this area the committee can assist teachers by acquainting them with available materials. The committee can mount book displays, make evaluations of instructional materials, and check the readability of materials. Particularly important here also is guidance in choosing textbooks. For example, how clearly written is the textbook? What aids should be given to the students if the style of writing is not clear? A subcommittee to the reading committee could study the issue in depth and help teachers in analyzing their text materials.

Planning a Comprehensive Program

In this area the reading committee considers specific procedures and strategies to help teachers in the implementation of the complete program. Emphases are determined by the philosophy and scope of the program. Inservice activities, direct work with teachers, bulletins, and other efforts can address the following questions:

1. How can proficiency in the reading skills be diagnosed—general schoolwide standardized testing, or within the classroom through informal means?
2. What types of grouping or techniques of individualization should be employed? Are we concerned here with schoolwide grouping, or with individualization within the classroom, or both?
3. What criteria do we use for the selection of student materials?
4. What basic lesson procedures do we advocate?
5. What are the skill needs of the students?
6. How do teachers meet these needs?
7. What are the responsibilities of various personnel?
8. How do they dovetail in the complete program?
9. What timetable will we follow for the complete implementation of the program?
10. How can we evaluate the effectiveness of the program?

Developing Community Interest and Support

Obviously, this area is an important one for the committee to consider. PTA presentations, newsletters, special programs, and involvement of persons from the community in program planning are all ways to communicate with parents and the community. Community knowledge of what the school is attempting to do usually engenders community support. This support can be instrumental to the success of the program—if for no other reason than that budgetary requirements will be approved.

SUCCESS OF THE PROGRAM

The success of the program can be governed by extrinsic factors such as the interest of administrators, teachers and the community; budget; and the school philosophy. Even more important are the attitudes of teachers toward the place of reading in the high school; their classroom procedures reflect these attitudes. For instance, are the teachers planning their lessons to:

1. Provide motivation?
2. Adapt techniques and materials to help students on various levels of ability?
3. Extend help in developing a broad vocabulary?
4. Use recommended reading procedure?
5. Provide a balance among all the skills in their development in each discipline?
6. Guide the students in purposeful reading?
7. Foster understanding as the end goal of skill instruction?

The reading committee of a school may evaluate its program by asking the following questions:

1. What are the basic premises underlying the school reading program?
2. Do the teachers have a well-founded philosophy of reading instruction?
3. Is provision made to teach the reading skills sequentially, systematically, and continuously?
4. Are thought and relationship questions used as well as fact questions?
5. Are the reading skills taught in the context of a story or subject matter, or are they isolated?
6. Are the understandings and concepts emphasized with the appropriate skills needed for comprehending them?
7. Is practice work related to student needs?
8. Are reading materials of varying levels and topics available?
9. Is there a well-stocked school library with a qualified librarian?
10. Are there classroom collections of books supplementary to the textbooks?
11. Is reading isolated from the rest of the curriculum—is it taught as a subject apart?
12. Is reading taught in all subjects, whenever the students use printed materials?
13. Do teachers follow the steps of a directed reading activity?
14. Are the students reading books on their instructional level (material that is challenging but can be read successfully)?
15. Is instruction in reading differentiated to each student's needs or directed to the class as a whole?
16. Are we able to provide instruction in reading for superior readers?
17. Are we able to provide instruction in reading for less able readers?

18. Is there provision for all types of classroom organization as needed for effective instruction?
19. Are teachers flexible in their classroom organization?
20. Do teachers know how to diagnose and evaluate?
21. Do teachers continuously diagnose the needs and evaluate the progress of students in reading?
22. Are the students enjoying reading; are they reading widely?
23. Do teachers have the necessary background to interpret the reading program to the public?
24. Are opportunities for inservice instruction provided for teachers?
25. Is there systematic communication between the remedial teachers and the classroom subject teachers?

SUMMARY

The goal of schools is to foster literacy. Literacy enables students to function constructively in society, both as individuals and in groups. Being able to read is essential for becoming a self-sustaining person. Consequently, the thrust of reading instruction must be toward independence in learning. All school personnel must be concerned with ensuring reading competence, since it affects success in all educational pursuits.

QUESTIONS AND PROBLEMS FOR YOUR OWN CLASSROOM

For readers who are training to be teachers:

1. Describe a school reading program in which you would like to teach.
2. If you had a problem reader in one of your classes, to whom would you go for assistance? Describe the type of assistance you would expect.
3. If you were asked to serve on a school reading committee, what would you envision to be your duties and responsibilities?
4. What are your expectations in reading for the students in your classes? How would you use the school resources to meet their needs?

For readers who are teaching:

1. Analyze your school reading program and determine how and where reading instruction and provision for wide reading are provided.
2. Note a reading problem in your school and determine how it can be solved.
3. Survey the personnel roster for your school and determine who should be included in a school reading committee.
4. Note the various personnel assigned to your school and list the duties of each toward the implementation of total school reading program.
5. As a basis for the work of your school reading committee, survey your department or school for the apparent reading problems and suggestions for corrective action.

SELECTED REFERENCES

Burg, Leslie A.; Kaufman, Maurice; Korngold, Blanche; and Kovner, Albert. *The Complete Reading Supervisor, Tasks and Roles.* Columbus: Charles E. Merrill, 1978.

An excellent discussion of inservice education is presented.

Strang, Ruth, and Lindquist, Donald M. *The Administrator and the Improvement of Reading.* New York: Appleton-Century-Crofts, 1960.

The role of the administrator is described.

Appendix

Steps in a Unit Procedure

UNIT DEVELOPMENT	CLASSROOM ORGANIZATION TO MEET SPECIFIC NEEDS	READING SKILLS
I. *Introducing the Unit* A. Select a topic for study which may be divided into several problems for group and individual research. 1. Find out what the students know about it. (Determine what needs to be taught) a. List the facts on the blackboard. b. Discuss the sources of information. c. Decide on ways of judging the correctness of ideas such as contradictions or misconceptions. d. Have a record made of the information listed. 2. Find out what the students want to know about the topic. a. Use the same four points listed under #1 above. b. As the material is previewed, graphic aids and topical headings may alert students to information they wish to investigate. c. Note that very few questions may be forthcoming at this time. The suggestion can be made that other questions may come to mind as the topic is studied. 3. Help the students relate the topic to their experimental background. Relate the topic to present knowledge and understandings.	The entire class *Note:* If multitexts are used, the teacher may survey by using an overhead projector to select pertinent features from each. This will help students with their specific textbook and provide an enriched introduction based on all of the textbooks.	A. Prepare (readiness) for reading 1. Explore the student's background of information. Probe with questions to help students remember information in their background. 2. Develop meaning to basic concepts (vocabulary). 3. Survey the scope of the topic. When using printed materials, use typographical aids. 4. Set up purpose questions.

Steps in a Unit Procedure—Continued

UNIT DEVELOPMENT	CLASSROOM ORGANIZATION TO MEET SPECIFIC NEEDS	READING SKILLS
4. Use whatever materials may be available, appropriate, and necessary such as pictures, objects, models, current news, related stories or poems, TV and radio news or programs, and trips.		
B. The time needed for the introduction to a unit may require just one class period or a few days. This is the same as the introduction for an individual lesson procedure. The preparation depends upon (1) the length of the unit, (2) the fundamental nature of the material, and (3) the student's background in the data.		B. Diagnose student's proficiency in using the skills.
II. *Developing the Unit* A. Use basic materials to expand pupils' information about the topic. Initial reading will help the students to decide what problems they may wish to work on as well as to know more about the main topic. B. Determine the major problem and various subproblems. The problem should be stated as questions rather than as topics in order to implement the application of the skills of interpretative and critical reading. Identify problems to be used for research by groups.	A. The entire class B. Possible grouping according to the need of students for instruction in specific skills.	A. Use the information gained through the diagnosis to determine the skills which need to be taught further and practiced. B. Teach the following skills, if needed, as basic materials are used: 1. Review and teach all of the skills common to the content area. 2. Develop specific vocabulary. 3. Use typographical aids. 4. Teach how to use graphic aids (maps, pictures, etc.). 5. Give instruction in setting up purposes for reading.
III. *Student-Teacher Planning for Research* A. Organize the groups (committees) according to interest indicated in each problem. (Students may also be assigned to specific	A. Interest groups B. Social groups if indicated by needs of students	A. Set up purposes (problems) to guide reading. B. Teach locational skills:

groups if the teacher sees a student's social need which can be met.)

B. Discuss and review resource material.
   1. Have the students recall and determine what they know about resource materials.
   2. Discuss sources of materials.
      a. Determine where the materials may be located.
      b. Help students determine specific sources which may contain information about their problem.
         Formulate answers to the question: How can we solve our problem?
   3. Provide instruction in techniques of using various resource aids and resource materials, *i.e.,* card catalog, World Almanac, etc. The school librarian is a valuable resource person.

C. Set up standards for group work.
   1. Determine the role of the chairman, recorder, the process observer.
   2. Organize the work of the group so that each participant has a job he can do.
   3. Note effective work procedures—each student works so as not to annoy others, does not talk too loudly, works at the job at hand, does not waste time, works democratically, does some things even though they are not his first choice, does his own job, etc.

C. Total class (prior to actual beginning of research by groups)

D. Role of the chairman
   1. Direct discussion.
   2. Use the ideas of other participants—get all shades of opinion.
   3. Help all participants to take part in the discussions.
   4. Have a sense of organization.
   5. Lead the group in evaluating their work.
   6. See that facts are well supported by research.

E. Role of the recorder
   1. Maintain a record of group progress.
   2. Assist leader in summarizing work completed.

F. Role of the process observer
   1. Watches working of the group in accordance with standards of effective work.
   2. Assist leader in planning for participation.
   3. Assist group in providing information pertinent to group evaluation, such as reactions of group members.

G. Group member duties
   1. Participates by reading, doing his part, and discussing with group.
   2. Contribute ideas freely.
   3. Accept decisions of the group.
   4. Set standards for group work.

H. The students will need to delineate their problem—determine the scope and depth which they will need to develop.

1. Use of library skills
2. Use of references
3. Use of parts of a book

Steps in a Unit Procedure—Continued

UNIT DEVELOPMENT	CLASSROOM ORGANIZATION TO MEET SPECIFIC NEEDS	READING SKILLS
IV. *Conducting Research* A. Have a variety of materials on differing levels of difficulty. B. Encourage students to read widely and pool their information. C. Keep a bibliography. D. Teach the students to evaluate their group work; assist groups when necessary; help in further planning; try not to let group bog down. The teacher may find it necessary to guide the pupils through their group work, at least at first. The teacher may pace students by requiring the recorder to give her an account of what was accomplished in each day's group work and a statement of the next day's intentions. In this way the teacher can keep a close scrutiny of each group's progress and be prepared to assist if the group seems to be floundering. When groups begin to work, students should be directed to map first their total assignment within the time limit given and each day think through what is to be done at the meeting.	A. Interest groups conducting research B. Possible social groups C. Special need groups, as established groups of individuals needing further help in some research skill or grouping technique D. Groups organize the assignments in accordance with standards and duties of members as listed in *III. Student-Teacher Planning for Research* E. Entire class according to need for possible immediate evaluation. This may be done at any time to help the students rethink the mode of work through group processes.	A. Apply locational skills B. Use skimming techniques. C. Apply all skills for getting information common to research. D. Use outlining skills. E. Synthesize data from more than one source. F. Organize data into a report. G. Apply information to the problem. (Involves the use of interpretive reading skills.)
V. *Culminating the Unit* A. Help the students prepare their presentations to the class. 1. Determine what to report. 2. Determine how to report. Presenting information using types of projects such as dramatizations, original	A. Group participation in presentation B. Group evaluation of its work C. Total class evaluation of method of working; of need for further instruction in the skills of reading, etc.; of the entire unit's work.	A. Teach techniques of giving reports. Set up standards such as well-organized reports in student's own words. B. Teach techniques of taking notes. 1. Main ideas and supporting detail outline 2. Listening for any key words and phrases

descriptions or stories, models, dioramas, charts, pictures, collections, etc. B. Develop standards for an audience such as listening with a purpose, aking in outline the main ideas of the report, being courteous to the speaker, etc. C. Evaluate each group's presentation—through discussion and questionnaire. 1. Did each group solve its problem? 2. Was the presentation well-organized and interesting? 3. Were standards of group work maintained? D. Evaluate the solving of the main topic. 1. Has the main problem been answered? (Help students see the relationship of each group's information to he main topic.) 2. What improvements are necessary?		3. Listening for main ideas, structure of information in the report.

Note: The teacher should know what the groups are to do *before* they are to be expected to do it. Also, before students undertake the research, the teacher should know the references and see the organization of the unit and ways it may be culminated.

Index

Adjusting materials, 242–253
  factors affecting difficulty, 243–245
  readability, 245–248
  rewriting, 251–252
  supplementary materials, 252
  textbook evaluation, 248
Allen, Robert L., 91
Ames, Wilbur S., 99
Anderson, Bernice, 337
Anderson, Thomas H., 75
Andre, Marlie D.A., 75
Art
  applying reading skills, 360–362
Assessment. *See* Diagnosis
Attitudes
  effect on comprehension, 64
Aukerman, Robert C., 328
Automatic materials, criteria for, 206

Bamman, Henry A., 283
Barrett, Thomas C., 58–59, 60, 63, 68–69, 71
Basal reader, 6
Basic competency, 238–241
  guidelines, 240
Betts, Emmett A., 64
Bilingual students. *See* Culturally different students
Bilello, Jane C., 257–259
Black English, 225–226
  classroom activities, 226
Bloom, Benjamin, 58, 60, 62–64, 68–69, 71, 97
Bond, Guy L., 147, 241
Bormuth, John R., 166, 253
Botel Reading Inventory, 152
Bridges, Sydney, 210
Burg, Leslie A., 387
Burnett, Richard W., 146–147
Burns, Paul C., 102, 328, 356
Business education
  applying reading skills, 330–337
  classroom procedures, guidelines, 337–340
  questioning, 63
  style of writing
    English, 331–337
    mathematics, 330–334
    science, 334
    social studies, 336
  vocabulary, 330, 332, 334–335, 338–339

California Achievement Tests: Reading, 153
Call, Russell J., 15
Campbell, Anne, 247
Carroll, John B., 10
Carvo, Margaret, 236–237
Cassidy, Jack, 240
Chall, Jeanne S., 10, 248, 253
Chart reading, 111–112
Chomsky, Carol, 234
Clymer, Theodore, 97
Combs, Arthur W., 8
Combs, Warren E., 91
Comprehension, 53–97
  classroom procedures, 67–73
  emotions and attitudes, 64
  interest, 61-62
  levels, 57
  motivation, 62–64
  nature
    affective dimension, 59
    cognitive dimension, 54–59
  problems in, 73–96
  questioning, 67–73, 90–91
  rate of, 127–128
  split brain research, 60–61
  subject areas
    business education, 63, 332
    foreign languages, 359–360
    homemaking, 79, 80, 82, 348–352
    industrial arts, 64, 343
    mathematics, 77–78, 83, 306–322
    music, 75–76, 79, 80, 82, 363–365
    physical education, 75–76, 367–373
    science, 75–76, 77, 78, 80, 82, 83, 85, 87, 296–303

Comprehension *(continued)*
taxonomies, 58–59
Content fields reading
language, 10–13
premises, 14–15
Context, 5
Contextual analysis, 31, 32–34
Culturally different students, 221–225
classroom activities, 223–225

Dale, Edgar, 248, 253
Davis, Carol A., 249–250
Davis, William W., 149
Dechant, Emerald, 127
Deating, Daniel, 214
Deighton, Lee C., 51–52, 92
Developmental stages, 3
middle school, 6–7
preschool, 3–4
primary and elementary school, 4–6
beginning reading, 4–6
the secondary school, 7–13
Diagram reading, 114–116
Diagnosis, 145–168
guidelines, 148–149
levels of, 146–147
methods of appraisal, 149
autobiography, 166
cloze procedures, 166–7
cumulative school records, 165
daily schedule, 165
interview, 165–166
observation, 163–164
standardized tests, 149–153
teacher-made tests, 153–163
Diagnostic Reading Test: Pupil Progress Series, 152
Diagnostic Reading Tests, 151
Dictionary usage, 21, 48–50
Differentiated assignments, 200–201
Disabled readers, 219–221
needs of, 220
classroom activities, 220–221
Durkin, Dolores, 73

Early, Margaret J., 264
Edwards, Peter, 101
Elliott, Peggy Gordon, 134
Ellsworth, Ralph E., 140
Emotions
effect on comprehension, 64
English
applying reading skills, 256, 260–265
free reading, 265–267
lesson procedure, guidelines, 265
EVOKER (study formula–poetry), 102
Exceptional students, 208–227
Black English, 225–226
cultural different and bilingual students, 221–225
disabled readers, 219–221
reluctant readers, 221
slow-learning readers, 216–219
superior readers, 209–215

Farr, Roger, 168
Fay, Leo, 101
Figurative expressions, 94–95
Figurel, J. Allen, 92
Fillmer, H. Thompson, 6
Finder, Morris, 95
Flesch, Rudolf, 248, 253
Following directions, 122–123, 322
Foreign languages
applying reading skills, 358–360
Foster, Alan G., 93
Fox, Patricia L., 60, 61
Free reading. *See* Wide reading
Fry, Edward, 247, 248, 253

Gates, Jean Key, 141
Gentile, Lance M., 132, 133, 367, 374
Goodman, Kenneth S., 19, 20, 52
Goodman, Yetta M., 222
Graphic aids, 107
charts, 111–112
diagrams, 114–116
graphs, 119–121
maps, 108–111
pictures, 121–122
tables, 116–118
Graph reading, 119–121
Grapho-phonemic skills
generalizations, 46–48
Greek roots, 41-42
Grouping, 194–200
Guilford, J. P., 54–57, 63–64, 97, 170

Harris, Albert J., 2, 57, 99
Harzell, T. Stevenson, 171
Hatcher, Catherine W., 90–91
Havighurst, Robert J., 19
Health education
applying reading skills, 367–373
Herber, Harold L., 67, 124, 129, 144
High School National Achievement Test, 152

Hittleman, Daniel R., 2, 3
Hodges, Carol A., 73
Hoeffner, Ralph, 54, 55
Holmes, Janis, 105
Home economics. *See* Homemaking
Homemaking
  applying reading skills, 348–352
  directed lesson, 183
  classroom procedure, 352–355
  comprehension, 79, 80, 82
  questioning, 64
Horn, Thomas D., 227

Individualized instruction, 191–207
  approach, 6
  considerations for, 192–193
  forms of, 193
    differentiated assignments, 200–201
    grouping, 194–200
    job sheets, 203
  materials, 204
Industrial arts
  applying reading skills, 340–346
  classroom procedure, 346–348
  questioning, 64
  wide reading, 348
Intelligence
  Guilford's model of, 54–57
Interest, 61–62, 130
  effect on comprehension, 61–62
  guidelines for developing, 134–136
  why adolescents read, 131–134
Iowa Tests, 151
Irwin, Judith Westphal, 249–250
Ives, Sumner, 91

Job sheets, 203
Johnston, Joyce D., 341

Kaufman, Maurice, 387
Klare, George K., 253
Klein, Howard A., 241
Korngold, Blanche, 387
Kovner, Albert, 387

Laffey, James L., 227
Lamb, Charles E., 328, 356, 374
Lamberg, Walter J., 328, 356, 374
Language arts skills, 12–13
Language experience approach, 6
Lapp, Diane, 207
Larrick, Nancy, 265–266
Latin roots, 40–41
Lefevre, Carl A., 256
Lerch, Harold H., 305
Library
  classroom, 135, 252
  school, 139–143
Lindquist, Donald M., 387
Literacy, 10

Maffei, Anthony C., 102
Manzo, Anthony V., 19, 102
Manzo, Marilyn G., 102
Map reading, 108–111
Marien, Michael, 9
Mathematics
  comprehension, 77–78, 83
  diagrams, 114
  directed lesson, 181–183, 324–325
  graphs, 119–121, 317–320
  the inadequate reader, 322–324
  nature of mathematical writing, 306
  objectives, 305–306
  questioning, 63
  relevant reading skills, 306–322
    following directions, 322
    graphic representations, 317–320
    purpose, 307
    statistical reports, 311–315
    symbols, 311
    vocabulary, 311
    word problems, 315–317
  study formulas
    PG4R, 102
    SQRQCQ, 101
  syntax, 92, 93
  tables, 114, 118, 311–315
Marksheffel, Ned D., 21, 22
Mayo, Bernard, 8
McCullough, Constance, 57
McDonald, Arthur S., 31
McKay, William, 99, 103
McLaughlin, G. Harry, 248, 253
McMillan, Merna M., 132–133
Melnik, Amelia, 147
Meredith, Robert, 20, 52
Michaels, Melvin, 11
Milulecky, Larry, 101
Mindell, Phyllis, 214
Morphological clues, 34–45. *See also* Structural analysis
Motivation
  effect on comprehension, 62–64
Music
  applying reading skills, 363–365

Music *(continued)*
  comprehension, 75–76, 79, 80, 82
  vocabulary, 363

Nelson, Joan B., 67
Niles, Olive S., 203
Newspaper reading, 275–276
Norman, Maxwell H., 101
Notetaking, 104–107

OARWET (study formula), 101
O'Brien, Carmen, 227
Olsen, Arthur V., 99
Organizing information, 100–104
Orlando, Vincent P., 102

PANORAMA (study formula), 101
Paragraph patterns, 75–83, 244
  art, 362
  social studies, 276–282
PARS (study formula), 101
Passaw, A. Harry, 227
Petre, Richard M., 266
PG4R (study formula–mathematics), 102
Phonic analysis, 5–6, 31, 45–48
Physical education
  applying reading skills, 367–373
  comprehension, 75–76
Picture reading, 121–122
Poetry
  study formula, 102
Polya, George, 188, 190
Postman, Neil, 10
PQ4R (study formula), 102
PQRST (study formula—science), 101
Prefixes, 35–38
Principles of learning, 13–14
  applied to procedure, 170–172
Procedures, 169–190
  basic plan, 174–179
  comparison with study formula, 179
  planning the lesson, 173
  study guides, 183–184
  unit plan, 184, 187
  guidelines, 188
Programmed materials, 205
PSC (study formula), 102

Questioning, 64, 73, 90, 91

Rate of comprehension, 127–128
Rath, James N., 93
Rauch, Sidney J., 241
Readability, 245–248
  formulas, 246–248
Reading process, 2–3
  language structure, 267–268
Reading program
  checklist for success, 385–386
  implementing, 376–380
  organizing, 380–384
  parts, 376
  personnel, 379–380
  philosophy, 376–378
  practice, 378–379
Reading skills, 16
Reading-study skills, 98–129
Reading Versatility Test, 15
REAP (study formula), 102
Redundancy, 5, 33
Reluctant readers, 221
Remedial readers, identification of, 229
Remediation, 228–241
  basic competency, 238–241
  programs, 229–232
  guidelines, 231–232
  in content area classroom, 232–235
Report writing, 126–127
Research reading, 124–126, 142–143
  steps of, 125–126, 141–143
Richards, John P., 90–91
Robertson, Jean E., 93
Robinson, Francis P., 99, 129
Robinson, H. Alan, 102, 241, 356, 374
Roe, Betty D., 102, 328, 356
Russell, David H., 21
Russell, Ivan L., 144

Sanders, Norris M., 65–67, 97
Scanning, 127–128
Science
  applying reading to science, 282, 283
  comprehension, 75–76, 77, 78, 80, 82, 83, 85, 87, 296, 303
  diagrams, 114–116, 292–296
  directed lessons, 181
  following directions, 122–123, 301–302
  formulas, 291
  fusing reading to scientific method, 303–304
  graphic aids, 291–296
  map reading, 108, 109
  problems in reading, 283–284
  questioning, 63, 70–71
  study formula PQRST, 101
  syntax, 92
  tables, 116–117

unit plan, 185–187
project, 304
vocabulary, 32, 290–291
Self-help materials, 204–205
Shane, Harold, 9
Shane, June Grant, 9
Shapiro, Jon E., 144
Shepherd, David L., 124, 141–143, 303–304
Sherer, Peter A., 94–95
Sherk, J. K., 19
Shuman, R. Baird, 230–231
Shuy, Roger, 227
Sipay, Edward R., 2
Skimming, 127–128
Slow learning readers, 216–219
characteristics, 216
classroom activities, 217–219
Smith, Carl B., 101
Smith, E. Brooks, 20, 52
Smith, Henry P., 127
Smith, Nila Banton, 57, 241
Smith, Richard J., 59
Smith, Sharon L., 101
Social studies
applying skills, 268
charts, 111–112
comprehension, 80–81, 84, 86–7, 271–282
directed lesson, 179–181
graphs, 119–120
map reading, 108–110
paragraph patterns, 276–282
problems in reading, 269
questioning, 63, 67–69
study skills, 271–273
syntax, 92, 93
tables, 116–117
vocabulary, 32, 270–271
Spache, George D., 97–131
SPIRE Individual Reading Evaluation, 152
Split brain research, 60–61
SQRQCQ (study formula–mathematics), 101
SQ3R (study formula), 75, 99–100, 105
comparison with directed lesson, 179
SRA reading record, 152
Standal, Timothy C., 246–247
Stauffer, Russell G., 174–190
Steinhellner, Lesley Linda, 134
Steinley, Gary, 61
Steurer, Stephen J., 235
Stoodt, Barbara D., 102, 328, 356
Stracher, Dorothy A., 214–215
Strong, Ruth, 146–7, 168, 387
Structural analysis, 31, 34–45
classroom activities, 43–45
Greek roots, 41–42
Latin roots, 40–41
prefixes, 35–38
suffixes, 38–39
Structure words, 88–89
Study formulas, 99–100, 101–102
EVOKER, 102
OARWET, 101
PANORAMA, 101
PG4R, 102
PQ4R, 102
PQRST, 101
PSC, 102
READ, 102
SQ3R, 101
SQRQCQ, 101
Study guides, 183, 184
Suffixes, 38–39
Summers, Edward G., 107
Superior readers, 209–215
classroom activities, 211–213
characteristics, 210
needs, 210
Syllabication, 42–43

Table reading, 116–118
Tapes, 206
Tatham, Susan M., 59
Taxonomy, 58
Bloom, 58
Barrett, 58–59
Teacher-made tests, 153–163
English inventory, 154–157
mathematics inventory, 161–162
science inventory, 159–161
social studies inventory, 157–159
Tests, 149–193
standardized, 149–153
Diagnostic Reading Test, 151
Reading Versatility Test, 151
Iowa Tests, 151
Traxler High School Reading Test, 152
Traxler Silent Reading Test, 152
SRA Reading Record, 152
Botel Reading Inventory, 152
High School National Achievement Test, 152
Diagnostic Reading Test: Pupil Progress Series, 152
SPIRE Individual Reading Evaluation, 152

Tests *(continued)*
California Achievement Test: Reading, 153
Teacher-made, 153–163
English inventory, 154–157
mathematics inventory, 161–162
science inventory, 159–161
social studies inventory, 157–159
Textbook evaluation, 248–250
Thelen, Judith, 166
Thomas, Ellen Lamar, 102, 356, 374
Thralls, Zoe A., 109
Tinker, Miles A., 241
Toffler, Alvin, 17
Tovey, Duane R., 255
Tutolo, Daniel J., 183–184

Unit plan, 184–187, 389–393

Vocabulary, 18–52
basis for development, 20–21
classroom activities, 25–31
forming concepts, 21–22
principles, 22–24
reasons for poor vocabulary, 19–20
subject areas
business education, 330, 332, 334–335, 338–339
foreign languages, 358–359
general, 34–35
homemaking, 349
industrial arts, 341–343
mathematics, 311
music, 363
science, 32, 290–291
social studies, 32, 270–271
word analysis, 31–51

Wagener, Hobart D., 140
Weingartner, Charles, 10
Wide reading
business education, 340
English class, 205–267
industrial arts, 348
techniques for developing, 136–139
Wiggin, Neal A., 115
Winters, Leslie J., 93
Word analysis, 31
contextual analysis, 31, 32–34
dictionary usage, 31, 48–50
phonic analysis, 31, 45–48
structural analysis, 31, 34–45
Wright, Brenda, 105

Ziegler, Warren L., 89
Zuck, Louis V., 222